Sociologists generally study macrolevel institutions and social processes with little reference to the individual. Psychologists, on the other hand, tend to study individual-level processes with little reference to society. This new volume, featuring contributions from some of the most influential scholars working in U.S. social psychology today, brings the link between the individual and society into focus.

The chapters in the volume are distinguished by their concentration on either cognitive, emotional, or behavioral processes. These analyses eschew the traditional psychological approach to individual-level processes and instead offer intriguing accounts of how thought, emotion, and action are embedded in social context and are central to the dynamic between self and society. Together, the 15 chapters present a synthesis of theory and research that promises to be a major force in stimulating and influencing future investigations of the link between the individual and the larger society.

The self–society dynamic

The self–society dynamic

Cognition, emotion, and action

Edited by

JUDITH A. HOWARD
University of Washington

PETER L. CALLERO
Western Oregon State College

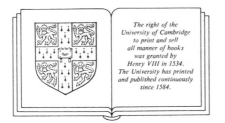

The right of the
University of Cambridge
to print and sell
all manner of books
was granted by
Henry VIII in 1534.
The University has printed
and published continuously
since 1584.

CAMBRIDGE UNIVERSITY PRESS

Cambridge

New York   Port Chester   Melbourne   Sydney

Published by the Press Syndicate of the University of Cambridge
The Pitt Building, Trumpington Street, Cambridge CB2 1RP
40 West 20th Street, New York, NY 10011, USA
10 Stamford Road, Oakleigh, Melbourne 3166, Australia

First published 1991

Printed in the United States of America

Library of Congress Cataloging-in-Publication Data
The Self–society dynamic: cognition, emotion, and action / edited by
  Judith A. Howard, Peter L. Callero.
      p.   cm.
    Papers presented at a conference entitled, Self and society: a
social cognitive approach, held at University of Washington, July,
1988.
    1. Social perception – Congresses.   2. Social interaction –
Congresses.   3. Social psychology – Congresses.   I. Howard, Judith A.
II. Callero, Peter L.
  BF323.S63S44   1991   90–41672
  302.5–dc20   CIP

British Library Cataloguing in Publication Data
The Self–society dynamic: cognition, emotion, and action.
  1. Social psychology. Interactionism
  I. Howard, Judith A.   II. Callero, Peter L.
  302

ISBN 0–521–38433–8 hardback

DEDICATION

One of the names of the initial list of participants for this conference was Louis Zurcher, a sociologist who has conducted important work on self and the self–society interface, and a scholar whose many works are referenced frequently in this volume. During the months of planning this volume, Louis Zurcher died of cancer. We dedicate this volume to his memory, in recognition of the many contributions he made not only to research on the relationship between self and society, but also to sociology as a whole and to humanity.

Contents

vii

Contributors

VICTORIA BILLINGS
Department of Sociology
University of California
at Los Angeles

PHILIP BLUMSTEIN
Department of Sociology
University of Washington

PETER J. BURKE
Department of Sociology
Washington State University

PETER L. CALLERO
Division of Social Science
Western Oregon State College

KATHLEEN CARLEY
Department of Sociology
Carnegie–Mellon University

VIKTOR GECAS
Department of Sociology
Washington State University

JUDITH A. HOWARD
Department of Sociology
University of Washington

PAULA NURIUS
School of Social Work
University of Washington

JANE ALLYN PILIAVIN
Department of Sociology
University of Wisconsin-Madison

MORRIS ROSENBERG
Department of Sociology
University of Maryland

MICHAEL L. SCHWALBE
Department of Sociology
North Carolina State University

RICHARD T. SERPE
Social Science Research Center
Humanities and Social Sciences
California State University
at Fullerton

LYNN SMITH-LOVIN
Department of Sociology
University of Arizona

SHELDON STRYKER
Department of Sociology
Indiana University

RALPH TURNER
Department of Sociology
University of California
at Los Angeles

Preface and Acknowledgments

Manny Rosenberg observed, at a conference entitled "Self and Society: A Social Cognitive Approach," convened at the University of Washington in July 1988, that this was the first gathering in the United States of sociological social psychologists who study the self, despite the fact that such work has been central to sociological social psychology for decades. This volume is one outgrowth of this conference. The participants included those who have developed and guided the growth of the original theory and research in this area – scholars such as Sheldon Stryker, Ralph Turner, and Morris Rosenberg – and a younger generation of scholars who have recently begun their work in this area.

The participants were asked to prepare papers on aspects of the relationship between self and society, and to address how theories of social cognition, a perspective that dominates contemporary psychological social psychology, might inform this relationship. The conference focused primarily on a question relevant to sociologists, that is, How can sociological social psychology benefit from considering recent work in social cognition? Had the papers focused only on the conference topic, the target audience would include primarily sociological social psychologists. However, reflecting the conviction of the authors that sociological approaches to the self–society interface have substantial merit, there is much here for psychological social psychologists to learn from as well. Virtually all of the chapters present new models, extend in creative ways existing research, or explore entirely new empirical territory. Thus the work presented here is germane to any scholar interested in the contemporary thinking and research of some of the most active social psychologists of the self.

Support for this conference was provided by the American Sociological Association's Problems of the Discipline program, the Graduate School and College of Arts and Sciences at the University of Washington, and by Western Oregon State College. We also want to thank Peter Kollock, Susan McWilliams, Melanie Moore, Jodi O'Brien, and Kenneth Pike for their substantial assistance with and participation in the conference, and Jocelyn Hollander for her careful assistance with the index.

Introduction: The self–society dynamic

Judith A. Howard

The participants of the conference out of which this volume grew were asked to address how theories of social cognition, a perspective that dominates contemporary psychological social psychology, might inform the relationship between self and society. Thus in one sense this book is an update of the "two social psychologies" (or three, House, 1977) literature (Stryker, 1977; Cartwright, 1979) Stryker reviews briefly in chapter 1. This literature contends that there are substantial costs associated with the prevailing mutual ignorance among the three branches of social psychology – psychological, sociological, and personality and social structure. This volume is one attempt to redress this ignorance.

The book is organized into three sections. The first section includes four chapters that address the general interface between sociological theories of the self and theories of social cognition. The second section presents four chapters that address affective and motivational links with cognition, and the third section includes six chapters that illustrate links between the self and cognition as manifested in different forms of behavior. The organization of the volume as a whole thus echos a theme that emerges in a striking number of the individual contributions, that is, reference to the tripartite division of behavior, cognition, and affect.

Over the course of the twentieth century, social psychology has revolved around these three poles of behavior, cognition, and affect. The contemporary wave of social cognition emerged with the work of Lewin and the several subsequent generations of his students as a corrective to the heavily behaviorist emphasis of social psychology at that time. Recently, dissatisfaction with the prevailing strong emphasis on cognition has produced widespread recognition of the importance of affect and emotion, evidenced in the formation of a new American Sociological Association section on emotions, and production of a special issue of *Social Psychology Quarterly* (March 1989) on the topic. Thus over the span of this century, social psychology has emphasized, in turn, behavior, cognition, and emotion. What is lacking is a cogent theory of how these three aspects of human

1

beings work together, although many of the contributions that follow provide preliminary steps in the direction of such a theory. In this introductory chapter we consider how these various selections define the key terms of the self–society interface, how they draw on the concepts of cognition, affect, and behavior, and most important, how they approach the interface between self and society. We begin by considering the general interface between sociological theories of the self and theories of social cognition.

Self and social cognition

In chapter one, Stryker suggests that the main terrain for common dialogue between psychological and sociological social psychologies is the self. Preoccupation with issues of self characterizes contemporary cognitive, as well as sociological, social psychology. Given this parallel emphasis, it is essential to be explicit about what these terms mean. In psychology, self-conceptions are derivatives of traits or personality dispositions. In sociology, self is defined generally as a process of self-objectification. Despite considerable differences of definition, Stryker maintains that cognitive social psychology can assist sociologists in addressing some longstanding thorny problems. Cognitive social psychology poses a multifaceted and complex view of self, reminding that self is more than the role-linked identities emphasized by identity theory. Cognitive social psychology also emphasizes the self as system, incorporating linkages of multiple and interrelated parts; this notion of self as information systems and processes is not far afield from the work of George Herbert Mead (1934). Each of these emphases is a useful corrective to traditional sociological views of the self.

In chapter two, Peter Callero contends that to fully explain social action and the relationship between self and society, we must achieve an explicitly sociological understanding of cognition. He offers a framework for such an analysis by addressing four fundamental questions: (1) What is cognition, (2) when does cognition enter the social process, (3) how is social cognition related to action, and (4) how are cognitive processes linked to the social structure? Following the work of Mead (1934), Callero asserts that thought occurs within communities; social adaptation and interaction depend upon cognition. Furthermore, thought is a subvocal form of conversation that depends upon language, an inherently social medium. Thus cognition itself is at least implicitly a form of interaction. Social cognition cannot be uniquely private or subjective, because it depends upon language.

When does cognition enter the social process? Callero distinguishes among four types of what he calls action–affect episodes, characterized as either patterned or novel, and symbolic or nonsymbolic. Novel and nonsymbolic activity is basic stimulus–response behavior; patterned and nonsymbolic activity is labeled habit. Consistent with his view of social cognition as a covert form of symbolic interaction unique to humans, he suggests that cognition enters the social process when we engage in symbolic interaction. But he goes one further step in arguing that it is only problematic behavior or situations that evoke cognition. Nonproblematic or scripted symbolic interaction need not involve cognition, according to Callero (script theorists may well disagree with his implication that scripted interaction is not cognitive). Thus patterned and symbolic activity is labeled as ritual; cognition enters social interaction only with the conjunction of symbolic and novel behavior. This view of cognition is clearly in striking contrast to conventional psychological approaches, and suggests a number of potential revisions to cognitive social psychology.

Definitions: Self and identity

In contrast to the traditional psychological conception of self as an aggregate of traits or personality dispositions, the sociological conception of self is more interactive, social, and processual. Although these chapters emphasize different aspects of self, they share an emphasis on the reflexive process of self-objectification. We review these sociological definitions of the self with reference to three systems of categorization: (1) their relative emphasis on cognition, affect, and behavior; (2) their relative emphasis on structure and process; and (3) the degree of stability or mutability they attribute to the self.

Cognition

Identity theory's view of self and identity is primarily cognitive, structural, and, at least in the traditional formulations, relatively stable. Identity theory, developed primarily by Sheldon Stryker (1981), derives from the general symbolic interactionist position that self is the product of society and that self, in turn, organizes social behavior. Identity theory asserts that selves are produced in concrete networks of social interactions. In highly differentiated societies, so too are selves highly differentiated and organized. For Stryker, Burke, and Serpe, key proponents of identity theory, identities are internalized role designations carrying the shared meanings and behavioral expectations associated with roles and group memberships; self is a hierarchical ordering of identities, organized into a structure of salience. The salience of identities is a consequence of commitment, ties to networks of social relationships. Choices among behavioral options are presumed to be consequences of the location of identities in the salience hierarchy, connecting cognition and conation.

Although symbolic interactionist theory views self as both structure and process, as Serpe observes in chapter 3, short shrift has been paid empirically to cognitive activity. Other conceptions of self that derive from identity theory place more emphasis on the processual and reflexive development of self, following the traditional Meadian approach. Gecas views the self-concept as a product of reflexive activity, the dialectical relationship between I and me that emerges from symbolic interaction via role taking. Callero characterizes self as an internalized conversation, a covert form of interaction involving the self and both specific and generalized others. Serpe suggests that cognitive activity is the conative aspect of self, an aspect that has received less attention than cognitive parts of the self. In an empirical study, Serpe examines the relationship between cognitive activities, commitment, and identity salience, using four identities associated with college life. He demonstrates that cognitive activities do have an effect on identity salience over and above the effects of affective and interactional commitment. Serpe maintains that assessing the quantity and nature of cognitive activity relative to specific identities would inform the understanding of stability and change in self-structures.

Other cognitive views of the self focus on information and knowledge. Rosenberg refers to the self-concept as a body of knowledge, including the full range of beliefs, facts, opinions, values, attitudes, or other forms of knowledge the individual holds with regard to the self. Rosenberg stresses internal interaction in the form of self-objectification in accounting for the development of self. Carley also views self as an aggregate of information, but she focuses in chapter 4 on the external interactions that transmit knowledge and thus create the self. She contends that knowledge is a key construct in the self–society interface: Behavior is based on information; interaction opportunities affect what one knows and what information is currently salient. Thus what information or knowledge individuals have and what they share with others, is the key to the self–society interface. She applies these ideas in a computer simulation study of the transmission of knowledge between parents and children in 27 constructed societies that vary in several structural characteristics. She asks whether, across societies, children learn information that is social from their parents or develop their own social knowledge, and whether structural features of societies affect the existence of a generation gap in knowledge.

In direct contrast to these conceptions of self as mutable, Piliavin views much individual behavior as guided by habit, the unthinking patterns of past behavior. Her focus on habit, elaborated in chapter 12, suggests implicitly that the self includes habits, overlearned actions that may at one time have been a conscious part of self, but have receded into the realm of unthinking behavior. Although this conception of self as stable echoes the identity theory view of self, the source of stability is distinctly different.

Emotion

These conceptions of self are highly cognitive. Other chapters in this volume conceive of self as substantially more affective. Interestingly, emphasis on the emotional components of self appears to be associated with a sense of the mutability of self, probably reflecting a general conception of emotion as fleeting and situationally responsive. In the first of four chapters that stress the importance of affect and emotion, Turner and Billings go a step beyond many of those who have argued recently for the incorporation of affect into theories of cognition. Turner and Billings suggest that affect may precede cognition in defining self. They contend that feelings of authenticity and inauthenticity are closer to Cooley's original conception of the self than more recent cognitive conceptions. Furthermore, they stress the situational specificity of affect and, by implication, of self. According to Turner and Billings, self-discovery and recognition take place in identifiable social contexts, and some contexts are more potent than others in evoking self-feelings. In the empirical study they present in chapter 5 Turner and Billings explore self-in-situation interactions through which discovery and recognition of self occur. Among the more interesting findings are that conforming to internal expectations leads to true self-experience, as does the absence of a sense of pressure. When a person feels external pressure, compliance with those demands is necessary to experience inauthenticity. Conversation is overwhelmingly the most common activity in which both true and spurious selves are experienced. One curious finding that challenges much cognitive research on the self is that respondents' roles, beliefs, and self-conceptions did not play much part in determining the meaning respondents assigned to the situation. Turner and Billings conclude by emphasizing the diversity of situations in which people have self-experiences, noting that these contexts are differentiated more by the meanings the actor assigns than by objective characteristics.

Nurius's conception of self is not incompatible with Turner and Billings's. Like them, and in contrast to identity theory's view of the self as rather stable, biographical, and schematic, Nurius emphasizes the situated, responsive, mutable features of the self-concept, focusing in chapter 11 on what she calls the working self-concept, the functionally relevant self-concept at a given moment. This is a shifting configuration of self-conceptions, or possible selves, representations of oneself in future or past states, that wax and wane in salience according to situationally relevant cues. Possible selves are a motivational force, decreasing the perceptual distance between one's current state and a possible future or past state. They function as plans for action and in this motivational sense also contain an affective element.

Possible selves are also resources for coping. To become active they must be mobilized, and this occurs, at least in part, through social interaction. Indeed, Nurius suggests that we use social ties strategically to reconfigure prevailing conceptions of current or future self, as a means of coping. She applies these ideas in explaining health outcomes, asserting that possible selves are the cognitive underpinnings of appraisals of social support and health, linking social ties, individual mediation, and coping behavior. Nurius's concept of possible selves raises a host of intriguing questions, many of which are relevant for other concepts of self and identity. Most relevant to the topic of this volume, How do identities articulate with possible selves – when does a possible self become probable, and in turn, become an identity? What are the limits of possible selves? Not all selves are always possible; clearly structural factors can constrain not only actual selves but also the construction of imaginary selves.

In chapter 6, Morris Rosenberg turns more to matters of process than definition, asserting that the self-objectification of physiological arousal creates emotional experience and thus illustrates the close connection between cognition and emotion. According to Rosenberg, control of emotional experience is essential for the attainment of many personal and interpersonal goals. Given that we cannot control what we feel, Rosenberg contends that we attempt to control our thoughts, the causes of our emotions. Some techniques are designed to control the events in the external environment that impinge on the mind, for example, selective interaction or selective exposure. We may also act directly on emotion-evoking thoughts through selective attention, and interpretation, thought displacement, distraction, selectivity of focus, rationalization, selective ignoring, or selective comparison. All of these are methods of emotional self-control; all require self-objectification. Rosenberg concludes that humans are able to gain some control over their emotions by producing effects on their causes.

Action

At least two of the views of self presented in this volume place a primary emphasis on behavior. In chapter 13, Schwalbe begins with a conception of self much like that of Callero or Gecas, but he moves from internalized conversations to social communication and behavior. Schwalbe contends that the self arises not only through the cognitive rehearsals of action common to all symbolic interactionist conceptions of self, but also through actual problem-solving behavior. He views the self as inseparable from what he calls moral action. In introducing the notion of moral behavior, Schwalbe emphasizes the importance of content, of specific problem-solving situations, as against the often content-free models of cognitive activity. Schwalbe notes that according to Mead, moral problems are always social problems, in that they entail conflicts between interests and values arising in a community. Thus moral behavior cannot be abstracted from concrete social relations and situations.

Moral problems are communicative problems whose solutions arise out of negotiating meanings and new social relationships. When moral problems are defined in terms of discovering points of convergence and divergence between conflicting perspectives, role taking assumes great importance. Schwalbe develops the notion of the moral self, which relies in part on impulses to role-take, the expansiveness of the generalized other, conceptions of self as an object possessing moral characteristics, and a sense of self-efficacy that motivates action. Schwalbe thus defines the self in terms of action.

In chapter 14, Blumstein turns on its head the question of how self shapes behavior, asking instead how identity, what is presented behaviorally to others, creates the self. He conceptualizes self as private, reflexive, enduring, and identity as what is publicly displayed; identity requires no private commitment on the part of actor or audience to its being a true reflection of the self. In this dramaturgical argument, Blumstein asks whether what we present becomes who we see ourselves to be, much like Bem's (1972) theory of self-perception. He suggests that we make self-inferences on the basis of, for example, what types of influence strategies we use; indirect people are created through using indirect strategies. As this example suggests, Blumstein also maintains that situated identities are much more apt to have long-lasting implications for the self in close personal relationships than in nonintimate social interaction, hence he illustrates his argument through an analysis of how selves are created through intimate relationships.

Summary

Although these multiple conceptions of self are diverse, they share a belief in the reality of the experienced or phenomenal self. One contemporary view of self that has been popular primarily in the humanities and other interpretive disciplines, the postmodern self, is distinctively missing from this inventory (Henriques, Hollway, Urwin, Venn, & Walkerdine, 1984). From a postmodern perspective, a self does not exist. There is no such thing as an authentic self; what is under scrutiny then is the apparent felt need prevailing in this historical time to create and maintain a sense of an authentic self. This conception of self does not necessarily invalidate any of the more traditional conceptions already discussed, but does place them within a critical and historical context. Sociologists Michael Wood and Louis Zurcher (1988) have theorized what they call a postmodern self, by which they refer to a self that emphasizes impulse, process, and change. This self is conceived as the product of the many forces of modernization and is thus placed within a specific historical context. Although this self is substantially more mutable than any of those just reviewed, in its continued assertion of the possibility of an authentic experienced self this remains a conservative definition in contrast to the more radical view of the postmodern self. We suggest that the sociological emphasis on identifying the significance of self for specific social consequences, which requires a theory of human agency, accounts for these different approaches to the notion of self. A sociological conception of self must be concerned not so much with the validity of self as with the social consequences of the human tendency to conceive of a self.

Self and other cognitive structures

Whether the self is conceived as cognition, affect, behavior, or some combination of these three, a social cognitive perspective on sociological work on the self must articulate how the self relates to other cognitive structures. Whereas traditional cognitive structures include attitudes, values, and beliefs, the schema – organized knowledge about a given concept or stimulus – is most prominent among more recent conceptions of cognitive structures (Taylor & Crocker, 1981). There has been substantial research on self-schemas, organized knowledge about one's own personality, appearance, and behavior (Fiske & Taylor, 1984; Markus, 1977; Markus & Zajonc, 1985).

In chapter 1, Stryker begins to address how self-schemas relate to the conceptions of self articulated by sociologists, developing links between specific theories of social cognition, for example, theories of cognitive schemas, self-discrepancy, and self-complexity, and identity theory, the most prominent sociological theory of the relation of self and society. Self-complexity theory is a model of the organization of self. Self-complexity theory adds to identity theory the hypothesis that identities will be more salient if they are cognitively linked. In other words, the degree of in- or interdependence among cognitive structures is an important element of self. According to Stryker, theories of cognitive schemas also provide an empirical basis for the proposition that identities motivate interactional performance; schema theory helps put identity into action with the concept of possible selves, representations of oneself in future (and past) states. This notion of possible selves also suggests the need to incorporate a time dimension in considering identities and how they function. Stryker observes as well that existing self-schemas can impede changes in self by biasing information processing. He notes that self-schema theory raises questions about how deep changes in social relationships must be to overcome identity inertia.

In exploring possible interfaces between schema theories and identity theory, it will be important to consider how self-schemas articulate with identity salience hierarchies. Is a self-schema isomorphic with a hierarchy of identity salience, the closest concept within identity theory? If not, how is it different? How do such schemas – cognitive structures that are presumably resistant to change – constrain changes in hierarchies of identity salience? Self-schemas are generally considered to be a subtype of person schemas. The identity theory conception of self, however, seems closer to role schemas than to person schemas. Identity theory might profit from research on self-schemas, which would point to a broader conception of identity, and hence of self.

Other chapters also address directly the relationship between the self and other cognitive structures and concepts. Nurius relates the notion of possible selves to self-schemas, for example, defining possible selves as the future-oriented components of self-schemata. In chapter 9, Burke explicitly maps parallels between the self-concept and attitudes. He suggests that the literature on the attitude-behavior problem may be helpful in specifying the relationship between self and behavior, drawing on methodological approaches such as Fishbein and Ajzen's theory of reasoned action (1975) and a cognitive mediation perspective that focuses on the complex links among the roles of cognition, experience, and perception. He argues that the importance of self in attitude research has been evident implicitly in assumptions about the self in Festinger's (1957) theory of cognitive dissonance, Heider's (1958) model of the balance and congruity of cognitive elements, and more recently in affect control theory, which implicates attitudes (Smith-Lovin, chapter 7; Smith-Lovin & Heise, 1988). He also raises the problem of nonidentity and nonattitude, that is, the possibility that attitudes and identities may not exist in certain domains. This points to the need for substantially more creative measurement devices.

Piliavin's emphasis in chapter 12 on the concept of habit is fully compatible with the general perspective of social cognition, although she does not locate her discussion within this model. The guiding metaphor of social cognition is the view of the human being as an information processor and, in turn, given the limits of these capacities, a cognitive miser (Fiske & Taylor, 1984). We do not expend cognitive effort unless it is necessary; reliance on schemas frees us from gathering a full set of information anew each time we experience a given situation. Habit, which Piliavin conceives as repetitious behavior, serves the same purpose. Habit is analogous to scripted behavior, and thus is very much a cognitive concept. Although she does not explore the relationship between habit and self, habits would seem to reflect self-schemas. In stressing habit, Piliavin reminds us that cognition can refer to inactive and automatic activation of information or behavior, rather than to highly conscious and active information processing. She demonstrates this with an empirical study of blood donors, finding that among early career, uncommitted donors, those who have not yet developed a habit of donating, there are more errors of not giving when predicted to do so, in predicting donation from behavioral intentions, whereas among late career, committed donors, those who do have a habit of donating, there are more errors of giving when predicted not to, in predicting donation from intentions.

Self and situation: The person–situation interaction revisited

Another issue of increasing importance to sociological theories of the self is specification of the situations in which selves are expressed. This topic, addressed by several of the theories presented in this volume, recalls the attention of psychological social psychologists to the interaction between person and situation, a topic of substantial importance in the 1970s (Bowers, 1973; Endler & Magnusson, 1976). Within psychology, this question refers to the extent to which effects of personality characteristics are shaped by characteristics of situations. Although a number of studies generally demonstrated the existence of such interactions, this line of research ended here. The general failure to specify these interactions further is due to the striking absence of research on features of the situation, as opposed to the person (Frederiksen, 1972). Although psychologists have done little with this question, sociologists have more tools with which to address specification of the social context of behavior.

The approach most relevant to person–situation interactions is affect control theory, presented in chapter 7 by Smith-Lovin. Affect control theory is based on the proposition that people perceive and create events to maintain the meanings evoked by their definition of a situation. The theory conceptualizes meaning as specific and measurable; the empirical applications are based on a simulation program that models the process of affect control. One of the more significant aspects of the theory is its prediction that when events create transient impressions that differ from our fundamental understanding of what people and behaviors are like, we are likely to construct new events to confirm fundamental sentiments. In other words, people may manage their social life in ways that control their feelings about reality. Affect control theory provides an explicit statement of the connections between cognitive processes such as situation definition and labeling and affective reactions and emotions.

Other chapters also address the interaction between person and situation. Turner and Billings's exploration of the degree to which variations in situations are associated with evocation of a sense of true or spurious self demonstrates the diversity of situations in which people have self-experiences. Importantly, Turner and Billings note that these contexts are differentiated more by the meanings the actor assigns, than by objective characteristics of these situations. This "phenomenal situation" is the epitome of a person–situation interaction. Piliavin's discussion of habit is also relevant. She stresses the importance of external structural factors such as availability of occasions, as well as internal structural factors such as habit, in understanding how we do or do not come to perform repetitive behaviors. Piliavin suggests that person–situation interactions can become scripted, and thus lead semiautomatically to behavior.

Burke also stresses the necessity of a full recognition of how the self is situated, arguing for a principle of congruency among identity, attitudes, behavior, and situation, consistent with affect control theory. His analysis of the activation of identities demonstrates the importance of situating the self. Burke observes that if people take on different identities in different situations or in different roles, then we must specify what activates, and deactivates, given identities. Consistent with Turner's exploration of what situations generate a sense of true or spurious self, Burke has demonstrated in his own work (Burke & Franzoi, 1988) the situational sensitivity of the relationship between identity and behavior. When people are in a situation because they choose it, there is closer correspondence between the meaning of the situation and their identity. Presumably in such situations their behavior reflects a sense of authenticity.

There may be other tools relevant to this question within contemporary social cognition. For example, research on the three primary forms of schemas – person, role, and event – has focused primarily on identifying the components of such schemas and demonstrating that they influence information processing. Each type of schema has been considered in relative isolation from the others. More attention to how these schemas intersect might prove useful for specifying how person and situation interact. Thus, for example, it might be helpful to consider how self- and event schemas are interwoven in situated action, or to specify how far person or role schemas can vary from expectations with an event schema before the schema itself is considered inoperative.

The stability or malleability of self

As suggested, one of the enduring dimensions of diversity about conceptions of self is the relative emphasis on stability or malleability of the self. How much does a sense of self incorporate permanent, enduring qualities? How much does self vary in response to varying situations and social contexts? Contemporary theorizing suggests the unprofitability of viewing these as either–or propositions. More important is to specify when self is experienced as stable, when as responsive and shifting, and how the two relate to each other. What is the relationship between the selves we experience in specific situations and our sense of permanent self? Smith-Lovin's model is directly relevant to this question. Although she is concerned with the process whereby transient impressions are reconciled with fundamental self-sentiments through the construction of particular actions, this model could be used to address the opposite question: Under what circumstances are transient impressions not reconcilable with fundamental self-sentiments? In other words, in what situations is a new self-sentiment constructed? Nurius also offers a direct analysis of these questions with her notion of the working self-concept, the functionally relevant self-concept at a given moment. What is not specified in this model is how the sense of potential selves articulates with the more stable and biographical self. Nurius's emphasis on social support suggests that one variable that may mediate between a stable self and possible selves is the relative availability of a consistent and reliable network of social support.

The self–society interface in the 1980s: The micro–macro link

The sociological "hot topic" of the 1980s was attention to the "micro-macro" link, one organizing theme of the 1989 American Sociological Association convention (Alexander, Giesen, Munch, & Smelser, 1987). In a way this phrase simply restates the significance of the self–society dynamic. There is widespread recognition that sociologists (and psychologists) must recognize the dual aspects of the self–society problem:

the constraints on cognitive content and organization of self posed by social structure, as well as the limits of the impact of social structure on self. That is, we need to specify an account of social reproduction through the impact of society on self and social production, an account that specifies how new phenomena enter social life and social structure.[1] The most important challenge is to specify the precise mechanisms that link these levels; there are many points in these chapters that elucidate this link.

Many of the chapters in this volume address the micro–macro connection. In specifying the dependence of cognition on language, and distinguishing symbolic from novel behavior, Callero identifies key concepts. Carley puts these concepts into action, arguing that the transmission of information is the key to the self–society dynamic. She explores intergenerational knowledge transmission as one trace of this process, and specifies some structural features that might affect how this occurs. Carley demonstrates how a cognitive model of the individual can be used in conjunction with a model of communication to examine the self–society dynamic.

Smith-Lovin extends past applications of affect control theory to address the more general topic of micro–macro linkages, contrasting human agency and social constraint. She explores the relationships among emotions, norms, values, and ideology, demonstrating how the ritual means of emotional production is a potent tool in contests over power and legitimacy, and clarifying the central normative underpinnings of affect control. Smith-Lovin's analysis is one of the few that makes specific predictions about social change; she shows how the affect control model reveals societally important role strain, and thus can predict shifts in institutional arrangements. More generally, Smith-Lovin demonstrates that emotions can serve as the basis for institutional change. Viewing situations as the immediate conveyer of social institutions, she examines how situations constrain the immediacy of identities, and how human actors in turn shape situations, and thus implicitly, society.

In thus emphasizing the reciprocality of the interface between self and society, Smith-Lovin illustrates one contribution social psychologists are uniquely qualified among sociologists to make to this general topic. The phrase micro–macro suggests a neutrality of terms such that both terms are equally important. In practice, however, both theory and research generally have addressed the effect of macro institutions on microlevel phenomena, that is, the effect of society on the self.[2] Although social psychologists often assert the reciprocality of this link, few researchers actually address this (with the major exception of the line of research by Kohn & Schooler, 1973, 1978, 1983). Both Smith-Lovin's and Carley's empirical research are significant steps in this direction, as is Schwalbe's (1986) study of the psychosocial consequences of work and social action.

Other chapters also offer promising models for such research. Callero explores the interactive components of cognitive processing in asking how social cognition is related to action. Callero proposes the intriguing idea that one function of social cognition is to transform unique experiences into shared, socially familiar experiences, and then back again into particular acts. "Role thinking" is one mechanism for this. Indeed he asserts that thought is necessarily role based, in that cognition is a covert form of interaction among various roles. Cognitive structures are linked to social structures through processes of role thinking; structures cannot exist independent of cognitive role-using activities of the community.

Understanding how cognitive structures are implicated in the motivation of behavior is crucial for accounting for individual participation in social change; Gecas thus makes an important contribution in the sociological theory of motivation he presents in chapter 8. Gecas suggests that the self-concept is a particularly appropriate basis for developing a theory of motivation, because the self is a social product and as such dependent on social interaction for its maintenance. He identifies at least three motivations associated with the self-concept: self-esteem, self-efficacy, and authenticity. He argues that these motives not only affect individuals' actions, but also have implications for social change. For example, self-efficacy, the motive especially relevant for the social structural domain, influences how individuals respond to social problems. Although the specification of motives may not constitute a fully sociological theory of motivation, clearly Gecas moves social psychology toward that goal.

Howard addresses a similar question, but moves beyond intraindividual motivation into the social arena. Howard also emphasizes the impact of individuals on social systems. She argues in chapter 10 that phenomena such as social movements can be understood only with explicit attention to the phenomenal selves of individual actors. Reasoning that social change must derive in part from self-change, she attempts to identify those forces that impel the self to the redefinitions required to overcome the tendency toward self-definitional stability. All sociological social psychological theories of the self point to some degree of environmental and structural upheaval or change as the motivator of self-based change, but these theories do not identify specific mechanisms by which selves change. Howard suggests three such mechanisms: the cognitive concept of possible selves, the affective experiences of social behavior, and the interactive social networks in which action occurs. Each of these mechanisms shapes how general societal disruption affects specific individuals.

Howard applies these ideas to understanding social movements, emphasizing the problem of recruitment of members to social movements. She suggests that the degree to which cognitive and affective stimuli become linked to the self predicts who will become a recruit, and who will stay one. Particularly important are social networks and the degree of communication they promote among individuals. Howard proposes a model through which identity becomes linked to consciousness and eventually to social activism. She concludes by suggesting that the processes whereby selves and society change are reciprocally determined through their mutual reliance on social networks, communication, and affective experience.

Finally, Schwalbe's chapter also points to ways in which individuals shape society. Schwalbe takes up the question of how social structural experiences affect the development of the moral self, demonstrating how one's structural position affects the development of the propensity to role take, the expansiveness of the generalized other, conceptions of the self as efficacious, and hence the tendency to engage in social action. Schwalbe thus demonstrates the relevance of morality for macrosociological issues such as the reproduction of social structure.

Conclusion

There is a certain irony in the emphasis in this volume on exploring what current social cognition has to offer to sociological social psychologists. As Stryker points out, the key theoretical underpinnings of sociological social psychology – the writings of Cooley, Mead, and others – have always had a strong cognitive component, one predating the psychological emphasis on cognition. Thus I conclude by noting that psychological social psychologists, especially those who work within the framework of social cognition, have much to gain from attention to the work of their sociological colleagues. As Stryker himself has reminded psychologists, social structures are important sources of cognitions; persons' locations in differentiated structures are consequential for the differential activation of cognitions as well as the simultaneous activation of conflicting cognitions (and see Howard, 1990). Indeed, some psychologists have begun to borrow from sociologists. There are references to the work of Mead and occasionally Goffman in Markus and Nurius (1986), Linville (1987), and Swann (1983), among others, but references to contemporary sociological social psychologists are almost entirely absent. The chapters in this volume, authored by these contemporary sociologists, raise significant, challenging questions whose solutions will require the insights of interdisciplinary theories and research. We expect that these contributions will stimulate all readers, whatever their academic discipline, to make their own contributions to these challenging questions, questions likely to absorb the social psychology of the 1990s.

Notes

1 In some ways the phrase "self-society dynamic" is problematic. The very term reifies a distinction between these two levels of analysis that are so intimately intertwined.
2 This emphasis was reified in the program cover of the 1989 American Sociological Association convention program; the typeface of "macro" was approximately four times larger than the typeface of "micro."

References

Alexander, Jeffrey C., Bernhard Giesen, Richard Munch, & Neil J. Smelser (Eds.). 1987. *The micro–macro link*. Berkeley, CA: University of California Press.

Bem, Daryl J. 1972. Self-perception theory. In Leonard Berkowitz (Ed.), *Advances in experimental social psychology* (Vol. 6, pp. 1–62). New York: Academic Press.

Bowers, K. S. 1973. Situationism in psychology: An analysis and a critique. *Psychological Review* 80: 307–336.

Burke, Peter, & Stephen L. Franzoi. 1988. Studying situations and identities using experiential sampling methodology. *American Sociological Review* 53: 559–568.

Cartwright, Dorwin. 1979. Contemporary social psychology in historical perspective. *Social Psychology Quarterly* 42: 82–93.

Endler, Norman, & D. Magnusson. 1976. *Interactional psychology and personality*. Washington, DC: Hemisphere Publishing.

Festinger, Leon A. 1957. *A theory of cognitive dissonance*. Stanford, CA: Stanford University Press.

Fishbein, Martin, & Ajzen, I. 1975. *Belief, attitude, intention, and behavior: An introduction to theory and research*. Reading, MA: Addison-Wesley.

Fiske, Susan T., & Taylor, Shelley E. 1984. *Social cognition*. Reading, MA: Addison-Wesley.

Frederiksen, Norman. 1972. Toward a taxonomy of situations. *American Psychologist* 27: 114–123.

Heider, Fritz. 1958. *The psychology of interpersonal relations*. New York: Wiley.

Henriques, Julian, Wendy Hollway, Cathy Urwin, Couze Venn, & Valerie Walkerdine. 1984. *Changing the subject: Psychology, social regulation, and subjectivity*. New York: Methuen.

House, James S. 1977. The three faces of social psychology. *Sociometry* 40: 161–177.

Howard, Judith A. 1990. A sociological framework of cognition. In Edward J. Lawler, Barry Markovsky, Cecilia Ridgeway, & Henry Walker (Eds.), *Advances in group processes* (Vol. 7, pp. 75–103). Greenwich, CT: JAI Press.

Kohn, Melvin L., & Carmi Schooler. 1973. Occupational experience and psychological functioning: An assessment of reciprocal effects. *American Sociological Review* 38: 97–118.

Kohn, Melvin L., & Carmi Schooler. 1978. The reciprocal effects of the substantive complexity of work and intellectual flexibility: A longitudinal assessment. *American Journal of Sociology* 84: 24–52.

Kohn, Melvin L., & Carmi Schooler. 1983. *Work and personality: An inquiry into the impact of social stratification*. Norwood, NJ: Ablex.

Linville, Patricia W. 1987. Self-complexity as a cognitive buffer against stress-related illness and depression. *Journal of Personality and Social Psychology* 52: 663–676.

Markus, Hazel. 1977. Self-schemata and processing information about the self. *Journal of Personality and Social Psychology* 35: 63–78.

Markus, Hazel, & Paula Nurius. 1986. Possible selves. *American Psychologist* 41: 954–969.

Markus, Hazel, & Robert B. Zajonc. 1985. The cognitive perspective in social psychology. In Gardner Lindzey & Elliot Aronson (Eds.), *The handbook of social psychology* (3d ed., pp. 137–230). New York: Random House.

Mead, George Herbert. 1934. *Mind, self and society: From the standpoint of a social behaviorist*. Chicago: University of Chicago Press.

Schwalbe, Michael L. 1986. *The psychosocial consequences of natural and alienated labor*. Albany, NY: State University of New York Press.

Smith-Lovin, Lynn, & David R. Heise. 1988. *Affect control theory: Research advances*. New York: Gordon and Breach.

Social Psychology Quarterly. 1989. Vol. 52, no. 1.

Stryker, Sheldon. 1977. Developments in "two social psychologies": Toward an appreciation of mutual relevance. *Sociometry* 40: 145–160.

Stryker, Sheldon. 1981. Symbolic interactionism: Themes and variations. In Morris Rosenberg & Ralph H. Turner (Eds.), *Social psychology: Sociological perspectives* (pp. 3–29). New York: Basic.

Swann, William B., Jr. 1983. Self verification: Bringing social reality into harmony with the self. In Jerry Suls & Anthony G. Greenwald (Eds.), *Psychological perspectives on the self* (Vol. 2, pp. 33–66). Hillsdale, NJ: Erlbaum.

Taylor, Shelley E., & Jennifer Crocker. 1981. Schematic bases of social information processing. In Higgins, C., P. Herman, & M. P. Zanna (Eds.), *Social cognition: The Ontario Symposium* (Vol. 1, pp. 89–134). Hillsdale, NJ: Erlbaum.

Wood, Michael R., & Louis A. Zurcher, Jr. 1988. *The development of a postmodern self: A computer-assisted comparative analysis of personal documents*. New York: Greenwood Press.

1 Exploring the relevance of social cognition for the relationship of self and society: Linking the cognitive perspective and identity theory

Sheldon Stryker

Introduction: Context and limits

The topic of the working conference on self and society is premised on a fundamental theme in the "Two Social Psychologies" literature (Stryker, 1977; House, 1977; Cartwright, 1979; Stephan & Stephan, 1985). The literature argues the considerable costs attending the mutual ignorance characterizing the social psychologies produced by sociologists and by psychologists. It argues that much could be gained were practitioners of each social psychology familiar with the theories, conceptualizations, and findings of the other social psychology and were they to recognize those theories, conceptualizations, and findings in their own theorizing and research.

The conference topic asks participants to consider the relevance of the social cognitive perspective for sociological conceptions of the relationships of self and society. Since the social cognitive perspective per se characterizes contemporary psychological social psychology – Markus and Zajonc (1985: 137) go so far as to assert that contemporary social psychology is defined as the study of the social mind – and interest in the self–society relationship is fundamental to sociological social psychology, the conveners of this conference in defining its topic point participants to a focus on the potential contributions of contemporary theorizing and research in psychological social psychology to the sociological variety of social psychology. There is an irony in this formulation. Sociological social psychology, in particular that version owing a major debt to Cooley, Mead, and more generally to symbolic interactionism, has always had a strong cognitive cast; and psychological social psychology abandoned its behavioristic epistemology and metatheory for a cognitive epistemology and metatheory only relatively recently. Yet, on the contemporary scene, it is psychology that has recast and adopted wholeheartedly the cognitive framework, developing and extending it in a manner such that it can fairly be said, as

19

the citation to Markus and Zajonc avers, that its social psychology begins and ends with social cognitions.[1] Having made social cognition its raison d'être, it offers insights and suggestions that can inform the sociological concern with the relationship of self and society. At the same time, however, an indiscriminate adoption by sociologists of the social cognition framework could obviate the point of a sociological social psychology by leading it to abandon the demand, implicit in positing a self–society *relationship*, that cognitions be rooted in social structure and in social interaction.

Thus, along with a focus on the import of cognitive processes for the self–society relationship, there must be a correlative focus on the import of the self–society relationship for cognitive processes. That assertion owes its validity to the observation that social and cognitive processes are truly nonrecursive although not necessarily instantaneously reciprocal. We cannot fully understand cognitive structures and processes without seeing them as (at least in part) rooted in social structure and social processes; and we cannot fully understand social structures and processes without recognizing that implicated within these are cognitive structures and processes. Both sides of this coin of reciprocity must be examined if violence is not to be done to either side; to assume or to do otherwise is both unnecessarily artificial and unwisely limiting.

This said, it becomes pragmatically necessary here to consider only one side of the coin, how the cognitive perspective of psychological social psychology can inform the sociological concern with the relationship of self and society, leaving aside a consideration of its reciprocal.[2] Given this decision, the discussion must proceed primarily by addressing what the cognitive perspective has to suggest with respect to the concept of self.

The so-called cognitive revolution in experimental psychology subsequently imported into psychological social psychology sets the stage for and makes reasonable examining the interaction of social cognition and relationships of self and society, for that revolution makes a dialogue between the two subdisciplines possible and suggests how the two may be bridged. When internal processes like thought and mind were ruled out by psychologists' commitment to behavioristic premises, little could be done to bring sociologists and psychologists doing social psychology to attend to one another and few conceptualizations could be exploited across the boundary separating them. The cognitive revolution in psychology legitimated concern with internal, subjective processes generally and with self specifically. Contemporary cognitive social psychology as enunciated by psychologists makes self central to its concerns. The centrality of self in cognitive social psychology articulates with the centrality of self in the social psychology enunciated by perhaps most sociologists; and this coincidence of central concepts can be exploited in pursuing the agenda of this conference. More generally, this coincidence makes more promising than ever before a dialogue between the two social psychologies.

Not that self means the same thing in the context of theorizing in psychological and in sociological social psychology. In the former, self is typically defined by attaching trait conceptions to persons, or by attaching self to a particular activity of the person – as in self-monitoring, self-consistency, self-esteem – and then converting the process to a traitlike propensity. The concept thus becomes a substitute for earlier trait notions in personality theory formulations. In sociology, self is typically defined in terms of the process of self-referencing, in Mead's terms as "that which is an object to itself," then linked as consequence and source to interpersonal relations and social interaction. Still, there are commonalities in conceptualization open to exploitation; and, even in the absence of such commonalities, the use of a common term invites mutual attention where such is unlikely in the absence of that common term. It may be wise to remind that it also creates the possibility of the subdisciplines talking past one another while assuming they are communicating.

Some of the desirable dialogue has been and is already occurring – in the two social psychologies literature, in the increasing frequency of crossover attendance and participation in meetings, in the selection of research topics entailing the literatures of both subdisciplines (e.g., the literatures of self-presentation, self-attribution). But the dialogue in place is limited in its import and impact. That is, the extant dialogue has two dominant characteristics: It is largely hortatory and largely phrased in very general terms. The admonition to psychologists from sociologists is, in effect, never forget the explanatory power of social structure, social organization, and the ongoing social process. The equivalent admonition from psychologists to sociologists is, in effect, never forget the heterogeneity of the human organism and the import of resulting individual differences lost through aggregation processes.

There is virtue in both exhortation and generalized lesson; however, that virtue is limited and, if taken as final word, limiting. Exhortation argued only through generalized assertion, directed to one's children or kindred professional, is unlikely to have much impact on behavior. What is needed is demonstration that explicitly linking specific theories of social cognition with specific theories of the relation of self and society increases explanatory power and understandings relative to that available through one or the other separately (see Morgan & Schwalbe, 1990, for another statement of this theme). There are a few exceptions to my characterization of the extant dialogue that meet this need. On the sociological side, David Heise's (1979) affect control theory and research make quite self-conscious and effective use of the cognitive literature on impression formation; on the psychological side, Stefan Hormuth (1990) makes equivalent use of the sociological literature on identity formation and change in his ecology of self-theory and research. More such theories are needed; it is to this end that the current effort is directed.

Specifically, I propose to utilize identity theory (Stryker, 1981; Stryker & Serpe, 1982; Burke & Reitzes, 1981) as an instance of a sociological theory of the relation of self and society. I propose to use concepts and theoretical propositions general to the cognitive perspective in social psychology and some that are particular to cognitive schema theory (Markus, 1977; Markus & Sentis, 1982), self-discrepancy theory (Higgins, 1987; Higgins, Bond, Klein, & Strauman, 1986), and self-complexity theory (Linville, 1985, 1987), suggesting how these can inform identity theory. Doing so, I hope to meet the charge of the organizers of this conference to bring to bear work in social cognition on sociological appreciation of the relation of self and society. I choose these cognitive theories because I know something about each, finding them intuitively appealing and relevant to identity theory, because that relevance extends to seeing the potential utility of identity theory for them, and because I think the lessons available from them are relevant beyond identity theory.

Identity theory and relevant cognitive theories: Descriptions

Earlier, I noted that a coincident focus on a common concept, self, provided the opening that could be exploited in bridging psychological theories of social cognition and sociological theories of the self–society relation. It is largely the view of self as structure incorporated into (some) psychological and sociological theories implicating self that creates the perceived opportunity. That suggestion cues the following descriptions and discussion of particular theories and, later, linkages between particular theories.

Identity theory

Identity theory[3] derives from a symbolic interactionist meta-theoretical perspective or framework, a perspective that stems from the work of George Herbert Mead (1934), Charles Horton Cooley (1902), John Dewey (1930), W. I. Thomas (Thomas & Thomas, 1928), and Herbert Blumer (1969). For the most part, it represents a specification and formalization of symbolic interactionism's basic formula: Society shapes self, which in turn shapes social behavior. It departs from some, perhaps most, symbolic interactionist statements by making an effort to place symbolic interactionists' basic emphases on the social psychological processes joining interpersonal interaction, self, and social behavior in larger settings of social structure that facilitate or constrain these processes. That is, identity theory has been formulated in the context of what has been termed a "structural symbolic interactionism" (Stryker, 1981), an attempt to provide symbolic interactionist thought with a more viable sense of social structure than it typically contains by developing symbolic interactionism's affinities to role theory.[4] Structural symbolic interactionism asserts that it is social structures – including systems of positions and related roles as well as larger principles (e.g., age, sex, race, class) around which societies are organized – that shape interaction. With respect to positions and roles, it asserts that definitions or meanings attached to self as well as definitions or meanings attached to others are importantly built around positional and role designations. With respect to the larger principles, it argues that these facilitate or constrain the possibilities for role making, for the construction rather than the "mere" enactment of social behavior, doing so by facilitating or constraining who come together in what social settings to interact with what interactional resources for what social purposes.

Identity theory specifies the symbolic interactionist formula, representing the framework's most general claim, with which this discussion began by reconceptualizing self and by focusing the conceptions of society, self, and social behavior implicated in the formula. Identity theory accepts the symbolic interactionist dictum that self is the product of society and organizes behavior. It recognizes that it is in concrete networks of social interactions that selves are produced and that when societies are highly differentiated and organized, the selves that are produced will be equivalently differentiated and organized. The theory's specification is through the proposition that "commitment" shapes "self," which shapes choices among role options available to the person. Self is conceptualized as a hierarchical ordering of identities, defined as internalized role designations,[5] into a structure of salience, defined as the probability of invoking a given identity across or within situations of interaction. The salience ordering of identities is understood to be a consequence of commitment, defined as the costs to persons of relationships foregone were those persons no longer to have a given identity and play out the role associated with that identity. Commitment, so conceived, is a matter of ties to networks of social relationships. The theory as it has thus far developed recognizes two forms of commitment: interactional and affective. The former has its referent in the size and connectedness of social networks, the latter in the affect generated in role relationships. Choices among role options are presumed to be consequences of the location of identities containing those options in the identity salience hierarchy: the higher the relative salience of an identity, the more likely a choice of a role option associated with that identity.[6]

Self-complexity theory

Self-complexity theory, developed by Linville (1985, 1987), argues that the structure of self-representation – specifically, the degree of "complexity" of the self-representations – accounts for variation in how persons respond to occurrences in their lives. In particular, the more "complex" the self-representation, the less likely are responses to exhibit dramatic affective swings, that is, be extreme in their form and content.

Linville's model of self derives from James (1890) in asserting that self is composed of multiple aspects (and, it can be added, accords with identity theory's image of self as comprised of multiple identities, an image that also has its roots in James). Included in these aspects are cognitive categories whose referents are in social roles, traits, kinds of relationships, types of activities, category memberships, and so on. The self is complex insofar as it has many distinct aspects relatively independent of one another. In the degree that one cognitively organizes his or her self-knowledge in terms of a great variety of self-aspects, and in the degree that these self-aspects exist as separate, independent, nonoverlapping cognitive structures, one is characterized as having a complex self-representation.[7] Self-aspects are separate and independent if they are composed of different "features" and "propositions" (Linville, 1987).

If self has a simple (noncomplex) representational structure, it will be subject to a "spillover" process by which life events affecting one aspect of self impact the remaining aspects associatively linked to that initial aspect. All of the variables linked to the activation of cognitive representations in the more general cognitive literature are presumed to account for the activation of a given aspect of self-representation.

Self-discrepancy theory

This theory, articulated by Tory Higgins (1987), develops from the longstanding psychological premise that holding conflicting or incompatible beliefs leads persons to experience discomfort or distress,[8] and the related premise that inconsistencies internal to self produce emotional problems. It specifies such views by distinguishing the various kinds of discomfort (or emotional vulnerabilities) people experience and relating these systematically to types of discrepancies among self-beliefs. The theory asserts two basic clusters of negative emotions: a set that are dejection related (feelings of depression, dissatisfaction, depression), and a set that are agitation related (anxiety, guilt, fear); these clusters are linked to self-discrepancies.

Prior theories of belief incompatibility focus on the availability of cognitive constructs in memory for use in mental processes. As cognitive constructs, Higgins observes, belief incompatibilities can be either chronically or momentarily accessible, that is, ready to be used to process information; and individual differences in availability and accessibility of incompatible beliefs can be expected to influence persons' responses.

Underlying the patterning of discrepant self-beliefs or self-state representations are two cognitive dimensions: *domains* of self and *standpoints* on the self. Domains include actual self, persons' representations of attributes that someone (self or other) believes they possess; ideal self, persons' representations of the attributes someone (self or other) ideally would like them to possess; and the ought self, persons' representations of attributes that someone (self or other) believes they should or ought to possess – their responsibility, obligation, or duty. There are two basic standpoints on self, or vantage points from which the person can be judged, own and other, and there may be many significant others whose views are implicated in self-discrepancies.

A cross-classification of domains and standpoints serves to define the fundamental psychological situations hypothesized to link to emotional responses and vulnerabilities, which the theory conceives as motivational states. That is, the theory postulates that people are motivated to reach conditions where their self-concepts (actual-own or actual-other self representations) match their personally relevant self-guides (ideal-own, ideal-other, ought-own, ought-other self-representations). Each type of self-concept–self-guide discrepancy is presumed to reflect a particular negative psychological situation and to be associated with a specific emotional or motivational problem. In general, there are two kinds of negative psychological situations, each with a characteristic emotional state. The actual or expected absence of positive outcomes links to dejection-related emotions, and the actual or expected presence of negative outcomes links to agitation-related emotions. It is assumed that it is the significance or meaning attached to the possession of a self-concept that has emotional consequence, with significance or meaning being a function of the relation of the self-concept to a self-guide.

Persons may have no, many, or many different self-discrepancies and so no, many, or many different emotional vulnerabilities, not all equally active or active at the same time. Whether a particular discrepancy pattern is activated depends on its accessibility; accessibility depends on well-known cognitive variables: recency of activation, frequency of activation, and applicability to a stimulus event.

Observational, correlational, and experimental evidence is brought to bear on this theory (see, e.g., Higgins et al., 1986) and is generally supportive.

Self-schema theory

Contemporary cognitive theorizing, Zajonc and Markus (1985) note, requires the postulate that there exist systematic sources, in the form of internal cognitive structures and mechanisms with appropriate properties, of departures from normative models of information processing through errors, biases, and distortions. These cognitive structures, presumed to develop as generalizations of experiences with the concepts they reflect, filter information derived from the environment by determining how such information is represented, categorized, and stored. "Schema" is a commonly used term for these internal cognitive structures as organizations of conceptually related elements.

Markus (1977; Markus, Crane, Bernstein, & Siladi, 1982; Markus & Nurius, 1987; see also Nurius, this volume) applies this cognitive psychology to social psychology by conceptualizing self in schema terms. A self-schema is a summary and construction of past behavior that enables persons to understand their experience and organize information about themselves; such self-schemas may include identities, roles, traits, goals, abilities, preferences. When networks of meanings and representations of attributes are used in thinking about, describing, or evaluating oneself, a self-schema exists (Markus et al., 1982). "A self-schema in a particular behavioral or stimulus domain is, then, an intersection in memory of these behaviors or of these stimuli and the representations of the self" (Markus et al., 1982: 39).

Self-concept is defined as a union or conjoint of self-schemas. Self-schemas or self-concepts are cognitive structures; Markus theorizes that they operate as any cognitive structures in categorizing, explaining, and evaluating behavior.[9] Specifically, she argues, it can be expected that schematics (those with a self-schema for a particular behavioral domain) more than aschematics (those without such) will attend schema-relevant information more, better, and faster (Markus, 1977).

But beyond being an integration of past and present actions, a self-schema may be a "claim" of responsibility for future behavior in a given domain (Markus & Nurius, 1986, 1987). That is, some self-schemas represent what people would like to become, could become, fear becoming; they represent a vision of what is possible. Markus argues that as cognitive structures that are representations of potential and future linked to self, possible selves put the self into action by linking salient identities and role performances (Markus & Nurius, 1987: 159).

From cognitive social psychology to self–society theory

Having noted the limited utility in generalized dicta arguing the mutual relevance of the two social psychologies and the greater utility in demonstrating explanatory gains made by joining elements of specific cognitive theories and specific self–society theories, it may appear contradictory to introduce a discussion of what, in general, cognitive social psychology can do for self–society theory. I do so, however, to provide grounding for the more theory-specific discussion to follow.

Some of the potential general contribution of social cognition to self–society theory is on the relatively mundane level of method and measurement, some on the level of metatheory and concept. With respect to both, method and measurement as well as metatheory and concept, means are available by which fundamental ideas can be refined and even substantially modified, as well as given greater precision.

This last claim rests first of all on the recognition that self is a cognitive phenomenon, whether defined in "purely" individual terms as psychologists are wont to define it or person-other terms as sociologists are more likely to conceptualize it. Beyond that, it rests on recognizing that self–society theory focuses on a twin problem: (1) to root the process and cognitive structure of self in social structure and so understand constraints on the cognitive content and organization of self as well as on self-processes; and (2) to understand the limits of the impact of social structure on the content, organization, and processes of self. The first aspect of this twin problem points to an account of social *re*production – the process by which social structure reproduces itself through its impact on self. The second aspect of the twin problem points to an account of social production – the process by which something new or creative enters social life and (potentially) social structure.

Sociologists tend to account for the latter in terms of multiple social structures, multiple memberships in diverse social structures, multiple standpoints on self, and multiple selves (see the discussion of this issue is Stryker & Statham, 1985). Cognitive theory argues the existence of "indigenous" cognitive processes and experientially linked associations among cognitive elements relatively independent of social structure, as well as the existence of an active constructor and organizer of cognitive systems. Both principles of cognitive organization per se and the likelihood that at least some cognitive schemas reflect "random" events unaccountable for via social structure introduce "indeterminacy" into the self–society relation and open the way for self (at least under some, perhaps rare, conditions) to alter society. At a minimum, the potential independence of social structure and cognition argues the need to sort out when the relationship between the two is close, when distant, and what the consequences in given circumstances may be of a gap between the two.

A closely related utility resides in the reminder, available through cognitive social psychology, that self contains more than role-linked identities. Identity theory has developed explicitly as a *limited* theory, invoking a theoretically delimited set of explanatory variables and principles to deal with highly circumscribed behavior. Too, identity theory early recognized (Stryker, 1968) that self as an organized structure contained more than the cognitive modality of identity. Still, theoretical work always exhibits the tendency to push a limited explanation, however explicitly the limitations are recognized, beyond its capabilities. That is, identity theory makes identities, as internalized role designations, the content of self, and makes self so defined central to its explanations. Cognitive social psychology suggests that self contains traits, affect, social categories, "master statuses," attitudes, preferences, goals, and so on that may or may not be tied to specific identities. Thus, cognitive social psychology points to kinds of things that identity theory can seek to accommodate in order to make it more powerful as explanation and more general in what it explains. To some extent, a beginning has been made in this accommodation (see, e.g., Stryker, 1987a, 1987b); but the development of identity theory may well call for more, and more successful, treatment of self in other than "pure" identity terms.

In roughly the same vein, cognitive social psychology has a reasonably clear image of self as system, articulating the system-linked ideas of multiplicity of and interrelations among parts. Whereas these ideas are not foreign to identity theory – both are implicated in its image of self as made up of identities organized into a salience hierarchy – the terms in which systems ideas enter cognitive theory may permit an enriched vision of self as it mediates the relation of social structure and behavior.

The metaphor that undergirds and underwrites much conceptualizing and theorizing in cognitive psychology generally and in cognitive social psychology in particular is of the person as information processor akin to computer; in the latter, it is self that plays the processor role. Although sociologists sometimes bristle at what they take to be the overly rational presumption of the underlying human-as-computer metaphor (the information processor metaphor holds whether the person is taken to be inherently deficient qua computer or potentially perfectible), there is considerable comparability in this view of human behavior and the view found in Mead of the human as scientific problem solver. Recognizing that comparability as well as taking into account the cognitive social psychological literature pointing to the "biases" frequently if not necessarily present in human information processing (see the summary review of relevant literature in Markus & Zajonc, 1985) can inform sociologists' understanding of how self operates in relation to society.

Still on the level of metatheory and conceptualization, contemporary understanding in cognitive social psychology of cognition as a multistaged process (Markus & Zajonc, 1985: 149) offers opportunities for refinement of sociologists' views of the self–society relationship. Integral to those views, typically if not invariably, is some conception of "definition of the situation" (or conceptual equivalent playing the same theoretical role) having the quality of a unitary, seamless perceptual-cognitive event. Understanding cognitions to be multistaged opens the way for refinements of that concept, for appreciating that elements of situations may (or may not) be attended, the sensory input comprising the "situation" may (or may not) be encoded, may (or may not) undergo a sequence of transformation, may (or may not) be organized and stored, and may be called up in somewhat different forms, *and* recognizing that each of these stages may be under the control of somewhat different processes, begs for subtlety in invocations of the concept. Further, and as Markus & Zajonc (1985: 149) observe, a view of cognition as multistaged enables a beginning understanding of how preattentive or precognitive stages of encoding can affect subsequent reactions, thus freeing a concept like definition of the situation from the "conscious," overt labeling assumptions frequently attached to it. There is still another implication of a view of cognition as multistaged. Many sociologists working on the self–society relationship conceptualize both parts of that relationship in more or less pure process terms, as so much and so continuously in flux that structural concepts of either self or society are inadmissable (see, e.g., Blumer, 1969). Considering only the self part, a view of self-related processes in multiple stage terms permits a reasonable sense of self-as-process (now specified in terms of stages) while at the same time admitting a reasonable sense of self-as-structure (since the very idea of stages suggests there is some organized entity that proceeds from one stage to the next).

Finally, on the level of metatheory and conceptualization, cognitive social psychology incorporates a view of self as motivational that can enrich sociologists' sense of how self moves people to behave, whether in accord with the meaning of self-conceptions or in opposition to them. Self–society theory in sociology has long argued that self motivates behavior in accord with self-conceptions, but just how it energized behavior remained mysterious.[10] There is, of course, a long tradition of work in social psychology arguing the motivational force of cognitions, in particular of discrepancies between cognitions in one form or another: The balance theories of Heider (1958), Newcomb's (1953) cognitive consistency theory, and Festinger's (1957) theory of cognitive dissonance are variations on this theme, as are the more recent elaboration of affect control theory (Heise, 1979) and self-discrepancy theory (Higgins, 1987). However, only recently has the postulate underlying such theories, that cognitive discrepancies are sources of discomfort that give rise to efforts to remove the discomfort, received empirical verification (see the brief discussion in Markus & Zajonc, 1985). That belated verification suggests renewed effort by those interested in the relation of self and society to discover just what kinds of self-conceptions or relations among self-conceptions move people to behave in ways that reinforce or erode existing social order.

To say that part of the potential contribution of a cognitive social psychology to society–self theory is mundane is hardly to denigrate it. For an empirical discipline, research without theory is directionless, but theory without research is empty; thus, to elevate theory over research is a debilitating conceit. So considered, it is no small matter that historically self–society theory has been stronger on ideas than on the empirical examination of those ideas in the context of rigorous research,[11] and that there exists a stronger research tradition among cognitive social psychologists than among those coming out of intellectual traditions in which the self–society relation is at the core. The latter have much to learn from the former in terms of imaginative translation of abstract theories into concrete research designs. I have noted elsewhere (Stryker, 1989) that sociologists view Goffman's cognition-impregnated images as interesting and even lovely but as too evanescent to be reduced to anything recognizable as a research design, whereas cognitive social psychologists like Swann (1983),

Schlenker (1980), and Snyder (1974) assume not only that they can do this without great violence to the ideas, but that they must in order to do justice to those ideas. The persons just cited are experimentalists; although I see no grounds for dismissing experiments (only bad experiments) as a source of knowledge of self–society relationships, the same imaginative translation lesson is available from the nonexperimental research of Hormuth (1990) examining his ecological theory of self,[12] a theory very close to identity theory.

Corollaries of cognitive social psychology's research imagination and sophistication as a potential contribution to self–society theorizing are its conceptualization of cognitive structures and processes and its measurement procedures that can move us from conception to research variable. More on this topic is reserved for the next section.

From particular social cognition theories to identity theory

As earlier argued, there is need to move beyond generalized and hortatory statements of why those whose fundamental interests lie in self–society interrelations should know more than they typically do about cognitive social psychology. In some degree, however, these virtues derive from ideas and principles, already discussed, indeed general to the social cognition framework. I will call on these more general ideas and principles as well as the specifics of the particular cognitive theories invoked.

Self-complexity theory and identity theory

The linkages between self-complexity theory and identity theory appear to be reasonably straightforward. Most sociologists thinking about the cognitive complexity of self, defined a la Linville in terms of the existence of multiple, relatively independent self-cognitions, and certainly a sociologist using identity theory, would immediately ascribe the source of that phenomenon to the absence of what in identity theory is called "structural overlap." This term has been used to describe the situation in which a person is a participant in many overlapping social networks; and the theoretical argument underlying the sociologist's ascription is simply that if social networks are composed of different persons, what one does in the context of one network (or what happens to one in the context of one network) will not carry over to another network. Certainly, this sociological argument and resultant ascription of self-complexity to nonoverlapping social networks has some, perhaps considerable, validity.

If (the absence of) structural overlap and self-complexity were isomorphic because social structure completely determined the cognitions,[13] a theorist would not need to call upon the cognitive variable to explain any behavior; and parismony would demand that the theorist not do so. That one-to-one relationship, however, is undoubtedly absent except under very unusual if ever existing circumstance. It is far more likely that any person will have an experience that joins together two cognitive elements not connected through one's social memberships – a chance reading of a story joining an occupation and an odd recreational activity is an illustration. That is, something happens to link disparate roles and related identities not otherwise linked, creating a cognitive bond that does not reflect a social structural bond. Thus, self-representations may be linked in the absence of social structural links. Too, social structural bonds need not create cognitive bonds: Cognitive defense mechanisms (compartmentalization, denial, etc.) can create complex selves (in Linville's sense) even where there are social structural bases for linking cognitive elements.

Since social structures and self-structures are not likely to be totally isomorphic, they are not redundant variables. Since they are not redundant, identity theory must recognize both. It already recognizes self-structures in the form of the organization of identities into a salience hierarchy. But the complexity of self represents another, potentially important way that self is organized and therefore another, potentially important way that self ties back into social structure. Identity theory hypothesizes that social commitments in the form of interactional and affective ties to social networks lead to a salience ordering of identities on the basis of which those ties exist, and that the salience of an identity leads to behavior that recreates conditions giving that identity its initial salience. According to the theory, some identities are made more salient (than they otherwise would be) by the existence of structural overlaps. Self-complexity theory adds the hypothesis that identities will be more salient (than they otherwise would be) if they are cognitively linked, if the self that incorporates them is not complex in that it does not bound and isolate the identities one from the other. The "spillover" mechanism presumably operative to produce this result involves activating multiple aspects of self through the associative network that links them in a cognitive structure. The final hypothesis in this chain is that through the spillover process, identities cognitively tied together, even in the absence of social structural underpinnings, make more likely behavioral choices in line with the associated identities and make more likely as well behaviors that create the social structural underpinnings "justifying" the cognitive ties.[14] By hypothesis, this is one way self can ultimately alter extant social structure.

The conception of self-complexity points to the variable independence-interdependence of the cognitive structures comprising self. An equivalent view of self, in somewhat more general terms, is implicit in thinking about self as a multiple-system phenomenon. It is also implicit in the identity theory conceptualization of self as comprised of multiple identities and in visualizing self as having cathectic and conative as well as cognitive modalities (Stryker, 1968). These related conceptions – from general social cognition theory, from specific self-complexity theory, and from identity theory – lead almost necessarily to asking about conditions under which subsystems incorporated into the self are and are not interdependent and about consequences of varying degrees of interdependence. An especially intriguing question concerns the ways in which affective and cognitive systems entering self relate. The student of the self–society relationship is brought to ask what the social structural sources of interdependence-independence may be, and to hypothesize – as the earlier discussion suggests – that structural overlap is an important although neither total nor necessary source. With respect to consequences, from Linville's results one might expect social structural overlap to amplify and render more extreme emotional responses to life events, via its negative effects on complexity of self. Taking the matter further, one might expect amplification and "exaggeration" of affect to make more salient identities to which the affect attaches.[15] Then, consequences anticipated by identity theory of heightened salience for further social behavior would follow.

Self-discrepancy theory and identity theory

The potential linkages between self-discrepancy theory and identity theory appear to be many, even limiting consideration to what the first has to suggest with regard to the second. That this is the case should not surprise: Higgins draws heavily and explicitly on sociological sources in the development of his theory. Here, I will focus on a few linkages that seem to me to be most strategic for the further development of identity theory.

One such linkage is conceptual and methodological. Fundamental to self-discrepancy theory are distinctions among the availability, accessibility, and activation of cognitions, in particular self-cognitions. A self-cognition is available if experience has underwritten its construction and storage in memory so that it is possible to use the cognition in processing information. Available self-cognitions are differentially accessible, either chronically or momentarily, that is, more or less readily used to process information presented to the senses. Even accessible cognitions require activation: They must actually be used for information processing. Activation is presumed to depend on accessibility, and accessibility of a self-cognition will depend on how recently in the past it has been activated, how frequently it has been activated, and its applicability to a stimulus event (which in turn depends on the relation of the "meaning" of the cognition and its fit to the properties of the event). Methodologically, these distinctions and related discussion suggest that priming may be used to manipulate accessibility, and that response latency can be used to measure accessibility.

The link of such thinking to identity theory is made by recalling the definition of identity salience: An identity is salient in the degree it is invoked in or across situations. Conceived in this way, identity salience and self-cognition accessibility are conceptually equivalent. The obvious follows. One can in research manipulate identity salience by contextually priming it, drawing on a long tradition of research in cognitive psychology that capitalizes on recency effects. One can draw on the same tradition of research to rationalize the use of response latency to measure the differential salience of identities.

Of a host of possible comments only a few can be offered.

1. Use of priming and latency to methodological advantage in researching identity theory does not require resort to the experimental laboratory; these can be as readily used in a field or interview context. The importance of this observation for the development of identity theory can be underlined by noting that measurement procedures used previously in a survey context to gather data relevant to testing identity theory is potentially open to the criticism that the procedures confound identity salience and role choice, that is, an "intervening" and a "dependent" variable.

2. Those familiar with the history of the Twenty Statements Test (TST), touted as a way of getting at the equivalent of salience in self-research as early as the 1950s (Kuhn & McPartland, 1954), may assert that response latency is unlikely to measure salience well. That test, however, did not make use of priming, and it was typically administered in settings almost guaranteeing unreliable results[16] – they had no particular relevance to the range of identities making up subjects' selves, and they permitted subjects to make sense of their task by providing their own, likely variable in time, contexts.

3. The theoretical argument implicit in the distinctions among availability, accessibility, and activation – to the effect that inactive cognitions cannot impact behavior – is directly paralleled in the literature of role conflict and status inconsistency (Stryker &

Macke, 1978; Stryker, 1986), where the argument, now couched in terms of social roles and social status, is formally equivalent.

The heart of self-discrepancy theory is the postulate that self-view–self-guide discrepancies motivate attempts to match view and guide. Important to identity theory are the reminders that self-structures go beyond the actual self, that is, one's own or others' cognition of what one really is, and that there are strong normative elements, deriving from self and others, incorporated into the self. Ideals and standards, as applied to persons by themselves and by significant others, along with identities per se enter the process by which social behavior is produced.

If this is so, it is useful to ask how they enter. One possible way is by modifying identity both directly and indirectly through commitment. For example, it is reasonable to hypothesize that an actual-own/ideal-own discrepancy motivates attempts to match actual to ideal through behavior more closely approximating the ideal by creating affect that increases the salience of the identity involved in the discrepancy. It may be reasonable to hypothesize that an actual-own/ought-other discrepancy decreases commitment to that other (more accurately, to the network of relationships implicating that other), and through that mechanism decreases the salience of the identity underlying the person–other relationship. And conditional relationships can perhaps be asserted, for example, that an actual-own/ideal-other discrepancy results in heightened salience of the identity joining person and other if the other has high status or high power relative to the status or power of the person. Finally, a refinement of identity theory stimulated by thinking about a discrepancy that does not involve a norm or standard can be suggested: An actual-own/actual-other discrepancy may be expected to result in reduced commitment to the other by making the interaction in the self–other relationship problematic.

Self-schema theory and identity theory

Although the addition of "possible selves" (Markus & Nurius, 1987) to its repertory of concepts marks an important innovation and departure from standard social cognitive thinking, in its early statements (Markus, 1977; Markus & Sentis, 1982) self-schema theory represents a straightforward application of a social cognitive framework to the domain of self.

That fact, of course, hardly denigrates self-schema theory; nor does it demean the contribution that self-schema theory can make to clarifying the self–society relationship. Perhaps there can be no more significant contribution to identity theory than to make less ambiguous and to provide the empirical bases for accepting a fundamental assumption of that theory, namely, "that identities motivate interactional performances whose function it is to reaffirm in interaction that one is the kind of person defined by the identities" (Stryker, 1987a: 95). Self-schema theory, drawing on general cognitive theory principles, does this.

A self-schema is a cognitive structure, albeit a relatively complex cognitive structure. Environmental inputs are filtered, represented, categorized, stored, and recalled in terms in part dictated by self-schema. More pointedly put, schema-related environmental stimuli are attended to more, better, and faster than are schema-unrelated stimuli. Implied is that identities, particularly highly salient identities, render their possessor especially sensitive to cues that call for performances in terms of the identities, more ready to "read" (to give identity-relevant meaning to) ambiguous cues in ways that trigger such performances, more likely to "use" socially structured opportunities to behave in ways whose meanings accord with the meanings of the identities, and so on.

Apart from adding substance and even precision to identity theory's assumption that identities motivate performances in accord with their meaning, self-schema theory's argument that self-schemas "bias" information processing suggests there are impediments to changes in self in response to changes in social relationships – in the language of identity theory, there can be resistance to altering the structure of identity salience to align with changing commitments. How "deep" changes in social relationships must be to overcome "identity inertia" occasioned by biased information processing is an interesting question, even though no reasonable answer even can be attempted at this point. Answers to such questions are important to understanding limitations of the identity theory formulation.

There is yet another way self-schema theory contributes to clarifying motivational assumptions underlying identity theory. Markus and Nurius (1987: 157–159; see also Markus & Wurf, 1987) argue that "possible selves" are cognitive representations of enduring goals, motives, aspirations, fears, and threats and so give specific cognitive organization, direction, and meaning to these motivational dynamics. Explicitly making the link to identity theory, they suggest that possible selves put self into action, doing so in part by joining salient identities and role performances.

Possible selves, Markus and Nurius (1987: 159; see also Markus & Nurius, 1986, and Nurius, this volume) suggest, are importantly claims of responsibility for future behaviors in particular domains. That conception gives to the concept a normative element akin to that implied in identity theory's emphasis on expectations in defining social roles and consequently identities as well as conceptions of ideal and ought selves that figure prominently in self-discrepancy theory. Noting this linkage, it is not unreasonable to suppose that possible selves, in invoking representations of future states, have something of the character of ideal selves – even a future self projected in negative terms generally asserts what one does not wish to be and in that sense states an ideal – and function motivationally in relation to self-conceptions anchored in present or past as do self-discrepancies generally. Suggested is the need to explicitly incorporate into identity theory (really to reincorporate since the underlying emphasis on symbolic meanings as defined by Mead must imply the relevance of future) a time dimension in considering identities and how they function.

Conclusion

There are, I am certain, other important implications in social cognition theory generally and in the specific social cognitive theories treated for identity theory and through identity theory for sociological understandings of the self–society relation. Too, I am certain there are specific social cognitive theories other than those treated that have much to say to identity theory. But perhaps enough has been said about ways in which work in social cognition links to identity theory to make reasonable the underlying premise of this paper – namely, that sociological practitioners of social psychology can make good use of theories, concepts, and findings emanating from the work of psychologists doing social psychology.

It would not do, however, to leave the matter with this statement. It ignores the other side of the coin, speaking to what social cognition theory generally and particular social cognitive theories implicating self specifically can learn from sociological theories of the relation of self and society and from identity theory as a particular instance of such a sociological theory. To iterate, cognitions are not randomly assigned to persons but in important degree emerge from socially structured interaction and experience. To fully appreciate the impact of social cognition on understandings of the self–society relationship, both sides of the coin must be brought into focus.

Notes

1 We may be entering a period of reaction to the virtually total dominance of a cognitive perspective in psychological social psychology. With some exceptions (e.g., Higgins), as practiced by psychologists, cognitive social psychology has focused entirely on cognitions and cognitive processes to the virtual exclusion of interest in interaction, motivation, and even overt behavior. At a recent meeting of the Society for Experimental Social

Psychology, an organization whose membership is dominated by the most active researchers in psychological social psychology, one could hear mutterings in both sessions and hallways to the effect that it was time to rediscover social interaction and motivation.

2 How a sociological social psychology can inform social cognition work generally as well as specific cognitive social psychological theories is the topic of a paper (Stryker, 1988) presented at a meeting of the Society for Experimental Social Psychology, Madison, Wisconsin, October 21, 1988. In general, the lessons available in this direction have to do with the necessity of being aware that social structure cannot be reduced to perceptions and cognitions, that social structures are important sources of cognitions, that therefore persons' location in differentiated structures will be consequential for differential activation of cognitions as well as the simultaneous activation (or reducing the probability of simultaneous activation) of conflicting cognitions, etc. See also Callero, this volume, and Morgan and Schwalbe, 1990.

3 This statement of identity theory is fundamentally taken from Stryker (1987a) and Serpe and Stryker (1987).

4 See Stryker and Statham (1985) for a review of role theory and a thorough explication of the argument linking role theory and symbolic interactionism.

5 Cognitive representations or meanings do not constitute the whole of "self." In the initial paper presenting identity theory (Stryker, 1968), three hierarchical modalities of self including a cognitive, a cathectic, and a conative (an "I am" modality, an "I feel" modality, and an "I want" modality) self were postulated; but then the theory developed utilizing a totally cognitive conception of self. Recently, an attempt has been made to integrate affect into identity theory; see Stryker (1987b).

6 The structural symbolic interactionist framework recognizes that persons do not always have behavioral options. Identity theory, however, assumes that sometimes options in a realistic sense are available – that people sometimes can choose relatively freely among alternative behaviors representing various roles – and it focuses on the explanation of choices made when that is the case.

7 Linville's choice of wording followed in this paper when discussing her theoretical work is perhaps confusing given the usual implications of the term "complexity" when applied to thought processes. That is, we ordinarily take thought to be more complex when the thinker perceives subtle connectives among ideas or other elements entering the thinking, connectives that others fail to see. For Linville, it is the absence of connectives that in part defines complexity.

8 This premise, for a time thought untenable because evidence appeared to deny it, has now received empirical support; see the brief discussion of the point and appropriate research reference in Markus and Zajonc (1985: 140).

9 Markus and Zajonc (1985) ask whether self-schemas are in any way different from schemas not connected with the self and briefly review the status of this issue in the contemporary literature. They appear to conclude that schemas linked to self will have special qualities by virtue of that linkage, but do not specify what those qualities will be. One infers, however, that the relation to self will amplify the significance to the person of whatever role, trait, behavior, etc., is linked to self. Higgins and Bargh (1987) argue that information related to self is not processed in ways different from how other information is processed.

10 In the context of identity theory, e.g., the motivational force of identities has been assumed; i.e., it has simply been taken for granted that identities motivated behavior in keeping with those identities. Even Burke's (Burke & Reitzes, 1981) arguments regarding the link between identity and behavior in terms of meaning common to both leaves open issues of how the human is energized to act.

11 By rigorous, I do not mean and do not imply "quantitative." But rigor surely goes beyond

seizing on convenient illustration to argue the validity of theoretical ideas; and it surely includes the methodological devices of systematic observation and recording, the incorporation of relevant controls and control groups, etc.

12 Hormuth studies, e.g., how self reconstitutes identity-supportive environments by having subjects who have changed residential locales photograph household objects relevant to self.

13 Both identity theory and cognitive theory would agree in principle that the network membership variable be accorded causal priority, cognitive theory because network membership is an important aspect of the prior experience of persons that the theory presumes provides the elements and the linkages among elements that constitute cognitive structures.

14 Identity theory says that the higher the salience of an identity, the more likely the person having that identity will seek opportunities to engage in identity-expressive behaviors, read situations as calling for identity-related behaviors, interpret cues as identity-relevant, etc. Extending the argument, if cognitively linked identities lead persons to seek opportunities to express both at the same time, interpret cues as relevant to both at the same time, etc., they will cue behaviors from others responsive to both. Thus interaction can become premised on the joined identities; stabilized, these interactions are rudimentary social structures that can become institutionalized and feed into larger social structures.

15 The logic underlying this presumption is developed in Stryker (1987b).

16 See Spitzer, Couch, and Stratton (1970) for the evidence on which this assertion of TST's unreliability is based, even as these authors give this evidence a different reading.

References

Blumer, Herbert. 1969. *Symbolic interactionism: Perspective and method*. Englewood, NJ: Prentice-Hall.

Burke, Peter J., & Donald Reitzes. 1981. The link between identity and role performance. *Social Psychology Quarterly* 44: 83–92.

Cartwright, Dorwin P. 1979. Contemporary social psychology in historical perspective. *Social Psychology Quarterly* 42: 82–93.

Cooley, Charles H. 1902. *Human nature and the social order*. New York: Scribner's.

Dewey, John. 1930. *Human nature and conduct*. New York: Modern Library.

Festinger, Leon. 1957. *A theory of cognitive dissonance*. Evanston, IL: Row, Peterson.

Heider, Fritz. 1958. *The psychology of interpersonal relations*. New York: Wiley.

Heise, David R. 1979. *Understanding events*. Cambridge, UK: Cambridge University Press.

Higgins, E. Tory. 1987. Self-discrepancy: A theory relating self and affect. *Psychological Review* 94: 319–340.

Higgins, E. Tory, & J. A. Bargh. 1987. Social cognition and social perception. *Annual Review of Psychology* 38: 369–425.

Higgins, E. Tory, Ronald N. Bond, Ruth Klein, & Timothy Strauman. 1986. Self-discrepancies and emotional vulnerability: How magnitude, accessibility, and type of discrepancy influence affect. *Journal of Personality and Social Psychology* 51: 5–15.

Hormuth, Stefan E. 1990. *The ecology of the self. Relocation and self-concept change*. Cambridge, UK: Cambridge University Press.

House, James S. 1977. The three faces of social psychology. *Social Psychology Quarterly* 40: 161–177.

James, William. 1890. *Principles of psychology* (Vol. 1). New York: Holt.

Kuhn, Manfred H., & Thomas S. McPartland. 1954. An empirical investigation of self-attitudes. *American Sociological Review* 19: 68–76.

Linville, Patricia W. 1985. Self-complexity and affective extremity: Don't put all of your eggs in one cognitive basket. *Social Cognition* 3: 94–120.

Linville, Patricia W. 1987. Self-complexity as a cognitive buffer against stress-related illness and depression. *Journal of Personality and Social Psychology* 52: 663–676.

Markus, Hazel. 1977. Self-schemata and processing information about the self. *Journal of Personality and Social Psychology* 35: 63–78.

Markus, Hazel, M. Crane, S. Bernstein, & M. Siladi. 1982. Self-schemas and gender. *Journal of Personality and Social Psychology* 42: 38–50.

Markus, Hazel, & Paula S. Nurius. 1986. Possible selves. *American Psychologist* 41: 954–969.

Markus, Hazel, & Paula S. Nurius. 1987. Possible selves: The interface between motivation and the self-concept. In Krysia Yardley & Terry Honess (Eds.), *Self and identity: Psychosocial perspectives* (pp. 157–172). Chicester, UK: Wiley.

Markus, Hazel, & K. Sentis. 1982. The self in social information processing. In Jerry Suls (Ed.), *Psychological perspectives on the self* (Vol. 1, pp. 41–70). Hillsdale, NJ: Erlbaum.

Markus, Hazel, & Elissa Wurf. 1987. The dynamic self-concept: A social psychological perspective. *Annual Review of Psychology* 38: 299–337.

Markus, Hazel, & Robert B. Zajonc. 1985. The cognitive perspective in social psychology. In Gardner Lindzey & Elliot Aronson (Eds.), *The handbook of social psychology* (3d ed., pp. 137–230). New York: Random House.

Mead, George H. 1934. *Mind, self and society*. Chicago: University of Chicago Press.

Morgan, David L., & Michael L. Schwalbe. 1990. Mind and self in society: Linking social structure and social cognition. *Social Psychology Quarterly* 53: 148–164.

Newcomb, Theodore M. 1953. An approach to the study of communicative acts. *Psychological Review* 60: 393–404.

Schlenker, Barry R. 1980. *Impression management*. Monterey, CA: Brooks/Cole.

Serpe, Richard T., & Sheldon Stryker. 1987. The construction of self and the reconstruction of social relationships. In Edward J. Lawler & Barry Markovsky (Eds.), *Advances in group processes* (Vol. 4, pp. 41–66). Greenwich, CT: JAI Press.

Snyder, Mark. 1974. Self-monitoring of expressive behavior. *Journal of Personality and Social Psychology* 30: 526–537.

Spitzer, Stephan, Carl Couch, & John Stratton. 1970. *The assessment of self*. Iowa City, IA: Effective Communications, Inc.

Stephan, Cookie W., & Walter G. Stephan. 1985. *Two social psychologies*. Homewood, IL: Dorsey.

Stryker, Sheldon. 1968. Identity salience and role performance. *Journal of Marriage and Family* 30: 558–564.

Stryker, Sheldon. 1977. Developments in "Two social psychologies": Toward an appreciation of mutual relevance. *Social Psychology Quarterly* 40: 145–160.

Stryker, Sheldon. 1981. Symbolic interactionism: A social structural version. Menlo Park: Benjamin-Cummings.

Stryker, Sheldon. 1987a. Identity theory: Developments and extensions. In Krysia Yardley & Terry Honess (Eds.), *Self and identity: Psychosocial perspectives* (pp. 89–104). Chichester, UK: Wiley.

Stryker, Sheldor. 1987b. *The interplay of affect and identity: Exploring the relationships of social structure, social interaction, self and emotion*. Paper presented at the meeting of the American Sociological Association, Chicago, IL.

Stryker, Sheldon. 1988a. *Social structures and cognitive structures: specifying linkages*. Paper presented at the meeting of the Society for Experimental Social Psychology, Madison, WI.

Stryker, Sheldon. 1988b. Status inconsistency from an interactionist perspective: A theoretical elaboration. In Hermann Strasser & Robert W. Hodge (Eds.), *Status inconsistency in modern societies* (pp. 70–82). Duisburg: Verlag der Socialwissen schaftlichen Kooperative.

Stryker, Sheldon. 1989. The two social psychologies: Additional thoughts. *Social Forces* 68: 45–54.

Stryker, Sheldon, & Anne S. Macke. 1978. Status inconsistency and role conflict. *Annual Review of Sociology* 4: 57–90.

Stryker, Sheldon, & Richard T. Serpe. 1982. Commitment, identity salience and role behavior: Theory and research example. In William Ickes & Eric Knowles (Eds.), *Personality, role and social behaviour* (pp. 199–218). New York: Springer-Verlag.

Stryker, Sheldon, & Anne Statham. 1985. Symbolic interaction and role theory. In Gardner Lindzey & Elliot Aronson (Eds.), *The handbook of social psychology* (3d ed., pp. 311–378). New York: Random House.

Swann, William B., Jr. 1983. Self-verification: Bringing social reality into harmony with the self. In Jerry Suls & Anthony G. Greenwald (Eds.), *Psychological perspectives on self* (Vol. 2, pp. 33–36). Hillsdale, NJ: Erlbaum.

Thomas, William I., & Dorothy S. Thomas. 1928. *The child in America*. New York: Knopf.

2   Toward a sociology of cognition

Peter L. Callero

A complete explanation of the social world must at some level articulate the relationship between self and society. In many ways this is the fundamental theoretical task of sociological social psychology. Consequently, sociologists have developed a diverse set of conceptual systems and theoretical perspectives that seek to explain the nature of social action as it relates to our larger societal structures. Many of these theories rely (whether explicitly or implicitly) on various cognitive processes in their explanations of society. In fact, there is a long tradition of concern for cognitive issues within the discipline. Durkheim's analysis of collective representations, Marx's discussions of ideology and class consciousness, and Weber's "idealist" orientation and verstehen method all clearly place cognition in a central role. Yet, despite this tradition of general appreciation, there has been little explicit theoretical articulation of cognition from a sociological perspective. Indeed there has been conspicuously little in the way of contemporary developments even of the work of Mead, where the basis of a truly sociological approach to the mind is found. As Collins (1985: 225) has recently noted,

Mead still provides the basic outlines of a theory of thinking as an internalized social process, which remains the best building block available....The only drawback is that we have not been used to building on it....Nevertheless the potential is here for a sophisticated sociological theory of the mind.

If we are to fully explain social action and the relationship between self and society, we must at some point achieve an explicitly sociological understanding of cognition. In this chapter I attempt to aid in the development of a sociological theory of the mind by proposing a general framework for analyzing cognition within a sociological context. Discussion of four fundamental questions will guide the presentation of this framework: (1) What is cognition; (2) when does cognition enter the social process; (3) how is social cognition related to interaction; and (4) how are cognitive processes linked to the social structure?

43

What is cognition?

One major roadblock to the development of a sociological theory of cognition undoubtedly has been the belief that cognitive processes are too psychological and too individualistic to be relevant to social theory. Such a position is largely justified under the popular psychophysiological conceptualization of thought. When cognition is defined by brain activity, memory structures, and associative learning, and when empirical analyses rely on measures of electrical impulses, tests of recall, and reaction time, the study of cognition is only indirectly relevant to social thought.[1] Under traditional psychological conceptualizations, cognition tends to be viewed as an individual skill that develops with slight variability among humans. Thus conceived, cognition does appear as tangential to the major issues in sociological theory.

More recent efforts in psychology have been directed toward the study of *social* cognition. These analyses clearly begin with the assumption that cognition is central to understanding social action; the dominant model sees the actor as an "information processor" within a social context. The important question then is to discover how the actor organizes and processes objective information in his or her environment. Ironically, however, the models of social cognition tend not to be any more relevant to sociology than those developed within the tradition of cognitive psychology. Thus, in a recent review and analysis of the social cognition field, Forgas (1983: 130–131) concludes,

It is remarkable that even though much of the critical impetus for a reformed social psychology over the past decade came from an intellectual tradition which objected to the extreme individualism of the discipline, the recent social cognition paradigm turned out to be even more individualistic than its predecessors. Its models and theories come nearly exclusively from cognitive psychology.

As long as cognition is defined psychologically, its relevance to sociology will remain distant. We must begin therefore with a sociological conceptualization of cognition. Such a conceptualization must treat thought as fundamentally social, not simply as an individual skill used in a social context. Fortunately, as Collins (1985, 1989) notes, the basis for just such a conceptualization is found in the work of George Herbert Mead.

Drawing from the philosophical tradition of American pragmatism, Mead conceptualized cognition, or the "mind," as emerging from the process of adjustment to the social and environmental conditions of the world. The sociological foundation of Mead's conceptualization is most clearly illustrated in three tenets. First, the developmental process that leads to full cognitive capacities and the existence of mind cannot occur independent of community. Second, the social processes of adaptation and interaction that characterize and define society are dependent upon cognition. Third, and most uniquely important, thought is itself social in that it is essentially an internalized conversation, or covert form of interaction involving the self and specific and generalized others. When we take the role of other, when we evaluate our own performance, when we imagine how others will respond, when we plan for the future, search for alternatives, or try to solve a problem, we are engaged in a subvocal form of conversation.

This last point is the least recognized and yet most crucial to developing the sociological implications of cognition. Viewing cognition as an internalized conversation means first of all that cognition depends upon language. We must have an external symbol system of communication before a similar system can be internalized for use as the basis of cognition. Second, if one is to engage in an internal conversation, a fully developed self is required. Without the ability to treat the self as object, a subvocal conversation would be impossible. Third, because language is composed of symbols that have a shared or common meaning in the community, cognition must also occur in a shared context. Thus, even though thought is covert, which means we may hide what we are thinking from others, it is never totally subjective or unique in the sense that others would be unable to understand our thoughts. On the contrary, thought is by definition an objective process because it always has the possibility of being externalized and shared. In this sense thinking occurs in terms of universals and not particulars.

If we follow Mead and take cognition to be a covert extension of the social act, we cannot treat it simply as a psychological skill or subjective process involving the storing, retrieving, and processing of information. Rather, like all social acts, social cognition must be conceptualized as being dependent upon a wide set of interlocking social relations, as occurring within a particular historical context, and as being part of an institutionalized struggle for power.

Finally, I should emphasize that this sociological definition of cognition is not meant to represent all thought process. There are certainly ways of thinking outside of conversing with one's self. Thus animals and infants think even though they do not exhibit a sense of self. Also, some adult human thought may simply involve the imagery of events in such a way that language and self-consciousness are not implicated. Nevertheless, I would argue that the most important cognitive processes from a sociological perspecitve are those that implicate the self in an internal form of social interaction, in other words, the cognitive activity that occurs during self-consciousness.

When does social cognition occur?

Central to developing a sociological conceptualization of thought is identifying when cognition enters the social process. Acknowledging the unique cognitive abilities of the human actor does not necessarily mean that cognitive processes are required of all cooperative social action. In fact, many social situations that we encounter are patterned, relatively predictable, and unproblematic. In such a context, the reflexive problem solving that characterizes self-conscious cognition is not required for successful cooperative action. Moreover, there are limits to our cognitive abilities (cf. Langer, 1978). We cannot be expected to maintain an endless series of covert conversations for every person in every situation and for every single act we engage in.[2]

But cognition is necessary at times.The question is, when? Mead is helpful to a point in approaching this question. He suggests that in nonproblematic situations we rely on habit. That is, we enter into a covert conversation only when we find ourselves in novel behavioral episodes that require self-conscious problem solving. Mead's use of habit, however, tends to be quite general. From a sociological perspective, there must be more to habit than what is ordinarily meant by the term. Defined as an acquired individual response, habit does not lend itself easily to the explanation of large-scale patterns of reoccurring interaction that characterize social structures. We need a conceptualization that is more explicitly sociological. I suggest that such a conceptualization can be found in distinguishing between two different types of cooperative behavior associated with symbolic and nonsymbolic interaction.

Nonsymbolic interaction is characteristic of all animal behavior. Without the ability to symbolize, animals do not develop the capacities for either language or self-conscious cognition. Despite this limitation, they obviously manage to communicate and develop basic patterns of social organization. Cooperative social behavior at the nonsymbolic level occurs in a stimulus–response environment where participants react consistently only after learning specific sequences of responses. We can call such nonsymbolic interaction patterns *habit*. Action and affect at this level are always particular, which is to say they have no meaning or significance beyond their utility for completing the immediate act. Habit and nonsymbolic communication are the social basis of cooperative action in animal societies.

Like animals, human societies also rely on habit and nonsymbolic inter-action. The difference, however, is that humans possess self-conscious-ness, which allows for language, cognition, and the ability to engage in symbolic interaction. Through symbolic interaction we are able to adjust to our environment in highly creative ways. It is important to stress, however, that symbolic interaction does not always require self-conscious cognition. Noncognitive symbolic interaction also takes place. Noncogni-tive symbolic interaction is similar to habit in that it is a common recurring pattern of interaction associated with learned behavior. It is distinct from habit, however, in that the episodes of action and affect that characterize noncognitive symbolic interaction have symbolic meaning in the commu-nity. In other words, they have significance beyond the completion of the immediate act. I will refer to patterned noncognitive symbolic interaction as *ritual*.

Although a complete discussion of the nature of ritual is beyond the scope of this chapter, two important dimensions of ritualistic behavior need to be highlighted. First, like habit, ritual frees the actor from the heavy requirements of cognition by providing a sequence of cooperative activity that requires little self-conscious problem solving. Yet unlike habit, ritual also has a more distinctly sociological dimension. Because it is nec-essarily symbolic, ritual also works to uphold the uniquely human aspects of social structure.

The significant sociological implications of ritual have been elaborated by a number of sociologists working in the Durkheimian tradition, but these have been most explicitly articulated at the microlevel by Goffman. Goffman (1967) has argued that certain patterns of everyday interaction are as ritualistic as the religious ceremonies and public festivals described by Durkheim. Moreover, the function of interaction rituals is similar to larger societal rituals in that they serve to create and sustain a collective reality. Similarly, Collins (1981) argues that interaction ritual is at the basis of power relationships defining the stratification system, and that chains of interaction ritual translate microevents into macrostructures.[3] Thus, episodes of noncognitive symbolic interaction may be as important to the explanation of the self–society relationship as the problem-solving activity that characterizes the self-conscious episodes of social cognition.

Since episodes of ritual and habit are by definition patterned and unprob-lematic, they do not involve self-conscious cognitive activity. This means that social cognition occurs outside of habit and ritual during episodes of novel behavior. But not all novel behavior requires self-conscious cogni-tion. At times we act within a basic stimulus–response environment. This is true, however, only when the action–affect episode is nonsymbolic. When

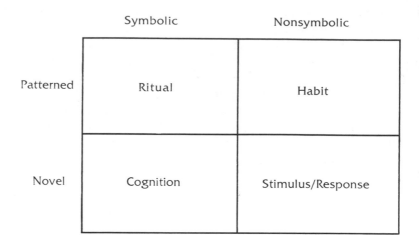

Figure 1. Four types of action–affect episodes

the action–affect episode is characterized as both novel and symbolic, self-conscious cognitive activity is required.

Thus, we have four distinct types of action–affect episodes represented in the two-dimensional relationship diagramed in Figure 1.

The conceptualization of cognition along these two basic dimensions may clarify our understanding of the social context in which cognition appears. In addition, this framework can also serve as a starting point for an explanation of how social cognition is related to interaction.

How is social cognition related to interaction?

The relationship between cognition and overt symbolic interaction must be at the core of a sociology of cognition. Moreover, the explanation of this core relationship must take explicit account of the complexities of social structure. As noted already, an important first step is to conceptualize cognition as a covert form of symbolic interaction. Too often the differences between the covert and overt phases of the act are overemphasized, treating them as almost independent. I will argue that it may be beneficial to treat cognition as one phase of a unified social act. There is, however, an important difference between the overt and covert phase. Overt action and affect become sharable only after symbolic transformation in the covert phase.

Nonsymbolic interaction is primary. Before we develop the capacity for symbolic interaction we communicate at this level. Moreover, we retain the capacity for nonsymbolic interaction even after we have developed the capacity for symbolic interaction. In fact, when communication at the symbolic level breaks down, we resort to the more basic nonsymbolic level of communication. In this sense, our nonsymbolic world is quite stable and dependable but our symbolic world is potentially precarious. In metaphysical terms, the difference between our symbolic and nonsymbolic lives has to do with the fact that episodes of nonsymbolic action and affect are "particular," whereas symbolic systems of communication are by definition "universal." An object or experience is particular when it is unique and not part of a larger category of meaning. On the other hand, a universal experience generalizes across the specifics of particulars to produce a common level of understanding. Social cognition is central in that it helps transform unique experiences of action and affect into shared, socially familiar experiences, and then back again into particular acts. Thus, our overt acts and verbal utterances have no general symbolic meaning unless they are first comprehended at the cognitive level. Similarly, we could not act with the anticipation of shared meaning unless we first recognized the universal significance (meaning) of our particular act or utterance. This relationship between the overt and covert phases of the act is characterized in part by a process I will call "role thinking."

Role thinking

As noted, interaction at the cognitive level (i.e., subvocal communication with the self) is necessarily symbolic. This means that when the self and other become "participants" in covert interaction it is as symbolic representations of particular actors. When others are represented in terms of universal symbols, we can say they are represented in terms of social roles. Because of this, I will argue that interaction at the covert level is very often in terms of social roles.

The use of social roles in this theoretical context is unique. Most traditional approaches to this concept tend to suffer from problems related to either dualism or idealism. Under dualism, the actor and the social role are divorced to the point where social roles are seen as outside the actor, determining behavior through social expectations or internalized behavior patterns. Under idealism social roles are seen as reifications, and as having only subjective reality. Both conceptualizations tend to separate the self, action, and social structure.

A more useful approach is one that recognizes roles as simultaneously both "social object" and "perspective" (cf. Callero, 1986). To say that a role is a social object is to acknowledge that it is a universal, objective, and real feature of the community. Thus despite the fact that roles are symbols, they are not solely cognitive; they are necessarily tied to action and exist as part of the social environment. As such, roles must be taken into consideration during action and, as a result, will often constrain and limit behavior. As elements of the self, however, roles also function as "perspectives." According to Mead, all living organisms are "in" perspectives, which is to say they engage the environment actively, selecting stimuli as opposed to passively responding. In this sense, perspectives represent particular ways of structuring the world. For animals, perspectives are conditioned largely by their physiological capacity, but for the self-conscious human actor perspectives are more flexible. Thus, the community one enters at birth provides a general approach to organizing and structuring one's environment.

Within the limits of this general community perspective, individual differences are possible. Self-definition using social roles as objects is an important source of difference in individual perspectives. Once a role has emerged as a social object in the community, it becomes a social tool and can be used for a variety of social tasks. For example, roles may be used to define self, they may be used to define other, and they may be used as a basis for completing the social act. When social action is successful using one's role-as-perspective, then role-as-object is sustained. It is important to emphasize that roles must be both object and perspective; this is the key to avoiding the problems of traditional conceptualizations. One can only be in the perspective of a social object recognized by the community. The social object, however, must be used in the social act for it to be recognized as a social object.

This particular conceptualization of role allows for a more precise articulation of the relationship between social cognition and action. Since cognition is a covert form of interaction among various roles, thought is necessarily role based. In other words, cognition in the form of self-conscious covert interaction is not possible outside of role use. For symbolic interaction to occur, particular acts must be represented (symbolized) in terms of universal roles. At the same time, roles (as objects) must be sustained in the particular practical activities of interaction. Thus, although roles are represented cognitively, they are not simply combinations of "trait dimensions" or "dispositional schemata," as Wiley and Alexander (1987) have recently argued. Roles are defined by the social act and their meaning is found in the social act. Yet, at the same time, they are symbolic universals, generalizing across a category of acts. This distinction helps clarify the confusion in the literature over the relationship between action and role. Role is not the same as a bundle of acts; acts are particulars that are essentially unique. A literal translation of a role into specific behavioral requirements for specific actors in specific situations is simply not possible (cf. Hilbert, 1981). But roles also are not merely metaphors or reifications since the universality of a symbolic representation must be grounded in the particulars of action. When a role is used successfully as the basis for action, its objectivity is sustained.

Thus, although psychologists have demonstrated how cognition is structured and organized in terms of various representations, schemas, prototypes, and scripts, they have not recognized that these organizational forms have a larger sociological significance. The cognitive structures identified by psychologists can be viewed in many ways as specific features of more unifying and central role categories. Conceptualizing cognition as fundamentally role based also allows us to articulate with greater ease the relationship between social cognition and social structure.

How is social cognition related to social structure?

Complex human social structures are inextricably tied to symbolic interaction in episodes that are both novel and ritualistic. Thus, social structure cannot exist independent of the cognitive role-using activities of the community. This view of social structure parallels that which has been developed at some length by Giddens (1984: xxi), who argues that "the structural properties of social systems exist only insofar as forms of social conduct are reproduced chronically across time and space." Structure in this sense is "carried" in reproduced practices and relationships that have become stabilized (ritual and habit). But social structure is also seen as a set of resources within a dynamic social system. Social roles are one important type of cultural resource. As a resource, social roles can enable the actor to accomplish certain interactional goals. For the same reason, if one is denied access to a certain role, action could be limited and constrained.

The value of Giddens's theory of "structuration" is that it avoids the agent–structure dualism inherent in traditional conceptualizations of social structure, and thus compliments the Meadian conceptualization of role presented in this chapter. Under Giddens's conceptualization, structure is not seen as standing outside the actor, independently compelling or forcing certain patterns of behavior. At the same time, Giddens's conceptualization of social structure avoids the subjectivism of certain phenomenological and interpretive approaches. Acknowledging that social structure is a property of human agency does not necessarily imply that actors create social structures. To view social structure as a product in the subjectivist sense is to view actors as somehow preconstituted or independent of social structure. This subjectivist position also leaves little room for any notion of social structural constraint, or a recognition that social structure can endure beyond the lifetime of particular individuals. The key, as Giddens has noted, is in recognizing that social structure is *both* enabling and constraining.

By way of analogy it is helpful to think of social structure as similar to language. Quoting Giddens (1984: 170),

No one "chooses" his or her native language, although learning to speak it involves definite elements of compliance. Since any language constrains thought (and action) in the sense that it presumes a range of framed, rule-governed properties, the process of language learning sets certain limits to cognition and activity. But by the very same token the learning of a language greatly expands the cognitive and practical capacities of the individual.

Like the process of language use, the use of roles in the role-thinking process can be both enabling and constraining. Social role is one type of available resource defining social structure. As a resource, social roles enable action. They must be used or be drawn upon if one is to act competently. Moreover, role use involves both overt and covert action. Because of this, social structure depends upon cognition. But this does not mean that social structure is mental, subjective, a reification, or a metaphor. Since action has both an overt and covert phase, social structure is necessarily tied to action. Consequently, the externalization of the covert act is in some ways the nexus of the self–society relationship. Roles and cognition radiate out from primary and nonsymbolic episodes of action and affect. Together, webs of symbolic interaction carry social structure across time. Because the process is open and dynamic, one can expect variation in the extent to which the cognitive process affects change in the social structure. Change can be slow or swift. Identifying the factors that are associated with rates of change is an important sociological task, one that must inevitably consider the role of social cognition.

Summary

A sociology of cognition is critical for a complete explanation of the self–society relationship. However, current theories of cognition tend to conceptualize cognitive processes as an individual skill, largely ignoring the necessary relationship between cognition and society. In this chapter I have tried to develop an initial framework for thinking about cognition from a sociological perspective. The framework can be summarized by the following key principles:

1. Self-conscious social cognition is a covert form of symbolic interaction unique to humans.
2. Because social cognition depends upon language, it cannot be uniquely private or subjective and is always potentially sharable.
3. Not all situations require social cognition. Both novel and patterned nonsymbolic interaction are possible outside of cognition. Patterned symbolic interaction can also be sustained with little cognition.
4. Self-conscious social cognition occurs in novel situations requiring symbolic interaction.
5. Nonsymbolic action–affect episodes are primary and particular, meaning communication takes place in a limited stimulus–response environment before the capacity for symbolization emerges.
6. Social cognition translates action–affect particulars into symbolic universals.
7. Social cognition requires social roles – universal, symbolic social objects referencing the self.
8. Social roles are used as perspectives in covert symbolic interaction.
9. Social structure exists largely in the patterned action–affect episodes of symbolic interaction and the social resources required for interaction patterns to proceed.
10. The social structural resources necessary for symbolic interaction both enable and constrain the actor.
11. Social structure is carried through time and undergoes change as a result of the cognitive role-using processes of symbolic interaction.

Within this framework we thus have a number of explicit avenues for exploring the sociological dimensions of cognition. Pursuing a truly sociological conceptualization should help improve our understanding of both cognition and the self–society relationship.

Notes

1 My criticism here is directed toward the dominant theoretical and empirical approaches in psychology and I do not mean to suggest that all empirical analyses that rely on individual measures of recall and reaction time are irrelevant to sociology. As Stryker has suggested in chapter 1, it is certainly possible to use such measures as a means for investigating important sociological aspects of thinking.
2 For similar reasons there must also be limits on our use of role taking. If not, it would be easy to imagine an endless loop of reciprocal role taking developing out of each actor's need to understand other in a constantly dynamic encounter. In fact, Garfinkel (1967) and other ethnomethodologists argue a similar point when they demonstrate how we avoid

recognizing the "indexicality" of our interactions by employing certain "ethnomethods" for maintaining interaction.
3 Although Collins's definition of ritual is more general than the one I have proposed, his theory of interaction ritual chains remains quite relevant (see especially, Collins, 1989).

References

Callero, P. L. 1986. Toward a Meadian conceptualization of role. *The Sociological Quarterly* 27: 344–358.

Collins, R. 1981. On the micro-foundations of macro-sociology. *American Journal of Sociology* 86: 984–1,014.

Collins, R. 1985. *Three sociological traditions*. New York: Oxford University Press.

Collins, R. 1989. Toward a neo-Meadian sociology of the mind. *Symbolic Interaction* 12: 1–32.

Forgas, J. P. 1983. What is social about social cognition? *British Journal of Social Psychology* 22: 129–144.

Garfinkel, H. 1967. *Studies in ethnomethodology*. Englewood Cliffs, NJ: Prentice-Hall.

Giddens, A. 1984. *The constitution of society*. Berkeley: University of California Press.

Goffman, E. 1967. *Interaction ritual*. New York: Doubleday.

Hilbert, R. 1981. Toward an improved understanding of "role." *Theory and Society* 10: 207–226.

Langer, E. 1978. Rethinking the role of thought in social interaction. In J. Harvey, W. Ickes, & R. Kidd (Eds.), *New directions in attribution research*. Hillsdale, NJ: Erlbaum.

Wiley, M. G., & C. N. Alexander. 1987. From situated activity to self-attribution: The impact of social structural schemata. In K. Yardley & T. Honess (Eds.), *Self and identity: Psychosocial perspectives*. New York: Wiley.

3   The cerebral self: Thinking and planning about identity-relevant activity

Richard T. Serpe

In 1979, Morris Rosenberg began his book, *Conceiving the Self*, with the following statement: "It is somewhat astonishing to think that after decades of theory and research on the self-concept, investigators are as far as ever from agreeing on what it is or what it includes" (1979: 3). This statement is perhaps as timely today as it was when published. Over the last decade, however, the gap has been narrowing between theoretical statements of the nature of self and empirical investigations of those theoretical statements. Researchers have systematically developed measurement instruments for these conceptualizations. The result has been to sharpen the debate about what constitutes the self. Within this debate, identity theory has posited the link between commitment and identity, qua "self-structure" (Stryker, 1987a, 1987b). This chapter presents a rationale for including cognitive activity, that is, the processes of thinking and planning about identity-relevant activity, within the model of self-structure offered by identity theory (Stryker, this volume). Specifically, the direct effect of cognitive activity on the structure of self is considered.[1]

Social cognition and symbolic interactionism's treatment of thinking and planning

Cognitive social psychologists have been asserting that processes exist by which individuals "think" about self. These processes, they suggest, help determine the behavior of the individual. Much research in the area of social cognition has focused on the functions of the self that relate to affect, perception, and behavior. (For a review of research in social cognition of the self, see Greenwald & Pratkanis, 1984.) Several of these formulations have direct relevance to the relationship between thinking and self-structure.

Work in self-schemata (Alba & Hasher, 1983; Judd & Kulik, 1980; Markus, 1977; Markus & Sentis, 1982; Markus & Smith, 1981; Swann,

55

1983; Swann & Read, 1981) demonstrates that individuals process schema-relevant information more rapidly, and in ways that are consistent with their self-structures. In other words, individuals process information about self selectively and assimilate that information differentially into their self-schemata. From this perspective, the mechanics of coding self-relevant information into schemata result in linkages among the structure, content, and process of self (Morgan & Schwalbe, 1990).

Research on self-knowledge assumes that self-concepts are constructed from information contained in unfolding life experiences (Greenwald & Pratkanis, 1984; Higgins & Bargh, 1987; Kihlstrom & Cantor, 1984; Markus, 1983; Markus & Nurius, 1986). The construction of self-knowledge is selective and creative, and reflects the social history, percep-tions, and actions of the individual. The area of self-knowledge most relevant to this paper is what Markus calls "possible selves" (Nurius, this volume; Markus, 1983; Markus & Nurius, 1986), the "type of self-knowledge that pertains to how individuals think about their potential and about their future" (Markus & Nurius, 1986: 954).

The link between social cognition and symbolic interactionism is clear in research on planned action. This work suggests that people act in self-relevant ways based on a set of "plans, goals, and scripts." People are viewed as purposive. Actions are considered and planned. This view is well articulated from a social cognition perspective by Harre (1980), Schlenker (1980), and Schank and Abelson (1977). The social cognition perspective views plans and scripts as somewhat different from other cognitive struc-tures because they are action structures that are most often associated with a temporal sequence of events, and are thus situational in nature. They are based on self-knowledge, but are a product of social action and of individual's perceptions of their places within social action (Harre, 1980).

Symbolic interactionists also view people as purposive (Lindesmith & Strauss, 1968). McCall and Simmons (1978), for example, present a set of propositions suggesting that "man is a planning animal." For them, the self-structure of an individual has meaning in relation to social action, which is a product of planning. Heise (1979: 24), considering affect and situated action from a symbolic interactionist frame, points out the rela-tionship between planning and self:

One's sense of self may be largely determined by long-term plans that are in process of being implemented; each plan corresponds to some intended event in which the self is acting in a particular identity, and the identities involved in "what am I doing?" can be named to describe "who I am."

Traditionally, symbolic interactionists have always viewed the self as a cognitive process. The focus on the cognitive aspect of the self is located in their view of "society." This perspective is easily identified in Mead (1934: 173):

Emphasis should be laid on the central position of thinking when considering the nature of the self. Self-consciousness, rather than affective experience...provides the core and primary structure of the self, which is thus essentially a cognitive rather than an emotional phenomenon. The thinking or intellectual process – the internalization and inner dramatization, by the individual, of the external conversation of significant gestures which constitutes his chief mode of interaction with other individuals belonging to the same society....The essence of the self, as we have said, is cognitive; it lies in the internalized conversational of gestures which constitutes thinking, or in the terms of which thought or reflection proceeds. And hence the origin and foundations of the self, like those of thinking, are social.

Symbolic interactionists have identified the cognitive nature of the self as the "I am" conceptions. These conceptions are most often related to social position or action. Although thinking also has been part of the explicit and implicit formulations of self, symbolic interactionists have not pursued "thinking" empirically. Arnold Rose's (1962: 12) discussion of the role of thinking clearly states the central view of symbolic interactionist thought:

Thinking is strictly a symbolic process because the alternatives assessed are certain relevant meanings, and the assessment is made in terms of the individual's values. In thinking, the individual takes his own role to imagine himself in various possible relevant situations. Thinking is a kind of substitute for trial-and-error behavior in that possible future behaviors are imagined (as "trials") and are accepted or rejected (as "successes" or "errors").

The theoretical views of symbolic interactionism and social cognition regarding thinking and planning are similar. Both perspectives maintain that:

1. thinking is related to social action;
2. thinking (thought) is important to the development of the self;
3. planning based on social situation has an impact on the self.

The differences between symbolic interactionism and social cognition's treatment of thinking and planning lie in their relative basis in empirical investigation. For social cognition, these topics have been studied empirically. For symbolic interactionism, these topics have been asserted theoretically without empirical investigation.

Identity theory, and thinking and planning

Researchers working from a symbolic interactionist frame of reference have begun to develop empirical agendas to investigate theoretical statements (Stryker, 1987c). Growing out of what Stryker (1980) calls "structural symbolic interaction," identity theory systematically addresses the link between social interaction and the development of self-structure (Stryker, this volume; Stryker & Serpe, 1982, 1983).

Identity theory's early formulations suggested that the self-structure organized self-relevant responses. These responses were differentiated into three general categories: cognitive (I am), cathectic (I feel), and conative (I want) (Stryker, 1968: 560). These differentiated responses of self were viewed as reflexive and interdependent. Early identity theory research defined and investigated empirically the "I am" dimension. This direction was based on the propensity of symbolic interactionists to focus on socially situated aspects of self (the "I am" statements), and on a general tendency within symbolic interactionism not to emphasize the role of affect, or the "I feel" dimension (see Stryker, 1987b).[2]

Identity theory subsequently has incorporated affective responses into empirical investigations (Stryker, 1987a, 1987b; Serpe, 1987; Serpe & Stryker, 1987), but has not yet dealt with conative, the "I want," responses. Conation is defined here as "the act of wanting or making an effort toward identity-relevant activity." When one spends time thinking and planning about identity-relevant activity, one is engaged in the "act of wanting or making an effort toward identity-relevant activity."[3]

Combining the positions of symbolic interactionism and social cognition, the conative acts of thinking and planning may be identified further as representative of "cognitive activity," which is directly relevant to the development and maintenance of one's self.[4]

Identity theory and cognitive activity

Identity theory (Stryker, 1980) asserts that the self can be conceptualized as a set of identities that are tied to positions and imbued with shared expectations for social action. The relationship between self and social structure is central to an understanding of social action. From the perspective of identity theory (Stryker, 1980, 1987a, 1987b; Stryker & Serpe, 1982), the structure of self is assumed to be relatively stable over time as a consequence of the stability of social relationships (Serpe, 1987; Serpe & Stryker, 1987). Changes in the structure of self are assumed to be related directly to the person's movement within the social structure, either by choice or by force of circumstances, including normal life course changes (Wells & Stryker, 1988). Thus, the theory presumes both relative constancy in the structure of self, given the absence of movement within the social structure, and relative change in the structure of self, given such movement.

Identity theory emphasizes relationships among self, society (social structure), and role performance in seeking to understand how and why individuals make *choices* among role performances, given a variety of possible alternatives (Serpe, 1987; Serpe & Stryker, 1987; Stryker & Serpe, 1983). For example, why does one person choose to work on the weekend while another chooses to spend time with his or her child? Identity theory suggests that such choice behavior can be understood through the concept of "identity salience," the relative salience of a given identity in relation to another.[5]

From a structural symbolic interactionist perspective, choice has also been conceptualized as reflecting constraints that operate on any given set of identities. The appropriate referent for the concept of choice is the manner in which choice operates within a given social structural context. Notably, not all social structural contexts are equally constraining to all actors. For example, consider the identities of parent and worker from the standpoint of expected or appropriate actions associated with each identity from both a male and female perspective. The choice associated with each identity is, by nature of social structure, constrained differently for men and women. Men have *less* choice with respect to the identity of worker, but *more* choice with respect to the identity of parent. The opposite is true for women (at least from a traditional sex-role perspective). (For empirical evidence regarding the impact of social structure on choice, see Serpe, 1987.)

Identity theory integrates social structural elements into identity salience by emphasizing the importance of social relationships, which reflect the individual's location in the social structure. Social relationships define and constrain patterns of commitment, defined by the social and personal costs entailed in no longer fulfilling a role that is based on a given identity (Stryker, 1980). Commitment is defined in two potentially independent forms: (1) interactional commitment, referring to the "extensiveness" or number of social relationships associated with a given identity; and (2) affective commitment, referring to the "intensiveness" of affect attached to the potential loss of social relationships and activity associated with a given identity (Serpe, 1987; Serpe & Stryker, 1987; Stryker, 1987a).

Within identity theory, commitment is viewed as a social structural variable representing society. Commitment reflects the structure of a person's relationships with others, and thus affects the development of a reflexive understanding of self. Identity theory presumes that cognitions are more readily alterable than social structure and thus hypothesizes that commitment has a direct effect on identity salience. Considerable evidence supports the existence of this relationship between identity salience and commitment (Stryker & Serpe, 1982; Serpe, 1987; Serpe & Stryker, 1987; Hoelter, 1983, 1985a, 1985b, 1986; Callero, 1985; White, 1984). Social structural constraints thus operate directly on commitment, a social structural variable, but not on identity salience, a cognitive variable.[6]

In summary, identity theory strives to develop an understanding of the choices individuals make within social action. In assuming that cognitions are easier to change than social structure, it follows that, in addition to the social structural impact of commitment on identity salience, thinking and planning about identity-relevant activity (defined as cognitive activity) should also have a direct effect on identity salience. In this sense, cognitive activity represents one important way by which a person makes choices regarding self.

When individuals spend time thinking and planning about activities related to a specific identity, they are making choices both in terms of that identity and in relation to other identities. It is unlikely that spending time thinking or planning about activities related to one identity does not have either an explicit or implicit impact on other identities. This impact may be because of overlap between activities related to identities, or simply because of time constraints, that is, spending time on one identity may preclude spending time on another.

Theoretically, cognitive activity is not viewed as orthogonal to either interactional or affective commitment. It is assumed that cognitive activity will be correlated with both interactional and affective commitment. The pattern of correlations between cognitive activity and both interactional and affective commitment will vary according to the identity in question.

> HYPOTHESIS 1. *The greater the extent to which a given identity requires social interaction with others, the larger the correlation between cognitive activity and commitment. The greater the extent to which an identity can be enacted without social interaction with others, the smaller the correlation between cognitive activity and commitment.*

The hypothesized patterns are consistent with the role that choice plays in enacting identities. Identities requiring the individual to choose to engage in activities that are not dependent on others or exist because of the presence of others, require by nature more effort from the individual. Conversely, when enacting an identity is dependent on the existence of a social organization, that existence should reduce the amount of time a person must spend thinking about and planning activities related to the identity.

For cognitive activity to be integrated into identity theory, it must have either a direct or indirect impact on identity salience.

HYPOTHESIS 2. *Cognitive activity will have a direct effect on the identity salience of each identity.*

The impact of cognitive activity on identity salience will vary across identities and will reflect the nature of each identity, as well as the relationship between cognitive activity and both interactional and affective commitment.

HYPOTHESIS 3. *The greater the required social interaction, the smaller the effect of cognitive activity on identity salience.*

HYPOTHESIS 4. *The larger the correlation between commitment and cognitive activity, the smaller the effect of cognitive activity on identity salience in relation to the effect of commitment on identity salience.*

These hypotheses make the assumption that interactional and affective commitment and cognitive activity, although interrelated, have independent impacts on identity salience. Differences in the patterns of effects will reflect differences in the characteristics of the identities.

Methods

The sample consisted of 320 college freshmen enrolled in introductory psychology classes at a large midwestern university in a small city.[7] The sample was two-thirds female (215) and one-third male (105). It was representative of college students at the university as indicated by age, racial, and religious profiles. The average age of the sample was 18.5 years. The racial makeup was 88% (282) white, 6.3% (20) black, and 5.7% (18) Hispanic, Asian, or other. Responses regarding religious affiliation were: 45.6% (146) Protestant, 30.6% (98) Catholic, 9.1% (29) Jewish, 6.6% (21) other, and 8.1% (26) no preference. Only minimal differences were apparent on these dimensions between men and women.

Subjects were asked to complete a self-administered questionnaire shortly after their arrival on campus in September, and again in October and December of the same year. The subjects provided information about themselves on a variety of interactional and social psychological variables in relation to five identities relevant to college students: academic (coursework), athletic-recreational, extracurricular, nonorganization friendship (personal involvement), and dating.

The data for these analyses are from the third time point within the data set. The nature of the question addressed within this chapter does not require longitudinal data. The third data point was chosen for these analyses because respondents had a full semester to establish patterns of interaction relevant to these identities. Therefore, the third data point is relatively stable with respect to change in the identities.

Variables

Interactional commitment was measured by two items:

1. How many of the people you have met through (one of the identities) have become close friends? The response is the number of people each respondent reported.
2. How often do you do things or have activities related to (one of the identities)? Response categories were: never, once a month, twice a month, once a week, several times a week, and daily.

Affective commitment refers to the intensiveness of affect associated with the loss of any given identity. Because of the nature of the sample (entering college freshmen), it seemed unrealistic to attempt to assess the potential effect of loss on very new identities. Since this aspect of commitment is viewed as being a product of affect, the use of "reflected appraisals" of the subject's parents and best friend serves as a reasonable substitute, albeit theoretically distinct from assessment of loss.[8] Thus, reflected appraisals are conceptualized here as indexing affective commitment. It is assumed that those who receive highly positive evaluations from significant others, based on particular role performances, have much to lose should they no longer function in those roles. That is, the greater the positive evaluations of self from significant others, the greater the affective commitment. Affective commitment was measured by two items for each identity. The subjects were asked the following questions.

1. How good or successful (at a specific identity) do you think your parents think you are?
2. How good or successful (at a specific identity) do you think your best friend thinks you are?

Cognitive activity was measured by asking the respondents to answer a set of questions that addressed the amount of time they spend thinking and planning about activities related to an identity. These questions were phrased as follows: In addition to actually doing things that we are required or choose to do in our daily activities, we might spend time thinking and planning about our daily activities. We would like you to tell us how often you think and plan about those activities.

1. How often do you spend time thinking about (a given identity)?
2. How often do you spend time planning about (a given identity)?

Categories for this scale were: never, seldom (hardly ever), a couple of times a week (one or two days), several times a week (three or four days), almost every day (five or six days a week), at least once a day, and several times a day.

Identity salience was measured by the method of paired-comparison scaling (Thurstone, 1927; Schuessler, 1971). The subjects were asked to chose one identity over another, using all possible unique pairs, in terms of which identity was more characteristic of how they thought of themselves (e.g., Which of the following is more important to the way you think of yourself: coursework or dating?). This strategy resulted in an index for each identity that was referenced to all other identities, thus approximating the notion of an identity salience hierarchy.

Results and discussion

Figure 1 represents the theoretical model to be estimated. A separate model was estimated for each identity using LISREL VII, a maximum-likelihood structural equation program (Joreskog & Sorbom, 1988). The results of the analysis for each identity are reported in tables 1 through 5. All coefficients shown were significant at $p < .05$ or lower. The three structural coefficients (γ's) representing the effects of interactional commitment, affective commitment, and cognitive activity on identity salience were significant at $p < .01$ if the coefficient was larger than .25. In general, the models fit well for all five identities, as evidenced by the probabilities that ranged from .12 to .51 and the low χ^2 to degrees-of-freedom ratios.

Hypothesis 1 addressed the relationship between commitment and cognitive activity. It posited that the correlations between commitment and cognitive activity would be larger to the extent that the nature of an identity requires social interaction with others. This hypothesis did not receive support from the patterns of correlations between cognitive activity and either interactional or affective commitment. The ϕ coefficients ranged from .113 to .247 with no apparent pattern of effects across identities. The pattern hypothesized would have been supported if the ϕ coefficients for the extracurricular and dating identities had been considerably larger than the ϕ coefficients for the coursework and athletic-recreational identities.

Hypothesis 2 asserted that cognitive activity would have a direct effect

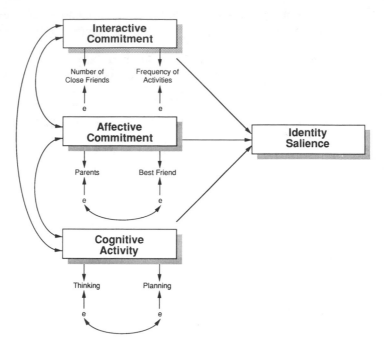

Figure 1. Theoretical model

on identity salience. This hypothesis received strong support. For each identity, there was a significant ($p < .01$) γ coefficient for the effect of cognitive activity on identity salience. The γ coefficients ranged from .271 to .376.

Hypothesis 3 stated that identities that require social interaction, for example, extracurricular, would exhibit smaller effects of cognitive activity on identity salience than would identities requiring less social interaction, for example, coursework. Clear support was found for this hypothesis. The smallest effect for cognitive activity was found in the extracurricular identity, $\gamma = .271$, while the largest effect was found in the personal involvement identity, $\gamma = .376$. Effects of the remaining three identities ranked as follows from smallest to largest: athletic-recreational, $\gamma = .296$; dating, $\gamma = .321$; and coursework, $\gamma = .341$.

Hypothesis 4 posited that the larger the correlation between commitment and cognitive activity, the smaller the effect of cognitive activity on identity salience. This hypothesis was not supported by the pattern of ϕ coefficients between cognitive activity and interactional and affective

Table 1. *Measurement model and structural coefficients for the coursework identity*

	Measurement model						Structural model
	Interactive commitment		Affective commitment		Cognitive activity		
	No. close friends	Frequency of activities	Parents	Best friend	Thinking	Planning	Identity salience
Interactive commitment	$\lambda_x = .645$	$\lambda_x = .311$					$\gamma = .154$
Affective commitment	$\phi = .101$		$\lambda_x = .479$ $\theta_{\delta PAR,BF} = .341$	$\lambda_x = .411$			$\gamma = .292$
Cognitive activity	$\phi = .182$		$\phi = .232$		$\lambda_x = .802$ $\theta_{\delta T,P} = .311$	$\lambda_x = .747$	$\gamma = .341$

Note: $\chi^2 = 7.47$, $df = 8$, $\chi^2/df = .933$, $p = .32$, $n = 320$

Table 2. *Measurement model and structural coefficients for the athletic-recreational identity*

	Measurement model						Structural model
	Interactive commitment		Affective commitment		Cognitive activity		
	No. close friends	Frequency of activities	Parents	Best friend	Thinking	Planning	Identity salience
Interactive commitment	$\lambda_x = .541$	$\lambda_x = .479$					$\gamma = .234$
Affective commitment	$\phi = .165$		$\lambda_x = .451$ $\theta_{\delta PAR,BF} = .091$	$\lambda_x = .529$			$\gamma = .345$
Cognitive activity	$\phi = .213$		$\phi = .169$		$\lambda_x = .652$ $\theta_{\delta T,P} = .387$	$\lambda_x = .623$	$\gamma = .286$

Note: $\chi^2 = 6.98$, $df = 8$, $\chi^2/df = .873$, $p = .39$, $n = 320$

Table 3. *Measurement model and structural coefficients for the extracurricular identity*

	Measurement model						Structural model
	Interactive commitment		Affective commitment		Cognitive activity		
	No. close friends	Frequency of activities	Parents	Best friend	Thinking	Planning	Identity salience
Interactive commitment	$\lambda_x = .794$	$\lambda_x = .687$					$\gamma = .394$
Affective commitment	$\phi = .196$		$\lambda_x = .717$	$\lambda_x = .671$ $\theta_{\delta PAR,BF} = .057$			$\gamma = .328$
Cognitive activity	$\phi = .113$		$\phi = .242$		$\lambda_x = .632$	$\lambda_x = .713$ $\theta_{\delta T,P} = .391$	$\gamma = .271$

Note: $\chi^2 = 5.72$, $df = 8$, $\chi^2/df = .715$, $p = .51$, $n = 320$

Table 4. *Measurement model and structural coefficients for the dating identity*

| | Measurement model | | | | | | Structural model |
| | Interactive commitment | | Affective commitment | | Cognitive activity | | |
	No. close friends	Frequency of activities	Parents	Best friend	Thinking	Planning	Identity salience
Interactive commitment	$\lambda_x = .526$	$\lambda_x = .674$					$\gamma = .239$
Affective commitment	$\phi = .217$		$\lambda_x = .621$ $\theta_{\delta PAR,BF} = .119$	$\lambda_x = .727$			$\gamma = .275$
Cognitive activity	$\phi = .123$		$\phi = .247$		$\lambda_x = .612$ $\theta_{\delta T,P} = .322$	$\lambda_x = .663$	$\gamma = .321$

Note: $\chi^2 = 9.82$, $df = 8$, $\chi^2/df = 1.228$, $p = .12$, $n = 320$

Table 5. *Measurement model and structural coefficients for the personal involvement identity*

	Measurement model						Structural model
	Interactive commitment		Affective commitment		Cognitive activity		
	No. close friends	Frequency of activities	Parents	Best friend	Thinking	Planning	Identity salience
Interactive commitment	$\lambda_x = .752$	$\lambda_x = .696$					$\gamma = .340$
Affective commitment	$\phi = .257$		$\lambda_x = .534$ $\theta_{\delta PAR,BF} = .129$	$\lambda_x = .647$			$\gamma = .268$
Cognitive activity	$\phi = .147$		$\phi = .231$		$\lambda_x = .722$ $\theta_{\delta T,P} = .301$	$\lambda_x = .743$	$\gamma = .376$

Note: $\chi^2 = 5.86$, $df = 8$, $\chi^2/df = .733$, $p = .46$, $n = 320$

69

commitment, or by the pattern of γ coefficients for cognitive activity on identity salience.

Cognitive activity had a strong effect on identity salience in the presence of both interactional and affective commitment across all five identities. Additionally, the magnitude of the effect was relatively consistent across all five identities. Notably, whereas both interactional and affective commitment were correlated with cognitive activity, these correlations did not appear to affect the relationship between cognitive activity and identity salience. This suggests that cognitive activity's contribution to understanding identity salience is independent of the effects of either interactional or affective commitment.

These analyses provide reasonable support for the inclusion of cognitive activity variables in empirical models of identity theory. The results suggest that cognitive activity affects identity salience over and above the social structural effects of interactional and affective commitment, and are thus consistent with early theoretical statements of identity theory (Stryker, 1968). It is also important to note that research in social cognition has demonstrated clearly that cognitive activity is part of the formation of the self (Greenwald & Pratkanis, 1984). Further, social cognition indicates that estimation of cognitive activity will add to our understanding of behavior (Morgan and Schwalbe, 1990).

Since identity theory assumes that cognitions are easier to change than social structure, and strives to develop an understanding of the choices individuals make within social action, cognitive activity must be incorporated in models that seek to represent both stability and change in self-structure. The inclusion of a cognitive activity variable within a symbolic interactionist frame should be viewed as an extension of the assumption that the self is cognitive in nature. Within an identity theory research program, a cognitive activity variable could be useful in furthering the understanding of the reflexive nature of interactional and affective commitment, and cognitive activity, as predictors of identity salience. In longitudinal research designs, a cognitive activity variable would help specify the processes of stability and change in identity salience by indexing modifications in the quantity and nature of cognitive activity relative to specific identities.

Notes

1 Rosenberg (1979) draws a distinction between self and self-concept, focusing on issues related to the self as it "is" and the self as it is "known" to the person. Within this chapter, the terms "self" and "self-concept" are used interchangeably to refer to "self-concept" as elaborated by Rosenberg.

2 Stryker (1987b) develops both a theoretical and an historical explanation for symbolic interactionism's lack of focus on the area of affect. I assert here that, for similar reasons, cognitive activity has not been addressed.

3 It is clear that conation as used here is very different from its use by others. The present formulation is developed from Stryker's (1968) early view of identity theory. As such, conation as it is used here is distinct from the normal attitudinal definition of conation.

4 As used here, "cognitive activity" (I wants) is different from the "cognitive" (I am) notions of self.

5 The notion of the salience or relative importance for self-definition of one identity over another has been addressed theoretically in terms of several other concepts: identity prominence (McCall & Simmons, 1978), role-person merger (Turner, 1978), and psychological centrality (Rosenberg, 1979). Although these conceptions are similar, the notion of identity salience differs significantly by explicating the relationship between identities and social structure.

6 Symbolic interactionism asserts that society and self are reflexive in nature. Given the reflexive nature of society and self, identity theory does not deny the effect of identity salience on commitment, but does assert, on theoretical grounds, that the effect of commitment on identity salience is stronger. Empirical evidence concerning the temporal relationship and strength of effects between commitment and identity salience has been presented elsewhere (Serpe, 1987; Serpe & Stryker, 1987).

7 The generalizability of the college sample is not an issue for this research, which is concerned primarily with process rather than prediction. Other populations may exhibit different patterns of relationships because of different investments and commitments.

8 The use of reflected appraisals as an antecedent of identity salience and as a proxy variable for affective commitment is not without precedent. Serpe (1987) used reflected appraisals to represent affective commitment. Hoelter (1984) utilized reflected appraisals along with role evaluation to predict identity salience.

References

Alba, J. W., & L. Hasher. 1983. Is memory schematic? *Psychological Bulletin* 93: 203–231.

Callero, P. L. 1985. Role-identity salience. *Social Psychology Quarterly* 48: 203–214.

Greenwald, A. G., & A. R. Pratkanis. 1984. The self. In R. S. Wyer & T. K. Srull (Eds.), *Handbook of Social Cognition* (Vol. 3, pp. 129–178). Hillsdale, NJ: Erlbaum.

Harre, R. 1980. *Social being: A theory for social psychology*. Totowa, NJ: Littlefield, Adams.

Heise, D. R. 1979. *Understanding events*. New York: Cambridge University Press.

Higgins, E. T., & J. A. Bargh. 1987. Social cognition and social perception. *Annual Review of Psychology* 38: 369–425.

Hoelter, J. W. 1983. The effects of role-evaluation and commitment on identity salience. *Social Psychology Quarterly* 46: 140–147.

Hoelter, J. 1984. Relative effects of significant others on self-evaluation. *Social Psychology Quarterly* 47: 126–134.

Hoelter, J. 1985a. The structure of self-conception: Conceptualization and measurement. *Journal of Personality and Social Psychology* 49: 1,392–1,407.

Hoelter, J. 1985b. A structural theory of personal consistency. *Social Psychology Quarterly* 48: 118–129.

Hoelter, J. 1986. The relationship between specific and global evaluations of self: A comparison of several models. *Social Psychology Quarterly* 49: 129–141.

Joreskog, K. G., & D. Sorbom. 1988. *LISREL VII: A guide to the program and applications*. Chicago: SPSS Inc.

Judd, C. M., & J. A. Kulik. 1980. Schematic effects of social attitudes on information processing and recall. *Journal of Personality and Social Psychology* 38: 569–578.

Kihlstrom, J. F., & N. Cantor. 1984. Mental representations of the self. In L. Berkowitz (Eds.), *Advances in experimental social psychology* (Vol. 17, pp. 1–47). New York: Academic Press.

Lindesmith, A. R., & A. L. Strauss. 1968. *Social psychology*. New York: Holt, Rinehart and Winston.

Markus, H. 1977. Self-schemata and processing information about the self. *Journal of Personality and Social Psychology* 35: 63–78.

Markus, H. 1983. Self-knowledge: An expanded view. *Journal of Personality* 51: 543–565.

Markus, H., & P. Nurius. 1986. Possible selves. *American Psychologist* 41: 954–969.

Markus, H., & K. Sentis. 1982. The self in social information processing. In J. Suls (Eds.), *Psychological perspectives on the self* (pp. 41–70). Hillsdale, NJ: Erlbaum.

Markus, H., & J. Smith. 1981. The influence of self-schemata on the perception of others. In N. Cantor & J. Kihlstrom (Eds.), *Personality, cognition and social interaction* (pp. 233–262). Hillsdale, NJ: Erlbaum.

McCall, G. J., & J. L. Simmons. 1978. *Identities and interactions*. New York: Free Press.

Mead, G. H. 1934. *Mind, self and society*. Chicago: University of Chicago Press.

Morgan, D. L., & M. L. Schwalbe. 1990. Mind and self in society: Linking social structure and social Cognition. *Social Psychology Quarterly* 53: 148–164.

Rose, A. 1962. A systematic summary of symbolic interaction theory. In A. Rose (Ed.), *Human behavior and social process* (pp. 3–19). Boston: Houghton-Mifflin.

Rosenberg, M. 1979. *Conceiving the self*. New York: Basic.

Schank, R., & R. Abelson. 1977. *Scripts, plans, goals and understanding*. Hillsdale, NJ: Erlbaum.

Schlenker, B. R. 1980. *Impression management: The self-concept, social identity, and interpersonal relations*. Monterey, CA: Brooks/Cole.

Schuessler, K. 1971. *Analyzing social data: A statistical orientation*. New York: Houghton-Mifflin.

Serpe, R. T. 1987. Stability and change in self: A structural symbolic interactionist explanation. *Social Psychology Quarterly* 50: 44–55.

Serpe, R. T., & S. Stryker. 1987. The construction of self and the reconstruction of social relationships. In E. J. Lawler & B. Markovsky (Eds.), *Advances in group processes* (Vol. 4, pp. 41–66). Greenwich, CT: JAI Press.

Stryker, S. 1968. Identity salience and role performance: The relevance of symbolic interaction theory for family research. *Journal of Marriage and Family* 30: 558–564.

Stryker, S. 1980. *Symbolic interactionism: A social structural version*. Menlo Park, CA: Benjamin-Cummings.

Stryker, S. 1987a. Identity theory: Developments and extensions. In K. Yardley & T. Honess (Eds.), *Self and identity: Psychosocial perspectives* (pp. 89–104). London: Wiley.

Stryker, S. 1987b. *The interplay of affect and identity: Exploring the relationships of social structure, social interaction, self and emotion*. Paper presented at the meeting of the American Sociological Association, Chicago, IL.

Stryker, S. 1987c. The vitalization of symbolic interactionism. *Social Psychology Quarterly*, 50: 83–94.

Stryker, S., & R. T. Serpe. 1982. Commitment, identity salience and role behavior. In W. Ickes & E. Knowles (Eds.), *Personality, roles and social behavior* (pp. 199–218). New York: Springer-Verlag.

Stryker, S., & R. T. Serpe. 1983. Toward the theory of family influence in the socialization of children. In A. Kerchoff (Ed.), *Research in the sociology of education and socialization* (Vol. 4, pp. 47–74). Greenwich, CT: JAI Press.

Swann, W. B. 1983. Self-verification: Bringing social reality into harmony with the self. In J. Suls & A. G. Greenwald (Eds.), *Psychological perspectives on the self* (Vol. 2, pp. 33–66). Hillsdale, NJ: Erlbaum.

Swann, W. B., & S. J. Read. 1981. Self-verification processes: How we sustain our self-conceptions. *Journal of Experimental Social Psychology* 17: 351–372.

Thurstone, L. L. 1927. A law of comparative judgment. *Psychology Review* 34: 273–286.

Turner, R. 1978. The role and the person. *American Journal of Sociology* 84: 1–23.

Wells, L. E., & S. Stryker. 1988. Stability and change in self over the life course. In P. B. Baltes & D. L. Featherman (Eds.), *Life-span development and behavior* (pp. 191–198). Hillsdale, NJ: Erlbaum.

White, C. L. 1984. *Ethnic role identity: Processes and consequences for academic performance among black and white college students.* Unpublished doctoral dissertation, Indiana University, Bloomington.

4   Growing up: The development and acquisition of social knowledge

Kathleen Carley

Sociologists are generally concerned with understanding the interface between self and society. A variety of interface mechanisms have been suggested including, but not limited to, "role taking" and "role making" (Cicourel, 1974; Stryker, 1980; Smith-Lovin, this volume; Heise, 1987), development of shared meanings (Stryker, 1980; Burke, this volume; Smith-Lovin, this volume), development of common language (Cicourel, 1974; Shibutani, 1961; Luria, 1981; Callero, this volume), development of common response (Goffman, 1963; Heise, 1987; Smith-Lovin, this volume), and identity formulation (Stryker & Serpe, 1982; Serpe, 1987, this volume; Howard, this volume; Smith-Lovin, this volume; Blumstein, this volume; Burke, this volume; Stryker, this volume). Underlying all of these conceptions is the notion that what information[1] individuals have, and what information they share with others, is somehow key to the self–society interface. It is generally acknowledged that individuals do not acquire this information in a vacuum, but that the social context affects what information they acquire and what information they consider salient. For example, the extant social context impacts the individual's notion of self (Turner & Billings, this volume; Smith-Lovin, this volume; Stryker, this volume) and the individual's conception of others (Heise, 1987; Smith-Lovin, this volume). Two of the aspects of social context that have been explored include social structure and social knowledge. Social structure is often described in terms of the following: setting – for example, church; relative status and memberships – police officers, white, female; or opportunities for interaction – clubs one might join (Serpe, 1987; Schwalbe, this volume; Serpe, this volume; McPherson & Smith-Lovin, 1987); or the network of ties between individuals (White, Boorman, & Breiger, 1976; Burt, 1980; Granovetter, 1974; Carley, 1986a; for example). Social knowledge is often modeled as tacit shared knowledge (Smith-Lovin, this volume; Polanyi, 1962; Carley, 1986a, 1986b, in press-a).

In general, the extant social context is taken as a given, that is, a static phenomena. Neither social structure nor social knowledge, however, is static. And as suggested by Howard (this volume), social change may be a product of individual change. Since the social context is generally treated as static, the dynamics of a society where what knowledge is social is continuously changing, where social structure is changing, where individuals are continually acquiring information and constructing their notion of self, have not been addressed in a systematic analytical fashion.

In this chapter, an analytic framework (referred to as constructuralism) for exploring the relationship between self and society when neither the self nor the society is static is presented. The proposed model is based on the fundamental propositions that (a) interaction leads to shared knowledge and (b) relative shared knowledge leads to interaction. The utility of this model is demonstrated by looking at the question, Is it inevitable that parents and children have different views of the world?

People often speak of there being a generation gap. Evidence exists both anecdotally and in the literature that such gaps exist (Berkner, 1972; Netting, 1981; Caldwell, 1982). Further, such gaps are worse, that is, produce more tension and disagreement, as children get older and enter adulthood (Berkner, 1972; Netting, 1981). Explanations for such gaps include economic explanations (tension created by differentials in the means to control production), psychological explanations (desire for independence and tendency toward rebelliousness), cultural explanations (reverence of parents, age of marriage, etc.), and socialization explanations (difference in education). These explanations lead one to expect that if these differentials did not exist there would be no intergenerational gap and that this gap is peculiar to the process of becoming an adult. In this chapter it will be demonstrated that if individuals are not static, if they are continually learning, if they are continually engaged in the process of self-construction, then such gaps are inevitable. Further, it will be demonstrated that the degree to which such gaps occur is a function of structural factors, for example, the type of education provided and the level of homogeneity in the society.

Statements such as *I just don't understand my kids* and *Parents see things in a totally different way* suggest that the gap is a gap in not just age but in information. If growing up is a process of acquiring information, and parents and other caregivers are the ones imparting this information, then why is it that this gap exists? Part of the explanation surely lies in the fact that discoveries are made, and there is technological change. But even if there were not such systemic changes, would the gap still accrue? Further, do structural features of the society such as the relative scarcity or preponderance of children in the society affect the formation of this gap?

This chapter addresses these questions by exploring via simulation the effect of different educational choices and structural features of the society on both what the individual knows and on what information is considered "social" by the child and by the parent. The simulation model used is CONSTRUCT1, a model based on constructural theory, a cognitively and socially based theory of individual and social development. Using CONSTRUCT1, changes in social knowledge for a family, cultures within a society, and the society as a whole are tracked for a set of 36 societies. These societies differ initially in terms of social structure, educational choice, and family size. Like earlier work on self-construction, social structure as in the size of the population and the composition of groups, will be treated as static. Social knowledge, however, will be treated as dynamic.

The model to be presented centers around the acquisition, exchange, and utilization of information or knowledge. Prior to presenting this model, two questions need to be addressed. What is the relationship between individual knowledge and social knowledge; that is, how can we go from the self to the social? And, why is knowledge a key construct in understanding the interface between self and society?

To address the relationship between individual and social knowledge the following assumption is made. Knowledge is divisible into a set of discreet items, for example, *I am an artist* and *Artists look at the world differently than psychologists*. Individuals either know a piece of information or they do not. Individuals share information, if they both know that piece of information. Social knowledge thus becomes that information which is shared by a majority of individuals in the society.[2] Defined in this way, social knowledge has the properties associated with it when people talk about social knowledge as mediating the relationship between self and society.

That knowledge is a key construct in understanding the interface between self and society has been argued in a variety of ways, not the least of which are the almost axiomatic claims that (a) individual behavior is predicated on what information the individual knows (e.g., Goffman, 1963; Heise, 1987; Smith-Lovin, this volume); (b) interaction opportunities affect what information the individual knows (e.g., Granovetter, 1973, 1974); and (c) interaction opportunities affect what information is currently salient (Heise, 1987; Smith-Lovin, this volume; Burke & Reitzes, 1981; Stryker, 1980; Turner & Billings, this volume). Further, it has been argued that social knowledge performs a variety of interfacing functions. Consider the following. Social knowledge constrains behavior by limiting, for a particular task or social situation, the range of possible interpretations of the available information. Thus, social knowledge enables such feats as story understanding and interpreting newspaper headlines (Schank, 1975; Lehnert, 1981; Rumelhart, 1976; Wilensky, 1981; Carbonell, 1981; Schank & Riesbeck, 1981; Schank & Abelson, 1977), and behaving in a restaurant or a doctor's office (Schank & Abelson, 1977; Heise, 1977, 1979, 1987; Smith-Lovin, 1987a, 1987b, this volume; Goffman, 1974). Social knowledge can be used to judge social membership. That is, one way of distinguishing groups is by whether or not the members of that group share a core set of knowledge that is distinct from other groups. Individuals are judged to be part of that group on the basis of whether or not they share that core set of knowledge. For example, in science shared paradigms can segregate individuals into groups (Price, 1963, 1965; Price & Beaver, 1966; Crane, 1970). Social knowledge is necessary in order for the individual to establish his or her frame of reference, make decisions, and perform tasks (Heider, 1958; Festinger, 1954; Wegner & Vallacher, 1977; Goffman, 1974; Rumelhart, 1978b; Schank & Abelson, 1977). Social knowledge is assumed by members of the society, and is necessary for interpreting communications (Whorf, 1956, Rumelhart, 1978a, 1978b; Collins, Brown, & Larkin, 1977; Charniak, 1972). Social knowledge can be thought of as shared culture or social background information (Polanyi, 1962; Whorf, 1956; Cicourel, 1974; Bar-Hillel, 1960; Carley, 1986a, 1986b). Without social knowledge the members of the group would have no common basis that would admit discussion, let alone agreement (Shibutani, 1961; Cicourel, 1974; Carley, 1984).

Despite the importance of knowledge, and in particular social knowledge, to social behavior, analytic models of the dynamics relating knowledge, social knowledge, and knowledge acquisition have rarely been forwarded. An exception here is the work by Cicourel (1974), and to some extent that by Garfinkel (1968) and Garfinkel, Lynch, and Livingston (1981). Statements such as Cicourel's (1974: 86) that without such a base, "everyday interaction would be impossible for nothing could pass as 'known' or 'obvious,' and all dialogue would become an infinite regress of doubts" and Shibutani's (1961: 40) that "men are able to act together with relative ease because they share common understanding as to what each person is supposed to do" demonstrate both the importance of systematically and analytically examining the development and acquisition of social knowledge and the fuzziness with which the concept has been treated.

A great deal of research has, however, been devoted to understanding individual knowledge acquisition. It has been demonstrated that individual knowledge acquisition is a function of (a) the individual's interaction patterns (Festinger, Schachter, & Back, 1950; Festinger et al., 1947; Granovetter, 1973, 1974, 1982; Carley, 1984, 1986a, 1987b); (b) the opportunities for interaction (Festinger et al., 1947; Burt, 1980); (c) the individual's cognitive processes for acquiring information (Roloff & Berger, 1982; Laird, Newell, & Rosenbloom, 1987; Laird, Rosenbloom, & Newell, 1986a, 1986b; Carley, in press-a, in press-b); and (d) the way in which the information is structured (Winston, 1975; Carley, 1987a). Despite the dual importance of both social and cognitive factors on knowledge acquisition, most research has concentrated on either the cognitive aspects (e.g., Anderson, Spiro, & Montague, 1976; Collins & Gentner, 1978) or the social (e.g., Blau, 1977; Granovetter, 1974; Burt, 1973, 1980) to the exclusion of the other. In addition, most theories of individual knowledge acquisition either ignore social knowledge or treat it as a static item, thus overlooking that in the process of acquiring information, individuals are creating and recreating social knowledge (Garfinkel et al., 1981; Cicourel, 1974). In contrast, constructural theory treats knowledge acquisition as a function of both social and cognitive factors and it treats social knowledge as a dynamic entity that is continually constructed as individuals acquire information and the number of individuals that share a particular piece of information increases.

According to constructural theory the social and the cognitive worlds of the individual are being continuously constructed as individuals move through the series of tasks that constitute their daily lives. In performing these tasks individuals interact, communicate, and acquire knowledge. For the individual, knowledge acquisition and hence cognitive development, can and does occur as a by-product of human interaction. The individual's cognitive structure, that is, what is known and the relationship between pieces of knowledge, is continuously constructed as the individual moves through the series of tasks that constitute his or her daily experience. The social world is continuously constructed as tacit consensus and temporal regularities form across the individuals in the society. Much of the social world is thus an artifact of the parallel construction of individuals' cognitions and the physical act of interacting. The social world and the individuals' cognitive worlds develop reflexively. As individuals' knowledge bases coevolve, their propensity to interact changes and the social world changes. Thus, who you talk to affects what you know and what you know affects whom you talk to. For a more detailed discussion of constructural theory the reader is directed to Carley (1986a, 1990a).

Model – CONSTRUCT1

A basic premise of constructural theory is that interaction leads to shared knowledge and the amount of information individuals share relative to what they share with everyone else affects their level of interaction.

This model is based on this premise. A consequence is that the process of self-construction is viewed as a three-stage process: (1) Individuals interact; (2) they exchange information; and (3) on the basis of their information they reconceptualize their relationship to all other members of the society by determining whether or not they are more or less similar than they were previously, thus altering the likelihood that they interact in the future. Further, the individual's identity becomes both what information the individual knows and the individual's interaction propensities. To use other terms, the individual's identity is both the sum of what he or she knows and who his or her friends are.

Individual behavior

Individuals are characterized by their propensity to interact with other members of the society and by the information that they know. These two characteristics control future interactions and exchanges of information. The individual's life is modeled as a series of interactions – reconceptualization moments. Each time period the individual first interacts with someone, perhaps himself or herself. The individual can interact with at most one other person during this time period. Mass communication is beyond the scope of this model. During this interaction information is exchanged. After all individuals have interacted they reconceptualize their relationships to all other individuals in the society.

Whether or not two individuals interact is a function of their interaction propensities. Each individual, i, has a nonnegative propensity to interact with every other member of society, j:

$$0 \leq INTPRO_{ij}(t) \leq 1$$

Each time period, the individual must interact:

$$\sum_{j=1}^{I(t)} INTPRO_{ij}(t) = 1$$

This interaction, however, may be with one's self, $INTPRO_{ii} \geq 0$; for example, when having an internalized conversation. The interaction propensity is a subjective facet of individual behavior. Consequently, $INTPRO(t)$ is not necessarily symmetric, that is, it may be the case that

$$INTRO_{ij}(t) \neq INTPRO_{ji}(t)$$

Whether or not two individuals actually interact is a chance occurrence weighted by the initiating individual's propersity to interact with the individuals who are not already interacting with someone else. That is, a forward chaining search for the most likely interaction partner is conducted among the remaining individuals. By definition, if there are an odd number of people in the society, then each time period at least one individual will partake in self-interaction. Due to this process, the propensity to interact and actual interaction are expected to be highly correlated, although not identical.

The individual, i, knows a set of information. At any point in time there are a number of pieces of information that are potentially available to the members of the society for communication: $K(t)$. Potentially available information includes that information that is known by at least one member of the society. For each piece of the potentially available information, k, the individual either knows or does not know that information:

$$KB_{ik}(t) = \begin{cases} 1 & \text{if } i \text{ knows } k \text{ at time } t \\ 0 & \text{if } i \text{ does not know } k \text{ at time } t \end{cases}$$

The information known by the individual forms the individual's knowledge base. Individuals do not forget information that they know; that is,

$$\text{if} \quad KB_{ik}(t) = 1, \quad \text{then} \quad KB_{ik}(t + 1) = 1$$

Consequently, over time the size of the individual's knowledge base grows:

$$\sum_{k=1}^{K(t)} KB_{ik}(t) \leq \sum_{k=1}^{K(t+1)} KB_{ik}(t + 1).$$

The knowledge representation scheme described is list structured. That is, each piece of information is distinct and unrelated to the next. There is no intrinsic way to link pieces of information together using this scheme.[3]

Each time an individual interacts there is the possibility that the individual will acquire a piece of information and communicate a piece of information. Whether or not the individual acquires or communicates information is a function of the type of communication channel with the interaction partner and the individual's current knowledge base.

The communication channel between two individuals (CC_{ij}) defines who can send information:

$$CC_{ik} = \begin{cases} > 0 & \text{if } i \text{ can send information to } j \\ 0 & \text{if } i \text{ cannot send information to } j \end{cases}$$

The communication channel is not time dependent. The interaction propensities reflect the communication channel. That is, if two individuals cannot send information to each other, their propensity to interact with each other is zero. Two individuals can interact even if the communication channel is unidirectional. If the channel is unidirectional, then only one of the individuals can send information and the other individual can only receive information, and who can send or receive does not change over time.

There are two ways in which the individual can acquire information – via independent discovery or communication. Independent discovery can occur only if the individual is self-interacting. During self-interaction the individual can discover new information or reflect on known information. If the individual is interacting with another individual, then knowledge acquisition can occur only if knowledge can be and is communicated. Thus, if individuals i and j are interacting, j will learn information as long as the communication channel is open $(CC_{ij}(t) > 0)$ and i has something to communicate. An individual has something to communicate if at least one piece of information is known. That is, an individual can only communicate a piece of information if it is currently in his or her knowledge base:

$.i$ can communicate k if $KB_{ik}(t) = 1$

All pieces of information known by the individual are equally likely to be communicated. An individual always accepts, that is, learns, a communicated piece of information, unless he or she already knows it.

The level of shared knowledge, SK, is the intersection of the two individuals' knowledge bases:

$$SK_{ij}(t) = \sum_{k=1}^{K(t)} KB_{ik}(t) \cap KB_{jk}(t)$$

The relative level of shared knowledge, RSK, for two individuals is defined as:

$$RSK_{ij}(t + 1) = \frac{\sum_{k=1}^{K(t)} KB_{ik}(t) \cap KB_{jk}(t)}{K(t)}$$

After each round of interaction the individuals automatically reposition themselves cognitively on the basis of relative shared knowledge; that is, they reconceptualize their identity and redetermine with whom they are most similar. This causes an adjustment in their interaction propensities:

$$Adjustment_{ij}(t) = RSK_{ij}(t) - \frac{\sum_{j=1,i \neq j}^{I(t)} RSK_{ij}(t) + \sum_{i=1,j \neq i}^{I(t)} RSK_{ji}(t)}{2 \times (I(t) - 1)}$$

The individual's interaction propensity changes through a small adjustment in the individual's previous interaction propensity. If individual i is now more cognitively similar to individual j than to others, that is, $Adjustment_{ij}(t) \geq 0$, then i's propensity to interact with j increases:

$$INTPRO_{ij}(t) = \frac{INTPRO_{ij}(t-1) + Adjustment_{ij}(t) \times (1 - INTPRO_{ij}(t-1))}{\sum_{j=1}^{I(t)} INTPRO_{ij}(t)}$$

Whereas if they are less cognitively similar, that is, $Adjustment_{ij}(t) < 0$, then the interaction propensity decreases:

$$INTPRO_{ij}(t) = \frac{INTPRO_{ij}(t-1) + Adjustment_{ij}(t) \times INTPRO_{ij}(t-1)}{\sum_{j=1}^{I(t)} INTPRO_{ij}(t)}$$

At the individual level, interaction propensities will track shared knowledge. At the social level, social structure – shared patterns of interaction – will track sociocognitive structure – shared patterns of knowledge.

Groups

Groups can be defined on the basis of a priori information. For example, in this chapter one group is the set of all parents, another group is the set of teachers. An individual may be in more than one group. What group(s) the individual is in does not directly affect individual behavior.

Implementation

The model just described was implemented as a computer simulation model that is referred to as CONSTRUCT1. CONSTRUCT1 has been used to explore the relationships among social structure, interaction, and consensus (Carley, 1987a), and to investigate social stability (Carley, 1990b). CONSTRUCT1 is also described in Carley (1987a, 1988). A modified version appears in Carley (1990a).

Given a description of a society CONSTRUCT1 simulates interactions between individuals, the resultant acquisition of knowledge, and the development of shared and hence social knowledge. CONSTRUCT1 takes as input a text file containing a description of a society and produces as output text files of various statistics at the overall social, subculture, or dyad level.

Table 1. *Parameters to describe society*

Parameter	Representation
Length of simulation	Number of interaction-reconceptualization cycles
Number of people	
Number of groups	Defined a priori
Group characteristics	Membership list
Number of pieces of information	
Interaction propensities	A matrix indicating for each dyad their initial propensity to interact
Distribution of knowledge	A matrix indicating for each individual for each fact whether or not the individual initially knows that fact
Rate of immigration	Number of new people who enter society each time period (actual or as percentage of current population)
Startup values for immigrants	Initial interaction propensities and knowledge for each immigrant
Rate of emigration	Number of individuals in society who leave each time period (actual or as percentage of current population)
Rate of rediscovery	Frequency with which individuals discover a fact that is new to them but already known by someone in the society
Rate of discovery	Frequency with which a fact that is new to the society is discovered
Amount of fixed knowledge	Number of facts that individuals may or may not know that cannot be communicated. This can be interpreted as facts about self that cannot be changed such as age or sex.
Social knowledge level	Percentage of group that must know a fact for it to be considered social

These statistics can be produced for each of several time periods. The society is described by providing values for the set of parameters described in Table 1.

The model is analyzed via simulation because it is mathematically intractable for societies with even moderate numbers of individuals and pieces of information, for example, five people and seven facts. Simulation offers the advantage of being able to explore individual and social behavior in more realistically sized groups. A drawback to the simulation approach is that the behavior of the model, and hence the behavior of the societies explored, can only be approximated.

Method

This chapter uses simulation to explore the relationships among social structure, educational choice, and family size and their effects on the development and acquisition of social knowledge. Using CONSTRUCT1 36 societies are simulated, each for 100 time periods. Statistics on the acquisition and development of social knowledge are collected for each time period. Using these statistics it is possible to consider whether, across each society, children learn that information that is social for their parents or develop their own social knowledge, and whether the gap in children's and parents' social knowledge increases or decreases over time. Since statistics on a single family are also collected, it is possible to contrast social knowledge acquisition within a prototypical family to that in the society as a whole.

Societies modeled

A set of 36 distinct societies was created by varying three basic social parameters: the base social structure, the educational choice, and the number of children per family. The base social structure reflects the overall homogeneity of the society. Three different base social structures are explored: the homogeneous society, the heterogeneous society, and the two-culture society. Educational choice reflects the way in which childen arc educated in the society. Three different educational choices are explored: state-operated day care, private day care, home care. In both of the day-care situations it is assumed that children and parents still interact. Four different levels of the number of children per family are explored: 1, 2, 3, and 4. In all other ways, the societies are set up to be comparable, for example, with a similar number of people and the same number of pieces of information. Refer to Table 2 for those parameters that are held constant across all 36 societies.

Each of these 36 societies is characterized by a specific pattern of interaction propensities and a specific pattern in the distribution of knowledge. These are initial descriptions. Given the dynamic nature of CONSTRUCT1 the pattern of knowledge and interaction propensities can change over time. All societies simulated are comparable in size. Within these societies three types of individuals are identified – parents, children, and teachers – as are family units – two adults and n children.

Interaction propensities are described in terms of levels. For example, Zebadiah and Aaron have an interaction propensity at level 5, Zebadiah

Table 2. *Social parameters held constant*

Parameter	Value	Parameter	Value
Length of simulation	100	Number of people	*
Rate of immigration	0	Number of groups	*
Rate of emigration	0	Number of pieces of information	100
Rate of rediscovery	0	Startup values for immigrants	random
Rate of discovery	0	Interaction propensities	*
Size of fixed knowledge base	0	Knowledge base	*

* Items are varied for different societies.

and Deety at level 5, and Deety and Aaron at level 2. Levels indicate the relative ratio of the interaction propensities to each other. Given the level of interaction propensity, L_{ij}, between all dyads, the actual interaction propensity can be found by:

$$INTPRO_{ij} = \frac{L_{ij}}{\sum_{j=1}^{I(t)} L_{ij}}$$

A set of assumptions is made in setting up all societies. Individuals are assumed to interact more with family members than with nonmembers. This is represented by giving family members an interaction level of 4 with each other and lower levels of interaction with non–family members. Individuals are assumed to spend most of their time interacting with others. This is represented by giving each individual an interaction level of 1 for interacting with themselves. Parents are assumed not to interact with teachers (level 0). Parents are assumed to interact only with their own children (interaction with other children is set to level 0). Children are characterized as starting out with no knowledge. Children interact with their own parents, other children, and teachers. All teachers know the facts that are social knowledge for their community (see section on groups and initial shared knowledge). All teachers at the same day-care facility know the same set of facts. Teachers interact with children and other teachers. If there are teachers, then the number of teachers is one-third the number of children. Teachers interact more with children than with other teachers. Children interact more with teachers than they do with other children. This is modeled by setting the teacher–child interaction level to 3. Teachers can communicate information to children but cannot learn from children. Although these assumptions are not entirely realistic, they do present a description of society that is plausible. Further, these assumptions make the societies modeled distinct and characteristic of different sociocultural environments. Thus, if there are effects from varying the structural parameters (social structure, educational choice, and family size) such results will be observable.

Social structure. In the homogeneous society there is a uniform level of interaction between non–family members, and a high level of shared knowledge. This is modeled by setting the level of interaction between parents, excluding spouse, and the level of interaction between children, excluding siblings, to level 2, and by having each parent know 75% of the facts. In the heterogeneous society there is a lower overall level of interaction and less uniformity in the interaction, and there is a lower level of shared knowledge. This is modeled by setting the level of interaction between parents, excluding spouse, and the level of interaction between children, excluding siblings, to either level 1 or 2 determined randomly. Each parent knows 40% of the facts. In the two-culture society the society is divided into two subcultures each with an equal number of parents and children. The set of facts is divided in half, so that one-half is associated with each subculture. Within a subculture the individuals are treated as a homogeneous society, whereas there is less interaction and shared knowledge between subcultures. The level of interaction between parents in different subcultures, and between children in different subcultures is set to level 1. Each parent knows 15% of the other subculture's facts. Regardless of the social structure, which facts are known by whom is determined at random.

Educational choice. Whether or not there are teachers depends on the educational choice. What knowledge two teachers share and what knowledge a teacher shares with other members of the society depends on the educational choice. If there are teachers and it is the two-culture society, then the teachers are equally divided between the two subcultures. When the choice is state-operated day care all children go to the same set of teachers. When the choice is private day care there are two day-care centers with half of the teachers in each center, and which children go to which center is chosen on the basis of social knowledge shared between parents and teachers. When the choice is home care there are no teachers.

Number of children per family. A family unit is composed of two parents and a certain number of children. Four different sizes of family units are explored, those with one, two, three, or four children. When the family unit has four children there are 16 family units in the society. When the family unit has three children there are 20 family units in the society. When the family has two children there are 26 family units in the society. When the family unit has one child there are 36 family units in the society.

Groups and initial shared knowledge

In order to determine whether the gap in social knowledge for parents and children changes over time at the family, subculture, or societal level the following groups are identified. For each group, social knowledge can be identified. A piece of information is considered to be social knowledge for a group if 60% of the individuals in that group know that piece of information. Since children start out with no knowledge, they have no initial social knowledge. There are two societal-level groups, four subcultural-level groups, and two family-level groups.

All parents. This group contains the complete set of parents. If the social structure is the homogeneous society or the heterogeneous society, then the social knowledge for this group are those facts that are known by 60% of all parents in the society.

All children. This group contains the complete set of children.

Parents group 1. This is the first half of the parents in the society simulated.

Parents group 2. This is the second half of the parents in the society simulated.

Children group 1. This is the first half of the children in the society simulated.

Children group 2. This is the second half of the children in the society simulated.

If the social structure is the homogeneous society or the heterogeneous society, then there is no systemic difference between the first and second group of parents or children. Any apparent difference is the result of chance. If the social structure is the two-culture society, then the two groups differ systemically both in the pattern of their interaction propensities and the distribution of knowledge. Further, if the social structure is the two-culture society, then group 1 data is for one subculture and group 2 is for the other subculture.

Teachers group 1. If the educational choice is state-operated day care, then all teachers are in this group. The social knowledge for the group is the social knowledge for all the parents in the society. If the educational choice is private day care, then the first half of the teachers are in this group. In this case, these teachers share the social knowledge of the first group of parents.

Teachers group 2. There is a second group of teachers only if the educational choice is private day care. If there is a second group of teachers, these teachers will share the social knowledge of the second group of parents.

Family parents. This group contains the parents of a particular family selected at random. A fact is considered to be a social knowledge for this group if both parents know it.

Family children. This group contains the children in the selected family.

Measures

For each time period the following measures are collected for the society as a whole, for each subculture, and for the selected family: total social knowledge, amount of original social knowledge, amount of new social knowledge, and amount of unique social knowledge. Using these measures the information gap between children and parents can be calculated. The last three of these measures are based on knowing what information was originally social knowledge for the parents. The parents' original social knowledge is the set of facts that were known by 60% of the parents in that group at time 0.

Total social knowledge. This is measured as the number of facts that are known by 60% of the individuals in the group at that time. This is referred to as *total*.

Amount of original social knowledge. This is measured as the number of facts that are known by 60% of the individuals in the group at that time and that were part of the original social knowledge for the corresponding parents' group. This is referred to as *original*. For groups of parents the amount of original social knowledge is constant over time.

Amount of new social knowledge. This is measured as the number of facts that are known by 60% of the individuals in the group at that time and that are now social for the corresponding parents' group and that were not originally social for the parents. These facts are referred to as *new*. For groups of parents $new(t) = total(t) - original$.

Amount of unique social knowledge. This is measured as the number of facts that are known by 60% of the individuals in the group at that time and that are not social for other corresponding groups. These facts are referred to as *unique*. For groups of children $unique(t) = total(t) - new(t) - original(t)$.

Three measures of the information gap between children and parents are calculated: gap(0), gap(100)-original, and gap(100).

Gap(0). This is the gap in parents' and children's social knowledge at time 0. Since the children begin by not knowing anything, this is just the number of facts that are originally social for the parents.

Gap(100)-original. This is the gap in parents' and children's social knowledge that is measured when the parents' social knowledge is treated as static. It is measured as the difference in the amount of original social knowledge for the parents and the amount of original social knowledge for the children.

Gap(100). This is the gap in parents' and children's social knowledge that is measured when the parents' social knowledge changes over time. It is measured as the difference in the total social knowledge for the parents and the original and new social knowledge for the children.

Results

This analysis provides a variety of insights into the acquisition of social knowledge at the family, subculture, and societal level. A variety of these findings are general, that is, based on the average behavior across all 36 societies simulated (see Table 3).

Knowledge becomes social for children very slowly. For both the society and the subculture in 100 time periods only an average of 18 pieces of

Table 3. *General results for children (amount of social knowledge for that group at time 100)*

Level	Total	Original	New	Unique	Gap (0)	Gap (100)-original	Gap (100)
Social	18.19	9.31	8.22	0.66	48.75	39.44	79.14
Subculture	18.03	12.17	3.52	2.34	62.58	50.41	71.37
Family	41.86	17.47	22.09	2.30	42.67	25.20	55.13

information come to be shared by the children. Within a particular family, however, the children in that family may come to share much more information with each other than all children in the society share; however, the variance across families is quite high (mean = 41.86, sd = 34.59). What about the information gap between parents and children? If we looked only at the knowledge that was part of the parent's original social knowledge, it appears that (a) there is still a large gap (see gap(100)-original column in table), and (b) this gap has decreased, albeit slowly, over time (see difference in gap(0) and gap(100)-original columns). This is true regardless of the group level. And the decrease in the gap may be the most pronounced at the family level. During this time, however, both children and parents have been acquiring new information. The parents at time 100 have new social knowledge. When this knowledge is considered the gap between parents and children actually increases over time (see gap(100) column). This, also, is true regardless of level. The increase in this gap appears the worst at the overall social level.

At the societal level, children sometimes develop social knowledge that is different than the parents' social knowledge. This happen in 10 of the 36 societies. This generally happens in two-culture societies (9 of the 10 societies).

The impact of social structure, educational choice, and family size on social knowledge acquisition and development is complex. These structural factors do impact the rate at which children acquire the parents' original social knowledge, the parents' new social knowledge, and social knowledge that is not shared by the parents. Regardless of level of analysis or which of these structural features is considered, if parental social knowledge had been treated as static, the gap between children and parents appears to decrease over time. Whereas, when you take into account that the parents are also learning new information the gap is seen to actually increase (contrast the difference between gap(0) and gap(100)-original, and the difference between gap(0) and gap(100) in tables 4, 5, and 7).

Table 4. *Social structure results for children (amount of social knowledge for that group at time 100)*

Level	Total	Original	New	Unique	Gap (0)	Gap (100)-original	Gap (100)
Homogeneous							
Social	15.67	15.50	0.17	0.00	98.00	72.50	84.33
Subculture	15.92	14.67	1.25	0.00	91.75	77.08	83.83
Family	39.25	23.58	15.67	0.50	60.00	36.42	60.08
Heterogeneous							
Social	17.00	12.25	3.57	0.08	47.75	35.50	82.91
Subculture	16.67	11.58	4.92	0.17	50.00	38.42	82.08
Family	40.92	15.33	25.00	0.59	38.00	22.67	57.34
Two-culture							
Social	21.92	0.17	19.83	1.92	0.50	0.33	70.17
Subculture	21.50	10.25	4.42	6.83	46.00	35.75	48.16
Family	45.42	13.50	26.00	5.84	30.00	16.50	40.00

Effect of social structure

Social structure does affect the acquisition of social knowledge (refer to Table 4). The less homogeneous the society, the more social knowledge the children develop (see total column), the more social knowledge children develop that is not shared by the parents (see unique column), and the smaller the gap between parents and children. For both a homogeneous and a heterogeneous society at both the subculture and societal level, children learn more of the parents' original social knowledge than of the parents' newly acquired social knowledge. For a two-culture society children will adopt more unique social knowledge, that is, knowledge that is not shared by the parents, than will the children in either the homogeneous or heterogeneous societies. This is an indicator that the two-culture society is inherently unstable. Children in such societies are prone to develop their own set of social knowledge, thus changing the character of the society. At the family level children learn the most of the parents' original social knowledge if the social structure is homogeneous.

In a highly homogeneous society children are most likely to learn the parents' social knowledge because interaction with other children and teachers tends to reinforce the values taught at home, whereas in the heterogeneous society and the two-culture society children are less likely to adopt their parents' original social knowledge as there is less reinforcement outside the family. This lack of reinforcement may also be seen as

Table 5. *Educational choice results for children (amount of social knowledge for that group at time 100)*

Level	Total	Original	New	Unique	Gap (0)	Gap (100)-original	Gap (100)
State							
Social	19.33	11.25	6.92	1.16 ·	48.75	37.50	76.16
Subculture	19.00	13.00	3.25	2.75	62.58	49.58	69.33
Family	42.92	17.83	25.09	3.00	42.67	24.84	53.08
Private							
Social	20.67	10.42	9.75	0.50	48.75	38.33	77.16
Subculture	20.75	14.42	4.00	2.33	62.58	44.16	69.08
Family	45.67	19.50	24.08	2.09	42.57	23.17	51.50
Home							
Social	14.58	6.25	8.00	0.23	48.75	42.50	84.08
Subculture	14.33	9.08	3.34	1.91	62.58	53.50	75.66
Family	37.00	15.08	20.09	1.83	42.67	27.67	60.83

encouragement to adopt the knowledge of the entire society, or socialization not to the subculture but to the society. Thus children develop more social knowledge in the two-culture society and the heterogeneous society that is not shared by their parents. At the same time, however, the parents are also being socialized. Thus as the society is less homogeneous, the actual gap between parents' and children's social knowledge will decrease but the uniqueness of the children's social knowledge will increase.

Effect of educational choice

Educational choice also influences the acquisition and development of social knowledge (refer to Table 5). At the social and subculture level when either state or private day care is used, most of the social knowledge acquired by the children is part of the parents' original social knowledge. Both state and private care lead to the children gaining more social knowledge that is unique. The more children are segregated (private and home care versus state care), the greater the gap between parents and children (gap(100) and gap(100)-original columns) and the less the gap decreases over time (difference in gap(0) and gap(100)-original columns). Segregation, however, does not lead the children to necessarily develop more social knowledge.

Administrators will perceive children overall as acquiring the most original social knowledge if the form of day care is state day care. At the

Table 6. *Educational choice results by society for children (amount of social knowledge, subcultural level, at time 100)*

Level	Total	Original	New	Unique	Gap (0)	Gap (100)-original	Gap (100)
State							
Homogeneous	16.75	15.75	1.00	0.00	91.75	76.00	83.25
Heterogeneous	18.75	13.25	5.00	0.00	50.00	36.75	79.50
Two-culture	21.50	10.00	3.25	8.25	46.00	36.00	45.25
Private							
Homogeneous	18.75	17.00	1.75	0.00	91.75	74.75	80.75
Heterogeneous	18.25	13.75	4.25	0.25	50.00	36.25	80.50
Two-culture	25.25	12.50	6.00	6.75	46.00	33.50	46.00
Home							
Homogeneous	12.25	11.25	1.00	0.00	91.75	80.50	87.50
Heterogeneous	13.00	7.75	5.00	0.25	50.00	42.25	86.25
Two-culture	17.75	8.25	4.00	5.50	46.00	37.75	53.25

social or subcultural level in a private day-care system children will acquire less of the parents' original social knowledge, more of the parents' new social knowledge, and less unique social knowledge than they will in either the state or home care system. When home care is used overall children acquire the least of the parents' original social knowledge.

Thus, at the social level, state day care leads to the most stability in terms of social knowledge transference. If parents want their children to adopt their original social knowledge, they are better off sending them to either state or private day care than keeping them at home. That is, home care does not guarantee that the original social knowledge will be transferred within the family.

At the subculture level, a private day-care choice leads to the highest transference of the parents' original social knowledge. Thus for a subculture, developing private day care for the subculture helps ensure the transfer of original social knowledge. This is true even if that subculture is arbitrarily formed, as in the case of the arbitrary homogeneous and heterogeneous subcultures (see Table 6). In homogeneous societies, regardless of type of day care, children adopt more of the parents' original social knowledge. Home care leads to the lowest transference of parents' original social knowledge to the children.

In the two-culture society home care leads to the children acquiring the least unique knowledge, that is, social knowledge not shared by parents.

Table 7. *Family size results for children (amount of social knowledge for that group at time 100)*

Level	Total	Original	New	Unique	Gap (0)	Gap (100)- original	Gap (100)
1 child							
Social	17.00	9.22	7.11	0.67	49.00	39.78	80.11
Subculture	17.22	11.33	2.67	3.22	65.00	53.67	71.44
Family	10.00	42.67	51.22	6.11	42.67	0.00	0.00
2 children							
Social	18.78	8.78	9.33	0.67	48.33	39.55	79.45
Subculture	19.00	12.78	3.44	2.78	65.00	52.22	70.56
Family	24.44	8.44	14.56	1.44	37.67	29.23	71.67
3 children							
Social	18.89	10.00	8.44	0.45	48.00	38.00	77.89
Subculture	18.44	12.22	4.67	1.55	57.00	44.78	71.89
Family	19.56	9.11	9.89	0.56	45.00	35.89	76.33
4 children							
Social	18.11	9.22	8.00	0.89	49.67	40.45	79.11
Subculture	17.44	12.33	3.34	1.77	63.33	51.00	71.55
Family	23.44	9.67	12.66	1.11	45.33	35.66	72.56

When children are educated at home, however, the greatest gap between children and parents occurs and the decrease in this gap over time occurs at the slowest rate. Again, the lack of reinforcement from teachers leads to the children not learning as much of their parents' social knowledge as they could. Further, when the children interact with other children, including those outside their culture, they acquire not only new information but information not shared by their parents. Going to school has a reinforcing effect not because it prohibits children from interacting, but because it educates all children with the same information so that when they interact with each other they reinforce this information.

Effect of family size

Family size, that is, the number of children in the family, has little impact on the acquisition and development of social knowledge when viewed at the social level. At the family level, however, it has a major impact (refer to Table 7).

The relationship between family size and social knowledge is complex. Within a family single children may quickly learn that knowledge that is social for their parents, thus decreasing the gap between children and parents, whereas at the social level, if all the children are single children, the gap between children and parents will be the highest. It is not the case that the more children in the family, the lower the gap or the higher the gap. For families with either two or four children, less of the parents' original social knowledge is learned, more unique social knowledge is developed, the overall gap is higher, and the decrease in the original gap is less. When there are fewer children (two and three as opposed to four), children acquire more of the parents' new social knowledge.

Conclusion

Constructuralism is a theory about the relationship between the cognitive world of the individual and the social world, that is, about the interface between self and society. According to this theory the social world is continually reconstructed as regularities form across individuals who are in a continual process of self-construction. In this chapter, one of the basic tenets of constructural theory – that interaction leads to shared knowledge and relative shared knowledge leads to interaction – was applied to the area of education.

This chapter illustrates how a cognitively based model of the individual can be used in conjunction with a model of communication to examine both individual and social behavior. The information presented demonstrates that valuable insights regarding the self–society interface can be drawn even when a simplistic model of cognition and a simplistic model of the self-construction process is used. This chapter also demonstrates that social change, modeled herein as change in social knowledge, can occur simply because all individuals in the society are simultaneously constructing their notions of self.

This work, like that of Heise and Smith-Lovin on affect control theory (Heise, 1977, 1978; Smith-Lovin, this volume), utilizes a mathematical modeling and simulation approach. Such an approach is extremely valuable for sociology as it allows us to develop experimental testbeds where questions of self and social change can be explored and the implications of complex theories precisely derived. Such models can be used to examine how sensitive empirical findings are to small changes in structural factors, such as the ratio of groups sizes, over which the data analyst may have little control. Further, such models can be used to noninvasively study the potential impact of social policies prior to their implementation. As our theories increase in complexity and become more dynamic, mathematical modeling and simulation become increasingly important tools for doing theory development. It is important to be careful in applying these models, however, as the modeling task necessitates not only being precise but simplifying. For example, in the analysis in this chapter, it was assumed that over the time period examined individuals did not forget and no discoveries were made.

In this study, through simulation a variety of predictions and explanations can be derived from constructural theory. These were listed in the previous section as results. Let us reconsider two of these.

The model suggests that if parents' social knowledge is treated as static, then the gap between parents and children should decrease over time, whereas, given that the parents are also learning, the gap should actually increase. Anecdotally, there is evidence that this is the case; that is, parents complain more of not understanding their teenagers than they do their toddlers. In addition, intergenerational tension not only does exist but appears to mark the transition of children to independence and adulthood (Berkner, 1972; Netting, 1981). The explanation for this transition is often given in terms of there being a difference in power, wealth, and status between adults and children and the parents being unwilling to transfer to the children the means of production. Constructural theory, on the other hand, suggests that the tension is the result of an intergenerational gap in information, a gap that is inevitable as long as both children and parents continue to acquire information.

The model also suggests that children who are more isolated, for example, those educated at home, will be less likely to acquire social knowledge, will be less likely to acquire parents' original social knowledge, will be less likely to acquire information different than their parents', and will exhibit greater intergenerational gaps. Due to the presence of fewer interaction partners, children educated at home will acquire less information overall, including social knowledge. In the literature it is generally argued that schooling, by increasing economic opportunities, literacy, and opportunities for accessing more new ideas than their parents, has increased the educational gap between children and parents (Ogburn & Nimkoff, 1955; Thornton & Fricke, 1987; Caldwell, 1982). Constructural theory suggests that schooling does not necessarily lead to a gap. Schooling will lead children to acquire information not shared by their parents. In addition, schooling will reinforce the knowledge taught at home. Thus schooling may actually decrease the gap between children and parents.

In interpreting this last prediction it is important to remember that direct interaction with an actual other, for example, face-to-face exchanges, is not distinguished from indirect interactions with a symbolic other, for example, through reading a book. Thus, the prediction that children with fewer interaction partners learn less social knowledge means children who play with fewer other children, who talk to fewer adults, and who read fewer books are more isolated in all these respects and acquire less social knowledge. An interesting expansion of the model would be to disaggregate direct and indirect interaction and to explore their relative effects. Without such an extension, the model does suggest, however, that children educated at home, even if they read the same number of books and watch the same amount of TV and so on as other children, will still acquire less social information.

With respect to education and intergenerational gaps, this chapter demonstrates that observed behavior can be explained by the simple process of interaction that leads to shared knowledge and shared knowledge relative to others leads to interaction. Differentials between parents and children in terms of control over the means of production, literacy, access to new technology, and motives are not needed to produce intergenerational gaps. This suggests that by clearly specifying the mechanisms of self-construction we will be able to produce more parsimonious theories.

It is clear that the social context influences individuals' behavior and the construction of self (e.g., Stryker, this volume; Schwalbe, this volume; Serpe, this volume; Howard, this volume; Smith-Lovin, this volume). In the model presented social context is represented by social structure (the set of groups and their interrelationships) and shared knowledge. In CONSTRUCT1 social contexts are not as differentiated as they are, for example, in affect control theory or role theory. To illustrate this, in CONSTRUCT1 whether a child interacts with a teacher or a parent, all the information known by the child is equally likely to be communicated. Thus, the context has no effect on what information is exchanged. If a more complex scheme for representing information were used, then in fact context effects on information exchange might be able to be explored. This is one direction in which constructural theory could be expanded.

Since the social context is generally treated as static, the dynamics of individual behavior in a changing society and the dynamics of change for the society are rarely explored. In this chapter a framework for exploring such dynamic concerns has been forwarded. Using this framework it was demonstrated that individual change does lead to social change. It was also demonstrated that structural features of the sociocultural environment affect both individual and social change. And, finally, it was demonstrated that social policies by producing certain social structures – for example, the type of educational opportunities available – establish and limit interaction opportunities, thus affecting not only how the individual identifies himself or herself but the opportunity for social change or stability. All this is to suggest that we cannot understand the self–society interface unless we situate our model of the constructed actor not only within social contexts, but within a dynamic model of social contextual change. If this is not done, then it is important to consider whether the propositions forwarded about individual behavior are in fact only short-term effects where the social context is relatively stable.

Notes

1 In this paper the terms *information*, *knowledge*, and *fact* will be used interchangeably.
2 This is an application to information of, and hence a simplification of, the meaning nominalist perspective (Grice, 1969; Bennett, 1976).
3 In CONSTRUCT1 there is no structure to the information. Hence CONSTRUCT1 is not a complete description of constructural theory as presented in Carley (in press-a, in press-b). This simplification is useful, however, as it makes it possible to address analytically the relationship between shared knowledge and interaction. This simplification is limiting in that it does not make it possible to address how organizing information into structures affects behavior. In fact, we know that it is not just how much information people know that determines their behavior but how that information is structured (Carley, 1987a; Morgan & Schwalbe, 1990; Fiske & Taylor, 1984).

References

Anderson, R. C., R. J. Spiro, & W. E. Montague (Eds.). 1976. *Schooling and the acquisition of knowledge*. Hillsdale, NJ: Erlbaum.

Bar-Hillel, Y. 1960. The present status of automatic translation of languages. In F. L. Alt (Ed.), *Advances in computers 1* (pp. 91–163). New York: Academic Press.

Bennett, J. 1976. *Linguistic behavior*. New York: Cambridge University Press.

Berkner, L. 1972. The stem family and the development cycle of the peasant household: An 18th-century Austrian example. *American Historical Review* 77: 398–418.

Blau. P. M. 1977. *Inequality and heterogeneity*. New York, NY: The Free Press, Macmillan.

Burke, P., & D. Reitzes. 1981. The link between identity and role performance. *Social Psychology Quarterly* 44; 83–92.

Burt, R. S. 1973. The differential impact of social integration on participation in the diffusion of innovations. *Social Science Research* 2: 125–144.

Burt, R. S. Dec. 1980. Innovation as a structural interest: Rethinking the impact of network position innovation adoption. *Social Networks* 4: 337–355.

Caldwell, J. 1982. *Theory of fertility decline*. New York: Academic Press.

Carbonell, J. 1981. Politics. In R. C. Schank & C. K. Riesbeck (Eds.), *Inside computer understanding* (pp. 259–307). Hillsdale, NJ: Erlbaum.

Carley, K. M. 1984. *Constructing consensus*. Unpublished doctoral dissertation, Harvard University, Cambridge, MA.

Carley, K. M. 1986a. An approach for relating social structure to cognitive structure. *Journal of Mathematical Sociology* 12(2): 137–189.

Carley, K. M. 1986b. Knowledge acquisition as a social phenomenon. *Instructional Science* 14: 381–438.

Carley, K. M. 1987a. *Increasing consensus through interaction and social structure*. Unpublished working paper, Carnegie-Mellon University, Pittsburgh, PA.

Carley, K. M. 1987b. *Separating the effects of structure and interaction*. Unpublished working paper, Carnegie-Mellon University, Pittsburgh, PA.

Carley, K. M. 1990a. Group stability: a socio-cognitive approach. In E. Lawler, B. Markovsky, & C. Ridgeway (Eds.), *Advances in group processes: Theory and research* (Vol. 7, pp. 1–44). Greenwich, CT: JAI Press.

Carley, K. M. 1990b. *Social and cognitive stability*. Unpublished working paper, Carnegie-Mellon University, Pittsburgh, PA.

Carley, K. M. In press-a. Knowledge, interaction, and language. In K. M. Carley, R. Lawler, & G. Drescher (Eds.), *Experiments in epistemology*. Norwood, NJ: Ablex.

Carley, K. M. In press-b. The social construction of knowledge. In K. M. Carley, R. Lawler, & G. Drescher (Eds.), *Experiments in epistemology*. Norwood, NJ: Ablex.

Charniak, E. 1972. *Toward a model of children's story comprehension*. Unpublished doctoral dissertation, Massachusetts Institute of Technology, Cambridge.

Cicourel, A. V. 1974. *Cognitive sociology*. New York, NY: The Free Press, Macmillan.

Collins, A., J. S. Brown, & K. M. Larkin. 1977. *Inference in text understanding* (Tech. Rep. Report No. 3684). Cambridge: Bolt Berenek and Newman.

Collins, A., & G. Gentner. 1978. *A framework for a cognitive theory of writing*. Cambridge: Bolt Beranek and Newman.

Collins, A., E. H. Warnock, & J. J. Passafiume. 1974. *Analysis and synthesis of tutorial dialogues* (Tech. Rep. Report No. 2789). Cambridge: Bolt Berenek and Newman.

Crane, D. (1970). *Invisible colleges: Diffusion of knowledge in scientific communities*. Chicago: University of Chicago Press.

Festinger, L. 1954. A theory of social comparison processes. *Human Relations* 7: 117–140.

Festinger, L., D. Cartwright, K. Barber, J. Fleisch, A. Keysen, & G. Leavitt. 1947. The study of a rumor: Its origin and spread. *Human Relations* 1: 464–486.

Festinger, L., S. Schachter, & K. Back. 1950a. *Social pressures in informal groups*. New York: Harper and Brothers.

Fiske, S., & S. Taylor. 1984. *Social cognition*. Reading, MA: Addison-Wesley.

Garfinkel, H. M. 1968. *Studies in ethnomethodology*. Englewood Cliffs, NJ: Prentice-Hall.

Garfinkel, H., M. Lynch, & E. Livingston. 1981. The work of a discovering science construed with material from the optically discovered pulsar. *Philosophy of the Social Sciences* 11: 131–158.

Goffman, E. 1963. *Behavior in public places: Notes on the social organization of gatherings*. Glencoe, IL: Free Press.

Goffman, E. 1974. *Frame analysis: An essay on the organization of experience*. New York: Harper and Row.

Granovetter, M. S. May 1973. The strength of weak ties. *American Journal of Sociology* 68: 1,360–1,380.

Granovetter, M. S. 1974. *Getting a job: A study of contacts and careers*. Cambridge: Harvard University Press.

Granovetter, M. S. 1982. Alienation reconsidered: The strength of weak ties. *Connections* 5.2: 4–15.

Grice, H. P. 1969. Utterer's meaning and intentions. *Philosophical Review* 78: 147–177.

Heider, F. 1958. *The psychology of interpersonal relations*. New York: Wiley.

Heise, D. 1977. Social action as the control of affect. *Behavioral Science* 22: 163–177.

Heise, D. 1978. *Computer-assisted analysis of social action* (Tech. Report). Chapel Hill, NC: Institute for Research in Social Science.

Heise, D. 1979. *Understanding events: Affect and the construction of social action*. New York: Cambridge University Press.

Heise, D. 1987. Affect control theory: Concepts and model. *Journal of Mathematical Sociology* 13: 1–34.

Laird, J. E., Newell, A., & P. S. Rosenbloom. 1987. Soar: An architecture for general intelligence. *Artificial Intelligence* 33: 1–64.

Laird, J., Rosenbloom, P., & A. Newell. 1986a. Chunking in soar: The anatomy of a general learning mechanism. *Machine Learning* 1: 11–46.

Laird, J., Rosenbloom, P., & A. Newell. 1986b. *Universal subgoaling and chunking*. Boston: Kluwer Academic Publisher.

Lehnert, W. G. 1981. Plot units and narrative summarization. *Cognitive Science* 4: 293–331.

Luria, A. R. 1981. *Language and communication*. New York: John Wiley and Sons.

McPherson, J. M., & L. Smith-Lovin. 1987. Homophily in voluntary organizations: Status distance and the composition of face-to-face groups. *American Sociological Review* 52: 370–379.

Morgan, D. L., & M. L. Schwalbe. 1990. Mind and self in society: Linking social structure and social cognition. *Social Psychology Quarterly* 53: 148–164.

Netting, R. 1981. *Balancing on an Alp: Ecological change and continuity in a Swiss mountain community*. Cambridge, UK: Cambridge University Press.

Ogburn W., & M. Nimkoff. 1955. *Technology and the changing family*. Boston: Houghton Mifflin.

Polanyi, M. P. 1962. *Personal knowledge: Towards a post-critical philosophy*. Chicago: University of Chicago Press.

Price, D. J. de S. 1963. *Little science, big science*. New York: Columbia University Press.

Price, D. J. de S. 1965. Networks of scientific papers. *Science* 149: 510–515.

Price, D. J. de S., & D. Beaver. 1966. Collaboration in an invisible college. *American Psychologist* 21: 1,011–1,018.

Roloff, M. E., & C. R. Berger (Eds.). 1982. *Social cognition and communication*. Beverly Hills: Sage.

Rumelhart, D. E. 1976. A problem solving schema for stories. In D. LaBerge & S. J. Samuels (Eds.), *Basic processes in reading* (pp. 265–304). Hillsdale, NJ: Erlbaum.

Rumelhart, D. E. 1978a. Notes on a schema for stories. In D. G. Bobrow & A. Collins (Eds.), *Representation and understanding: Studies in cognitive science* (pp. 47–73). New York: Academic Press.

Rumelhart, D. E. 1978b. Understanding and summarizing brief stories. In D. LaBerge & S. J. Samuels (Eds.), *Basic processes in reading* (pp. 211–236). Hillsdale, NJ: Erlbaum.

Schank, R. C. 1975. *SAM – a story understander*. Research Report 43, Yale University, New Haven, CT.

Schank, R., & R. Abelson. 1977. *Scripts, plans and goals, and understanding*. New York: Wiley.

Schank R. C., & C. K. Riesbeck (Eds.). 1981. *Inside computer understanding*. Hillsdale, NJ: Erlbaum.

Serpe, R. 1987. Stability and change in self: A structural symbolic interactionist explanation. *Social Psychology Quarterly* 50: 44–55.

Shibutani, T. 1961. *Society and personality*. New York: Prentice-Hall.

Smith-Lovin, L. 1987a. The affective control of events within settings. *Journal of Mathematical Sociology* 13: 71–102.

Smith-Lovin, L. 1987b. Impression formation from events. *Journal of Mathematical Sociology* 13: 35–70.

Stryker, S. 1980. *Symbolic interactionism*. Menlo Park, CA: Benjamin-Cummings.

Stryker, S., & R. Serpe. 1982. Commitment, identity salience, and role behavior. In W. Ickes & E. Knowles (Eds.), *Personality, roles and social behavior* (pp. 199–218). New York: Springer-Verlag.

Thornton, A., & T. Fricke. 1987. Social change and the family: Comparative perspectives from the West, China, and South Asia. *Sociological Forum* 2: 746–779.

Wegner, D. M., & R. R. Vallacher. 1977. *Implicit psychology: An introduction to social cognition*. New York: Oxford University Press.

White, H. C., S. A. Boorman, & R. L. Breiger. 1976. Social structure from multiple networks. I. Blockmodels of roles and positions. *American Journal of Sociology* 81: 730–780.

Whorf, B. L. 1956. *Language, thought and reality*. Cambridge: MIT Press.

Wilensky, R. 1981. PAM. In R. C. Schank & C. K. Riesbeck (Eds.), *Inside computer understanding* (pp. 136–179). Hillsdale, NJ: Erlbaum.

Winston, P. 1975. Learning structural description from examples. In P. Winston (Ed.), *The psychology of computer vision* (pp. 157–210). New York: McGraw-Hill.

5   The social contexts of self-feeling

Ralph H. Turner and Victoria Billings

Two historically important themes in sociological thought often receive only lip service in current sociological examinations of the self-conception. First, the self-conception is often treated strictly as a cognitive phenomenon, divorced from affect.[1] In contrast, Charles Horton Cooley (1902), the first major sociologist to make the self central in understanding the person in social structure, asserted the primacy of the self-sentiments. He identified the sense of *my* and *mine* and the associated emotional experiences as the first manifestations of a sense of self. If Cooley was correct, and *affect* precedes the cognitive formulation of who I am, we may be asking too much when we assume that people can easily translate the vague sense of who they are into words. Rather than asking people to answer the question, Who am I? we may learn more by asking people when they feel real and when they feel unreal.

A second common practice among sociologists is to describe the self as merely an internalized organization of social roles, memberships, and personal dispositions. However, a distinctive sociological theme in behavioral studies has been the importance of the situational contexts in which attitudes and behavior are manifested. A key orienting hypothesis in the sociological study of self-processes should be that self-discovery, self-recognition, and self-presentation take place in identifiable social contexts. A disproportionate emphasis on ascertaining each individual's internalized conception of self has diverted attention from exploring self-in-situation interactions through which discovery and recognition of self occur.

As a first step toward bringing affect and social context back into the study of self-conceptions, our aim in this chapter is to suggest a framework for the study of social contexts of self-feeling and to report some preliminary descriptive findings. We shall be dealing only with the sense of authenticity and inauthenticity and not with self-esteem and other self-evaluative sentiments. Our goal is principally descriptive and inductive, though we shall also ask to what extent some popular theoretical approaches to self help to illuminate our findings.

103

The nature of the data

The method and data we employ have been described elsewhere (Turner & Schutte, 1981; Turner & Gordon, 1981). In questionnaire format the subject is asked to answer two pairs of open-ended questions. The first question begins at the top of the page and reads as follows:

On some occasions my actions or feelings seem to express my true self much better than at other times. On these occasions the person that I really am shows clearly, I feel genuine and authentic, I feel that I know who I am.
Try to recall one such occasion when your true self was expressed. Please describe the occasion and what you did or felt in detail.

The entire page is left blank for the answer, broken only at mid-page by the probing question:

What was it about your actions or feelings on this occasion that made them an expression of your true self?

The second pair of questions begins similarly at the top of another page, with the probe placed halfway down the blank page:

On some other occasions my actions or feelings do not express my true self, and even misrepresent or betray the person that I really am. On these occasions I feel unreal and inauthentic, I sometimes wonder if I know who I really am. Afterwards I am likely to say something like, "I wasn't really myself when that happened."
Try to recall one such occasion when your actions or feelings contradicted your true self. Please describe the situation and what you did or felt in detail.
[space]
What was it about your actions or feelings on this occasion that made them a contradiction of your real self?

These questions were administered to subjects in the United States and two other English-speaking countries. The results reported here are from 355 students at the University of California, Los Angeles (UCLA). Names were drawn from the registrar's list of currently enrolled undergraduates, using random numbers. Requests were mailed to 800 students whose names were drawn in this fashion, asking them to come to a designated room on campus at an hour of their choice during a two-day period to fill out an anonymous questionnaire. Two rounds of follow-up requests went to students who had not responded. Because of subsequently verified errors in the registrar's list, we estimate the true response rate as approximately 50%. The codes we shall describe were first developed on a different set of protocols, secured in pretests before the main data were gathered.

The nature of situations

One of the greatest difficulties in classifying social contexts is the confusion between "objective" and "subjective" accounts and between ego's and alter's subjective accounts. Some features of social context can be called objective in the sense that all competent observers could agree upon the facts. Whether the subject is at home, at work, at school, or in the wilderness; whether the experience occurred in the daytime or the night-time; whether the subject was alone, with one other person, with a few other persons, or in a crowd; whether sex, alcohol, or drugs, food, entertainment, a religious service, an automobile accident, or a physical injury was part of the context; all are features that should be agreed upon by observers of the event.

Often, however, the most significant features of the social context are largely or entirely subjective. The mood of the gathering may be crucial, as may also be the attitudes of participants toward each other, the operative social norms and social pressures, the task or challenge posed by the situation, and the aesthetic and value features of the setting. With these variables we move further from an objectively describable situation toward W. I. Thomas's (Thomas & Znaniecki, 1927) *definition of the situation*.

We move even further into the subjective when we note that a naive subject's description of a situation or event is seldom sharply separated from an account of the feelings and images that the situation arouses in the subject. For example, to characterize a situation as "dreadful" means that the observer experienced a sense of dread or attributed such feelings to the participants.

Rejecting either a strict objectivism or an unrealistic subjectivism, we define a social situation as an external context consisting of a mixture of objective conditions and the subjective attributes of others in the situation, which acquires meaning for ego by selective perception and through the resonance between what ego brings to the situation and its other objective and subjective features.

In describing situations based on our protocols, we must bear in mind two interrelated difficulties. First, we are dependent upon the subject's report. Not all observable features of the context will be mentioned in the account. Second, there is no way to be certain which features of the social context were critical to the self-experience. We are prepared to assume that these two departures from objectivity are correlated, that the subject is likely to mention features that are critical to the self-experience and to ignore features that are not, though the correlation is surely far from perfect.

Coding social contexts

The code is intended to encompass all aspects of the social situation that subjects commonly see fit to mention in their accounts. Moving from the more objective to the more subjective features of the situation we code the physical location and properties of the *setting*, the size and composition of the *cast* of characters, the nature and motif of the *occasion*, the nature of the *activity* taking place, the overall *ambience*, and any *external demands* felt by ego in the situation. Ego is part of the situation and we recognize this contribution by coding the nature of *ego's actions*, any of *ego's roles* that become germane to the situation, and any *outcomes of actions* in the situation. Ego also contributes more subjectively in assigning meaning to the situation as relevant to ego's own *self-conception*, *beliefs*, *social characteristics*, *personal mood*, or *internal demands* sensed in the situation. Finally, we have coded indications of whether the situation is *exceptional* or frequent and have attempted to identify that feature of the situation that seems most *salient* in evoking the subject's self-feeling. In the next section we shall briefly describe each of the major headings, the broad dimensions for classification within each heading, and the relevant frequencies in the UCLA sample. This description will provide a concrete overview of the structure of social situations as we conceive them and of the relevance of situational characteristics to self-experience.

Self-feeling and the characteristics of situations

The analysis of situations will be guided by two orienting questions. First, to what extent are the situations evocative of true- and spurious-self feelings similar or different? We might hypothesize that the self is more intensely engaged in some kinds of situations than in others, so that both authenticity and inauthenticity feelings occur disproportionately in these situations. The contrasting hypothesis is that authenticity feelings are evoked when there is a basic harmony between self and situation, and feelings of inauthenticity reflect disharmony between self and situation. Hence authenticity and inauthenticity feelings should occur in contrasting types of situations. A variant on the second hypothesis comes from the earlier finding that the "upper" and "lower" boundaries of self are often not anchored to social structure in the same way (Turner & Gordon, 1981). Accordingly, meaningfully different – but not opposite – kinds of situations should evoke true- and spurious-self feelings. With this general question in mind we shall first examine percentage distributions by situational categories, separately for true- and spurious-self protocols, and then compare the two distributions.

A second question is whether self-feeling is more responsive to interaction and events that are strictly symbolic, such as conversations and private musings, or to interaction episodes and events that have more objectively demonstrable consequences, such as achievements, failures, physical injuries, and acquisition or loss of tangible resources.

Self-feeling and objective characteristics of situations

Setting. A drama always takes place in a physical setting. We coded *physical location*, with the difference between natural and artificial settings being most prominent, and *properties* such as decor, landscape features, cultural items, personal belongings, and consumable substances. Except for a few references to natural scenery, most subjects glossed over or ignored the time, place, and properties of the setting. In dramaturgical terms, our subjects could experience self as well in the stark context of the original Shakespearean theater as against the rich backdrops characteristic of the modern stage and motion picture.

Cast of characters. We continue with the stage metaphor in noting that every drama requires a cast of characters. We identified the *composition* of the cast in considerable detail, from self alone to self with parents, siblings, lover, friends, teammates, coworkers, authorities, acquaintances, strangers, and so on. The modal context for both true- and spurious-self experience is a dyad (39% and 43%, respectively, with 21% and 25% uncodable). For larger groups the number of persons present was seldom specified, for example, "I was with friends." Although solitary settings are not frequent (15%, 5%), individualistic experience is much more likely to give rise to authenticity than to inauthenticity experience. This observation is surprising in light of widespread concern for alienating effects of loneliness, even among college students. Over half of the protocols involving two or more people failed to include any unambiguous clue to the sex of the partners. When identifiable, sex composition does not distinguish between true- and spurious-self settings.

The relative flatness of the distributions for the detailed cast compositions indicates the variety of associations within which self-feeling can be evoked. As expected, friends (21.1%) are the most important setting for experiences of authenticity, but they are also the second most important setting for inauthenticity experiences (11.0%). Unspecified others (17.7%)

Table 1. *Cast of characters and self-feeling*

Cast of characters	True self (%)	Spurious self (%)
Charges, customers	4.8	1.1
Alone or others irrelevant	14.9	4.5
Friends, teammates, roommates	24.5	11.8
Lover, spouse, parents, siblings, extended family	16.6	15.5
Authorities	3.7	5.6
Others, strangers, acquaintances, coworkers, classmates	19.4	39.4
Date	1.7	5.6
Accounts not codable	14.4	16.3
Total accounts	100.0	99.8

(the faceless crowd?) constitute the most important setting for an experience of inauthenticity.

In order to illuminate any differences in settings conducive to true- and spurious-self experiences, we grouped the detailed categories in two ways. First, we distinguished intimate others, encompassing friends and family, from nonintimate others and authorities and formal relationships. Only slightly more true-self than spurious-self experiences occur among intimate others (39.4%, 32.1%), though considerable more inauthenticity experiences (40.3%) than authenticity experiences (22.8%) occur with nonintimates. Authorities are unimportant as a context for either authenticity (8.5%) or inauthenticity (6.8%) experience, perhaps because we learn to accommodate even unpleasant relations with authority within our *customary selves* (Turner & Gordon 1981).

Searching inductively for a differentiating principle, we combined cast categories into relatively homogeneous groups according to the ratio of true-self to spurious-self experience in the sample (Table 1).[2] The highest ratio – though involving small numbers – applies to the category "charges and customers," which consists of relationships in which the execution of a formal responsibility toward another person becomes transformed into a bonded personal relationship in which the other(s) are dependent on ego. The greatest disproportion of not-self experiences occurs in dating relationships, which are clearly distinguished from relationships with lovers and more casual interaction with members of the opposite sex. True- and spurious-self experiences are evenly balanced in family and lover relationships, whereas the less intensely intimate and committing friend, teammate, and roommate relationships are relatively more conducive to

Table 2. *Occasion and self-feeling*

Type of occasion	True self (%)	Spurious self (%)
Crisis or turning point	13.8	4.5
Casual	29.0	14.9
Routine	18.0	19.4
Ceremonial or ritual	7.3	8.5
Other, accounts not codable	31.8	52.7
Total accounts	99.9	100.0

authenticity experience. Secondary group relationships in general are disproportionately conducive to inauthenticity experiences, though nearly one-fifth of true-self experiences occurred in these contexts.

Occasion. Occasions are interruptions or highlighted segments in what pioneer students of human behavior like John Dewey (1922) identified as the continuous stream of human activity. We classify occasions as routine, occurring regularly, usually out of habit or necessity, and having no higher meaning for ego at the time; casual, occurring without regularity or planning, informal and lacking ceremony; ritual or ceremonial, an established social form having a collective social meaning; and crisis or turning point, putting ego or others or their plans or reputations in jeopardy, often but not always unexpectedly.

Many of the protocols – especially spurious-self accounts – were insufficiently specific to permit reliable classification of the occasion (Table 2). If we consider only the codable accounts, the modal occasions for authenticity experience are casual and the modal occasions for inauthenticity are routine. True-self experiences were significantly more likely to occur on casual or crisis occasions and spurious-self experiences on routine or ceremonial occasions. But comparison between true- and spurious-self experience must be balanced by observing that routine occasions are also the second most frequent category for true-self experience, and casual occasions are the second most frequent for inauthenticity. In spite of much advertised alienation from routine, many of these students were able to experience authenticity on routine occasions. In spite of the casual occasion's conduciveness to true-self experience, it also leaves many subjects vulnerable to feelings of inauthenticity.

Reflecting on the accounts that are nonspecific concerning occasion, we believe that ceremonial and turning-point occasions would have been readily identifiable in the subjects' accounts. Hence our cautious coding

Table 3. *Activity and self-feeling*

Primary activity	True self (%)	Spurious self (%)
Contemplation	9.6	2.5
Task activity	11.8	8.2
Recreation, socializing	16.9	13.8
Conversation	45.1	44.2
Affection, sex	.8	2.0
Aggression, conflict	.8	3.1
Accounts not codable	14.9	26.2
Total accounts	99.9	100.0

has probably underestimated the frequency of casual and possibly routine occasions. Indeed, an earlier coding that allowed the coder greater discretion to infer what was apparent but not explicit in the accounts showed the highest proportion of both true-self and spurious-self experiences occurring on casual occasions.

Activity. An occasion gives rise to some kind of joint activity involving the subject and any interacting others. The activity may be contemplation of either a structured or unstructured sort; conversation divorced from more active aims or pursuits; recreation, both active and passive, and socializing; expressing affection and engaging in sex; and work or task performance. Because of the importance assigned to it by some respondents as an overriding context for spurious-self feeling, we also included a category of conflict and aggression.

The two clearest impressions from Table 3 are the identical ordering of the three principal categories (conversation, recreation and socializing, and task activity) for true- and spurious-self experience, and the overweening importance of conversation as the context for both kinds of experience. The subjective or symbolic focus of experiences evocative of self-feeling is further accented by our effort to code accounts for their outcomes. Only 21.7% of true-self and 8.5% of spurious-self accounts included any reference to outcomes, and most of these were intangible.

Because conversation plays so great a part in these accounts we coded "type of conversation" and "speaker and topic." The commonest conversation type of true-self feeling was confession (27.4%); confessional conversations seldom evoke a sense of inauthenticity (4.9%). Confessions imply relationships of special trust. When they are combined with personal value statements, just over half of the true-self conversations involve self-clarifying conversation. The commonest conversation type of spurious-self experience is small talk (20.3%). With its low level of personal engagement, small talk seldom evokes true-self feeling (2.3%). For the same reason it is surprising that small talk should evoke feelings of inauthenticity, unless we understand small talk as a device for managing difficult or unpleasant situations.

In other respects, the ordering of conversation types is fairly similar for true- and spurious-self experiences, with personal value statements ranking second for each (22.9% true, 18.9% spurious). Conversations about tasks and problem solving evoke both true-self (16.6%) and inauthenticity (9.8%) feelings among substantial minorities of students.

Conversation about oneself is the commonest context for both true-self (35.4%) and spurious-self (26.8%) experience. Similarly double-edged and third ranking for both true- (20.0%) and spurious-self (12.3%) is conversation about others who are present. A more mutual conversation about selves and interests is much more likely to evoke true-self (30.3%) than spurious-self (8.7%) feelings. On the other hand, a conversation in which others talk primarily about their own interests is especially likely to evoke feelings of inauthenticity (25.4%; 6.3% true).

Self-feeling and subjective characteristics of situations

External and internal demands. Although sociologists assume that social expectations and pressures are ubiquitous, actors are not always conscious of these influences. Awareness and effectiveness of most pressures depend on the individual's own attitudes and sensitivities, but the actor externalizes some of the demands so that they become integral parts of the situation as he or she defines it.

Surprisingly few subjects described what our coders could recognize as external pressures, although more such pressures were indicated in spurious-self (31.8%) than in true-self (13.0%) accounts. In addition, 17% of the true-self accounts mentioned the absence of pressures or expectations as a factor in the situation. Peer or group pressures to conform or fit in were most disproportionately associated with an experience of inauthenticity (24%; 4% true), followed by the pressure of work and unreasonable rules (16% spurious, 13% true). Verbal or physical challenges provided the most scope for true-self experience (33%; 19% spurious).

Subjects also often mentioned pressures that they attributed to themselves. Like the external demands, these internal pressures were more often experienced in connection with inauthenticity (22.3%) than with authenticity (12.4%). In addition, another 6% of subjects associated the feeling of authenticity with a sense of being free from one's usual inhibitions and restraints. Inauthenticity feelings were most often associated with a sense of internal conflict (24%; 7% true), wanting to act on impulse or ignore responsibility (22%; 20% true), and a desire to be accepted or close to others (19%; 11% true). True-self experiences occurred most often with a desire to express oneself (25%; 18% spurious), impulse (already mentioned), a need for excellence or self-mastery (18%; 3% spurious), and a need to live by one's own values (18%; 11% spurious).

In order to understand the significance of these felt demands, we asked whether the subjects complied with them or not. For external demands in true-self situations, accounts divide about equally between compliance (50%) and noncompliance (46%), whereas in spurious-self situations the response is overwhelmingly compliance (91%; 8%). Although compliance with external demands is almost a necessary condition for the experience of inauthenticity when the individual experiences external pressures, it is not at all a sufficient condition for inauthenticity experience. The findings for internal expectations, although not as strong, almost mirror (i.e., reverse) the findings for external pressures. Thus inauthenticity experience is moderately more often associated with noncompliance (56%; 41%), whereas true-self experience is strongly associated with compliance (86%; 14%) to internal demands.

Ambience. Ambience refers to global characterizations of the situations, highly subjective in nature and describing a relationship or atmosphere rather than the behavior or attitude of separate individuals. It seemed clear in the accounts that our subjects often attributed their personal self-feeling to this quality of the situation. A codable ambience was indicated in the great majority of cases (76% for true self; 70% for spurious self). Of all the situational codes, this one distinguishes most strongly between true-self and spurious-self situations (Table 4). Disregarding categories with very small numbers in both columns, we find that atmospheres of acceptance or sympathy, time out or vacation, and openness or frankness are most distinctively associated with experiences of authenticity. Together these three types of ambience account for 60% of codable true-self experiences. At the other pole, a dominating mood of sociability and superficiality, a sense that the situation is somehow out of sync or awkward, and hostility are most distinctively associated with a sense of being unreal. They account for 58% of codable spurious-self experiences. A serious, no-nonsense, or decorous mood is more often associated with a spurious-self experience, though also not infrequently with a true-self experience. A sense of

Table 4. *Ambience and self-feeling*

Ambience	True self (%)	Spurious self (%)
Hope, confidence	1.4	0
Sympathy, acceptance	20.8	.6
Time out, vacation	10.1	1.1
Openness, frankness	14.9	3.4
Glum, defeated	1.7	1.1
Taken-for-granted alikeness	11.3	10.7
Repressiveness, coerciveness	.6	.6
No nonsense, serious, decorous	4.8	7.3
Difference in values	.8	2.0
Hostility, antagonism	3.1	7.6
Out of sync	4.8	13.5
Hedonistic, uninhibited	.3	2.0
Sociability, superficiality	1.7	20.3
Other, accounts not codable	23.7	29.9
Total accounts	100.0	100.1

common identities or interests is equally conducive to both true- and spurious-self experiences.

Self-feeling and the individual's contribution to the situation

Individuals contribute to the situations they find themselves in both objectively and subjectively. Objectively each individual plays a situational role that helps to structure the interactive situation. Subjectively each individual defines the situation with reference to predispositions that he or she brings into the situation.

Like ambience, the actions (situational roles) are sharply polarized in their relevance to true-self and spurious-self experience (Table 5). The two categories of revealing feelings and telling someone off or standing up for ones rights describe 42% of the coded true-self experiences. Combined with altruism and self-examination they encompass 71%. Antialtruistic behaviors of lying, bullying, and ignoring account for 40% of codable inauthenticity experiences, and the antithesis to expressing one's feelings by suppressing feelings, pleasing others by conforming, and impressing others, applies to 36%. Together the three efficacy-related categories of self-sufficiency, high performance, and leading include only 15% of coded true-self experiences. Bungling or failing to act accounts for a similar 15% of spurious-self accounts.

Table 5. *Actor's situational role and self-feeling*

Actor's situational role	True self (%)	Spurious self (%)
Helping, hosting, gift giving	14.6	0
Demonstrating self-sufficiency	4.8	0
Performing well in arts, sports, etc.	4.8	0
Leading positively	2.5	0
Revealing feelings positively	23.7	.3
Telling off, standing up for rights	9.9	.3
Goofing off, playing around	3.1	.3
Analyzing others or ideas	3.1	.3
Examining oneself	8.5	2.5
Conforming to conventional norms	1.1	3.9
Ignoring, refusing, withdrawing	1.1	6.8
Impressing others	.8	7.3
Pleasing others by conforming	.6	10.1
Bungling, waffling, failing to act	.6	12.1
Suppressing feelings, appearing normal	.3	12.4
Bullying, domineering	.3	16.1
Lying, manipulating	0	9.6
Other, accounts not codable	20.3	18.0
Total accounts	100.1	100.0

To what extent did respondents' social structural roles, beliefs, and self-conceptions play an important part in determining the meanings that respondents assigned to the situations? In surprisingly few instances did the confirmation or disconfirmation of a respondent's role appear significantly in the account. In only 23 cases (6.5%) for true-self experience and 9 cases (2.3%) for spurious-self experiences were there such mentions. Prior beliefs were a more frequent factor, but still not of widespread importance. In 57 true-self cases (16.1%) and 76 spurious-self accounts (27.0%), support or lack of support for one's beliefs, respectively, was crucial in evoking self-feeling. In only three and four cases, respectively, were the cited beliefs political. They more often dealt with ethics, religion, or prejudices.

Self-conceptions were cited more frequently, in 47.9% of true-self experiences and 49.9% of spurious-self accounts. Thus in about half the cases confirmation of an explicit prior self-conception evoked a real-self feeling, and disconfirmation of a self-conception evoked a sense of inauthenticity.

Complementary to the situational roles that subjects played are their personal moods. We were able to identify a dominant mood for every account, since personal feelings were more effectively communicated than

Table 6. *Personal mood and self-feeling*

Subject's personal mood	True self (%)	Spurious self (%)
Relaxed, carefree, relieved, comfortable	13.1	0.0
Competent, self-confident, proud	10.5	0.0
Fulfilled, self-satisfied, unique, happy	7.6	0.0
Belonging, oneness with people & nature	7.3	0.0
Good, wholesome, self-righteous	4.5	0.0
Altruistic, concerned	4.2	0.0
Honest, open, genuine, frank	2.0	0.0
Not rational, emotional, many moods	6.8	3.1
Romantic love, infatuation	1.7	.8
Curious, fascinated, stimulated	36.6	45.4
Helpless, hurt, rejected, depressed	3.1	8.7
Angry, moody, irritable to others	1.7	11.3
Ashamed guilty, mean, self-degraded	.8	14.6
Tense, phony, out of place, bored	.3	16.1
Total accounts	100.2	100.0

any other feature (Table 6). Personal moods were both generalized and polarized between true- and spurious-self accounts. Respectively, 37% and 45% of true- and spurious-self accounts revealed a mood that we classified as curious, fascinated, or stimulated. True-self experiences are most distinctively associated with a mood of relaxation, competence, fulfillment, or belonging. Spurious-self experiences are associated especially with feelings of being phony or out of place, ashamed, angry, or helpless or hurt. Thus the principal message is the variety of positive moods associated with a true-self experience and the variety of negative moods associated with feelings of inauthenticity.

One other feature of the situations warrants our attention. For both true- and spurious-self experience we found that the situations seemed to be common rather than unusual ones in the majority of cases, though the feelings or actions were often unusual. There may be a slight tendency for feelings of inauthenticity to occur in common situations more often than true-self feelings.

Matching subjective and objective features of situations

Whereas a subject's definition of the situation is crucial in determining a situation's self relevance, the objective features of the situation should make it more conducive to some meanings than to others. With this assumption in mind, we cross tabulated selected classifications with each other, studying especially relationships between the subjective variables of ambience and personal mood and the more objective variables of activity, cast, and occasion. Here we report only modal patterns.

When subjects experience their true selves in various activities, it is because conversation provides scope for feelings of openness, because recreation allows them to feel relaxed, carefree, and self-realized, and because tasks allows them to feel either altruistic or competent – most often the former. Different casts likewise facilitate different experiences: Close couple relationships (but not dating relationships) facilitate feelings of openness; friends provide opportunities to feel open or relaxed and carefree; family groups are contexts for altruistic feelings, as are acquaintances; in groups of coworkers one can feel either altruistic or competent; and being alone can be associated with feelings of competence and sometimes freedom from external demands. True-self experience on routine occasions is most often associated with an ambience of seriousness and a personal mood of curiousness or competence. Casual occasions mean time out, and again the personal mood can be one of curiousness or competence. Authenticity-evoking ceremonial situations are most often marked by a sense of taken-for-granted likeness, producing a mood of competence, relaxation, or self-righteousness. The ambience in crisis situations is most often hedonism, being out of sync, or seriousness, and the personal mood is altruism, though the meanings of crisis situations are quite variable.

Among the sources of inauthenticity feelings, conformity and lack of autonomy become special problems in large groups and with acquaintances and in other secondary relationships; maintenance of virtue, goodness, and maturity can be problems in pair relationships. Conversation shares all inauthenticity meanings proportionately, but the sense of being unreal is evoked disproportionately from recreation, socializing, and sexual or affectionate relationships that seem superficial. Task activity can become excessively serious. The ambience of routine occasions can be too serious, out of sync, or hostile, inducing a personal mood of anger, shame, or helplessness. Inauthenticity on casual occasions is most often associated with an ambience of superficiality or feeling out of sync, and a personal mood of tenseness or phoniness. Four-fifths of all inauthenticity-evoking ritual occasions are marked by superficiality or excessive seriousness, with the most common personal mood being tenseness and phoniness. Ambience was uncodable in a disproportion of crisis situations, but an ambience of defeat and personal moods of helplessness, tenseness, anger, and shame were most common.

Interpretation and conclusions

The clearest finding from these data is the diversity of situations in which people have self-experiences. Although there are clear modal patterns, there is no deterministic relationship between situations and the self. It is also clear that the contexts for true- and spurious-self experiences are more sharply differentiated according to the meanings that ego assigns to the situation than to the "objective" characteristics of situations. In answer to one of our orienting questions, the self-experiences of these university students occur much more often in connection with symbolic activity, such as nonutilitarian conversation, than in the course of activity with instrumental objectives.

The question of whether true- and spurious-self experiences occur in similar or dissimilar situations must be answered both Yes and Yes, and requires more extended discussion. In some respects, the same characteristics of situations are modal for both kinds of self-feeling. In addition, several characteristics are associated with substantial rates of both true- and spurious-self feelings. Both kinds of self-feeling are most common when the subject is with just one other person, when the activity is merely conversation, probably when the occasion is casual, and when the subject's mood is one of curiosity, fascination, or stimulation. Both kinds of experience occur with significant frequency when the subject is with just one other person, and when the other or others are friends, family members, or a lover; on routine occasions; when engaged in either recreation and socialization or task activity; when engaged in argument or making personal value statements; and when resisting or conforming to either external or internal pressures.

Several of these double-edged characteristics suggest situations that are more informally than formally structured, so that if one becomes "ego-involved" (Sherif and Cantril, 1947), the outcome depends mostly on the developing course of interaction. The neutral character of the mood of curiosity, fascination, and stimulation fits this observation. Other double-edged characteristics suggest the kinds of situations in which people are ego-involved – with intimates, engaging in argument, making value statements, and dealing with internal or external social pressures. We offer this as an important tentative conclusion, that *depending upon the emergent course of interaction, either a true-self or a spurious-self experience is likely to occur in situations that are informally rather than formally structured, in which the individual becomes ego-involved*. Generalized ego-involvement is disproportionately likely to occur among more rather than less intimate associates, in conversation dealing with values, when interaction takes the form of argument, or when the individual must cope with either internal or external pressures.

However, there are also situations in which people are much more likely to experience one type of self-feeling rather than the other. True-self experience is most common when the other or others are close enough associates to permit easy interaction but the relationship is not intimate or binding, when other is dependently bonded to ego, or when the individual is alone; when the occasion is casual or a crisis; when conversation is confessional or problem-solving and/or concerns mutual interests; when the subject is able to meet some external challenge or to resist complying with some other kind of external social pressure; when the individual is able to comply with his or her own internal standards of excellence or self-mastery, values, or self-expression; when the situational ambience is sympathy and acceptance, time out, or unusual frankness and openness; when the subject's situational role is marked by altruism, constructive self-expression or self-examination, or standing up for one's rights; and when the subject's mood is either one of relaxation and comfort, competence and pride, fulfillment, or belongingness. There are obviously several themes here that probably represent the different kinds of situations in which different people feel authentic. Perhaps the most recurrent theme depicts a situation that fosters relaxation, comfort, freedom from pressure, and fitting in. One secondary theme is situational freedom for self-expression. Another theme is situational opportunity to engage in altruistic behavior. A final major theme is a situation posing a challenge, providing an opportunity for achievement.

In contrast, spurious-self experience is most common when the other or others are associated through secondary rather than primary group relationships or the relationship involves precarious mutual testing as in dating; when conversation consists of small talk or centers on a request or invitation of some sort; when others in the group are talking principally about their own interests or about the subject individual; when external social pressures exact compliance from the individual, or when the individual is unable to comply with internal pressures; when the situational ambience is superficial sociability, hostility, or out of sync; when the subject finds himself or herself behaving antisocially, ineffectually, or ingratiatingly and conformingly, with the result that the subject feels phony or out of place, ashamed, angry, or helpless. The themes implicit in this list are quite complementary to the themes for the true-self, though the emphasis on situations that require one to maintain an appearance of being a certain kind of *person* is dominant. One can perform a role at work without feeling inauthentic because it is known to be a role; the self is more vulnerable at a party, in a dating relationship, or in a sacred ceremony because one must appear to *be* the part one is playing.

Relevance of self-theories. We found no theories in social psychological literature that directly addressed situational contexts for self-feeling. However, we conclude by briefly asking whether certain leading self-theories are useful or relevant in shedding light on our findings.

Most relevant to situations evocative of either true- or spurious-self feeling is the classic proposition from John Dewey (1922) that *self-consciousness* arises when habit or custom cannot guide behavior. Except for the crisis turning-point occasion, however, the situations evoking true-self experience for our subjects do not seem essentially problematic. Self-consciousness theory may be more applicable to inauthenticity situations, such as those that seem out of sync and in which ego or others act badly.

According to *identity* theory, in the honored tradition of Robert Park (1927), Manford Kuhn (1954), and Sheldon Stryker (1968, 1987), the self is constituted out of social structural identities organized into individually distinctive hierarchies.[3] However, our subjects' true-self experiences cluster in situations that free them from occupational, age, or gender identities, and spurious-self situations, if seen as assaults on identities, deal with social types rather than social structural identities. Although identity theory tells us a great deal about the *customary self* (Turner & Gordon, 1981), it tells us less about self-boundary experiences.

Another important approach treats the achievement of *self-efficacy* as the key self-process (Bandura, 1977; Gecas, 1982; Gecas & Schwalbe, 1983).[4] Self-efficacy theory illuminates a substantial minority of true-self experiences that take place in crisis situations, though altruism rather than competence is the meaning most commonly self-assigned to ego's behavior in those situations. It also sheds light on a significant minority of spurious-self experiences. Although self-efficacy is important in understanding self-esteem, it is not the crucial element in the most salient self-experiences for this group of university students.

Closely related to self-efficacy theory is the view that identifies authenticity with *autonomy*. Autonomy as a supreme personal value is the basis for Riesman's (1950) exposition of the "autonomous men," is implicit in Zurcher's (1977) positive characterization of the "mutable self," and was a major theme in youthful protest in the 1960s. With its emphasis on being in control of one's destiny, autonomy differs from *individuality* with its stress on being different. In light of the well-documented individualistic values

(Bellah, Madsen, Sullivan, Swidler, & Tipton, 1985) in American society, it is striking that we found little evidence of an individualistic theme in our protocols. The theme of autonomy, however, is recurrent, though the number of accounts that explicitly cite felt external pressures is surprisingly small.

It is generally assumed that individuals enter situations with at least moderately stable self-conceptions, which are then confirmed or disconfirmed by ensuing events, as described in Turner's (1968) exposition of the interplay between self-image and self-conception. Any fairly dramatic *self-confirmation* or disconfirmation of the prior self-conception should evoke self-feeling. According to a related *self-enhancement* approach, self-experiences should occur when a favorable or unfavorable self-conception is unusually strongly confirmed or disconfirmed. This approach is clearly derivative from Cooley's (1902) looking-glass self. Both of these theories can shed significant light on many but not all of the findings. Confirmation of prior self-conceptions was explicit in many of the true-self accounts, and disconfirmation was equally prevalent in spurious-self accounts. The focus of conversation on self in true-self accounts and on others in spurious-self accounts suggests that self-enhancement was often crucial.

Although he did not directly address self-theory, Durkheim's (1915, 1947) view of the intensified sense of reality evoked in collective behavior suggests that one might discover one's true being on ceremonial occasions. By contrast, mass society-alienation theory would lead us to expect not-self experiences most frequently on routine and possibly ceremonial occasions, and true-self experiences on casual and turning-point occasions. Our evidence fits well with mass society theory, but not with our extrapolation from Durkheim.

Few of these accounts could match Maslow's (1959, 1961) descriptions of *peak experiences* in intensity, comprehensiveness, and personal consequences. But themes of detachment from time and place, wholeness, and oneness with another person are frequent in true-self accounts, suggesting a lesser version of peak experiences.

From this sketchy review, we conclude that none of the theories provides a full explanation for our findings, but that some theories are more promising than others. There is clearly much work to be done in developing a suitable theory of self-boundary experiences, and in clarifying their relationship to the self-conceptions that sociologists usually study. We believe there is merit in further exploration of both the nature of authenticity and inauthenticity experiences and the relationship of these experiences to the social situations that evoke them.

Notes

1 See chapter 7 by Lynn Smith-Lovin in this book for a different treatment of affect and self.
2 In this and all other tables we have listed categories according to the rank order of ratios of true-self accounts to spurious-self accounts.
3 Cf. chapter 1 in this book by Sheldon Stryker.
4 Cf. chapter 8 in this book by Viktor Gecas.

References

Bandura, Albert. 1977. Self-efficacy: Toward a unifying theory of behavior change. *Psychological Review* 84: 191–215.

Bellah, Robert N., Richard Madsen, William M. Sullivan, Ann Swidler, & Steven M. Tipton. 1985. *Habits of the heart: Individualism and commitment in American life.* Berkeley: University of California Press.

Cooley, Charles H. 1902. *Human nature and the social order.* New York: Charles Scribner's Sons.

Dewey, John. 1922. *Human nature and conduct: An introduction to social psychology.* New York: Henry Holt.

Durkheim, Emile. 1947. *The elementary forms of the religious life* (Joseph Ward Swain, Trans.). New York: Free Press. (Original work published 1915)

Gecas, Viktor. 1982. The self-concept. *Annual Review of Sociology* 8: 1–33.

Gecas, Viktor, & Michael Schwalbe. 1983. Beyond the looking-glass self: Social structure and efficacy-based self-esteem. *Social Psychology Quarterly* 46: 77–88.

Kuhn, Manford H. 1954. Factors in personality: Socio-cultural determinants as seen through the Amish. In Francis L. K. Hsu (Ed.), *Aspects of culture and personality* (pp. 43–60). New York: Abelard-Schuman.

Maslow, Abraham H. 1959. Cognition of being in the peak experiences. *Journal of Genetic Psychology* 94: 43–66.

Maslow, Abraham H. 1961. Peak-experiences as acute identity-experiences. *American Journal of Psychoanalysis* 21: 254–260.

Park, Robert E. 1927. Human nature and collective behavior. *American Journal of Sociology* 32: 733–741.

Riesman, David. 1950. *The lonely crowd: A study of the changing American character.* New Haven, CT: Yale University Press.

Sherif, Muzafer, & Hadley Cantril. 1947. *The psychology of ego-involvements: Social attitudes and identifications.* New York: Wiley.

Stryker, Sheldon. 1968. Identity salience and role performance: The relevance of symbolic interaction theory for family research. *Journal of Marriage and the Family* 30: 88–92.

Stryker, Sheldon. 1987. Identity theory: Development and extensions. In Krysia Yardley & Terry Honess (Eds.), *Self and identity: Psychosocial perspectives* (pp. 89–103). Chichester, UK: Wiley.

Thomas, William I., & Florian Znaniecki. 1927. *The Polish peasant in Europe and America* (Vol. 1). Boston: Richard G. Badger.

Turner, Ralph H. 1968. The self conception in social interaction. In Chad Gordon & Kenneth Gergen (Eds.), *The self in social interaction* (Vol. 1, pp. 93–106). New York: Wiley.

Turner, Ralph H., & Steven Gordon. 1981. The boundaries of the self: The relationship of authenticity to inauthenticity in the self-conception. In Mervin D. Lynch, Ardyth A.

Norem-Hebeisen, & Kenneth Gergen (Eds.), *The self-concept: Advances in theory and research* (pp. 39–57). Cambridge: Ballinger Press.

Turner, Ralph H., & Jerald Schutte. 1981. The true-self method for studying the self conception. *Symbolic Interaction* 4: 1–20.

Zurcher, Louis A., Jr. 1977. *The mutable self: A self-concept for social change*. Beverly Hills, CA: Sage.

6   Self-processes and emotional experiences

Morris Rosenberg

In recent years there has been a veritable explosion of interest in the emotions among social scientists. Sociologists, psychologists, and anthropologists are all involved in this intellectual ferment. Sociocultural processes have been shown to play a major role in the formation and expression of the emotions (e.g., Gordon, 1990; Hochschild, 1979, 1983; Thoits, 1985). The aim of this chapter is to show how processes centering on the self can add to our understanding of the emotional lives of human beings.

Reflexivity and emotions

By self-processes, I refer to all the processes involving the self as the object of its own cognition and regulation (Rosenberg, 1990). These processes are features of human reflexivity, that is, phenomena in which the subject and object have the same referent. By virtue of reflexivity, the human being is able to adopt a "third-party" perspective on the self. When one views oneself as an object, one looks at oneself from the outside, observing oneself as one might observe any other object in the world.

All cognitive processes (e.g., attention, classification, evaluation, judgment, reasoning) whose content involves any feature of the self are expressions of *cognitive* reflexivity. Human reflexivity is also expressed in the control or regulation of the self, called *agentive* reflexivity (Rosenberg, 1990). Just as human beings strive to affect the external environment in order to meet their needs, so do they strive to produce intentional effects upon the self. Cognitive reflexivity and agentive reflexivity are the chief self-processes.

These self-processes are not simply the results of the unfolding of a given

The preparation of this paper was facilitated by the award of a Guggenheim Fellowship.

123

genetic potential. Both Cooley (1902) and Mead (1934) stressed that the self is a product of social interaction. It is only as the result of taking the role of the other – of coming to see oneself from the viewpoint of others – that the individual develops an awareness of self. In the course of time, these cognitive processes result in the construction of that attitudinal entity that we refer to as the self-concept. Although there are different ways of classifying the components of the self-concept, there is one broad division that is of major importance and that has been shown to follow a character-istic developmental course: the division between the internal and external features of the self (Shantz, 1975; Livesley & Bromley, 1973).

One of the most important internal features of the self is the emotions. The emotions are an important feature of human experience, represent a major source of human motivation, and have a significant effect on human behavior. It will soon become apparent, however, that thoughts and feelings are not readily separated – that it is not possible to speak of emotions without taking account of cognitions. My contention is that self-processes involve cognitions about these internal events and that these cognitions play a major role in human emotions.

There are at least three ways in which self-processes enter the emotional lives of human beings. First, they affect emotional identification; second, emotional display; and third, emotional experiences. Elsewhere (Rosen-berg, 1990) I have discussed emotional identification and emotional dis-play. In this chapter I shall focus on what I consider to be the most intriguing of the emotional self-regulation processes, namely, the self-regulation of emotional experiences.

Importance of emotional self-regulation

Before turning to the question of how self-processes affect the emotions, it is first necessary to ask, Why is the self-regulation of emotions important to human beings? I will first consider its importance for the individual and then turn to its importance for society.

Importance for the individual

There are at least three major reasons why emotions are important to individuals. The first is *instrumental*. Emotions are a means for the attainment of one's ends or, in the negative case, an obstacle in the path of such achievement. The second is *hedonic*. Some emotions are inherently pleasurable, others painful. The third is *normative*. Well-socialized actors strive to adhere to the emotional norms of society both because they have internalized these norms and because of the reinforcing consequences of adherence. In other words, people prefer those emotions that enable them to get what they want out to life (instrumental), that are inherently pleasurable (hedonic), and that are socially appropriate (normative).

Instrumental reasons. The regulation of emotional *intensity*, it is apparent, has instrumental relevance. First, emotional intensity can have a major impact on performance. Someone who can remain calm during a job interview is likely to perform better than someone who is extremely nervous. Intense emotions can also interfere with motor control. They may impair manual performance by producing hand trembling, disturbances in hand–eye coordination, and so on. Intense emotions can also exercise a disorganizing effect on thought processes. A person in a towering rage may be unable to mobilize the necessary clarity of thought and dispassionate analysis that will optimize problem-solving success. Under the influence of powerful internal turmoil, concentration may be lost, thoughts may become jumbled, racing ideas and random, irrelevant associations may come to dominate the mind. A vivid illustration is the thought processes of the manic. When people experience manic episodes, ideas sometimes race through their minds with seemingly little order or arrangement. Needless to say, judgment is often impaired.

Although excessively intense emotions may interfere with the attainment of one's goals, insufficiently intense emotions may be equally damaging. Flat affect, ennui, and lack of interest tend to be enervating, and can seriously impair performance. Consider an athlete preparing for an athletic contest. Athletes know that there is an optimal level of arousal for the most effective performance. Total relaxation or lassitude is apt to produce a lackluster performance. For this reason, athletes may attempt to "psych themselves up" by engaging in certain mental or physical activities.

Insufficiently intense emotions may also sap creativity. It appears to be part of the conventional wisdom to assume that intellectual challenges are best mastered by the application of cold, dispassionate reason, shorn of emotional charge. I believe that is a gross misconception. Indeed, it is difficult to think of any creative work – singing, dancing, writing, composing, painting – that is the product of pure dispassionate cognition. In the absence of such feelings, there is no drive, no spirit, no inspiration. Such work may be competent but it is likely to be flat, uncreative, pedestrian.

Emotions may hamper, restrict, or harm the individual in various ways. A dramatic example is the feeling of terror or panic associated with the phobias. From an instrumental viewpoint, the consequences today of being afraid to fly in an airplane, ride in an elevator, or walk in a crowded street may range from mild inconvenience to the frustration of important life goals.

Because emotions affect behavior, they may also lead to impulsive actions that the individual may have later cause to regret. In a towering rage, one person quits his job, a second drops out of graduate school, a third walks out on her husband, a fourth punches a policeman in the nose, and so on. The practical consequences of such impulsive behavior are obvious.

Of particular importance to people are emotions that affect their inter-personal relations. Much of what we want out of life depends on the goodwill of others, and this goodwill is significantly affected by emotions. For example, to express one's anger is to risk the danger of being fired, disliked, divorced, subjected to physical attack, rejected socially, eval-uated negatively, and much more. In general, the person who exhibits love, warmth, respect, admiration, and so on is more likely to elicit the desired response from other people than the one who displays hostility, contempt, boredom, irritation, and the like. This is especially true of role-related interpersonal emotions. Other things equal, a good-natured salesman, a kindly doctor, a cheerful girl will sell more goods, see more patients, and receive more marriage proposals than their peers with un-attractive emotions.

Emotions thus have major consequences for the lives of people. They may make the difference between success and failure, between the realiza-tion or frustration of one's goals. The ability to experience the desired emotions has monumental effects on the individual's life.

Hedonic reasons. Emotions are also central to the hedonic concerns of human beings. Some emotions are experienced as pleasurable, others as painful. It is interesting to note that in the English language, negative emotions greatly outnumber positive ones (Averill, 1980b), raising the possibility that emotional self-regulation may focus more on avoiding or eliminating negative feelings than on eliciting positive ones. But whether positive or negative emotions are involved, it is clear that the search for human happiness is at bottom a striving to maximize positive and minimize negative affect.

Normative reasons. Finally, emotional self-regulation plays an important part in producing adherence to the emotional norms of society. Sociolo-gists and anthropologists have provided abundant evidence showing that every society is characterized by a distinctive system of emotional norms. An example of contrasting emotional norms is Ruth Benedict's (1935) classic description of Dionysian and Appolonian cultures. According to

Benedict, the Dionysian culture is wild and uninhibited; emotional expression is encouraged. In this society (on socially prescribed occasions) restraint is cast to the winds; emotional inhibition is abandoned – indeed, it is severely condemned. The Appolonian culture, in contrast, values serenity and contentment. The expression of intense emotions is greatly deplored. Inner peace, contentment, quiet pleasure, and sobriety are the socially valued emotions.

Emotional norms are also attached to *social roles* or positions. In our society, a familiar example of such role-related feeling rules is the system of gender-based emotional norms. Early in life males are taught that "big boys don't cry" (Thoits, 1985), whereas such behavior is tolerated among girls. Among adults, men may condemn themselves (and be condemned by others) for emotional experiences that would be perfectly acceptable in a woman. Fear is a familiar example. Though a man may be quaking in his boots, it is normatively prescribed that he not experience or express such feelings, whereas for a woman the expression of such emotions may be perfectly acceptable.

Emotional norms may also be prescribed for various *situations*. Through instruction or example, society teaches children that different situations call for different emotions. At a funeral one is expected to be sad; at a party, happy; at an athletic contest, excited; and so on (Hochschild, 1983).

Because people have different "role-sets" (Merton, 1968), they are socially expected to experience different emotions toward different *categories of others*. Thus, it is socially appropriate to hate an enemy or a renegade but not appropriate to hate one's parents, one's country, or one's family. It is all right to feel sexual desire toward one's spouse but not toward one's parent, child, sibling, or pet. Freud's (1969) famous example of the Oedipus complex – the boy's sexual attraction to the mother combined with hatred and jealousy of the father – is a vivid example of the normative inappropriateness of emotions directed toward certain categories of others.

One of the main reasons why people strive to abide by the emotional norms of the society is that they fear the punishment that others will mete out to them for such norm violation. But there is also an inner audience (Greenwald & Breckler, 1985) that passes judgment on the behavior of the self and that affects the emotions that take the self as their object. Shott (1979) has directed attention to what she calls "reflexive role-taking emotions." These include such emotions as guilt, shame, embarrassment, pride, vanity, and so on. The feature common to these emotions is that they all involve self-esteem. The evidence indicating that negative self-esteem emotions are painful is abundant. Low self-esteem has been shown to be associated with depression, anxiety, irritability, resentment, anomia, and other distressing feelings (Rosenberg, 1985). One of the many factors contributing to low self-esteem is the derogation of the individual by both others and the self that stems from the violation of emotional norms.

Importance for society

In the evolutionary struggle for survival, the human species has been spectacularly successful. I believe that emotional self-control has played a significant role in this development. Although emotions in other animals serve the function of mobilizing the animal for appropriate action, the survival and success of the human species is not primarily attributable to the emotional properties of individual biological organisms. It is primarily attributable to the existence of human cooperation. In order to gain the evolutionary advantages of human cooperation, people must be able to live together in society. By virtue of society, people are able to accomplish collectively what vastly exceeds their capacities individually (Rosenberg, 1988). If we are to speak of the adaptive value of emotional control, then, we must speak of the contribution of emotional self-control to the survival of society.

It would exceed the scope of this chapter to attempt to do justice to this complex topic, but, to put the matter in a nutshell, I believe that society could not survive in the absence of emotional self-control. Unconstrained emotions would damage or destroy social order, would seriously interfere with essential role performance, and would pit people against one another in that apocalyptic vision of the "war of all against all" of which Hobbes (1968) warned. The existence of society thus depends on emotional control, and such control depends on self-processes. As Shott (1979: 1,324) expresses it, "Social control is, in large part, self-control."

The societal need for emotional self-regulation is acknowledged even by those most sensitive to its noxious consequences for psychological well-being. Freud (1961) reluctantly accepted society's need to regulate human biological impulses or appetites despite the damage that such emotional repression inflicted on the organism. Neurosis, he said, is the price we pay for civilization.

Involuntary nature of emotional experiences

Human beings thus have ample incentive to take charge of their emotional experiences. But when they attempt to do so, they come squarely up against a peculiar feature of the human organism, namely, that *people lack direct control over their emotional experiences.* In contrast to emotional *display*, which is largely under voluntary control, emotional *experience* is not. I may be able to make myself *look* interested but I cannot make myself *feel* interested. I can keep myself from showing anger but I cannot keep myself from feeling anger. The emotions I show and the emotions I feel may be poles apart.

The involuntary nature of the emotions tends to be taken for granted by both professionals and laypersons. According to Averill (1985: 89), "The emotions are generally portrayed in psychology texts as noncognitive responses, mediated by phylogenetically older portions of the brain, and manifested peripherally by arousal of the autonomic (involuntary) nervous system and reflexive, expressive reactions."

The same view tends to be held by the general public, and is expressed in several ways. The first is the common idea that an emotion comes upon us without reference to our wishes or desires. People say that they were *overcome* by sadness, that they were *gripped* by feelings of panic, that they were *seized* by fear, that they were *swept along* by the excitement, that they *fell* hopelessly in love, and so on (Thoits, 1985). So viewed, the emotion is not seen as something that the individual controls; it is seen as something that controls the individual.

The second is the idea that the emotions are spontaneous and involuntary reactions to stimulus events. Thus, if I see a car bearing down at me at high speed, I feel fear. If I see a baby sleeping peacefully in a crib, I feel affection. If I am subjected to a gratuitous insult, I feel anger. These emotional responses appear to be things that "happen" to us. They are not part of our plan or intention. We play no part in eliciting them.

The third is the familiar idea that emotions are not responsive to our volitional control. I cannot, through a simple act of will, call forth a desired emotional experience. I may want to feel loving toward a child, cheerful at a party, or sad at a funeral, but I cannot simply will these feelings into existence. Nor can I readily discard unwanted emotions. It is not within my power to eliminate feelings of rage, love, or fear by fiat.

The key problem of emotional self-control, then, is that emotional experience appears to be subject to the control of the autonomic rather than the central nervous system. Emotions are seen as biologically primitive, instinctive features of the organism. In general, people appear to have no more control over their emotional experiences than they have over their digestion, metabolism, or filtering of body wastes.

Given the importance of emotional control for the individual and society, and given the fact that emotional experiences appear to be outside the individual's control, what can be done about it? The solution that people usually adopt, I suggest, is not to attempt to control the emotional experiences directly but to attempt to control the *causes* of the emotional experiences.

Where are these causes to be found? In terms of proximal influences, I believe that the causes are primarily located in two places. The first is in the mind, the second in the body. In this chapter I will limit my discussion to those causes that are located in the mind.

Since the chief causes of emotions are mental events, the main way of controlling one's emotions is to exercise control over one's thoughts. This means that people must be able to observe and recognize their thoughts and must figure out ways to regulate those thoughts in a manner best calculated to produce the intended emotional effects. They must, in other words, draw upon the self-processes that are features of human reflexivity.

The idea that people can inspect their own thoughts struck William James (1950: 296) as a mysterious phenomenon. James was puzzled by the process of "our abandoning the outward-looking point of view...of our having become able to think of subjectivity as such, *to think ourselves as thinkers.*" James failed to remark on the still more peculiar fact that the mind can attempt to regulate its own content. The mind can tell itself what to think about and how to think about it. One important reason for doing so, I shall argue, is in order to gain its emotional objectives.

Before discussing these mental self-manipulation devices, it is relevant to ask, Just who or what is doing the observing or regulating of itself? Explicitly or implicitly, most writers appear to postulate the existence of some internal agent that is both observer and regulator of the self. According to Blankstein and Polivy (1982: 2), "Psychoanalytic writers have posited within the organism some kind of internal agent that makes deliberate decisions relating to the individual's controlled behavior." Various terms have been used to refer to this central guiding influence – the observing ego, the agent, the executor. Some philosophers view the mind as a panoptical scanner, looking inward as well as outward, busily peering into its own nooks and crannies, judging what it has observed, and making decisions about the thoughts it wishes to have. Whether or not one wishes to subscribe to this kind of homuncularism, it is nevertheless clear that the mind is taking an active part in observing itself and in attempting to determine its own content.

Stimulus events and emotional experiences

In dealing with the question of emotional self-regulation, it is helpful to consider Plutchik's (1980) observation that the analysis of an emotion must take account of (among other elements) (1) a stimulus event, (2) a cognition or interpretation, and (3) an emotion. For example, the stimulus event (threat by the enemy) leads to the cognition (danger) that produces the emotion (fear).

In general people tend to attribute their emotional experiences to stimulus events rather than to cognitions. The reason I feel depressed is that I have just failed the exam. The reason I feel angry is that I have just witnessed a cruel injustice. The reason I feel happy is that I have just met a delightful friend. In each instance it is the external stimulus event that is viewed as responsible for the internal emotional experience.

On what bases do people learn to associate particular stimulus events with specific emotional experiences? In part their expectations are based on standard cultural scenarios or scripts (Averill, 1985; Harre, 1986). A man whose veracity has been challenged expects himself to feel insulted. A bride on her wedding night expects herself to feel bliss (Thoits, 1985). These cultural scenarios or schemata are social constructions. People do not have to undergo these experiences themselves, or even observe them in others, in order to learn the expected connection between the event and the emotion. These messages are clearly transmitted through movies, television, and other mass media as well as through interpersonal communication.

Emotional expectations also rest on the development of a socially learned logic that connects stimulus events to emotional experiences. It is logical for me to feel angry if I have just been insulted, but illogical to feel elated. It is logical for me to feel resentful toward someone who has unfairly attacked me, but not logical to feel grateful for the attack. The violation of this logic can be a very serious matter in society. When people are unable to discern the logical link between a stimulus event and emotion, they may be driven to question the actor's sanity (Thoits, 1985; Rosenberg, 1984). (Indeed, failure to detect this link may even cause the actor to question his or her own sanity.) An example of the logical inconsistency between stimulus event and emotion, drawn from the *Diagnostic and Statistical Manual of Mental Disorders* (American Psychiatric Association, 1980: 183), is the following: "While discussing being tortured by electrical shocks, an individual with Schizophrenia, Paranoid Type, laughs or smiles."

Although people ordinarily attribute their emotions to stimulus events, Lazarus and Folkman (1984) argue that the stimulus event per se does not produce the emotional effect. What produces the emotional effect is the intervening cognition – the interpretation or appraisal of the stimulus event. In this view it is not the objective fact but the subjective meaning assigned to it that is responsible for the immediate emotional effect. How else can one explain the fact that the same objective event so often produces such different emotional reactions? The antics of a companion that so strongly irritate me fill you with amusement and delight. Music that produces feelings of sublimity in one person produces boredom in another. Emotionally, it makes all the difference in the world whether I interpret your remark as an insult or a joke.

Emotional self-control

Bodily effects aside, then, the main way to control one's emotions is to control one's thoughts. In this chapter I would like to discuss one broad strategy of mental self-manipulation that is widely used for purposes of emotional control. This is the strategy of *selectivity*, the motivated choice from among various options. Three types of selectivity will be considered: selective attention, perspectival selectivity, and selective interpretation.

Selective attention

Selective attention is a device designed to control the content of one's thoughts in the service of one's emotional objectives. The mind decides what it does or does not wish to think about and attempts to implant the desired content or eliminate the unwanted thoughts. It may do so indirectly by controlling the stimulus events or directly by controlling the thoughts themselves.

Indirect control: The method of selective exposure. Indirect control of emotions is exercised by controlling the stimulus events that impinge on the mind. Far and away the most common expression of this process is the phenomenon of *selective exposure*. Although people cannot always make their worlds, they are often able to choose the worlds that enter their awareness. Through selective exposure people are able to gain a large measure of control over what they think about. In the interest of their emotional objectives, desired thoughts are encouraged to enter awareness and unwanted thoughts are displaced or extruded.

Selective exposure, I suggest, is not simply one more device in a vast armamentarium of weapons of emotional control. It is, on the contrary, the master blueprint for the conduct of one's life. It is surely no accident that people, if given the choice, will usually elect to expose themselves to beauty and avoid ugliness, to associate with those who bring them pleasure rather than pain, to engage in activities that interest rather than bore them, and so on. Although many factors enter into each choice, certainly one of the main factors is the wish of people to optimize their hedonic emotional experiences by exposing themselves to appropriate stimulus events.

A related tactic is to expose oneself selectively to situations that, though not in themselves causes of emotions, are nevertheless conducive to their elicitation. As Averill (1980: 323) observes, "It is easier to become angry in a barroom than in a church, to fall in love on a summer cruise than on a work project, to become frightened at night than during the day, to become jovial at a party than in the classroom."

Let me stress that the use of selective exposure is designed to maximize *desired* emotions, not necessarily *pleasurable* emotions. A spouse mourning the death of a loved one may refuse invitations to a party or the theater for fear of being put in a good mood – a mood that would appear unseemly or might appear to reflect lack of respect or affection for the departed mate. In the past members of certain religious groups eschewed pleasurable stimulus events, such as dances or other frivolities, on the grounds that these ran counter to their religious commitments. Settings that arouse pleasurable experiences may also be avoided if they interfere with the accomplishment of one's goals (for example, going to a party rather than studying for a test).

In sum, I suggest that people seek to control their exposure to events, situations, and circumstances as a way of producing within themselves desired emotions. In fact, it is no exaggeration to say that people, to the extent that they are able, generally elect to live their lives in settings that they hope will arouse in them the emotions they wish to experience.

Direct control of mental content. Instead of depending on the mediation of stimulus events, people may attempt to control their emotions by acting on their mental events directly. One way to control one's emotions is *thought displacement* – that is, evicting certain thoughts and inserting others in their stead. Greenwald (1988) suggests that one such method is *thought stopping*. When people observe that their thoughts are focusing on subjects that arouse unpleasant emotions, they can sometimes block the continuation of these thoughts by instructing themselves to think about other things. Another example of thought displacement is *distraction*. Thoits (1986) cites research showing that widows and widowers often try to distract themselves from ruminating on their losses by turning their thoughts to other subjects. Another method is to displace unwanted thoughts with attention-commanding intellectual challenges. For example, the conventional wisdom tells us that one way to control anger is to count from one to ten (though I think it would be more effective to count from ten to one). In either case the purpose is to displace the anger-arousing cognition with an arithmetic challenge that is devoid of emotional charge. In recent years a more direct method of thought displacement – transcendental meditation – has gained a number of adherents. An important feature of transcendental meditation is that by providing methods of reducing the activity of one's mind, one can alter one's emotional states (Rubottom, 1975).

Another direct attention-selective tactic is to shift one's focus of attention. Simpson and Simpson (1959), studying psychiatric attendants, found that they attempted to boost their self-esteem by shifting the admirable features of their work from ground to figure in their phenomenal fields. They note (p. 392):

Attendants tend to minimize the less glamorous features of their work and focus on the most highly valued element in the sub-culture: care of the patient.... The data thus support the hypothesis that people in a low status occupation can develop and maintain a favorable occupational self-image by focusing on some highly valued aspect of the work situation.

Another attention-selective tactic is the phenomenon that Pearlin and Schooler (1978) have called "selective ignoring." In their investigation of people's ways of coping with the recurrent role-related stresses of marriage, parenting, work, and finances, Pearlin and Schooler found that people often dealt with these problems by deciding to ignore, overlook, or pay no attention to these problems. The purpose was to avoid negative emotion-evoking cognitions.

Perspectival selectivity

Whereas selective attention refers to *what* one elects to think about, perspectival selectivity refers to the *angle of vision* that one brings to bear upon events. Pearlin and Schooler (1978) found, for example, that people sometimes attempted to cope with their stresses by altering their time perspectives ("Time solves most problems on my job"). Another method of coping was to change their comparison reference groups. People searched for, and succeeded in discovering, others who were even worse off than themselves. These tactics diminished the intensity of the negative emotions stimulated by their thoughts about their current difficulties.

A well-known perspective-altering device is *minimization*. Here again the stimulus event remains in consciousness but the way of looking at it is altered. Although some of Pearlin and Schooler's (1978) respondents admitted that they had marital or financial problems, they insisted that these were not really important. Sykes and Matza's (1957) delinquent boys often alleviated their feelings of guilt by insisting that they had not seriously harmed their victims or, if they had, their victims were so worthless that it did not matter. Perhaps the prototype of the minimization phenomenon is the example of the young woman who was reproached by her parents for having an out-of-wedlock baby and attempted to minimize her transgression by explaining that, "Well, it was only a little baby."

Selective interpretation

Selective interpretation deals with the construction the individual chooses to place on stimulus events. To the extent that they are able, people tend to assign those meanings to events that will produce the desired emotions.

A well-known example is the phenomenon of *selective attribution*. Research consistently shows that when people are asked to account for their successes, they tend to attribute these outcomes to themselves, but when they are asked to account for their failures, they attribute these outcomes to external causes (e.g., bad luck, task difficulty, unfortunate external circumstances) (Bradley, 1978). This is true for both collective and individual tasks. When subjects in a two-person task were asked how much they had contributed to a successful outcome, they said that they were chiefly responsible; if the outcome was a failure, however, they considered their partners chiefly responsible (Johnston, 1967). Selective attribution protects self-esteem whether one succeeds or fails.

Another self-esteem protective device is to attribute one's failure to lack of effort rather than to lack of ability. According to Snyder, Higgins, and Stucky (1983: 104) "In a review of 17 studies in which people are given success or failure feedback about their performance on a variety of tasks, 13 studies show that failure condition subjects report significantly lower effort than do success condition subjects."

Surprisingly, self-esteem can even be protected by acting in ways that *promote* failure. Jones and Berglas (1978) have described these as "self-handicapping strategies." Examples of such strategies would be intentional lack of effort (Covington & Omelich, 1979) and the use of such performance-impairing agents as alcohol or certain drugs (Tucker, Vuchinich, & Sobell, 1981). If one fails, then the cause of the failure is not oneself but the alcohol, drugs, or lack of effort. And if one succeeds despite these handicaps, then one's achievements are all the more impressive.

Another type of selective interpretation is *selective comprehension*. In a study of prejudice by Cooper and Jahoda (1947), subjects were presented with a series of cartoons centering on a ridiculous-looking figure named Mr. Biggott. In each cartoon, Mr. Biggott expressed some kind of minority group prejudice. When asked what they thought the purpose of the cartoons was, the unprejudiced respondents replied that they were intended to lampoon prejudice, whereas the prejudiced respondents said that they were simply intended to amuse the reader.

Selective credulity is another device that is often recruited in the service of self-esteem maximization. Snyder and Clair (1976) report that when subjects are given negative feedback about their performance on a test, they are more likely to question the validity of the test. This is also the case when alleged personality tests reveal personality defects (Snyder, Shenkel, & Lowery, 1977).

A related mental self-manipulation device is the selective attribution of *authenticity*. Chapter 5 in this volume by Turner and Billings offers a good example of this phenomenon. In their investigation of people's views about their "real selves," Turner and Billings show that people tend to feel that certain admirable feelings (e.g., relaxed, carefree, comfortable, competent) are expressions of the real self, whereas certain undesirable characteristics (e.g., angry, irritable, guilty, phony) are expressions of their false or unauthentic selves.

Selectivity, then, includes a range of devices designed to produce desired emotion-evoking cognitions. By controlling what they think about, what aspect of the situation they focus on, what angle or perspective they bring to bear on it, or what construction they place on it, people act to produce within themselves the emotions they desire. Furthermore, in pursuing this general objective, it should be recognized that the individual is not necessarily limited to the use of a single device. Harvey, Kelley, and Shapiro (1957) showed that subjects simultaneously utilized a number of devices in order to undermine the credibility of a negative evaluator. In this study, subjects were told that a friend (or a stranger) had rated them more negatively than they had rated themselves. Harvey et al. found that the more negative the other person's alleged rating, the more likely were the subjects to say that (1) the rater had used the scale differently than they did, (2) the rater was not really being serious, (3) the rater had not followed the instructions, (4) the rater was careless and insensitive, (5) the rater did not really know them well, and (6) the other person had never actually made the rating.

This discussion is only a sample of the broad range of mental self-manipulation devices that are recruited in the service of one's emotional objectives. (For a discussion of other devices, see Snyder et al., 1983; Allport, 1961; Rosenberg, 1986.) It is apparent that as a consequence of human reflexivity, the mind takes an active role in controlling its own content. The mind tells itself what to think and how to think about it. In so doing, it brings to attention a particularly mysterious and remarkable feature of human cognition – the phenomenon of self-deception.

Self-deception

In discussing self-deception, it is relevant to compare the process of manipulating other people's minds with one's own. In many ways, these processes are similar. For example, if I want to console a man for a mistake he has made, I may assure him that it is only a minor mistake (minimization), that other people often make worse mistakes (selective comparison), that, viewed from a different angle, it is really a blessing in disguise (perspectival selectivity), that the mistake is not really attributable to him but to someone else (external attribution), that the people who blame him for the mistake don't know what they are talking about (selective credulity), that the mistake does not bear on an important feature of the self (selective valuation), that the mistake is an aberration and not an accurate reflection of the "real self" (selective authenticity), and so on. But human beings can so objectify their internal mental events that they adopt the same stance toward their own minds that they do toward others' minds. It is this fact that has suggested to Thoits (1986) that the concepts of "social support" and "emotion-focused coping" are essentially opposite sides of the same coin.

There is, however, an important difference between the manipulation of other people's minds and one's own. This is the degree of awareness. When I manipulate another person's mind, I may be fully aware that my purpose is to deceive or mislead him or her. Such deception, incidentally, is not necessarily self-interested. I may actually be acting for the other person's benefit, for the benefit of some third party, for the benefit of some abstract cause, and so on. For example, I may try to convince my failing friend that the test was really unfair not because I believe it to be so, but because I want to make him feel better. It is essential, however, that my friend be unaware of what I am doing. If he knew I was lying in order to make him feel better, my manipulative tactic would not work.

Although I may be fully aware that I am attempting to deceive someone else, I cannot, in full awareness, lie to or deceive myself. If I know that I am lying to myself, then the self-deception must fail. For example, if I realize that I am telling myself that the test was unfair in order to make myself feel better, I experience no emotional gain. In order to be effective, the self-deception must be outside of awareness.

Seen in this way, many of the mental self-manipulation devices described are actually instances of self-deception, in the sense that if the individual were fully aware of what he or she was doing, the tactic would not work. Let me stress that I am not suggesting that all mental self-manipulation devices are necessarily outside of awareness. On the contrary, in many cases the actor is fully aware of what he or she is doing. For example, if I am having unpleasant thoughts (or, to be more accurate, thoughts that produce unpleasant emotions), I may consciously decide to change these thoughts by listening to music or watching television. In so doing, I am fully aware that I am attempting to manipulate the contents of my mind in the service of my emotional objectives. In such instances, I make no effort to hide my intention from myself. In other instances, however, the awareness of the mental self-manipulation tactic in use automatically defeats its purpose. If I know that I am rationalizing, then the rationalization cannot work.

If this is so, then it suggests one possible function of the unconscious in human beings. For present purposes I will define the unconscious as those mental events that are outside of explicit awareness. One question one might ask is, Why does the unconscious exist? What purpose does it serve for the individual? I suggest that whatever other functions it may serve, one of its main ones is to make possible the use of a wide variety of mental self-manipulation ploys in the service of emotional objectives. The ability to keep certain mental self-manipulation tactics out of awareness is thus an important requirement in the exercise of emotional self-control.

In sum, although there are a number of ways in which the manipulation of others' minds and one's own are similar, one important difference is that the manipulation of one's own mind is more likely to operate on an unconscious level. We can consciously deceive or mislead another but we cannot consciously deceive or mislead ourselves. Yet if we are to be able to call out in ourselves the desired instrumental, hedonic, or normative emotional experiences, such self-deception is indispensable. Emotional self-regulation, which is so important for both the individual and society, is heavily dependent on our ability to maintain our ignorance of the various devices we use to regulate our thoughts. Although the unconscious doubtlessly serves other functions, there are probably few that match emotional self-regulation in importance.

Effectiveness of mental self-manipulation

Readers may well question the desirability of using such mental self-manipulation tactics. In the realm of depth psychology, no proposition is more fundamental than the view that illusion and self-deception are damaging to the individual. The central task of the therapist is to lead the patient to penetrate the curtain of falsehoods and self-deceptions that people use to defend themselves against their anxieties and to confront reality squarely.

Yet there is growing evidence to suggest that self-deception is an adaptive mechanism (Sackheim, 1988; Lockard & Paulhus, 1988). The use of certain mental self-manipulation devices, it has been found, is more likely to be associated with *superior* than with inferior emotional satisfaction and adjustment. For example, it has been found that people who fail to engage in self-deception, that is, people who see themselves as they really are, are those most likely to be judged as clinically depressed (Lewinsohn, Mischel, Chaplin, & Barton, 1980). It has also been shown that depressives and people with low self-esteem are *less* likely than others to make self-serving attributions (Tennen & Herzberger, 1987). Taylor and Brown (1988) have accumulated an impressive body of evidence to show that people who have "illusions" about their own worth, their ability to control events, and their expectations about events are more likely to be characterized by various indicators of mental health, such as "the ability to care about others, the ability to be happy and contented, and the ability to engage in productive and creative work" (p. 193). Veenhoven (1984) has found that happy subjects are more likely than unhappy ones to use certain defensive strategies, leading him to consider what he calls "the comforts of self-deceit" (p. 295). Alloy and Abramson (1982) found that depressed subjects were less likely than nondepressed subjects to overestimate their level of control. Among children, Harter (1986) showed that those with low self-esteem were less likely to utilize the tactic of value selectivity. Whereas the high self-esteem children were more likely to care about those things they were good at, this was much less true of those with low self-esteem. At least in these instances, the disposition to employ various mental self-manipulation devices is associated with more positively toned emotional experiences. And that, it is reasonable to assume, is their purpose.

This does not mean, of course, that mental self-manipulation tactics always work. Far from it. The causal process is multistaged and the possibility of slippage between emotional intent and outcome is strong. By looking at emotional control as the outcome of self-processes, we can discern a number of reasons why our success in controlling our emotional experiences is so limited.

First, the external event to which we choose to expose ourselves may not produce the desired cognitions (e.g., the movie we choose to watch fails to amuse us). Second, the cognition may fail to produce the desired emotion (e.g., the pleasant thought on which we concentrate may fail to cheer us up). Third, we may be unable to control our thoughts (e.g., our effort to eliminate persistent perseverative thoughts from our minds may fail). Fourth, the state of physiological arousal that is the foundation of the emotion may persist even when the mental events that aroused it are no longer present (e.g., we may continue to experience inner excitement even after the exciting incident has passed). Fifth, our efforts at self-deception may fail (e.g., we may recognize that we are rationalizing or kidding ourselves). Finally, the cognitions that are the source of the emotions may be unconscious and therefore outside our control (e.g., our chronic depression may be caused by unconscious feelings of guilt about some imaginary injury we have inflicted).

The self-regulation of emotional experiences is thus strewn with obstacles and pitfalls. The basic reason is that the process is essentially indirect. People rarely, if ever, are able to produce emotional effects at will. They must depend on a series of devices (perhaps one should call them tricks) of mental self-manipulation to produce the desired emotional results. Nevertheless, it is (bodily effects aside) the method on which they most depend. And what makes it possible is the phenomenon of reflexivity – the human being's virtually unique ability to stand outside the self, to observe and reflect on it (including such internal features as thoughts and feelings), and to produce intentional effects upon these internal processes. Despite the limited effectiveness of mental self-manipulation devices, the importance of emotional self-control for both the individual and society is profound.

References

Alloy, Lauren B., & Lyn Y. Abramson. 1982. Learned helplessness, depression, and the illusion of control. *Journal of Personality and Social Psychology* 42: 1,114–1,126.

Allport, Gordon W. 1961. *Pattern and growth in personality*. New York: Holt, Rinehart and Winston.

American Psychiatric Association. 1980. *Diagnostic and statistical manual of mental disorders* (3d ed.). Washington, DC: Author.

Averill, James R. 1980a. A constructivist view of emotion. In R. Plutchik & H. Kellerman (Eds.), *Emotion: Theory, research, and experience* (pp. 305–339). New York: Academic Press.

Averill, James R. 1980b. On the paucity of positive emotions. In K. R. Blankstein, P. Pliner, & J. Polivy (Eds.), *Assessment and modification of emotional behavior* (pp. 6–45). New York: Plenum Press.

Averill, James R. 1985. The social construction of emotion, with special reference to love. In K. J. Gergen & K. E. Davis (Eds.), *The social construction of the person* (pp. 89–109). New York: Springer-Verlag.

Benedict, Ruth. 1935. *Patterns of culture*. London: Routledge and Kegan Paul.

Blankstein, Kirk, & Janet Polivy. 1982. *Self-control and self-modification of emotional behavior*. New York: Plenum Press.

Bradley, Gifford W. 1978. Self-serving biases and the attribution process: A reexamination of the fact or fiction question. *Journal of Personality and Social Psychology* 36: 56–71.

Cooley, Charles H. 1902. *Human nature and the social order*. New York: Scribners.

Cooper, Eunice, & Marie Jahoda. 1947. The evasion of propaganda: How prejudiced people respond to anti-prejudice propaganda. *Journal of Psychology* 23: 15–25.

Covington, Martin, & Carol Omelich. 1979. Effort: The double-edged sword in school achievement. *Journal of Educational Psychology* 71: 17–31.

Freud, Sigmund. 1961. *Civilization and its discontents*. New York: Norton.

Freud, Sigmund. 1969. *An outline of psychoanalysis*. New York: Norton.

Gordon, Steven L. 1990. The sociology of sentiments and emotions. In M. Rosenberg and R. H. Turner (Eds.), *Social psychology: Sociological perspectives* (pp. 562–592). New Brunswick, NJ: Transaction Publishers.

Greenwald, Anthony G. 1988. Self-knowledge and self-deception. In J. Lockard & D. L. Paulhus (Eds.), *Self-deception: An adaptive mechanism?* (pp. 113–131). Englewood Cliffs, NJ: Prentice-Hall.

Greenwald, Anthony, & Steven J. Breckler. 1985. To whom is the self presented? In B. R. Schlenker (Ed.), *The self and social life* (pp. 126–145). New York: McGraw-Hill.

Harre, Rom. 1986. An outline of the social constructionist viewpoint. In R. Harre (Ed.), *The social construction of emotions* (pp. 2–14). Oxford, UK: Blackwell.

Harter, Susan. 1986. Processes underlying the construction, maintenance, and enhancement of the self-concept in children. In J. Suls & A. G. Greenwald (Eds.), *Psychological perspectives on the self* (Vol. 3, pp. 136–181). Hillsdale, NJ: Erlbaum.

Harvey, O. H., Harold H. Kelley, & Martin M. Shapiro. 1957. Reactions to unfavorable evaluations of the self made by other persons. *Journal of Personality* 25: 398–411.

Hobbes, Thomas. 1968. *Leviathan*. New York: Penguin.

Hochschild, Arlie. 1979. Emotion work, feeling rules, and social structure. *American Journal of Sociology* 85: 551–575.

Hochschild, Arlie. 1983. *The managed heart: Commercialization of human feelings*. Berkeley: University of California Press.

James, William. 1950. *The principles of psychology*. New York: Dover.

Johnston, William A. 1967. Individual performance and self-evaluation in a simulated team. *Organizational Behavior and Human Performance* 2: 309–328.

Jones, Edward E., & Steven Berglas. 1978. Control of attributions about the self through self-handicapping strategies: The appeal of alcohol and the role of under-achievement. *Personality and Social Psychology Bulletin* 4: 200–206.

Lazarus, Richard S., & Susan Folkman. 1984. *Stress, appraisal, and coping*. New York: Springer-Verlag.

Lewinsohn, Peter M., Walter Mischel, William Chaplin, & Russell Barton. 1980. Social competence and depression: The role of illusory self-perceptions. *Journal of Abnormal Psychology* 89: 203–212.

Livesley, W. J., & Dennis B. Bromley. 1973. *Person perception in childhood and adolescence*. London: Wiley.

Lockard, Joan, & Delroy L. Paulhus (Eds.). 1988. *Self-deception: An adaptive mechanism?* Englewood Cliffs, NJ: Prentice-Hall.

Mead, George H. 1934. *Mind, self and society*. Chicago: University of Chicago Press.

Merton, Robert K. 1968. *Social theory and social structure* (Enl. Ed.). New York: Free Press.

Pearlin, Leonard I., & Carmi Schooler. 1978. The structure of coping. *Journal of Health and Social Behavior* 19: 2–21.

Plutchik, Robert. 1980. A general psychoevolutionary theory of emotion. In R. Plutchik & H. Kellerman (Eds.), *Emotion: Theory, research, and experience. Vol. 1. Theories of emotion* (pp. 1–31). New York: Academic Press.

Rosenberg, Morris. 1984. A symbolic interactionist view of psychosis. *Journal of Health and Social Behavior* 25: 289–302.

Rosenberg, Morris. 1985. Self-concept and psychological well-being in adolescence. In R. L. Leahy (Ed.), *The development of the self* (pp. 205–246). Orlando, FL: Academic Press.

Rosenberg, Morris. 1986. *Conceiving the self.* Malabar, FL: Krieger.

Rosenberg, Morris. 1988. Self-objectification: Relevance for the species and society. *Sociological Forum* 3: 548–565.

Rosenberg, Morris. 1990. Reflexivity and emotions. *Social Psychology Quarterly* 53: 3–12.

Rubottom, Al E. 1975. Transcendental meditation and its potential uses in schools. In T. B. Roberts (Ed.), *Four psychologies applied to education* (pp. 514–524). New York: Schenkman.

Sackheim, Harold A. 1988. Self-deception: A synthesis. In J. S. Lockard and D. L. Paulhus (Eds.), *Self-deception: An adaptive mechanism?* (pp. 146–165). Englewood Cliffs, NJ: Prentice-Hall.

Shantz, Carolyn. 1975. The development of social cognition. In E. M. Hetherington (Ed.), *Review of child development theory and research* (Vol. 5, pp. 257–323). Chicago: University of Chicago Press.

Shott, Susan. 1979. Emotion and social life: A symbolic interactionist perspective. *American Journal of Sociology* 84: 1,317–1,334.

Simpson, Richard L., & Ida H. Simpson. 1959. The psychiatric attendant: Development of an occupational self-image in a low-status occupation. *American Sociological Review* 24: 389–392.

Snyder, C. Richard, & M. S. Clair. 1976. Effects of expected and obtained grades on teacher evaluation and attribution of performance. *Journal of Educational Psychology* 68: 75–82.

Snyder, C. Richard, Raymond L. Higgins, & Rita J. Stucky. 1983. *Excuses: Masquerades in search of grace.* New York: Wiley.

Snyder, C. Richard, Randee J. Shenkel, & Carol R. Lowery. 1977. Acceptance of personality interpretation: The "Barnum" effect and beyond. *Journal of Consulting and Clinical Psychology* 45: 104–114.

Sykes, Gresham M., & David Matza. 1957. Techniques of neutralization: A theory of delinquency. *American Sociological Review* 22: 640–670.

Taylor, Shelley E., & Jonathon D. Brown. 1988. Illusion and well-being: A social psychological perspective on mental health. *Psychological Bulletin* 103: 193–210.

Tennen, Howard, & Sharon Herzberger. 1987. Depression, self-esteem, and the absence of self-protective attributional biases. *Journal of Personality and Social Psychology* 52: 72–80.

Thoits, Peggy. 1985. Self-labeling processes in mental illness: The role of emotional deviance. *American Journal of Sociology* 91: 221–249.

Thoits, Peggy. 1986. Social support as coping assistance. *Journal of Consulting and Clinical Psychology* 54: 416–423.

Tucker, Jalie A., Rudy E. Vuchinich, & Mark B. Sobell. 1981. Alcohol consumption as a self-handicapping strategy. *Journal of Abnormal Psychology* 90: 220–230.

Veenhoven, Ruut. 1984. *Conditions of happiness.* Boston: D. Reidel.

Lynn Smith-Lovin

Jessica and Jim meet in a Hotel room, where they've come to do some work together. Jessica is a Virtuous Secretary; she knows Jim as a famous Evangelist. Jim would rather see their relationship as two potential Lovers. Thinking in these romantic terms, Jim *desires* Jessica; he *applauds* her recent work and her appearance, attempting to *amuse* her. As a Virtuous Secretary, Jessica wasn't expecting this. She tries to *address* Jim, intends to *pacify* him if he makes requests, to *consult* with him about their work for the ministry. Because of his greater power in the situation, Jim grabs the moment and Amuses Jessica with a joke. Jim's reactions to this lively interaction are in keeping with his romantic view of the situation; he feels *in love, passionate, pleased*, and *cheerful*. Jessica is somewhat taken aback at this loverlike behavior from her esteemed Evangelist – she is *touched* but feels *moved, awestruck, emotional* in response to his expressive attention.

Jim's impulses have not died down; he continues to *Entertain* Jessica with amusing stories. He *desires her sexually*. Jessica's somewhat agitated emotional state leads her to try and cool out the interaction by *Consulting* the Evangelist in a more formal manner about their work plans. He prevails, however (not unlikely, given her inclination to pacify him). He *Sleeps With* her. He feels great; she feels good but flustered.

Only when her religious counselors later describe her experience as a Virtuous Secretary being Corrupted by the Evangelist, does she begin to feel *afraid, embarrassed*, and *shaken*; she begins to think of herself as a *sinner* and Jim as a *ruthless, mean* Evangelist. Later the Ministers of

Some of the description of the theory here was presented originally in a paper, *A Quantitative Model of Affect Control*, at the American Sociological Association meetings in Chicago, 1987, and in Smith-Lovin (1990). The author would like to thank Mitch Abolafia, Steve Barley, Ronald Breiger, Peter Callero, Carolyn Ellis, John Freeman, David Heise, Judy Howard, David Krackhart, Miller McPherson, Beth Rubin, Sheldon Stryker, David Weakliem, and participants at the conference "Self and Society: A Social Cognitive Approach," Seattle, WA, in July 1988, for helpful comments on the paper.

the church say Jim has Betrayed them; they *summon* him before their governing board, and *silence* his ministry.

This scenario bears more than a passing resemblance to news events of 1988, when Jim Bakker's sexual indiscretions caused the downfall of the PTL[1] evangelist empire. It is not a news summary, however, but the output of a simulation program called INTERACT (Smith-Lovin & Heise, 1988; Heise & Lewis, 1988).[2] The capitalized words represent inputs to the program; italicized words are INTERACT's behavioral and emotional predictions.

INTERACT is a computer representation of affect control theory (Smith-Lovin & Heise, 1988; Heise, 1977, 1979, 1986), a model of social action incorporating the basic assumptions of symbolic interactionism. The interactionist tradition is heavily based in cognitive conceptualizations of the self and society. Sheldon Stryker (1987) has called for, and has begun in his own work, an effective integration of emotion into the theoretical structure of interactionist thought. In this chapter, I will summarize briefly recent advances in affect control theory that incorporate emotion into the theory's view of identity and social action. I will argue that the theory provides a useful framework for linking the cognitive processing so central to symbolic interactionism with the emotional responses that people have to situations in which they are involved. Recent work on emotion in sociology and research in the social cognitive tradition in psychology fit nicely with affect control predictions. I will attempt to highlight some of these points of reinforcement in my discussion of the theoretical ideas.

The affect control model

Heise (1977, 1978, 1979) developed affect control theory from symbolic interactionist ideas and from empirical work on the psychology of impression formation. The theory is based on the proposition that people perceive and create events to maintain the meanings evoked by their definition of a situation.

Definition of the situation

It is almost impossible to interact with someone else without having some sense of *who* that other person is. When we enter a situation, we see ourselves and others as occupants of identities such as Host[3] and Guest or Doctor and Patient. Often these identities are strongly determined by institutional structures and their reflections in physical settings. For example, a lecture hall supports the identities of Professor and Student (Goffman, 1959: 1, 124; 1963: 18, 20; 1974: 1–2; Gonos, 1977). Where ambiguity occurs, we may use key behaviors to place others in appropriate relationship to ourselves. If we are Students, and someone walks up to the front of a room and begins to lecture, the presumption is that the lecturing person is the Professor.

At other times we may be predisposed to take on identities that are more informal and less setting-specific, perhaps because of past history with specific others or because of physiological or affective states. Two Lovers, for example, may maintain their romantic relations in mundane sites like a city street.

When individual actors take on an identity either because of its salience for them or because of its place in a plan for action, they can transform the identities of others. This occurs because identity is not an *individual* feature of self, but rather a cognitive representation of the relationship of self to others in the setting. In routine instances, we know that the composition of a group can shape how we see ourselves; a single woman in a group of men is more likely to think of herself in gender-specific identities. More dramatically, a person with a gun can transform a bank setting with Managers, Tellers, and Customers into a robbery scene with a Thief and Hostages (Goffman 1974: 447).

Once identities are established, people recognize social events (like the Host is Ignoring me, his Guest) within this definition of the situation. As with identity assignment, event interpretation may be the source of individual variation in reaction to social interaction, but such idiosyncratic interpretation is not without limits. Cultural meanings of behavior labels and the prototypical events stored in memory serve to create consensus in event definition. When a Mother Spanks her Child, people may differ in seeing it as discipline or abuse; cigarette burns and skull fractures would be physical events that allowed little dispute about interpretation.

Note that this cognitive categorization or labeling of behavior determines its affective impact. We might approve of a Mother Disciplining her Child but would be unlikely to condone Abusing. One of the strengths of the affect control model is that it specifies how this cognitive labeling influences affective reactions. It also predicts how affective states feed back into labeling processes, to change the definition of the situation when disturbing, disconfirming events occur. It is to these aspects of the model that we now turn.

Affective meaning

The labels we use to characterize self, others, and social actions carry important meanings – fundamental sentiments about how good, how powerful, and how lively such people and behaviors are. A key feature of affect control theory is that it conceptualizes "meaning" in a specific, measurable way. The fundamental sentiments of goodness, powerfulness, and liveliness correspond to the three dimensions of affective meaning (evaluation, potency, and activity) that Osgood and his colleagues (Osgood, Suci, & Tannenbaum, 1957; Osgood, May, & Miron, 1975) discovered. These dimensions underlie reactions to many types of concepts in a variety of linguistic and national cultures. The semantic differential scales developed by Osgood measure the three dimensions.[4]

Such meanings are a part of our culture. Despite widely varying backgrounds, we largely agree that Mothers are nicer than Racketeers, that Physicians have more power than Patients, and that Children are livelier than Hermits. For example, in a Southern university undergraduate population, females rate a Mother as quite nice and good (as opposed to bad and awful, 2.33 on a scale that ranges from 4 to −4), quite big and powerful (1.90), and neither fast, young, and noisy nor slow, old, and quiet (0.04). A stigmatized identity like Racketeer has a profile of −0.85, 1.72, and 1.04 on the evaluation, potency, and activity dimensions.

Studies on topics ranging from word connotations to occupational prestige to severity of criminal acts find surprising agreement across social strata in the affective meanings associated with social identities and behaviors (Gordon, Short, Cartwright, & Strodbeck, 1963; Heise, 1966; Reiss, 1961; Osgood, 1962; Rossi, Waite, Bose, & Berk, 1974). Obvious exceptions occur when subcultures develop unique meanings for identities central to the group (e.g., homosexual identities in a gay church [Smith-Lovin & Douglass, forthcoming] or law enforcement identities within this professional subculture [Gilchrist project reported in Heise, 1979: 100–102]). Often, though, such subcultures develop a new set of identities (in effect, a new vocabulary) to reflect their differences from mainstream society; gang members may share the mainstream view of Police Officer, but be more likely to use slang words like Pig that carry a more negative and less potent connotation.

Affect control theory focuses on these three dimensions of affective meaning for four reasons:

1. The dimensions can be used to characterize many significant elements of social situations, including identities, actions, emotions, and settings, using the same three scales of goodness (evaluation), powerfulness (potency), and liveliness (activity).
2. These meanings are widely shared and represent important cultural information.
3. The three dimensions correspond to important social features of

identities and behaviors like status, power, and expressivity (see
review in Kemper, 1978: 26–42).
4. We can measure people's reactions on these dimensions. Our
    measurements of affective meaning allow us to link the qualitative
    features of situational definitions to the quantitative processes of
    impression change and control.

Impression change

Social events change impressions of people, making them seem
better or worse, stronger or weaker, livelier or quieter than they were
expected to be. For example, suppose that I attend a party and think that
the Host is Ignoring me, her Guest. Hosts and Guests normally are viewed
as pleasant people, with the Host being somewhat more powerful and
lively than the Guest. When rated by female undergraduates on a scale
ranging from -4 to $+4$, Host has an evaluation (goodness) of 1.5, a
potency (powerfulness) of 1.2, and an activity (liveliness) of 0.5; Guest has
an evaluation of 1.7, potency of 0.0, and activity of -0.2 (Heise & Lewis,
1988: 97, 98). The unpleasant and inappropriate act of Ignoring (with an
evaluation of -1.8, potency of -0.2, and activity of 0.2) damages the
reputation of both Host and Guest. A Host who has Ignored a Guest loses
goodness, power, and liveliness. The Guest also loses; victims are stigmatized by being the recipients of negative events, and lose power from being
acted upon in an insulting manner.

Affect control theory uses impression-change equations, estimated from
large numbers of such events, to predict the outcome (Smith-Lovin,
1987a). Calculations using the described input sentiments and impression-
change equations predict that such a Host will lose 2.2 units of evaluation
and 0.7 units of potency; she will gain slightly (0.2 units) in liveliness. One
might think of an identity as a point in a three-dimensional space; an event,
when recognized and processed by someone, may move the person in that
identity from its original, culturally given location to a new position.

The Host suffers because she has done a bad act to a good person;
Ignoring anyone is unpleasant, but Ignoring a nice person is worse than
Ignoring a nasty one. The equations capture notions of equity with an
interaction term that represents the traditional balance effect (Smith-
Lovin, 1987a: 47–49). That is, good unto bad and bad unto good damages
one's reputation; doing good to the deserving and punishing the villains
increases the evaluation of the actor.[5] The Guest also suffers from the
perception of being Ignored. The victim of a negative act loses evaluation,
as the impression-change equations capture the derogation of the victim

effect (Smith-Lovin, 1987a: 50–51). Power is lost, too, by being the object of another's inappropriate, unpleasant action (Smith-Lovin, 1987a: 55).

Events thus affect our impressions of pleasantness, powerfulness, and liveliness. They alter the feelings we have about all elements involved in an interaction: actors, objects, and even the acts themselves. Ignoring may seem less serious (less potent) when it is the behavior of a Host in a party setting, than when it is the behavior of a Judge toward a Lawyer in the course of a trial.

Control processes

When events lead us to create impressions that differ from our fundamental understandings of particular people and behaviors, we generate new events that restore these fundamental sentiments. (Heise [1979, 1986] uses the term "sentiments" to refer to fundamental meanings on the evaluation, potency, and activity dimensions.) In other words, people construct new events to *confirm* fundamental sentiments about self and others; they manage social life in ways that *control* their feelings about reality.[6]

In the established example, the Host and Guest have both lost status as a result of the Ignoring. The theory suggests that this event is somewhat unlikely, since it does not support the identities of the interactants. Such a behavior might be produced accidentally (if the Host is busy with other party arrangements, or if the Guest enters through a back door) or reflect a mood produced in another interaction (the Host is depressed because of a rejection by her boyfriend). If the Guest or someone else points out the event as Ignoring and the Host accepts this account of what has transpired, the Host is likely to produce a restorative act. According to the theory, such an act would be a behavior that, when processed, will move impressions back in line with fundamental meanings. Or the Guest might repair the situation with such an act. Possibilities for the Host include Appreciate, Soothe, and Apologize To; the Guest might Excuse or Caution the Host to restore her view of the occasion. Which of these expectations or intentions actually is realized depends on several factors, not all of which are understood. At a minimum, the action that is taken must be within the physical and social limits of the setting in which the interaction occurs. This restriction may eliminate some affectively appropriate behaviors (although not in this case, since all of the possibilities are reasonable ones). We might expect the source of the original disturbing action to repair the situation if the deflection was unintentional. If the Host fails to act, then the Guest would be expected to prompt action with a cautionary statement.

The theory produces predictions about impression-change and behavioral reactions with INTERACT, the computer program that produced the example with which this paper began (Heise & Lewis, 1988). The program contains the formal structure of the theory and empirical estimates of its parameters. Specifically, the program consists of equations that show how impressions change on three dimensions (evaluation, potency, and activity) for actor, object-person, and behavior (Smith-Lovin & Heise, 1988).[7] It uses a mathematical transformation to represent the proposition that people maintain fundamental meanings: The program solves for the three-number profile of behavior evaluation, potency, and activity that will move the identities of the actor and object closest to their original positions when the event is processed. The program uses evaluation, potency, and activity ratings of behaviors and identities from undergraduates to link words with the three-number profiles. The program represents the current form of the theory – the equations and the mathematical transformation – and allows us to link verbal descriptions to the numerical values, then to produce both quantitative predictions (the evaluation, potency, and activity levels of the expected behavior – the EPA profile) and verbal predictions (the verbal labels for the behavior, linked to the numerical EPA profile by searching the "dictionary" of undergraduate ratings).

Labeling

The program INTERACT can model more than behavioral reactions. It also provides a formal model for the processes through which new social meanings (e.g., deviant labels) become attached to individuals as the result of their own behavior or that of others toward them (see a review of labeling and attribution work in Howard & Levinson, 1985).

Sometimes events affect us so deeply that no new event could possibly restore our original sentiments about the participants in the scene. In our studies, the event "the Grandfather Rapes the Granddaughter" is an example of an incident that produces massive impression change. When we hear of such a disturbing situation, no action is sufficient to restore our original view of the relationship. Transient impressions that cannot be restored to fundamental sentiments through action may lead to redefinition of the situation.

In such cases, actions that are uninterpretable within a given set of identities may lead to a search for identities they do confirm. In effect, we search for a view of the situation that makes sense of the events at hand. The program INTERACT solves for a new identity EPA profile, rather than a three-number behavior profile. A Grandfather who Rapes a Child may be many things, but he no longer fits into our cultural view of what a Grandfather is. He may be a Rapist instead, or a Child-Molester; both are identities that are nasty and lively enough to do such a villainous thing. Of course, the Grandfather identity might remain as a less salient, central aspect of self; but the gruesome, vivid nature of the act leads the Child-Molester identity to be central in a large number of future interactions.

Reidentification also may occur in less criminal circumstances. A Wife announces she is divorcing her Husband; this event creates substantial deflections, leading to questions such as, How could she do this to me, her perfectly good, loving husband? What kind of a person would do such a thing? INTERACT suggests identities for the female spouse that could resolve the dilemma. They suggest that the rejecting Wife might be a Lesbian (She must be gay!), a Psychotic (She must be crazy!), or a Bitch (I hate her anyway. Good riddance!). Alternatively, a more introspective Husband willing to change his own identity might consider the possibility that his Wife wants to divorce someone she considers to be a Creep. These verbal labels come from matching the new EPA profile calculated by solving for the identity with the evaluation, potency, and activity ratings in the dictionary of average undergraduate ratings. The model therefore describes one avenue through which individuals attain complex, hierarchically organized selves (as posited by the structural symbolic interactionists like Stryker, Burke, and Serpe); we have some identities by virtue of our formal positions (e.g., Grandfather, ex-Spouse) and we acquire others through the labeling that goes on as our operation in these formal identities creates deflections.

Validation of the model

Affect control theory is mathematical in its form, but both qualitative and quantitative in its predictions. Although it is based on empirical equations and their mathematical transformations (Smith-Lovin, 1987a, 1987b; Heise & MacKinnon, 1987; Heise, 1987), and we use computer simulations to explore the theory's implications (Heise, 1978; Heise & Lewis, 1988), the computer program works with natural language descriptions of the social situation and the events within it. It produces natural language outputs showing how people might interpret the situation and how they might respond.

The behaviors predicted by the INTERACT program are, in effect, hypotheses derived formally from the theory. If people define the situation as we do in the program (e.g., as Host and Guest), and have viewed the action as we expressed it (e.g., as Ignoring), then the behavioral predictions should correspond to the intentions and expectations of the inter-actants (and, within physical limitations, to their actual behaviors). The theory has been tested by having people respond to vignettes and by recording actual behavior in a laboratory setting (Heise & MacKinnon, 1987; Wiggins & Heise, 1987). Roughly one-third of the variation in subjects' estimates of the likelihood of events can be explained with the model. After taking some simple cognitive constraints about the likelihood of actors appearing together in an institutional context into account, the theory can explain almost one-half of the variance in behavioral expecta-tions (Heise & MacKinnon, 1987).

When asked to place themselves into a hypothetical event as actor or object, deflection of transient impressions from fundamental sentiments was highly correlated with intentions and expectations for future behavior (for males, $-.42$ and $-.70$; for females, $-.50$ and $-.74$ for intentions and expectations respectively). The theory also correctly predicted the positiv-ity of a Student subject's response to another person (either another Student or a Delinquent) after having been Appreciated or Embarrassed by a Secretary (Wiggins & Heise, 1987). In another test, members of a religious subculture rated the likelihood of events generated by their own fundamental sentiments significantly higher than events generated from another church's sentiments or events created by random behavior selec-tions (Smith-Lovin & Douglass, forthcoming).

The affect control model of emotion

Early versions of affect control theory (Heise, 1977, 1978, 1979) were based on affective processing, but the theory did not deal explicitly with emotional reactions. Later work developed the empirical base neces-sary to describe emotions within an affect control framework (Averett & Heise, 1987; Smith-Lovin & Heise, 1988; Heise & Thomas, 1989).[8]

Affect control theory suggests that emotions provide signals about how well events are maintaining social meanings. Events may produce transient impressions that vary from our fundamental notions of how good, how powerful, and how lively we are, or ought to be. Emotions are the "code" for representing the degree and kind of confirmation or disconfirmation of our identities that is occurring. If someone Insults us while we are operating in a positive, institutionalized identity like Student, we may feel momentarily put down (unpleasant and bad). We have been deflected away from a fundamentally good, pleasant identity by a negative act. Specifically, Student has a profile of 1.2, -0.1, and 1.7 on the evaluation, potency, and activity dimensions (female ratings from Heise & Lewis,

1988: 99); being Insulted by a fellow Student leads to a loss of 2.2 on the evaluation dimension. (Potency and activity change only marginally, increasing 0.3 and 0.1 respectively.)

In our model, words used to describe feelings are labels that characterize the combination of a fundamental evaluation, potency, and activity profile (that is, the person's identity in a situation) and the transient profile produced by an event. A Student Insulted by a fellow Student might feel Flustered, Embarrassed, and Shook Up (predictions from INTERACT simulations). These are the emotion words that when combined with the Student EPA profile, produce the transient profile that is created by the event of Insulting. The emotion thus captures the disconfirmation of the Student identity resulting from the insult. The Student who does the insulting would be affected, too, of course (assuming that she saw the event in the same light). She would feel Spiteful and Bitchy for having done such an unpleasant thing to her fellow (a negative emotion, since her negative action has caused downward deflection on the evaluation dimension).

The model predicts that these emotions should be expected by others and actually experienced by those involved in the situation.[9] These outputs of the program are produced only by the theoretical assumptions (represented by the equations and their mathematical transformations) and by current empirical estimates of theoretical parameters (the coefficients in the equations and the average evaluation, potency, and activity ratings in the INTERACT dictionaries).

Identity and emotion

Averett and Heise (1987) estimated the parameters in equations that described how emotions and moods combined with identities to form impressions of emotion – identity composites (e.g., a Sad Friend). These equations play two roles within the theory. First, they allow actors to occupy identities that are described not only by role words (as discussed), but also by personality traits or status characteristics. Therefore, I might consider myself to be a Lively Professor or an Athletic Woman. Personality traits that we consider to be especially central to our self-conceptions may modify our identities in almost all situations (e.g., it may be central to my self-conception to be unusually Considerate in virtually all role-identities, allowing this characteristic to become a master trait analogous to a master status).

The emotion model turns these equations describing composite identities around mathematically to describe how identities and impressions from events imply emotion. The manipulated equations reveal that the character of an emotion is a function of (1) the transient impression created by an event and (2) the difference between the transient impression and the fundamental meanings (called *deflection* in affect control theory) (Averett & Heise, 1987: 124–128). Since nice events lead to positive transient impressions, they create positive emotions. A transient impression that is nicer than one's identity fosters an especially positive emotion. If one operates in very high status, positive identities, the nice things that are directed toward one are viewed simply as that which is expected and deserved from one's position in social life. If one's identity is more neutral, the positive event causes elation. An Apprentice glows from a compliment that an Expert takes as his due (see also Kemper 1978: 72–79).

If people interpret events and act to maintain their transient states near fundamental meanings, then affect control theory points to an interesting conclusion. The theory predicts that the character of one's emotions is sharply determined by his or her identity (Averett & Heise, 1987: equations 19, 20, and 21). Maintenance of positive identities – the kinds of roles[10] one occupies in normal, institutionalized life – typically creates positive emotions.[11] Maintenance of a negative identity (e.g., some type of deviant label) would foster negative emotions.

Anecdotal evidence and research provide many examples. For instance, Swann (1987) tells the story of an experience at a camp for disadvantaged youth that led him to thoughts about identity maintenance. He reports on a battered child with a very negative self-concept (i.e., who had a fundamentally negative self-evaluation). This child sought out an aggressive playmate named Crazy Louis. The emotional climate produced was powerfully negative. The negative identity led directly to identity-confirming interactions; the child was in emotional anguish most of the time, but still sought out his abusive peer.

Identity affects the potency and liveliness dimensions as well. Affect control theory suggests that people in powerful identities feel deep, high-potency emotions like Pride and Fury, whereas people in powerless positions experience emotions of impotency like Fear, Anxiety, and Depression.[12] People inhabiting less lively, older[13] identities are prone to quieter emotions (like Contentment or Remorse) and those who take on younger, more lively identities are inclined toward emotions like Euphoria, Fury, and Passion. From our computer simulations, we find that in normal identity-confirming circumstances a Boyfriend would typically feel Happy (a potent, lively emotion), an Old-timer would be Calm (a nice but quiet emotion), a Racketeer would feel Extravagant (a potent, lively but not so nice feeling), a Tightwad would be Smug (a negative, quiet affect), and a Braggart would be Dissatisfied and a Loafer would feel Disappointed (both emotions that are negative on all three dimensions) (Heise, 1982).

Obviously, occupying stigmatized identities require people to feel negative emotions, *if* they remain a part of the dominant culture. Indeed, we have many examples of such "proper" deviants. Mentally ill people often incorporate society's negative view and have low self-esteem (Marks, 1965). Many times, powerless people – those most likely to be stuck with stigmatizing labels by society – often share "normal" people's view of their worthlessness. Delinquent youth often report anxiety and distress associated with their negative identities (Rains, 1982).

Such negative emotions can be the mechanism by which sinners are reclaimed to normal society (Rains, 1982; Glassner, 1982). On the other hand, these negative emotions may undermine one's commitment to the dominant ideology. We might expect this effect when no avenues for identity change are available. In this case, deviants may create or search for a subculture where they are offered positive feelings through a competing ideology. They develop an ideology that makes their emotional life tolerable, even fulfilling. A gay church that we've studied with the affect control framework has done exactly this (Smith-Lovin & Douglass, forthcoming). The church group transformed homosexual identities and behaviors into positive, powerful meanings that engage religious ritual positively. As a result, the gay members experience the pleasant, deep emotions of worship.

Situations leading to disconfirmation and emotional response

The influence of identity on typical emotions holds during interactions when social events confirm identities. Affect control theory suggests that this will often be the case, as actors maintain their and others' identities. However, life is not always smooth confirmation; the affect control framework alerts us to situations in which events will fail to confirm identities. Since disconfirmation is experienced as an emotional response, the theory indicates the types of situations that are likely to lead to emotional arousal.

Disconfirmation of identity is likely when people differ in their definition of a situation (e.g., I think I'm a Professor but a Student who sees me in the department office thinks I'm a Secretary). In such cases, actors will intend and expect events that confirm differing views of the interaction. Actions that are confirming for one will be disconfirming for the other. In the present example, the behaviors that a Student directs at a

Secretary will not be deferential enough for someone thinking of herself as a Professor. (Notice that this confusion of institutionally based identities can be corrected by direct comment as soon as it is noticed. Such corrective action may not be feasible in the case of less formal identities: He thinks he is a Sophisticate, but I think he's a Bore.)

Disconfirmation of identity also occurs when people come from differing subcultures and have different meanings for identities and behaviors. Two people may agree on the definition of the situation (e.g., Professor and Student), but different cultural backgrounds may entail different EPA profiles for those identities. As a Professor from the relatively egalitarian U.S. educational system, I expect lively, collegial interaction with Graduate Students (including acts like Challenge, Question, and Josh). It is sometimes difficult to deal with the quieter, more deferential behaviors directed at me by Asian students who (I presume) see Professors as less nice but more powerful and who see Students as more quiet than my U.S. cultural view. Different fundamental meanings for Professor and Student lead confirming events from one person's viewpoint to be disturbing for the other.

The situations described produce identity disconfirmation because interaction partners come into association with differing views; either they disagree about the relevant identities or they hold different meanings for the same identities. Notice, however, that situations can produce disconfirmation (and emotion) without such full-scale disagreement. Events can push impressions away from fundamental meanings simply because few actions can confirm perfectly all identities and behaviors in a complex situation. Many situations require us to operate simultaneously in multiple identities of varying salience (Burke, 1980, this volume). Acts that confirm one identity may disconfirm another. (A devotion to work that reaffirms my identity as a Scholar may do violence to my view of myself as a Wife or a white-water Paddler.) Some settings have identity conflict built into them; Thoits (1985: 228–229) points out that these are likely occasions for strong emotion. When a Father remarries after divorce, his Son is dealing with a Stepmother whom the Father views as Wife (a more pleasant, powerful, and lively identity). The Son may have to do considerable emotion-work (Hochschild, 1979, 1983) to produce the appropriately positive reactions to the wedding.

Disconfirmation and emotion

When disconfirming events do occur, emotions signal the character of the deflection. When good fortune strikes, affect control theory predicts positive emotions. A Child who is Treated feels Delighted and Light-Hearted; the Mother who provides the Treat is Happy and Pleased. A Grandfather who Cuddles his Granddaughter feels Satisfied and Contented while the Granddaughter is Delighted and Amused.

Negative events cause negative emotions for both the actor and object. Parents who Punish a Child feel Annoyed, Disturbed, and Pained. Only people with very negative, deviant identities are glad when evil prevails.

Disconfirmation also operates to produce emotion on the potency and activity dimensions. Those who are deflected downward on the potency dimension feel Powerless, Meek, or Awkward. Those who get a boost in potency, relative to their identity, feel deep emotions like Creative, Faithful, Aggressive, or Forgiving (depending on the emotion's evaluation and activity profile). Activity variations lead one to feel Active and Adventurous (for positive deflections) or Conservative and Quiet (for negative deflections).

Emotion and labeling

Affect control theory predicts that emotion cues will be important in imputing identities or trait attributions. In particular, nonnormative emotional displays may lead us to suspect that an interaction partner is not who we thought he or she was. A key example is the affective response to victims of negative actions. Although victims may be blameless in principle, they suffer negative consequences beyond any material damage (Ryan, 1971). The tendency to derogate victims is strong and it shows up in our equations (Smith-Lovin, 1987a). Victimization may require that the object feel (and express) negative emotion in order to confirm the vileness of the act and show that it was truly inappropriate for the object (see a review of the victim-attribution literature in Howard, 1984).[14] If a victim looks happy or even relaxed after a negative act, he is signaling a positive deflection. He thereby shows that he views himself as occupying a negative identity – an appropriate recipient of evil. On the other hand, if one feels and displays the proper distress to signal the unfairness and inappropriateness of the act, one is then free to engage in constructive acts of recovery.

Similarly, when people appear distressed or nervous after positive events, we suspect that something is wrong with them (Heise, 1989). A person operating in a normally positive, powerful identity should have that identity supported by the pleasant event. The unease signals that the recipient does not view himself or herself in that fundamentally positive way.

Displays of appropriate emotion cues also are used by actors to *avoid* labeling during self-disclosure of negative information. Lazowski (1987) points out that negative information typically has high information value in interpersonal interactions; it leads to firm impressions and to dislike. But if we become close to others and disclose much information to them, some of this information must be negative. How is it that people sometimes like us anyway? Lazowski suggests that nonverbal expressions of emotion moderate listeners' reactions to negative self-disclosure content. Her experimental results showed that sadness led listeners to form more positive impressions of someone who admitted harming another. Anger also had this effect (although to a lesser degree), primarily because it was perceived by observers to be self-directed anger or shame.

Affect control theory has a ready explanation for this mitigating effect of emotion (Lazowski, Heise, & Smith-Lovin, 1989). We show through our sadness (or anger, if it appears to be self-directed) that we recognize the negative character of our behavior. Perhaps more importantly, we show that our self-concept or identity is fundamentally positive. Our emotion signals that the negative behavior that we have described has caused negative deflection. In a condition in Lazowski's experiment where no emotional reaction was shown, the viewer must infer that the negative behavior produced no deflection (or even positive impression-change). Since only bad people are expected to do bad things and feel neutral or good about them, the inference is that the speaker must be a fundamentally bad person. To avoid this inference, we display negative emotion when revealing our shortcomings to others. Such emotions often are played to and for an audience (Averill, 1980: 323) to authenticate identities and to mitigate the effects of negative information that is revealed through circumstance or self-disclosure.

Affect control and cognitive processes

Although the links between affective and cognitive processes are imbedded throughout my description of the model, in this section I will make these connections more explicit in order to relate the affect control perspective to other research traditions that focus on cognitive features, and point to areas where the confluence indicates useful new research directions.

Definition of situations

Since it is based on symbolic interactionist principles, it is not surprising that affect control theory views situational definitions as critical factors in determining both behavior and emotional response. Knowledge of persons' identities (or hierarchies of identities) and a cognitive labeling of their action is necessary for predicting what they will do and what they will feel. In this emphasis, affect control is closely linked to more traditional interactionist theorists like Stryker, Burke, and Serpe (all in this volume). All of these writers argue that identity is central to the production of social action. I think that affect control contributes to these other formulations a much more specific model of this linkage; it allows both qualitative (labeling) and quantitative (on the EPA dimensions) characterizations of the self within a situation; it also makes the processing of these cognitive and affective meanings that occurs as a result of social events more explicit.

When we consider the self as a configuration of identities (as Stryker, Burke, and Serpe do), affect control's emphasis on the definition of situation in producing emotion leads to some interesting insights. For example, it is clear how multiplex relationships can lead to conflicting and complex emotional response. When a person is simultaneously Lover and Employee, events that confirm one identity are disconfirming for the other. Clearly, one does not need affect control theory to generate this insight, but the model does give us a specific comprehensive framework with which to predict the degree of conflict that a wide variety of identities and behaviors will produce. For example, processing some events from two points of view (e.g., Lover and Employee) will lead to substantially differing emotions. When both are salient aspects of the self, a person will feel mixed emotions. Affect control theory can predict the mix specifically.

These mixed emotions prompt personal insight or social change. On the personal level, the strength with which various emotions are experienced can indicate how central an identity is to our global self-concept. If the pride of achievement at occupational pursuits is much stronger than the sense of having behaved too assertively for an appropriately feminine daughter, then one acknowledges the centrality of the work identity and relegates the daughter identity to a minor component, a stance to be elicited in a few social situations and with a limited set of traditional alters.

Perhaps more interesting are the implications of mixed emotions and the stresses they may imply for structural change. As the cooccurrence of two identities becomes more prevalent, problems in coordinating these identities will become a shared issue for a class of social actors. For example, the cooccurrence of Worker and Mother are much more likely now than several decades ago. If common events in modern organizational structure that are appropriate for a "good" Employee are simultaneously disconfirming for Mother, then negative emotion will result from engaging in normative occupational behavior. In a sense, the affect control perspective gives a greater specificity to the role strain idea proposed by earlier researchers (Rapoport & Rapoport, 1972; Poloma, 1972). It predicts when role strain should occur (when two identities cannot be maintained simultaneously in the same situation) and specifies the quality of the emotional experience that the strain implies. When large numbers of actors experience such strain, we are likely to see shifts in institutional arrangements to eliminate the problem, either through segregation of activities (either by setting or in time through the life course) or by modifying event structures so that both identities can be maintained simultaneously. When a group does not have the political or economic resources to engage in such structural change, we would expect emotional turmoil, and perhaps the potential for negative labeling as people display deviant emotions.

Another implication of the central role that situation definition plays for emotional production relates affect control theory to the network–social support literature. People occupying differing role-identities offer differential resources for restoring meanings. When identities have been disconfirmed (or when moods have been established through other, possibly physiological, forces), affect control theory predicts that people will expect and intend restorative events. What constitutes a restorative event will vary dramatically depending on the identities occupied by others with whom one might interact. For example, receiving a compliment from a Mentor would be much more edifying than the same compliment from a Schoolgirl. Even more dramatically, behaving nicely toward an esteemed other will increase self-evaluation much more than virtually *any* action directed at a stigmatized other. Network ties, and the role-identities that connected others occupy vis-à-vis us determine our resources for dealing with negative emotion (see related arguments in chapter 11 in this volume by Nurius). Who we know powerfully determines how we feel. Network ties create social support by providing us with a set of positive identities with whom we can create events to restore a fundamentally positive self-image.

Affective feedback into cognitive processing

Although it offers an explicit model for how cognitive categorizations of a situation and actions occurring within it can shape emotional reactions, affect control theory also specifies how affective processing can lead to cognitive labeling. Several dimensions of this feedback have already been mentioned. We use out-of-role behavior to attribute moods or traits to self and others. Adding a modifier like Depressed to a role-identity like Friend can "explain" systematically negative, quiet be-havior (e.g., such a cognitive reassessment reduces deflections and pro-duces more accurate predictions for future behavior).

Notice that affect control uses a logic parallel to the category-based information gain approach to trait attribution proposed by Jones and McGillis (1976) and to the consensus aspect of Kelley's (1973) covariational model of attribution. It is behavior distinct from that usually expected by someone in a social category (identity) that leads to trait attribution. Affect control's concept of deflection provides a metric for the amount of in-formation gain from an individual action; the equations and EPA values allow us to specify which traits will be implied by what behaviors.

In the cases of more extreme deviant behavior, serious affective deflec-tion leads us to change the social categories that we are using to view the scene. Therefore, Jessica becomes a Sinner rather than a Secretary when forced to view her sexual indiscretions as a corrupt act. Such relabeling can signal important changes in the social structure of the situations in which we are imbedded. When someone with structural power redefines us from Employee to Deadbeat, it affects not only our cognitive constructions but also our paycheck. When a Child has behaved so badly that his Parent is willing to consider him a Drug Addict, the disowning signals a potentially permanent shift in the personal networks of the two individuals involved. The Parent will no longer direct redemptive acts at the Child; the network tie is effectively broken for the purposes of social support. As Thoits (1985) points out, consistently inappropriate emotional displays can create pres-sures to apply the label of mentally ill, leading to institutionalization.

These examples refer to situations in which an initial definition is attained and supported by institutional mechanisms. Perhaps more excit-ing, however, are the insights that affect control processes offer in describ-ing how emotional displays help us to define ambiguous circumstances. Since emotional reactions reveal the extent of deflection experienced, they can tell us a great deal about how people view social action around them. The model can be solved for any element that is "missing" (i.e., ambi-guous) with the information that we *do* have. We can assess individuals' characters by observing others' (or their own) reactions to their behavior. In other situations, we can ascertain the appropriate labels for actions, if we are relatively sure of *who* is involved in the interaction. Should we consider this remark a Challenge, an Insult, a Joke, a Tease, or a Confidence? The emotional displays of the speaker and of other listeners are important clues. In many cases, it is likely that people process such ambiguous events at several levels. They use parallel interpretations, experience somewhat mixed emotions produced by the alternative views of the action, and perhaps create new events so that reactions will clarify which interpretation is correct.

Norms, values, and ideology

In the preceding discussion, I have concentrated on the relationship between emotion and definition of the situation. Other theorists, notably Collins (1975, 1981) and Hochschild (1977, 1983), emphasize the normative, ideological aspect of emotion. Ritual sequences of behavior can create powerful, predictable emotional outputs to support and reaffirm identity and meaning. This ritual means of emotional production is a potent tool for groups that contest for power and legitimacy. Emotions are not just reactions to events; they sustain and validate the norms, values, and expectancies that are the blueprint for their construction. Thus one of the surest ways for a religious or political convert to affirm the validity of a new system of beliefs is by experiencing (and displaying) the emotions considered authentic by the group (Averill, 1983: 1,158; see also the discussion in Howard, this volume). Conversely, Hochschild (1979: 567) points out that one can defy an ideological stance by inappropriate affect; lax emotional management is a clue to an ideology lapsed or rejected.

Affect control theory enriches the ideological interpretation of emotions because it claims that emotion is a direct outcome of the sentiments held for the actor, behavior, and object in an event. Once a group reaches agreement on what happened – who did what to whom – then the participants' emotions directly signal whether or not their sentiments correspond to the groups' definition. An appropriate emotion display implies that the participant has the same sentiments; an inappropriate display cues the observers that a participant has the "wrong" sentiment about the actor identity, the object-person identity, or the action. Identifying ideological deviance first instigates attempts to correct and resocialize sentiments into conformity; success is assessed by a display of "appropriate" affect from the violator. If that fails, the deviant may be stigmatized and expelled from the group. Thus a display of inappropriate affect – of ideological nonconformity – leads the violator either to strengthen the legitimacy of sentiments that originally were contrary to his or her own, or else to give up the benefits of status within the group.

The affect control view of the relationship between emotion norms, the emotion actually experienced, and the social display of emotions is similar to that proposed by Kemper (1981: 346): "First comes the social relationship, with its concrete behavior pattern and its characteristic emotions. Only later does a rule emerge to guard the relation pattern by guarding the emotions it evokes." Those who hold the sentiments associated with a dominant ideology and culture experience the proper emotions without regard to feeling rules or norms. Feeling rules are means of controlling those who do not maintain the ideologically appropriate meanings.

In a sense, all of affect control theory's predictions about emotions define norms since they are the responses generated by consensually held meanings. They will also be predictions for individual responses of members who share the definition of a situation and who share the culture. When members of differing subcultures meet, or when definitions of situations differ, or when people bring idiosyncratic meanings to interaction, emotion norms may be violated.

When such violations occur, interactants who wish to continue their relationship (or "pass" as an adherent to an ideology they have not yet thoroughly incorporated) may engage in emotion management to produce the desired affective displays (Hochschild, 1977, 1983; Thoits 1984, 1985). One may relabel an emotional display of self or other (I'm not angry, just surprised). Alternatively, one could "rethink" the situation in differing terms. Affect control theory would suggest that changing the identities and/or behaviors could lead to an authentic display of appropriate emotion. Hochschild (1983) reported that flight attendants manipulated their emotional life in this way by imagining that Passengers who Belittle them are actually recent Widowers from whom negative behavior would be expected.

Emotions, labeling, and attribution

One implication of the normative view of emotional display, developed by Thoits (1984, 1985) and supported by affect control theory, is that emotional deviants are at risk for labeling. When inappropriate emotional response is observed in another, we may surmise that either the person is not who we thought he was (i.e., we have labeled him with an identity that he is not operating within), he does not share our view of the situation, or he does not share our sentiments about the evaluation, potency, and liveliness associated with the situational definition.[15] When our own feelings fail to match our expectations, we may be sensitized to competing identities or may even begin searching for new ways to characterize the self. Segregating settings (e.g., not taking work home from the office) or ritual behaviors may help to restore appropriate feelings. In cases of extreme and repeated deviation from appropriate emotional response, Thoits (1985) points out that we may doubt our sanity and relabel ourselves as mentally ill. Such relabeling processes, whether carried out by self or other, are represented in affect control theory as reidentification. If emotion management does not work, we then ask the question, What kind of person could I be, to react in such a way?

Relating affective processing to rational action

Another exciting connection between affective and cognitive processing involves attempts to link affect control dynamics with models of rational action called *production systems*. Production systems are grammars for social action; they specify a system of rules by which role occupants generate appropriately organized sequences of action in relation to current conditions. Typically, such systems are composed of "if–then" rules and a priority structure that indicates which action will be taken when the conditions for more than one action are met. Fararo and Skvoretz (1984; Skvoretz & Fararo, 1979; Fararo, 1986) point out how production systems are linked to institutional action. In their view, institutions are sets of production systems that fit together to maintain higher-order institutional forms (e.g., in a restaurant, the major goal is to serve customers food in exchange for money). Heise (1989) has developed a new program called ETHNO that can use the production system idea to elicit and encode qualitative ethnographic information. Carley (1987) is working on making production system models more *social* by combining them with the affect control model.

The link between affective processing and rational action (as represented by production systems) is an important one for both perspectives. On the one hand, affect control theory currently describes behavior at a very general level: A Waitress might Serve a Customer, but the details of the service, the coordination of multiple customers, and other institutionalized routines would be impossible to anticipate. We might predict the negative emotion that would result if the Waitress Ignored the Customer, but we would not know that it was the cook's fault for letting the order sit too long before beginning the cooking process. Production systems handle such problems admirably.

Affect control theory also may contribute to some core problems in the production system approach. Affective processes may help us to explain the creation of behavioral goals, the impetus to achieve them, and the commitment to carry them out. Affective meanings are the values that provide stability to institutional systems. Emotions are signals about how well these systems are being maintained, and what type of work needs to be done to restore disturbed relations. I agree with Minsky (1986: 163), a well-known artificial intelligence researcher, when he says that "the question is not whether intelligent machines can have any emotions, but whether machines can be intelligent without any emotions." If machines, like people, had the ability to alter their own capabilities (one definition of artificial intelligence), they would have to have all sorts of complex checks and balances to guide their self-development. Emotional life plays this role for human actors. A complex self, with a hierarchically arranged set of identities, provides us with a mechanism for institutional change. When institutionalized processes cause distressful emotions (perhaps because of two or more identities operating simultaneously within the situation), these mixed emotions can provide the basis for institutional change.

Summary

I have described a new theoretical approach that links affective and cognitive information about social actions. Affect control theory models the connections of cognitive processes such as situation definition, trait inference, and labeling to affective reactions and emotions. It begins to link macrolevel concepts like ideology, value, norm, and institutional production system to the microlevel processes through which individuals produce actions and maintain identities.

Clearly the theoretical advances just claimed bear a close family resemblance to other current work in social psychology. Symbolic interaction and identity theory (e.g., Stryker, Burke, and Serpe, all in this volume) use many of the same assumptions and come to many of the same conclusions. Psychologists working in areas of attitude – behavior relations, attribution, self-cognition, and identity maintenance (see review in Stryker's and Burke's contributions to this volume) often have a more detailed view of some small piece of the puzzle. I hope that the affect control model contributes to these substantial efforts in two ways. First, it provides a specificity that is often lacking, particularly in the interactionist framework and in attribution studies. Affect control can show *how* identity affects action, both in normal interaction and in response to deviance. It can predict not only *when* attributions will be made, but *what* traits will be attributed to an actor engaging in atypical behavior for someone in a given social category. It provides an explicit link between quantitative measurements of affective meaning and the verbal descriptions that people use to think about their social world.

Affect control's second major contribution is its generality. Sociologists, in particular, have argued that thought, emotion, and action are tied irrevocably together in social process. Our model agrees, and gives an explicit formulation of how fundamental, apparently universal affective responses to events underlie a diverse set of social and cognitive outcomes.

Currently, the Achilles heel of the affect control approach is the lack of empirical research validating the model. The parameters are based on data analysis in the form of impression change studies (Heise & Smith-Lovin, 1979; Smith-Lovin, 1987a, 1987b; Averett & Heise, 1987; Heise & Thomas, 1989). Validation studies of the behavioral predictions are encouraging (Heise & MacKinnon, 1987; Wiggins & Heise, 1987; Smith-Lovin & Douglass, forthcoming). The theory's predictions about emotional response and about cognitive outcomes (labeling and trait attribution, e.g.) have not been tested yet. As Sheldon Stryker points out in his contribution to this volume, this area is one where sociologists can learn a great deal from our psychological counterparts. Psychological researchers often have excelled at translating subtle cognitive processes into laboratory procedures. Adopting some of their techniques may do more than provide us with useful tests of our model (e.g., Lazowski et al., 1989). It may provide a common ground for bringing the two social psychologies to a common focus on problems of mutual interest.

Notes

1 "Praise The Lord," "People That Love," or "Pass the Loot," depending on the time period and your general evaluation of the Bakkers' ministry.

2 This example was developed by graduate teaching assistants for use in introducing undergraduates in Sociology 101 (Introduction to Sociology) to the simulation program. Thanks to John Dumont, Kristen Esterberg, Raymond Liedka, and Scott Serneau. The actual output of program INTERACT from which this description was condensed is available from the author.

3 I use capital letters in the text of this chapter to indicate words that describe identities, social behaviors, emotions, traits or personal characteristics, and settings that one could use to define situations. These capitalized words come from a corpus of terms that can be used when running simulations of social events and emotional reactions using the INTERACT program (Heise & Lewis, 1988)

4 See Morgan and Heise (1988) for a description of how the semantic differential dimensions relate to other aspects of meaning and to dissimilarity ratings for emotion words.

5 Carolyn Ellis points out that social workers help criminals and ministers work with sinners without damaging their reputations. The impression-change equations indicate that these positive professional identities are maintained by the positive evaluation of the acts they direct at negative objects (like Rehabilitate and Pray For). Conversations with such practitioners also indicate some desire to distance themselves from the negative acts of their clients (creating other events like the Minister Criticizes the Sinner) and to stress the positive nature of their actions for the public (allowing a more positive object for some events, e.g., the Social Worker Aids the Probation Officer).

6 For those who prefer a spatial view of the process, the maintenance of meaning can be viewed as creating a new event that, when processed, will move the identity of actor, behavior, and object back to their original positions in the three-dimensional space defined by the evaluation, potency, and activity dimensions.

7 Extensions of the program described in later sections add consideration of emotions, personal traits, and settings.

8 Those familiar with the sociology of emotions will recognize that the affect control approach is similar in many respects to Kemper's (1978) social structural theory. He also argues that the basic dimensions of social relationships are status (regard, liking, or goodness), power, and technical activity. More importantly, Kemper views emotions as outcomes of interaction. His *structural* emotions parallel the affect control predictions about the influence of identity on emotion. What Kemper calls *consequent* emotions are analogous to the deflection or disconfirmation aspect of the affect control view. Both Kemper's structural theory and the affect control theory share an imagery of people moving through a multidimensional space, with their emotional experience determined both by their absolute position in the space and by their direction of movement.

9 The distinction between experienced emotion, expressed emotion, and feeling rules (or emotion norms) is implicit in affect control theory at this stage in its development. The INTERACT program predicts what people will feel, given their definition of the situation and the EPA meanings associated with the identities and behaviors. Their expression of that emotion may be managed, given that they recognize that their emotional reaction will provide information about the identity they occupy and their view of the situation (e.g., if I am Insulted but I want my Supervisor to believe that I interpreted his action as Teasing, then I will not display my flustered anger). The theory also predicts norms, in the sense that people who agree on meanings will predict the same emotional reactions; failure to experience the normative emotion indicates deviation either in the fundamental view of how good, powerful, and lively identities or behaviors are, or a difference in defining the situation. More discussion of this relationship between experienced emotion and normative expectations is presented in the rest of the chapter.

10 In affect control theory, a role is an identity taken in relationship to another identity. For example, Mother is an identity and is a role (with a corresponding set of behavioral predictions) when viewed in the context of the Mother–Son relationship.

11 This effect of identity on emotion does not imply, of course, that people in positive identities cannot feel bad. I can view my identity as a writer as a fundamentally positive, enjoyable one, but still experience negative emotion when events deflect me downward on the evaluation dimension (e.g., when an ill-formed sentence is pointed out to me).

12 Notice that a negative rating on the potency dimension does not imply that these emotions have little impact on the person experiencing them. Rather, they imply that the person experiences a sense of powerlessness or lack of control.

13 Chronological age is highly correlated with fundamental images of liveliness and expressivity (the activity dimension). Baby, Infant, and Schoolgirl are high on this dimension, whereas Grandparent is quite inactive.

14 Alternatively, Heise (personal communication) suggests that victims may mask emotion and appeal more directly to ideology by pointing out the evil character of the behavior. The effectiveness of this strategy may depend on the interaction partner – in situations where the victim has little status (evaluation) and power, and is interacting with the oppressor, to display negative emotion may invite further injury. When interacting with the oppressor, to display negative emotion may invite further injury. When interacting with a third party, appeals to ideology may be more effective. However, if the victim initially occupies a positive identity vis-à-vis the oppressor, displaying hurt may be more effective.

15 Carolyn Ellis provides an interesting example from a party. A friend was teased, became upset, and left the party in anger. The person had often initiated teasing interactions in the past and had seemed to enjoy them. His friends responded with the following interpretations of his behavior: (1) He was in a bad mood, but owes it to the situation to control himself, (2) the put-down has a history that we don't know about – others may have teased

him about this before, (3) the teasing may have meaning to him that we don't know about – the friend is gay and the behavior might be interpreted as a symptom of AIDS, (4) he is not who we thought, (5) he felt an inappropriate fleeting emotion and it took him over, (6) he came to the party already upset and this incident gave him an excuse to express the anger, (7) everyone has quirks that we have to accept in our friends. Possibilities 1 to 6 refer to potential reactions from earlier events; in affect control terms, we would view deflections from earlier events as potentially altering expectations for new events necessary to maintain one's identity. Possibilities 2 and 3 refer to the possibility that the friend may have defined the act differently than the other partygoers (possibility 6 also contains elements of this interpretation, since our moods may shape our perceptions of other's actions); the put-down may not have seemed like innocent teasing to him. Possibility 4 refers to the other partygoers' definitions of the situation and opens discussion of labeling the "friend" because of his inappropriate display; 1 also contains elements of emotional deviance and negative labeling. Possibility 7 suggests a more benign relabeling: We could consider the angry behavior a "quirk" and be willing to accept this not-so-negative reaction from our friend. Only possibility 5 is somewhat outside the affect control framework, in that it suggests an almost physiological urge image of emotion that "takes over" and has a life of its own, independent of the social context and the identity of the actor.

References

Averett, Christine, & David R. Heise. 1987. Modified social identities: Amalgamations, attributions and emotions. *Journal of Mathematical Sociology* 13: 103–132.

Averill, James R. 1980. A constructionist view of emotion. In R. Plutchik & H. Kellerman (Eds.), *Emotion: Theory, research and experience* (pp. 305–339). New York: Academic Press.

Averill, James R. 1983. Studies on anger and aggression: Implications for theories of emotion. *American Psychologist* 38: 1,145–1,160

Burke, Peter J. 1980. The self: Measurement requirements from an interactionist perspective. *Social Psychology Quarterly* 43: 18–29.

Carley, Kathleen. 1987. *Emotions and artificial intelligence.* Unpublished paper.

Collins, Randall. 1975. *Conflict sociology: Toward an explanatory science.* New York: Academic Press.

Fararo, Thomas. 1986. Action and institution, network and function: The Cybernetic concept of social structure. *Sociological Forum* 1: 219–250.

Fararo, Thomas, & John V. Skvoretz. 1984. Institutions as production systems. *Journal of Mathematical Sociology* 10: 117–182.

Glassner, Barry. 1982. Labeling theory. In M. M. Rosenburg, R. A. Stebbins, & A. Turowitz (Eds.), *The sociology of deviance* (pp. 71–89). New York: St. Martin's Press.

Goffman, Erving. 1959. *The presentation of self in everyday life.* Garden City, NY: Doubleday.

Goffman, Erving. 1963. *Behavior in public places: Notes on the social organization of gatherings.* Glencoe, IL: Free Press.

Goffman, Erving. 1974. *Frame analysis: An essay on the organization of experience.* New York: Harper and Row.

Gonos, G. 1977. "Situation" versus "frame": The "interactionist" and the "structuralist" analyses of everyday life. *American Sociological Review* 42: 854–867.

Gordon, Robert A., James F. Short, Jr., Desmond S. Cartwright, & Fred Strodbeck. 1963.

Values and gang delinquency: A study of street-corner groups. *American Journal of Sociology* 69: 109–128.

Heise, David R. 1966. Social status, attitudes and word connotations. *Sociological Inquiry* 36: 227–239.

Heise, David R. 1977. Social action as the control of affect. *Behavioral Science* 22: 163–177.

Heise, David R. 1978. *Computer-assisted analysis of social action*. Chapel Hill, NC: Institute for Research in the Social Sciences.

Heise, David R. 1979. *Understanding events: Affect and the construction of social action*. New York: Cambridge University Press.

Heise, David R. 1982, October. *Emotions as signals of self confirmation or disconfirmation*. Paper presented to the Society for Experimental Social Psychology, Nashville, IN.

Heise, David R. 1986. Modeling symbolic interaction. In S. Lindenberg, J. S. Coleman, & S. Novak (Eds.), *Approaches to social theory* (pp. 291–309). New York: Russel Sage Foundation.

Heise, David R. 1987. Affect control theory: Concepts and model. *Journal of Mathematical Sociology* 13: 1–34.

Heise, David R. 1989. Effects of emotion displays on the assessment of character. *Social Psychology Quarterly* 52: 10–21.

Heise, David R. 1989. Modeling event structures. *Journal of Mathematical Sociology* 14: 139–169.

Heise, David. R., & Elsa Lewis. 1988. *Introduction to interact*. National Collegiate Software Clearinghouse, Box 8101, North Carolina State University, Raleigh, NC 27695.

Heise, David R., & Neil J. MacKinnon. 1987. Affective bases of likelihood judgments. *Journal of Mathematical Sociology* 13: 133–152.

Heise, David R., & Lynn Smith-Lovin. 1979. Impressions of goodness, powerfulness, and liveliness from discerned social events. *Social Psychology Quarterly* 44: 93–106.

Heise, David R., & Linda Thomas. 1989. Predicting impressions created by combinations of emotion and social identity. *Social Psychology Quarterly* 52: 141–148.

Hochschild, Arlie R. 1977. Emotion work, feeling rules and social structure. *American Sociological Review* 85: 551–575.

Hochschild, Arlie R. 1983. *The managed heart*. Berkeley: University of California Press.

Howard, Judith A. 1984. The "normal" victim: The effects of gender stereotypes on reactions to victims. *Social Psychology Quarterly* 47: 270–281.

Howard, Judith A. 1985. Further appraisal of correspondent inference theory. *Personality and Social Psychology Bulletin* 11: 467–477.

Howard, Judith A., & Randy Levinson. 1985. The overdue courtship of attribution and labeling. *Social Psychology Quarterly* 48: 191–202.

Jones, E. E., & D. McGillis. 1976. Correspondent inferences and the attribution cube: A comparative reappraisal. In J. H. Harvey, W. Ickes, & R. F. Kidd (Eds.), *New directions in attribution research* (Vol. 1, pp. 389–420). Hillsdale, NJ: Erlbaum.

Kelley, H. H. 1973. The process of causal attribution. *American Psychologist* 28: 107–128.

Kemper, Theodore D. 1978. *A social interactional theory of emotions*. New York: Wiley.

Kemper, Theodore D. 1981. Social constructionist and positivist approaches to the sociology of emotions. *American Journal of Sociology* 87: 336–362.

Lazowski, Linda E. 1987. *Speakers' nonverbal expressions of emotion as moderators of listeners' reactions to disclosure of self-harm and social harm*. Unpublished doctoral dissertation, University of California, Santa Barbara.

Lazowski, Linda E., David R. Heise, & Lynn Smith-Lovin. 1989. Social inference within an identity negotiation framework: The impact of emotion displays. Unpublished paper.

Marks, I. M. 1965. *Patterns of meaning in psychiatric patients: Semantic differential responses in obsessives and psychopaths*. London: Oxford University Press.

Minsky, Marvin. 1986. *The Society of mind*. New York: Simon and Schuster.

Morgan, Rick L., & David R. Heise. 1988. Structure of emotions. *Social Psychology Quarterly* 51:19–31.

Osgood, Charles E. 1962. Studies on the generality of affective meaning systems. *American Psychologist* 17: 10–28.

Osgood, Charles E., W. H. May, & M. S. Miron. 1975. *Cross-cultural universals of affective meaning*. Urbana: University of Illinois Press.

Osgood, Charles E., George C. Suci, & Perry H. Tannenbaum. 1957. *The measurement of meaning*. Urbana: University of Illinois Press.

Poloma, Margaret M. 1972. Role conflict and the married professional woman. In Constantina Safilios-Rothschild (Ed.), *Toward a sociology of woman* (pp. 187–199). Lexington, MA: Xerox College Publishing.

Rains, Prue. 1982. Deviant careers. In M. M. Rosenberg, R. A. Stebbins, & A. Turowitz (Eds.), *The sociology of deviance* (pp. 21–41). New York: St. Martin's Press.

Rapoport, Rhoda, & Robert N. Rapoport. 1972. The dual career family: A variant pattern and social change. In Constantina Safilios-Rothschild (Ed.), *Toward a sociology of women* (pp. 216–245). Lexington, MA: Xerox College Publishing.

Reiss, Albert J., Jr. (Ed.). 1961. *Occupations and social status*. New York: Free Press of Glencoe.

Rossi, Peter H., Emily Waite, Christine E. Bose, & Richard E. Berk. 1974. The seriousness of crimes: Normative structures and individual differences. *American Sociological Review* 39: 224–237.

Ryan, William. 1971. *Blaming the victim*. New York: Pantheon.

Skvoretz, John, & Thomas Fararo. 1979. Languages and grammars of action and interaction: A contribution to the formal theory of action. *Behavioral Science* 25: 9–22.

Smith-Lovin, Lynn. 1987a. Impressions from events. *Journal of Mathematical Sociology* 13: 35–70.

Smith-Lovin, Lynn. 1987b. The affective control of events within settings. *Journal of Mathematical Sociology* 13: 71–102.

Smith-Lovin, Lynn. 1990. Emotion as confirmation and disconfirmation of identity: An affect control model. In T. D. Kemper (Ed.), *Research agendas in the sociology of emotions* (pp. 238–270). New York: SUNY Press.

Smith-Lovin, Lynn, & William Douglass. Forthcoming. An affect control analysis of two religious subcultures. In David Franks & Viktor Gecas (Eds.), *Social perspectives on emotion*. Greenwich, CT: JAI Press.

Smith-Lovin, Lynn, & David R. Heise. 1988. *Analyzing social interaction: Advances in affect control theory*. New York: Gordon and Breach Science Publishers.

Stryker, Sheldon. 1987. *The interplay of affect and identity: Exploring the relationships of social structure, social interaction, self and emotion*. Paper presented at the American Sociological Association meetings, Chicago, IL.

Swann, William B., Jr. 1987. *Self-verification and the cognitive-affective crossfire*. Paper presented at the American Sociological Association meetings, Chicago, IL.

Thoits, Peggy A. 1984. Coping, social support and psychological outcomes: The central role of emotion. Pp. 219–38 In Philip Shaver (Ed.), *Review of personality and social psychology* (Vol. 5, pp. 219–238). Beverly Hills, CA: Sage.

Thoits, Peggy A. 1985. Self-labeling processes in mental illness: The role of emotional deviance. *American Journal of Sociology* 91: 221–249.

Wiggins, Beverly, & David R. Heise. 1987. Expectations, intentions and behavior: Some tests of affect control theory. *Journal of Mathematical Sociology* 13: 153–169.

8 The self-concept as a basis for a theory of motivation

Viktor Gecas

It is becoming increasingly clear that social psychology, at least the sociological branch, needs to develop a theory of motivation. Calls for such efforts have taken several forms. Coleman (1986) and Giddens (1979) state that we lack a theory of action in sociology, which has hampered explication of the connection between the individual and society. Coleman's recommendation is to develop a voluntaristic theory of action along the lines initiated by Parsons in *The Structure of Social Action* (1937). Giddens's approach is to develop a theory of the subject (within his larger theory of "structuration") involving a stratified model of personality consisting of the unconscious, practical consciousness, and discursive consciousness – a creative utilization of ideas drawn primarily from Freud, Marx, and Mead. For Ralph Turner (1988), the issue is how do persons affect the institutions within which they live, and how are they in turn affected by these institutions? Turner suggests this connection could be developed by focusing on that aspect of personality involving social roles.

But the problem is most frequently stated in explicitly motivational terms, that is, that we need to develop a theory of motivation that is explicit, parsimonious, and sociologically defensible (McMahon, 1984; Emmet, 1976; Miyamoto, 1970; J. Turner, 1987). These authors maintain that our neglect of motivation in sociological social psychology has hampered theory construction (especially evident within symbolic interactionism), contributed to an "oversocialized view of man" (as I have argued elsewhere, Gecas, 1986), and handicapped our efforts to assess the relationship between institutions and individuals.

My purpose is to show how the self-concept can be used as the basis for a theory of motivation. This, of course, is not the first time such an effort has been attempted. Previous significant efforts include Foote's (1951) discussion of the motivational significance of identity, which Stryker (1980; Stryker & Serpe, 1982) has developed into identity theory; Miyamoto's (1970) attempt to bring the concept of motivation into symbolic

171

interactionism via several dimensions of self-concept; Ralph Turner's (1976) analysis of real and false selves as sources of motivation; much of the work on the self-esteem motive (especially Rosenberg, 1979); and a good deal of research in psychological social psychology on such motivational aspects of self-concept as self-efficacy, self-monitoring, self-consistency, and possible selves (see de Charms & Muir, 1978; Nurius, this volume, chapter 11). In developing my argument, I will build on this previous work and hopefully go beyond it in making the case for the motivational significance of self-concept. In so doing, I will emphasize a cognitive approach to motivation, since my perspective on self-concept is primarily cognitive.

The dubious status of the concept of motivation in sociology

"Motivation" is a slippery concept with various meanings in sociology and psychology. In its most elementary sense it refers to that condition of the organism that energizes action and gives it direction and intensity (Peters, 1958; Miyamoto, 1970). As such, motivation is not synonymous with "causes" of behavior (which might be located outside the individual) or with "reasons" for the behavior (to be discussed). Typically, to identify the motivation for a particular action is to largely explain why the action occurred. That is why the specification of motivational processes is usually at the core of most theories of human behavior (see Chein, 1972, and Csikszentmihalyi, 1985, for extensive treatments of the concept).

Sociologists, at least since Durkheim (1897/1951), have generally been uncomfortable with the concept of motivation. This antipathy for motivation is particularly apparent among symbolic interactionists, who (justifiably) associate the concept with biological, physiological, or genetic explanations of human action. G. H. Mead (1934/1964), in developing his sociologically oriented social psychology, was reacting against the individualistic psychologies of his day with their proliferation of drive and instinct theories of motivation, most of which have since fallen into disrepute.[1] Mead's pragmatic emphasis on action and its consequences, as well as Dewey's (1925/1958) influential statement that man is active by nature, set the basic symbolic interactionist stance on motivation. The "self-as-actor" is treated as a paradigmatic given, needing no further motivational elaboration.

Instead of motivation, symbolic interactionists have preferred the concept of motives (see, e.g., Lindesmith, Strauss, & Denzin, 1977: 246; Stone & Farberman, 1970: 467). "Motive" as typically used by symbolic interactionists does not refer to the causes of behavior, but rather is used in

C. Wright Mills's (1940) sense of "vocabularies of motive" to refer to the reasons or justifications for the action in question given by an actor or others in the situation. In this usage, motives do not "motivate" in the sense of giving impetus, intensity, and direction to action (although they could, as in Foote's [1951] association of motives with identities, and Mead's [1934/1964] discussion of "intending behavior"). Rather, motives serve primarily a linguistic and interaction function of justifying problematic or questioned conduct and thereby permitting interaction to continue. Vocabularies of motive are important topics of study in their own right, but they do not substitute for the concept of motivation (Gecas, 1986).

By avoiding motivation, symbolic interactionism is left with two positions on the directionality of behavior: (1) an emphasis on the indeterminacy of action, associated with the unpredictable, spontaneous "I" aspect of the self; and (2) an emphasis on the multiplicity of motivators in the form of goals, purposes, intentions, identities, and so on. Neither of these positions is very useful to theory development, as others have also observed (Giddens, 1979; Miyamoto, 1970).

The motivation picture in other sociological perspectives is not much better. When motivational concepts are used, they tend to be borrowed from other disciplines. For example, Parsons (1955) eventually turned to Freudian personality theory for his motivational concepts, as did Wrong (1961) and to some extent Giddens (1979); much of social exchange theory is based on reinforcement theories of motivation that emphasize costs and rewards (Homans, 1961; Blau, 1964). Others draw on economic models of decision making. For most sociological theories and perspectives motivational processes are more likely to be implicit and undeveloped. Jonathan Turner (1987) has recently attempted to develop a sociological theory of motivation by making *explicit* the various *implicit* theories of motivation within five contemporary sociological theories. This is certainly a step in the right direction, even if his attempt at synthesis of the various motivational schemes falls short of providing a coherent theory of motivation.

The motivational significance of the self-concept

The self-concept is a particularly appropriate locus for developing a sociologically adequate theory of motivation because the self is a social product, emerging out of and dependent on social interaction. The self is not based on biological, physiological, or strictly psychological processes (although it certainly may be influenced by such processes). Therefore a theory of motivation based on the self is also somewhat removed from these organismic processes. Following Mead (1934/1964), the self is viewed essentially as a reflexive phenomenon (referring to the dialectical relationship between the "I" and the "me") that emerges from symbolic interaction via role taking. The product of this reflexive activity is the self-concept, which is the conception an individual has of himself or herself. The content of self-concepts typically includes social and personal identities, traits, attributes, and even possessions.

Once the self-concept begins to form and develop, it takes on motivational properties. As I will argue, by virtue of having a self-concept the individual is motivated to maintain and enhance it, to conceive of it as efficacious and consequential, and to experience it as meaningful and real. On theoretical and empirical grounds a case can be made for at least these three motivations (or self-motives) associated with the self-concept: self-esteem, self-efficacy, and authenticity, respectively.[2]

There are some parallels between this set of self-motives and one proposed by Miyamoto (1970), and to a lesser extent Turner (1987). Miyamoto (1970) also looked to the self-concept for a theory of motivation. Building on Mead's point that the self is an object to itself, Miyamoto identified three possible orientations toward objects: evaluative, cognitive, and affective. Evaluative is associated with the self-esteem motive (on which we overlap completely); cognitive is described as the self-identity motive (partial overlap); and affective is described as the self-gratification motive (no overlap, and I would suggest that this category is too similar to "evaluative" to be considered a separate orientation). What is missing in Miyamoto's scheme is a discussion of self-efficacy. Also, the aspect of the cognitive category that he emphasizes is substantially different from my emphasis on authenticity.

Within Jonathan Turner's (1987) elaborate composite model of motivation there is a self-motive described as "need to sustain self-conception," which is a combination of two others: "need to sustain self-esteem" and "construction of substantive self-conception." The former is similar to my self-esteem motive and the latter falls within the cognitive dimension and is close to my authenticity motive. It remains to be explained how these self-motives are indeed motivational for individuals.

To argue that self-esteem, self-efficacy, and authenticity are motivational components of the self-concept implies that there are positive and negative states or conditions associated with each motive. Furthermore, it implies that individuals strive to establish or increase the positive condition and avoid the negative condition. The *self-esteem motive* refers to the motivation to view oneself favorably and to act in such a way as to maintain (protect) or increase a favorable evaluation of oneself. In general, people like to feel good about themselves and dislike feeling bad about themselves. These feelings are experienced in terms of such sentiments as pride and shame. Individuals are motivated to act so as to increase the probability of experiencing the former and avoiding the latter. Individuals also engage in various defensive and biasing activities, such as selective perception and cognition of self-relevant information, strategic self-presentations, and reconstructing the environment and redefining the situation to make it reflect a more favorable view of self (Rosenberg, 1979; Hales, 1985).[3] The self-esteem motive is the most prominent motive in the self-concept literature and is the motivational basis for a number of contemporary theories in social psychology. The self-esteem motive is the basis of Kaplan's (1975) theory of delinquent behavior, Brim's (1966) theory of socialization, Rokeach's (1979) theory of values, the reformulated cognitive dissonance theory (Aronson, 1968), Duval and Wicklund's (1972) self-awareness theory, Rosenberg's (1979) self-theory, and Alexander's (Alexander & Wiley, 1981) situated identity theory. It is also implicit in Goffman (1959) and much of the symbolic interactionist work on self-presentation and impression management. (For more extensive discussion of the self-esteem motive within these social psychological theories, see Gecas, 1982, 1986; Rosenberg, 1981; and Wells & Marwell, 1976.)

The direction of motivation for these self-motives is considered to be linear, from the negative to the positive condition. For self-esteem, it is easy to see what is undesirable about the negative condition (e.g., depression, feelings of worthlessness, self-contempt) and why people would wish to avoid it. The motive thrust is toward increasing or enhancing self-esteem and, in most of the literature on self-esteem, the higher the better. But the extreme positive condition can also be associated with some undesirable characteristics. An exaggerated sense of self-esteem is reflected in such pejorative terms as conceited, arrogant, vain, smug, and narcissistic. There are cultural proscriptions against displays of excessive self-esteem, as expressed in the aphorism, Pride cometh before the fall. Humility and modesty are valued qualities. These cultural elements serve to constrain the self-esteem motive. The self-esteem motive can also be curtailed by coming into conflict with other self-motives (to be discussed). So even though the self-esteem motive is not conceptualized as curvilinear, there are forces that lead individuals to avoid the extreme negative and positive conditions of self-esteem.

Self-efficacy refers to the motivation to perceive oneself as a causal agent in the environment, that is, to experience oneself in agentive terms. Much of the evidence for this motive comes from cognitive and developmental psychology (see Gecas, 1989, for a review). De Charms (1968) proposes that individuals strive to be "origins" of behavior rather than "pawns" of impinging forces. Deci (1975: 45) suggests that intrinsically motivated behaviors are based upon people's need to be self-determining: "People strive to be competent and effective in dealing with their environments, and an essential ingredient of this is that they be personally causative – that they be willful or self-determining." The motivation for causal agency in the self is also reflected in White's (1959) concept of effectance motivation, Brehm's (1966) concept of psychological reactance (i.e., the motivation to resist constraint or control), and McClelland's (1975) power motive.

Research on causal attributions is also relevant, although the emphasis is more on *beliefs* about causality and agency and less on motivations to hold such beliefs. Rotter's (1966) influential distinction between internal and external locus of control, and Bandura's (1977, 1982) work on self-efficacy expectations, suggest that beliefs about personal causation and efficacy are quite consequential for subsequent behavior.

Within sociology, the motivational significance of self-efficacy is most evident in the writings of Karl Marx (1844/1963) and some of the contemporary sociological literature on alienation (Seeman, 1959, 1983; Schwalbe, 1986). The central theme in Marx's view of human nature is that of self-creation through efficacious action in the context of work or "praxis." Under conditions of "natural labor" the self is created and affirmed through the individual's work activity. Under conditions of alienation, however, the sense of self-efficacy is frustrated or inhibited because of a disjuncture between action and self, wherein work activity is no longer a reflection and affirmation of self. For Marx, the heart of the problem of alienation is the issue of control, that is, the extent to which the individual has control over his or her labor and its products. If the locus of control is perceived to be outside the individual (e.g., in the boss, the company, the machine), the individual exists in a condition of alienation. To a large extent, this is the basis of Marx's critique of capitalism. A key feature of alienation, therefore, is powerless or lack of self-efficacy.

The deficit condition or negative state of the self-efficacy motive is experienced as powerlessness, helplessness (Seligman, 1975), inferiority, and even despair. It is easy to see why people would wish to avoid such feelings and perceptions of self. People are motivated to perceive themselves as efficacious. As with self-esteem, however, the extreme end of the self-efficacy motive may also be associated with perverse or undesirable manifestations, such as megalomania, lust for power, and various delusions of grandeur and omnipotence. Social sanctions, reactions of other people, and various other reality checks are some of the mechanisms that constrain individuals from going too far in their pursuit of self-efficacy.

The third self-motive, authenticity, is more complicated. At its core it refers to the individual's striving for meaning, coherence, and understanding. The psychological context within which the authenticity motive operates is primarily cognitive, including the realm of beliefs, meanings, and understandings about self. The symbolic interactionist proposition that human beings live primarily in a world of meaning created through symbolic interaction implies that humans are also *motivated* to create, attribute, and impose meaning on themselves and others. Miyamoto (1970: 281) describes the cognitive orientation toward the self-concept as motivating the individual "to maximize meaningfulness of his relations with others and minimize meaninglessness of self." Antonovsky (1979) argues that people have a need for coherence, by which he means the sense that our world is predictable and meaningful and that we can make sense of it and of ourselves. When this sense of coherence is diminished, Antonovsky argues, negative psychological and physical consequences result. Similar notions are also found in Turner's (1987: 18) motivational category, "need for a sense of identity," the need for answers to the question, Who am I? Authenticity, therefore, focuses on the motivational implications of beliefs about self with regard to what is real and what is false.

Beliefs about self, or self-meanings, typically take the form of identities. Some identities within the self-concept are more meaningful and real to the individual than are others – we feel that more of the true self is expressed in these identities. Turner (1976, 1987) draws on a similar idea of the "real self" in distinguishing between individuals who locate their sense of authenticity in the performance of institutional roles versus those whose sense of real self is located in the expression of impulse. Turner focuses on contexts of authenticity, that is, the types of situations and the kinds of activities within which individuals feel authentic and inauthentic. He suggests that there has been a shift in the locus of authenticity from institutional roles to impulsive behavior in the past few decades. Some would even argue that the issue of authenticity has become more central and more problematic in modern times (Weigert, 1988).

There is some congruence between the sociological literature on identities and the psychological literature on the self-concept as an organization of knowledge and beliefs. Both consider self-cognitions as having motivational implications. Lecky (1945), for example, viewed the maintenance of a unified conceptual system as the overriding need of the individual. Epstein (1980) and Markus (1977) suggest that individuals seek to maintain a coherent view of themselves in order to operate effectively in the world. However, when these cognitive processes are discussed in terms of an underlying self-motive, it is usually expressed as the consistency motive. This is a mistake. Individuals can live with considerable inconsistency in their belief systems. What is much more difficult to tolerate is the thought that their world is meaningless and, worse, that they themselves are meaningless (Frankl, 1939/1963; Antonovsky, 1979). If there is a tendency toward consistency in self-conceptions, as these cognitive social psychologists maintain, it is a by-product of the more fundamental motive here described as authenticity, since authenticity implies a degree of stability and consistency (see Antonovsky, 1979).

"Inauthenticity" refers to a condition of falseness, either to oneself or to others. This is a prominent theme in existentialist writings (Sartre, 1960; Zimmerman, 1981), where it is viewed as the major source of personal and interpersonal problems.[4] There is a strong element of false consciousness of one's self and one's social situation in Sartre's (1960) conception of inauthenticity, reminiscent of Marx's discussion of alienation and self-estrangement. Seeman (1966) relies on both of these theoretical strands in discussing inauthenticity as a condition of false identity arising from an individual's adjustment to a stigmatized or stereotyped identity (i.e., especially characteristic of minority status). This adaptation is characteristic of what Seeman (1983) later described as the "disguised self," a form of self-estrangement involving a deprivation of awareness of one's true condition or sentiments.

Drawing on these diverse theoretical strands, my conception of authenticity as a self-motive emphasizes beliefs about what is real and what is false as perceived by the individual and used as a basis for self-assessment. Authenticity is a function of commitment to systems of meaning in society, particularly to various identities embedded in systems of values and beliefs. Individuals are motivated to avoid the negative end of the authenticity continuum, characterized by feelings of meaninglessness, self-estrangement, and anomie. But the extreme positive state, characterized by certitude in one's beliefs and values, may also take undesirable forms, such as intolerance of different belief and value systems. A certain amount of ambivalence and uncertainty may be necessary to temper the possible excesses of the extreme positive states of authenticity.

Interrelationships among esteem, efficacy, and authenticity

These three self-motives typically tend to be interrelated in experience. Self-efficacy can give rise to self-esteem and, some have argued (Gecas & Schwalbe, 1983; Franks & Marolla, 1976), provides an important basis for the maintenance of self-esteem. Authenticity is also expected to be positively related to self-esteem, since it would be difficult to maintain high self-esteem if one were feeling inauthentic. Self-esteem, in turn, may increase feelings of efficacy. Individuals who are more secure in their self-worth and self-regard are more likely to undertake challenges and new experiences (Covington & Beery, 1976), thereby increasing their sense of agency and competence.

Authenticity and self-efficacy are also closely related. This is particularly apparent in the domain of morality. A number of scholars have suggested that moral choices are crucial indicators of the person as an active agent (Turner, 1968; Weigert, 1975; and Schwalbe, this volume). To consider the self as a moral agent is to underscore the interdependence of the efficacy and authenticity motives.

But sometimes these self-motives do not work in concert. Self-esteem may conflict with self-efficacy; acceptance of agency and responsibility for negative outcomes may, for example, have negative implications for self-esteem. Research on causal attributions suggests that individuals are more likely to make internal attributions (i.e., accept responsibility) for favorable outcomes and external attributions (i.e., deny responsibility) for unfavorable outcomes, which favors the self-esteem motive over the self-efficacy motive. Esteem and authenticity may conflict when negative beliefs about oneself (see Markus, 1977, on self-schemata) persist even in the face of evidence suggesting a more competent and worthy self. Specification of conditions under which each of these self-motives prevails over others is an important area to pursue empirically and theoretically.

So far I have argued for distinguishing among these three self-motives on the basis of the psychological importance of each, the different experiences generated by each, and the interrelationships (sometimes conflicting) among the three. The argument can be extended in two directions: (1) a consideration of the similarities and differences of *antecedents* of these self-motives; and (2) a consideration of the *consequences* of the self-motives for social change.

Antecedents of self-esteem, self-efficacy, and authenticity

To some extent, all of the processes involved in self-concept formation and socialization are relevant to the development of each of these self-motives. Reflected appraisals, social comparisons, self-attributions, and the process of role learning and commitment to social identities all affect self-esteem, self-efficacy, and authenticity. To be sure, these processes may not be equally relevant to each of the self-motives. Reflected appraisals and social comparisons are most frequently invoked in the study of self-esteem, self-attribution is most likely to be associated with the development of self-efficacy, and processes involved in commitment to social identities seem to be most relevant to the sense of authenticity. But there is probably more commonality than difference among the self-motives in these developmental processes.

The differences in antecedents are more apparent at a more abstract level, the level of social domains. If we distinguish among the interpersonal domain (characterized by face-to-face interaction), the social structural domain (involving hierarchies of power, status, and differential access to resources), and the cultural domain (systems of meaning, values, and beliefs), we can see an affinity between each of the self-motives and each of these domains. The self-esteem motive is most responsive to the interpersonal domain, within which the reactions of significant others and other audiences provide reflected appraisals for self-evaluations, and where strategies of self-presentation and impression management come into play in the service of maintaining a favorable self-image. This is the arena examined so deftly by Goffman (1959) and other symbolic interactionists focusing on presentations of self in everyday life (Alexander & Wiley, 1981). Self-esteem seems to be less affected by social structural (at least macrostructural) factors. Research on social stratification and self-esteem, particularly with regard to race and social class, has found very little difference in the self-esteem levels of blacks compared to whites (Yancey, Rigsby, & McCarthy, 1972; Taylor & Walsh, 1979; Hughes & Demo, 1989) and of middle- compared to lower-class persons (Wylie, 1979). A common explanation offered for this lack of association between social stratification and self-esteem is that self-esteem is more responsive to local, interpersonal relations.

The social structural domain is most relevant for the self-efficacy motive. Self-efficacy depends on one's actions in the world and the perception of these actions as having the intended effects. Actions tend to be circumscribed by power relationships and access to resources. These are major elements of the social structural domain. In general, the higher one's position within a social structure or stratification system, the greater one's opportunities for efficacious action and the greater one's sense of self-efficacy (Gecas & Schwalbe, 1983). Thus, as mentioned earlier, Marx criticized capitalism because it undermines workers' sense of efficacy and agency by severely limiting the amount of control workers have over the production process.

The cultural domain is most relevant for the authenticity motive. Authenticity, which deals with matters of reality and meaning for the individual, is primarily addressed at the symbolic level in terms of such cultural content as ideologies, systems of beliefs, and values. Commitment to identities and the ideologies within which they are embedded leads to a sense of authenticity. Conversely, authenticity is undermined when commitment to a central ideology wavers (because of challenge, a traumatic experience, or some other conflict), or when a central identity is lost or thrown into question, such as by the death of a spouse, loss of job, betrayal by a friend, or when one's own actions betray a valued conception of self. These circumstances may give rise to feelings of meaninglessness and anomie. At the least, they are circumstances that require a redefinition of self.

Consequences for social change

Self-esteem, self-efficacy, and authenticity evidently affect individuals' actions. I have argued that individuals are motivated to increase (or at least to maintain) their self-esteem and self-efficacy, and to feel authentic or meaningful. Thus, these self-motives are important factors in the stability and change of personality. But do these self-motives have any implications for social change, which Coleman (1986) considers the most difficult and neglected link in the society-personality connection? In this section, I will speculate on some possible effects.

In the area of political activism, the degree of self-efficacy and the attribution of cause may shape how individuals respond to social problems (see chapter 10 in this volume by Howard for a more extensive discussion of participation in social movements, emphasizing the importance of identity and identification). These two variables suggest a simple interaction scheme or paradigm. If we combine sense of efficacy (high or low) with attribution of cause for a particular social problem, such as poverty, crime, or pollution, (for simplicity, let us distinguish between only two types of attribution: "individual" and "institutional") we derive four types of individuals: (1) those who have a high sense of efficacy and attribute problems to individual causes, (2) those who have a low sense of efficacy and attribute problems to individual causes, (3) those with high efficacy who attribute problems to institutional causes, and (4) those with low efficacy who attribute cause to institutional sources. Each of these types of individuals would be expected to respond differently to the social problem in question[5] (see Figure 1).

Sociologically, the most interesting response pattern is associated with cell 3 in Figure 1. The combination of high self-efficacy with institutional attribution of cause should be most consequential for social change. If, for example, the problem is poverty, the solution would be sought through initiation of changes in the economic or political spheres – assuming that the issue is considered important enough for such action. When the activity

| Self-Efficacy | Attribution of Cause | |
	Individual	Institutional
High	(1) Self Improvement	(3) Political Action
Low	(2) Guilt/Inferiority	(4) Fatalism/Resignation

Figure 1. Paradigm of responses to social problems

takes on the character of a social movement, one of the important tasks for those in the vanguard of the movement is to transform individuals from cell 2 to 3. This is a major purpose of consciousness-raising groups in equal rights movements, for example. The task is (1) to overcome the minority members' sense of inferiority and increase their sense of efficacy and worth, and (2) to attribute the "problem" to institutional or societal factors. With this redefinition of self and relocation of cause, concerted political action is more likely.[6] Thus, individual action is most likely for those in cell 1, inaction for those in cell 2 and 4, and collective action for those in cell 3. Paige's (1971) study of riot participation provides some empirical support for the behavioral expectations associated with cell 3, as does Gurin and Brim's (1984) finding that those who challenged the political system during the 1970s were high on self-efficacy and low on judgments of system responsiveness (see Gecas, 1989, for a more extensive review of the literature on self-efficacy and political activism).

Authenticity also has implications for social change. Some of the literature on religious conversion and religious movements suggests that many converts are active seekers for a new ideology or belief system to alleviate their sense of meaninglessness and lack of authenticity (Richardson, Harder, & Simmonds, 1972; Richardson & Stewart, 1977). Similarly, it is within the ranks of the alienated and anomic that political activists often look for recruits for their cause. Howard (this volume) and others (Zurcher & Snow, 1981) also observe that feelings of inauthenticity and loss of meaning contribute to the development of social activism. Pervasive individual discontent or deprivation of self-esteem, self-efficacy, or authenticity produce an unstable social condition and provide a receptive milieu for social change.

Conclusion

Given the dubious history of the concept of motivation, because of its association with various biological and instinct theories of human behavior, the general neglect of motivational considerations within sociology is understandable. But we have paid a price for neglecting "motivation." This neglect has hampered theory development, given us an anemic, undeveloped conception of human beings, and resulted in too one-sided a view of the relationship between individuals and their social environments.

I have argued that the self-concept is a fertile and sociologically appropriate basis from which to develop a theory of motivation. The self-concept develops out of social (symbolic) interaction and is dependent on social interaction for its maintenance. By virtue of having self-concepts, individuals acquire certain powerful motivations identified as self-esteem, self-efficacy, and authenticity. I have briefly considered the nature of these self-motives, their interrelationships, their social antecedents, and speculated on their consequences for social change. This does not, of course, constitute a fully developed theory of motivation. A great deal of elaboration and specification of the nature of these relationships is still needed. Hopefully, this is a start.

Notes

1 The topic of motivation is not totally ignored by Mead. It enters Mead's social psychology in two ways: (1) as a biological impulse in the initial stages of the act and, more importantly, (2) as "intending" behavior (Mead, 1938). The first point acknowledges the relevance of biology to human action, but not much is done to develop this point and it does not fit very comfortably within Mead's overall perspective. The second point emphasizes the influence of an anticipated future (in the form of goals, aspirations, and beliefs) in motivating and directing action, and is more compatible with his overall sociological perspective.

2 If the self-concept is viewed as a set of self-*attitudes*, following Manford Kuhn's (Kuhn & McPartland, 1954) suggestion, we find that these three self-motives roughly correspond to the three main components of attitudes: evaluative (self-esteem), conative (self-efficacy), and cognitive (authenticity). See Triandis (1971) for a discussion of these attitude components.

3 Hales (1985), in an extensive review of the empirical evidence, concludes that the self-esteem motive, manifested in the psychological laboratory experiment as self-image management, has been a serious confounding influence on experimental research results since the inception of experimental social psychology.

4 Inauthenticity sometimes takes the form of self-deception, or what Sartre (1956: 49) called *mauvais fois* (sometimes translated as *bad faith*). All self-deception has as its point the evasion of responsibility by escaping oneself. Authenticity is a central concern for Sartre and other existentialists because it is the major criterion for evaluating personal existence as well as the basis for the moral order in society.

5 A somewhat parallel scheme is offered by Brickman, Rabinowitz, Karuza, Coates, Cohn, and Kidder (1982), who develop a four-fold typology on the basis of a distinction between "attributional responsibility for a social problem" and "attribution of responsibility for a solution." This combination, however, leads to different predictions.

6 There are many other psychological and situational factors that affect individuals' involvement in political action, e.g., risk taking and nonconformity (for an excellent discussion, see Tallman, 1976). Also important to this conceptualization is Bandura's (1977) distinction

between "efficacy expectations" and "outcome expectations." In order to direct their energies toward institutional change, individuals not only need to have confidence in their abilities, but also an expectation that their actions will have the desired effect. This is more likely to occur if individuals have a strong sense of what Bandura calls "collective efficacy" (1986: 449), i.e., individuals' judgments about their group's capabilities to engage in successful political action.

References

Alexander, C. N., & M. G. Wiley. 1981. Situated activity and identity formation. In M. Rosenberg & R. H. Turner (Eds.), *Social psychology: Sociological perspectives* (pp. 269–289). New York: Basic Books.

Antonovsky, A. 1979. *Health, stress, and coping.* San Francisco: Jossey-Bass.

Aronson, E. 1968. Dissonance theory: Progress and problems. In R. P. Abelson et al. (Eds.), *Theories of cognitive consistency: A sourcebook* (pp. 5–27). Chicago: Rand McNally.

Bandura, A. 1977. Self-efficacy: Toward a unifying theory of behavioral change. *Psychological Review* 84: 191–215.

Bandura, A. 1982. "Self-efficacy mechanism in human agency." *American Psychologist* 37: 122–147.

Bandura, A. 1986. *Social foundations of thought and action: A social cognitive theory.* Englewood Cliffs, NJ: Prentice-Hall.

Blau, P. M. 1964. *Exchange and power in social life.* New York: Wiley.

Brehm, J. W. 1966. *A theory of psychological reactance.* New York: Academic Press.

Brickman, P., V. C. Rabinowitz, J. Karuza, D. Coates, E. Cohn, & L. Kidder. 1982. Models of helping and coping. *American Psychologist* 37: 368–384.

Brim O. G., Jr. 1966. Socialization through the life cycle. In O. G. Brim & S. Wheeler, *Socialization after childhood: Two essays* (pp. 1–49). New York: Wiley.

Chein, I. 1972. *The science of behavior and the image of man.* New York: Basic Books.

Coleman, J. S. 1986. Social theory, social research, and a theory of action. *American Journal of Sociology* 91: 1,309–1,335.

Covington, M. V., & R. G. Beery. 1976. *Self-worth and school learning.* New York: Holt, Rinehart and Winston.

Csikszentmihalyi, M. 1985. Emergent motivation and the evolution of the self. *Advances in motivation and achievement* (Vol. 4, pp. 93–119). Greenwich, CT: JAI Press.

de Charms, R. 1968. *Personal causation.* New York: Academic Press.

de Charms, R, & M. S. Muir. 1978. Motivation: Social approaches. *Annual Review of Psychology* 29: 91–113.

Deci, E. L. 1975. *Intrinsic motivation.* New York: Plenum Press.

Dewey, J. 1958. *Experience and nature.* New York: Dover. (Original work published 1925)

Durkheim, E. 1951. *Suicide.* J. A. Spaulding & G. Simpson (Trans.). New York: Free Press. (Original work published 1897)

Duval, S., & R. A. Wicklund. 1972. *A theory of objective self-awareness.* New York: Academic Press.

Emmet, D. 1976. Motivation in sociology and social anthropology. *Journal for the Theory of Social Behavior* 6: 85–104.

Epstein, S. 1980. The self-concept: A review and the proposal of an integrated theory of personality. In E. Staub (Ed.), *Personality: Basic issues and current research* (pp. 27–39). Englewood Cliffs, NJ: Prentice-Hall.

Foote, N. N. 1951. Identification as the basis for a theory of motivation. *American Sociological Review* 16: 14–21.

Frankl, V. E. 1963. *Man's search for meaning*. New York: Simon & Schuster. (Original work published 1939)

Franks, D. D., & J. Marolla. 1976. Efficacious action and social approval as interacting dimensions of self-esteem. *Sociometry* 39: 324–341.

Gecas, V. 1982. The self-concept. *Annual Review of Sociology* 8: 1–33.

Gecas, V. 1986. The motivational significance of self-concept for socialization theory. In E. Lawler (Ed.), *Advances in group processes* (Vol. 3, pp. 131–156). Greenwich, CT: JAI Press.

Gecas, V. 1989. The social psychology of self-efficacy. *Annual Review of Sociology* 15: 291–316.

Gecas, V., & M. L. Schwalbe. 1983. Beyond the looking-glass self: Social structure and efficacy-based self-esteem. *Social Psychology Quarterly* 46: 77–88.

Giddens, A. 1979. *Central problems in social theory*. Berkeley & Los Angeles: University of California Press.

Goffman, E. 1959. *The presentation of self in everyday life*. Garden City, NY: Doubleday.

Gurin, P., & O. G. Brim, Jr. 1984. Change in self in adulthood: The example of sense of control. In P. B. Baltes & O. G. Brim, Jr. (Eds.). *Life-span development and behavior* (Vol. 6, pp. 115–148). New York: Academic Press.

Hales, S. 1985. The inadvertent rediscovery of self in social psychology. *Journal for the Theory of Social Behavior* 15: 237–282.

Homans, G. C. 1961. *Social behavior: Its elementary forms*. New York: Harcourt.

Hughes, M., & D. H. Demo. 1989. Self-perceptions of black Americans: Self-esteem and personal efficacy. *American Journal of Sociology* 95: 132–159.

Kaplan, H. B. 1975. *Self-attitudes and deviant behavior*. Pacific Palisades, CA: Goodyear.

Kuhn, M. H., & T. S. McPartland. 1954. An empirical investigation of self-attitudes. *American Sociological Review* 19: 68–76.

Lecky, P. 1945. *Self-consistency: A theory of personality*. New York: Island Press.

Lindesmith, A. R., A. L. Strauss, & N. K. Denzin. 1977. *Social psychology*. New York: Holt, Rinehart and Winston.

Markus, H. 1977. Self-schemata and processing information about the self. *Journal of Personality and Social Psychology* 35 (2): 63–78.

Marx, K. 1963. *Early writings*. T. B. Bottomore (Ed. and Trans.). New York: McGraw-Hill. (Original work published 1844)

McClelland, D. C. 1975. *Power: The inner experience*. New York: Irvington.

McMahon, A. M. 1984. The two social psychologies: Postcrises directions. *Annual Review of Sociology* 10: 121–140.

Mead, G. H. 1964. *G. H. Mead on social psychology: Selected papers*. Anselm Strauss (Ed.). Chicago: University of Chicago Press. (Original work published 1934)

Mead, G. H. 1938. *The philosophy of the act*. C. W. Morris (Ed.). Chicago: University of Chicago Press.

Mills, C. W. 1940. Situated actions and vocabularies of motive. *American Sociological Review* 5: 905–929.

Miyamoto, F. S. 1970. Self, motivation, and symbolic interaction theory. In T. Shibutani (Ed.), *Human nature and collective behavior: Papers in honor of Herbert Blumer* (pp. 271–285). Englewood Cliffs, NJ: Prentice-Hall.

Paige, J. M. 1971. Political orientation and riot participation. *American Sociological Review* 36: 810–820.

Parsons, T. 1937. *The structure of social action*. New York: McGraw-Hill.

Parsons, T. 1955. *Social structure and personality*. New York: Free Press.

Peters, R. S. 1958. *The concept of motivation*. London: Routledge and Kegan Paul.

Richardson, J. T., M. Harder, & R. B. Simmonds. 1972. Thought reform and the Jesus movement. *Youth and Society* 4: 185–202.

Richardson, J. T., & M. Stewart. 1977. Conversion process models and the Jesus movement. *American Behavioral Scientist* 20: 819–838.

Rokeach, M. 1979, March. *Some unresolved issues in theories of beliefs, attitudes, and values.* Paper presented at the Nebraska Symposium on Motivation, Lincoln.

Rosenberg, M. 1979. *Conceiving the self.* New York: Basic Books.

Rosenberg, M. 1981. The self-concept: Social product and social force. In M. Rosenberg & R. H. Turner (Eds.), *Social psychology: Sociological perspectives* (pp. 593–624). New York: Basic Books.

Rotter, J. B. 1966. Generalized expectancies for internal versus external control of reinforcement. *Psychological Monographs* 80 (Whole No. 609).

Sartre, J. P. 1956. *Being and nothingness.* New York: Philosophical Library.

Sartre, J. P. 1960. *Anti-Semite and Jew.* New York: Grove Press.

Schwalbe, M. L. 1986. *The psychosocial consequences of natural and alienated labor.* Albany, NY: State University of New York Press.

Seeman, M. 1959. On the meaning of alienation. *American Sociological Review* 24: 783–791.

Seeman, M. 1966. Status and identity: The problem of inauthenticity. *Pacific Sociological Review* 9: 67–73.

Seeman, M. 1983. Alienation motifs in contemporary theorizing: The hidden continuity of the classic themes. *Social Psychology Quarterly* 46: 171–184.

Seligman, M. E. 1975. *Helplessness: On depression, development, and death.* San Francisco: Freeman.

Stone, G. P., & H. A. Farberman. 1970. *Social psychology through symbolic interaction.* New York: Wiley.

Stryker, S. 1980. *Symbolic interactionism: A social structural version.* Menlo Park, CA: Benjamin-Cummings.

Stryker, S., & R. T. Serpe. 1982. "Commitment, identity salience and role behavior: Theory and Research Examples." In W. Ickes and E. Knowles (Eds.), *Personality, roles and social behavior.* New York: Springer-Verlag.

Tallman, I. 1976. *Passion, action, and politics.* San Francisco: Freeman.

Taylor, M. C., & E. J. Walsh. 1979. Explanations of black self-esteem: Some empirical tests. *Social Psychology Quarterly* 42: 242–253.

Triandis, H. C. 1971. *Attitude and attitude change.* New York: Wiley.

Turner, R. H. 1968. The self-conception in social interaction. In C. Gordon & K. J. Gergen (Eds.), *The self in social interaction* (Vol. 1, pp. 93–106). New York: Wiley.

Turner, R. H. 1976. The real self: From institution to impulse. *American Journal of Sociology* 81: 989–1,016.

Turner, R. H. 1988. Personality in society: Social psychology's contribution to sociology. *Social Psychology Quarterly* 51: 1–10.

Turner, J. H. 1987. Toward a sociological theory of motivation. *American Sociological Review* 52: 15–27.

Weigert, A. J. 1975. Alfred Schutz on a theory of motivation. *Pacific Sociological Review* 18: 83–101.

Weigert, A. J. 1988. Self and authenticity, identity and ambivalence: Aspects of the modern predicament. In D. K. Lapsley & F. C. Power (Eds.), *Self, ego, & identity: Integrative approaches* (pp. 79–96). New York: Springer-Verlag.

Wells, L. E., & G. Marwell. 1976. *Self-esteem: Its conceptualization and measurement.* Beverly Hills, CA: Sage.

White, R. W. 1959. Motivation reconsidered: The concept of competence. *Psychological Review* 66: 297–333.

Wrong, D. H. 1961. The oversocialized conception of man in modern sociology. *American Sociological Review* 26: 183–193.

Wylie, R. C. 1979. *The self-concept* (Vol. 2). Lincoln: University of Nebraska Press.

Yancey, W. L., L. Rigsby, & J. D. McCarthy. 1972. Social position and self-evaluation: The relative importance of race. *American Journal of Sociology* 78: 338–359.

Zimmerman, M. E. 1981. *Eclipse of the self: The development of Heidegger's concept of authenticity*. Athens: Ohio University Press.

Zurcher, L. A., & D. A. Snow. 1981. Collective behavior: Social movements. In M. Rosenberg & R. H. Turner (Eds.), *Social Psychology: Sociological perspectives* (pp. 447–482). New York: Basic Books.

9 Attitudes, behavior, and the self

Peter J. Burke

Introduction

For the past several years, I have been exploring the effects of a cognitive view of the self-concept on behavioral decisions within the context of identity theory. Behavioral decisions have also been examined from a cognitive perspective as a function of general attitudes. Inasmuch as the self-concept is an attitude, a self-attitude, it seems worthwhile to ask how these three concepts of self, attitudes, and behavior fit together within a cognitive framework. This chapter reviews work in each of these traditions and suggests how identity theory can incorporate more general attitudes.

Behavior, the self, and meaning

The self

I begin with a short review of identity theory and some of my work on self and behavior, drawing on Burke and Tully (1977), Burke (1980), and Burke and Reitzes (1981), as well as some development and thoughts since then. From a symbolic interactionist perspective, a person's self is made up of a set of hierarchically organized identities. These identities are viewed as internal, reflexive, positional designations that are tied to social structural positions: doctor, mother, student, professor. In this sense, they are often referred to as role-identities (McCall & Simmons, 1978).

Identities arise and are developed from the different social situations, contexts, and relationships we encounter, but they take on their own coherence and integrity and come to transcend the situations in which they arise. Identities carry the shared meanings and behavioral expectations associated with roles and group memberships. The internalization and attribution of these expectations provides the basis of identities (Stryker,

189

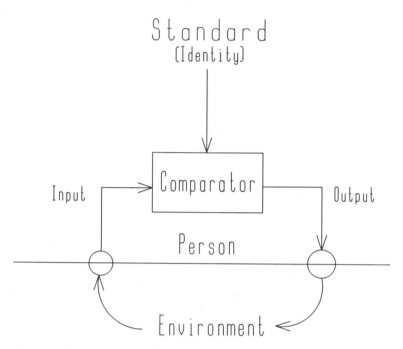

Figure 1. Simple control system

1980; McCall & Simmons, 1978). An identity is the internal component of a role-identity, whereas a role is the external component (McCall & Simmons, 1978; Burke, 1980). As roles do not stand in isolation but presuppose and relate to counterroles (Lindesmith & Strauss, 1956), so too do identities.[1] An identity consists of the internalized meanings (cognitive and emotional) of the self in a social position or role. The idea that identities are meanings a person attributes to the self (and others attribute to the person) is suggested in many writings (e.g., Lindesmith & Strauss, 1956; Rose, 1962; Heise, 1977). For this, it makes sense to think of meaning in the sense in which Osgood and colleagues (Osgood, Succi, & Tannenbaum, 1957) used the term as a "representational mediation process." The meaning of an identity is given by its *commonalities* with one class of persons similarly situated and its *differences* with other classes – those situated in counterpositions (Stone, 1962).

From a cognitive perspective identity processes are control systems as Powers (1975) uses this term (Burke, 1980). As illustrated in Figure 1, a control system consists of four components: an internal *standard*, an *input* from the outside, an *output* to the outside, and a *comparator* that compares the input with the standard. An everyday example of a control system is a

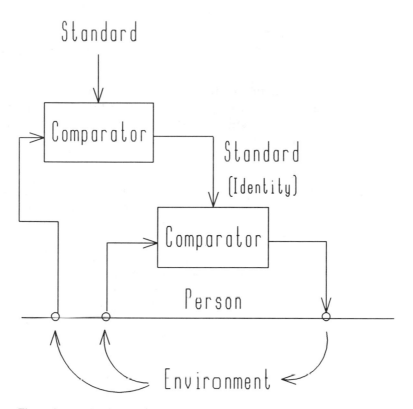

Figure 2. Two-level control system

thermostat, which works as follows: The input (current temperature) is compared to the standard (thermostat setting), and output (signal to the furnace) is a function of that comparison. Output is modified until the input from the outside matches the internal standard (current temperature matches the thermostat setting). The goal of the control system is to have the input match the standard. The input is what is controlled, often referred to as the *controlled quantity* (Powers, 1975). Inputs are controlled indirectly by the output of the system. Because the outputs are not directly linked to inputs but must filter through the environment, the exact way in which the output modifies the input is not under direct control. Indeed, the system does not have to "know" how to control the inputs, it can simply alter outputs randomly until the input matches the standard. Over time, and in a stable environment the system may "learn" to do this efficiently.

Control systems may be conceptualized in hierarchical form as illustrated in Figure 2 (Powers, 1975). In a hierarchical control system, the outputs on one level are the standards at a lower level. Hierarchical control systems may be many levels deep. Standards at a given level may change in response to a discrepancy between inputs and standards at a higher level.

This model of hierarchical control systems can be applied to identity processes.

1. An identity is the internal standard analogous to the thermostat setting. It can be thought of as a set (vector) of meanings of the self-in-social-position. But rather than being "set" at a particular temperature, it is positioned to the self-meanings.

2. In addition to the internal standard or identity vector, there is another vector of meanings that is the output. The output meanings become translated into meaningful (social) behavior that alters the situation (leading to modifications of the input).

3. A third vector of meanings corresponds to the input in the Powers model. In this case the input is the perceived vector of meanings attributed to the self-in-social-position in an interactive setting.

4. If the perceived self-in-social-position meanings (input) do not match the actual self-in-social-position meanings (the standard), then there is a feeling of psychological distress (Zanna & Cooper, 1976), and some change in behavior (output meanings) will occur. This change in behavior will have the effect of changing the perceived self-in-social-position meanings (controlled quantity). When given the opportunity, people learn what to do to make the input (perceived self-in-social-position meanings) match the standard (identity), and if what they do is not effective, they will do something else until a behavior is effective.

5. It is not always the case that people change their behavior; sometimes identities change. This model allows that possibility. Because identity processes exist in a hierarchical structure, an identity may change as the result of changes in the outputs of identity processes higher in the structure (see Figure 2).

6. This model reflects in a natural way the symbolic interactionists' view of the link between self (identity) and behavior in terms of meaning. Meaning becomes the medium of exchange, the standard against which social behavior is assessed. What we do conveys meaning. What others do conveys meaning. Meaning is what we assess as input; meaning is what we compare to our identities; meaning is what we offer as output (in the form of symbolic behavior).

As an example, consider a mother whose identity as a mother has a certain amount of *goodness, powerfulness*, and *activity* (these being the most general and universal dimensions of meaning – cf. Osgood et al.,

1957; Osgood, May, & Miron, 1975). Let us suppose that her mother identity is activated, and that the inputs she is receiving do not match the degree of goodness, powerfulness, and activity that is her identity setting. The model suggests that, as a result of this lack of semantic congruity, she will both feel a sense of distress and behave in such a way that will alter the inputs she receives in the interactive setting. If her inputs (perceptions) indicate that she is not as powerful as her identity, she may feel upset and alter her behavior by standing up for her rights, acting in a more firm fashion, being more forceful, and so on. This will continue until her perceptions of herself (directly and through others as her looking glass) match the identity she has. These perceptions or inputs are what is important, for they are what is being controlled, and they are what must match the standard or identity when the identity is activated.

Meaning

As implied in the stated example, my view of meaning is derived from the work of Osgood and his associates (1957) who view meaning as a *representational mediation process*. It is an internal response that is a reduced portion of the total response originally elicited by a significate. It consists of both cognitive and emotional responses. This idea is in accord with Mead's notions of meaning as a response and the symbol as that which calls out the same meaning (response) in the organism, using it as in the organism to which it is directed (cf. Mead, 1934: 146 ff). Additionally, I assume, as does Osgood, that meaning is multidimensional and contrastive. It can be characterized by the notions of *direction* (toward or away from one or the other end of the contrastive dimensions, e.g., good vs. bad) and *intensity* (the degree to which it approaches one extreme or the other).

The semantic differential was developed by Osgood and his coworkers to assess and measure the internal representational mediation process along as many dimensions as the investigator may wish to include. Empirically, however, Osgood has shown that the dimensions of evaluation (good–bad), potency (strong–weak), and activity (active–passive) are the three most important dimensions cutting across a wide variety of concepts (significates) and in a number of different cultures (Osgood et al., 1975). These three dimensions generally account for about 50% of the variance in semantic differential ratings.

Measuring the self

I have adopted the semantic differential to measure the meaning of different identities. In this procedure, people rate the meaning of a target role on the semantic differential, and then rate the meaning of a (set of) counterrole(s). It is assumed, of course, that the adjectives on the rating forms are relevant to the task of describing the target and counter-roles for the people doing the ratings. The selection of appropriate items requires some pretesting.

Following the ratings of the target and counterroles, the respondents rate themselves in the target role. For example, in a study of the effects of gender identity on school performance, boys and girls in grades six through eight were asked to rate the concepts of "Boys usually are...," "Girls usually are...," and "As a boy/girl I usually am..." (Burke, 1989). In another study college students were asked to rate the concepts "College students are," "Graduate students are," "High-school students are," "College graduates are," "Persons my age who didn't go to college are," and "As a college student I am."

A discriminant function analysis is then applied to the ratings of the target and counterroles, yielding a set of weights to be applied to the self-ratings. The discriminant function provides further selection of appropriate items by weighting them in terms of how well they actually distinguish between the target and counterroles. Some weights may be close to zero, indicating that the items are not relevant.

The linear combination of the weighted self-ratings is a score (or set of scores) that can be interpreted as distances along the underlying dimensions revealed by the discriminant function analysis. Thus for the gender identity measure, a score represents a distance along a continuum between the meanings of what boys are and what girls are. The self-meanings are located in a semantic space ranging from the meanings of being a boy to the meanings of being a girl. In the case of the student identities, the self-meaning of being a college student is located in a multidimensional space in which are located the meanings of being a college student, of being a high-school student, and so forth.

These self-meanings or identities have been found to predict various behaviors. For example, the gender identity of school children was related to their school performance (Burke, 1989). Student identities of college students were related to various activities in which they participated, for example, planning for graduate school or going to the movies (Reitzes & Burke, 1980; Burke & Reitzes, 1981).

What mechanisms are involved in the relationship between identity and behavior? It was hypothesized that the meaning of the behavior is what mattered, and that people selected behaviors whose meanings were congruent with their own identities. Thus, respondents were asked to rate the meanings of various activities. Results indicated that, indeed, people do tend to select activities whose meanings are congruent with their self-meanings.

In a later study, Burke and Franzoi (1988) have demonstrated the situational sensitivity of this relationship. They used an experiential sampling methodology in which people carried electronic timers with them over a period of two days. The timers were set to go off on the average of every 90 minutes. When the timer sounded the respondents filled out a short two-page questionaire asking them where they were, what they were doing, what identities they had, and what identities others in the situation had. They also rated the meaning of their own identity and the meaning of the situation. We found that variations in the meaning of the situations in which people found themselves were reflected in their own self-meanings. Further results showed that when people were in a situation because they chose it (rather than being there because they had to be for one reason or another), there was a closer correspondence between the meaning of the situation and their identity.

These studies demonstrate that people's self-meanings or identities are important to them and help them select situations and activities that are congruent with those identities. Such congruency both displays who they are to others and affirms their own identity to themselves.

Attitudes and behavior

Attitudes that people hold have also been used to predict choice behavior. The usual notion is that if people have a positive attitude toward an object (evaluate an object positively), then they will behave in a positive manner toward that object. Similarly, if they have a negative attitude toward an object, they will behave in a negative fashion toward the object.

Early conceptions often define attitudes as having three components: (1) cognitive or informational, (2) affective or emotional, and (3) conative or behavioral components. This early formulation was later changed; behavior was separated from attitude. Rather than treating behavior as one indicator of attitude, attitude was used to predict behavior. It soon became clear, however, that behavior was not predicted well by attitudes, and the "attitude–behavior problem" emerged.

Several approaches to the attitude–behavior problem have developed over the years. In one approach, DeFleur and Westie (1963) argued for a return to the earlier conceptualization of attitudes as having a behavioral component. They argued that the behavioral component is activated stochastically and therefore not expected necessarily to correspond with other parts of the attitude. In this way the attitude–behavior problem is

nullified. Similar conceptualizations have been held by others (Campbell,
1950; Krech & Crutchfield, 1948; Fuson, 1942).

Bem's (1967, 1972) theory of self-perception is a second approach to the attitude–behavior problem. His theory derives from a fairly radical behaviorist tradition – people come to know themselves (their attitudes) by observing their own behavior. Attitudes are thus derivative rather than causative of behavior. Attitudes cannot predict behavior because until people behave they cannot know their own attitudes.

Most attitude theorists generally reject the probability and self-perception conceptions of attitudes and continue to view attitudes both as latent processes and as important causes of behavior (Cooper & Croyle, 1984). They argue that the attitude–behavior consistency problem can be resolved by one of the following lines of reasoning.

1. If only we could measure attitudes better, or if only we measured attitudes at the same level of generality as we measure behavior. Ajzen and Fishbein (1977), Bagozzi (1981), and others argue that often attitudes are measured in very global and general terms, whereas we measure behaviors to be predicted from these attitudes in very specific terms. If we measure single-item behaviors, then we need to measure very specific attitudes; if we measure general attitudes, then we need multi-item measures of behavior.

2. If only we measure established attitudes and not more fleeting opinions or other related concepts. Additionally, it is possible that respondents construct "attitudes" in response to the questionaire when they have no established attitude.

3. If only we model the problem properly. Whereas some researchers see the problem as one of conceptualizing or measuring attitudes properly, others see the problem more as a question of the proper modeling of the attitude–behavior relationship.

Fishbein and Ajzen (e.g., 1975) have proposed the most extensive modification of the attitude–behavior model. First, they change the attitude target from attitude toward an object to attitude toward behavior related to the object. Thus persons who have a positive attitude toward a particular behavior are seen as more likely to perform that behavior. Second, they add the concept of behavioral intentions to the model. Attitudes are hypothesized to predict behavioral intentions, and behavioral intentions are hypothesized to influence actual behavior. In this way Fishbein and Ajzen close that gap between attitudes and behavior by inserting behavioral intentions between attitudes and behavior. Fishbein and Ajzen add some other components to the model, for example, subjective norms, whether people believe that specific individuals or groups think they should or should not engage in the behavior, but we will leave these aside for now.

All of these "if only" approaches and the model changes suggested by Ajzen and Fishbein are what might be termed *methodological* approaches to understanding the link between attitudes and behavior. They do not change the basic conception of the attitude–behavior link except in minor ways, by adding controls and by looking at intermediate steps in the process.

A very different approach has been suggested by Fazio and colleagues (Fazio & Zanna, 1978a; Fazio, Chen, McDonal, & Sherman, 1982) and by Sherman and colleagues (Sherman, Presson, Chassin, Bensenberg, Corty, & Olshavsky, 1982) who place attitudes within a cognitive framework. This approach might be called a *mediation perspective*; it focuses on the complex links among the roles of cognition, experience, and perception, among other things.

Cognition. Fazio and his coworkers (Fazio & Zanna, 1978a, 1978b; Fazio et al., 1982; Fazio, 1986) conceive attitudes as performing a functional role of organizing objects in the environment. For attitudes to play a role in the behavioral selection process, they must first be accessed from memory. Because social perception is assumed to be influenced only by accessed attitudes, the determination of how and when particular attitudes are brought into play is an important first step in understanding how and when attitudes will guide behavior. For example, experiments by Fazio and colleagues (Fazio et al., 1982; Fazio, Powell, & Herr, 1983) show that attitudes based on personal experience are more accessible, and that attitudes that have been primed recently are more accessible. More recent work (Fazio, Sanbonmatsu, Powell, & Kardes, 1986) has shown that attitudes are often automatically activated by the presence of the stimulus object, and that control or decision processes are not necessarily involved in the activation of attitudes.

Experience. As Fazio and Zanna (1978a, 1978b) and Sherman et al. (1982), among others, have pointed out, attitudes based on direct experience with the attitude object are typically more predictive of behaviors than attitudes not so based. Further, in a study of adolescent smoking intentions, Sherman et al. (1982) found that direct smoking experience increased the predictability not only of behavior, which Ajzen and Fishbein explain by the greater stability of attitudes based on experience over time, but also of intentions. This strengthened link cannot easily be explained by the Fishbein–Ajzen model, but is handled within a cognitive framework by the concept of accessibility of attitude.

Perception. Self-monitoring is a personality factor that has been explored in studying the complex relationship between attitudes and behavior (Snyder & Kendzierski, 1982). Individuals who are high self-monitors tend to be sensitive to, and thus influenced by, situational cues. Low self-monitors, however, tend to rely on their inner states and dispositions when making behavioral decisions. In the case of attitude–behavior correspondence, low self-monitors have shown higher correspondence between attitudes and later behavior than high self-monitors. Also, low self-monitors express attitudes that are more predictable from prior behavior than are attitudes expressed by high self-monitors. Snyder and Kendzierski (1982) have argued that low self-monitoring leads to greater behavioral consistency and a preference for social situations that will permit and/or encourage the expression of stable attitudes.

In summary, the concept of attitudes as an important determinant of behavior has undergone numerous changes over the years, culminating in the cognition based "mediation perspective." Recent work by Fazio and others demonstrates that attitudes, when activated, do play a role in behavioral selection. There are significant lessons from this cognitive perspective: (1) It is important to distinguish between attitudes and non-attitudes. Traditional attitude scales cannot always distinguish between deep-seated attitudes and attitudes that are constructed by the person during the measurement process. (2) It is important to demonstrate the conditions under which attitudes are activated. Behavioral choice is not solely a function of attitudes.

Attitudes, behavior, and the self

Advances can be made in both attitude theory and identity theory by bringing together attitudes and identities as determinants of behavior. The importance of identity in attitude research has been recognized from time to time. For example, Tittle and Hill (1967) compared the effectiveness (in terms of behavioral prediction) of three attitude scale construction techniques drawing items from a common pool. The Thurstone scale was the poorest, Guttman scaling was a little better, but the Likert scale proved to be the best predictor of behavior. The proportion of items with direct reference to the self was directly related to the predictiveness of the scales. This relationship was later replicated by Schulman and Tittle (1968). This suggests that behavioral predictions from attitude are enhanced when the attitudes take account of the self.

Festinger's (1957) theory of cognitive dissonance, which deals with attitude change, is well known for the "hidden" assumptions that are made about the self. The theory states that dissonance (psychological discomfort) occurs when cognitions (including attitudes) are inconsistent (one implying the negation of the other), and that as a result people will change their cognitions (attitudes) in order to reduce the dissonance. However, as Roger Brown (1965) points out, the logical contradictions among the cognitive components can only be generated when certain unexpressed premises are brought to the fore. These unexpressed premises include the following: (1) I say what I believe; (2) I do what I want to do; (3) If I willingly endure something unpleasant, it always turns out to have been worth it; (4) What I choose is better than anything I reject; and so on. Note that in each case it is a statement about the self that is implicit but necessary to the theory.

Attitude researchers in general have made assumptions about the self in constructing theories about the congruence of attitudes and behavior. For example, consider the prediction that we will behave positively toward a positively evaluated object. In fact, there are not just two elements here, one's attitude toward the object and one's behavior toward the object, that are congruent. There is a third element, one's attitude toward oneself. Explicitly bringing in the self as a component of the model, as in the Heider (1946) A-B-X model, reveals the hidden assumptions. Balance is achieved only when the model shows that one positively evaluates one's self. If I consider myself bad, I may behave negatively toward a good object, or I may behave positively toward a bad object. Neither of these cases can be handled by attitude theories without referring explicitly to the self.

Heise's (1979) affect control theory (ACT) is probably the most explicit attempt to bring the self into attitude–behavior relationship. This theory incorporates attitudes toward objects, attitudes toward the self, and attitudes toward behaviors in a complex but mathematically explicit fashion that is beyond the scope of this chapter to review (cf. Smith-Lovin & Heise, 1988). By bringing together all three sorts of attitudes, ACT can make correct predictions about the case of a bad person behaving badly toward a good object.

Nevertheless, there are problems with the way in which ACT brings together attitudes, self, and behavior. ACT uses the term "impressions" rather than "attitudes" in its formulations. Impressions, though like attitudes for the most part, seem in practice to be parts of the general culture rather than individual characteristics. Additionally, the theory does not generally talk about the self, but rather about an actor in a role, though that actor may be the self, and the actor-in-role may be taken to be an identity. There still remains the question of whether the dynamics of self-impressions differ from the dynamics of impressions of others.

All of these examples make the important point that in order to adequately predict behavior toward objects on the basis of attitudes, it is important to take account of the self. Attitude scale items that reference the self are better predictors; dissonance theory of attitude change implicitly takes account of the self; affect control theory works by taking account of the self and correctly predicts the negative action toward a bad object by a positively valued self.

Extensions: Where do we go from here?

Dimensions of the self

A number of years ago Rosenberg (1979) pointed out that there is more to the self-concept than self-esteem. This message was given at a point when almost all self-concept research focused on self-esteem; indeed, the notion of self-concept was often taken to be interchangeable with the term self-esteem.

Since that time, one important question raised by identity theory is what semantic dimensions in addition to self-esteem are needed to measure the essence of given identities. In the past I have suggested that we need to know the dimensions of meaning that separate and distinguish given role-identities from other role-identities in the same role-set (Burke, 1980). Thus, Reitzes and I (1980) distinguish among college student, high-school student, graduate student, college graduate, and a person who did not go to college in order to understand the meaning of being a college student. This set of other identities was selected with an idea that college student was one point in a temporal sequence of identities.

Other possibilities exist, however. College student may also be defined relative to professor, dean, registrar, bursar, and so on. Different dimensions may be relevant to distinguish college student from other roles with which the college student may interact. Other comparisons and dimensions are relevant if we think in terms of all the role-identities any given person may have. I am not only a professor, but also a father, a brother, a son, a friend, a science fiction buff, and so on. What dimensions of meaning distinguish these different identities, and how are they related? A general survey of people's identites (e.g., Burke & Franzoi, 1988) must answer this question.

I have argued (Burke & Tully, 1977) that the relevant comparisons are in the role-set in question. However, in doing a more general survey of all identities, it is obvious that (a) we did not know what identities people were going to have, and thus we could not anticipate all the comparisons that might be relevant, and (b) there would be no way to include in any single questionaire all the possible scales that would measure relevant dimensions.

The solution that Franzoi and I (1988) used was to incorporate the most general dimensions as discovered by Osgood and his colleagues (1957): evaluation, potency, and activity (EPA). This is, indeed, the strategy that Heise and his colleagues use in research on affect control theory. This strategy minimizes the measurement problem, and allows us to incorporate and compare many different identities. But I still have some misgivings about this solution. First, the EPA dimensions have never accounted for much more than 50% of the meaning of any object or concept, and although it is rather astounding to think that only three dimensions can do so well, it still leaves 50% of the relevant meanings not accounted for, so our empirical predictions will never be very strong.

I think the use of the EPA dimensions is an adequate solution for the general case, but it is clearly a compromise of convenience. We ultimately need to tap into the dimensions that people use to distinguish their identities from others and to assess their performance. Following this rule does not prohibit the use of the EPA dimensions, because there are certainly times, places, and identities for which one or more of these dimensions are the dimensions used by people. I am simply saying that it is important to capture the ethnomethodology of identities,[2] and this is a technical problem.

The first part of the solution is to find what dimensions are relevant and used by people who have particular identities to assess those identities and to assess their behavior in those identities. The total number of dimensions may be 10 or 30 or 50. Second, scales that measure each of the dimensions identified need to be constructed. Each dimension may take five or a dozen items to be measured with any reliability. Some items may be relevant for more than one scale or dimension, which would reduce the overall number of items needed; however, across all the scales it may be that 100, 200, or even 300 items are needed.

It is clear that computers are the only way to make such measurements possible. All of the items can be stored, all of the identities can be stored, and all of the rules that tell what items and dimensions go with each of the identities can be stored. In this way, if a respondent selects a particular identity, the proper scales to measure the particular meaning of that person's identity can be "constructed" on the spot and used to assess the identity relative to those identities that are part of the same role-set.

Dimensions of attitudes

If the self-concept is thought of as a "self-attitude" (cf. Rosenberg, 1979: 20), then extending the self-concept beyond the evaluative dimension suggests we do the same for the concept of attitude more generally. Do attitudes have more dimensions than evaluation? If so, what are they? Osgood et al. (1957: 198) equated the evaluation dimension of the mediation response (meaning) with attitude, but went on to say that "attitude is one – but only one – of the dimensions of meaning, and hence provides only part of the information necessary for prediction."

Following the work of Osgood and his associates (1975) that shows that evaluation, potency, and activity are widespread, if not universal, dimensions of meaning, I suggest that we consider the dimensions of potency and activity as candidates for additional dimensions of an expanded conception of attitudes. This would effectively equate *attitudes* toward objects with *meanings* of the objects and provide the capability to integrate self, attitudes, behavior, and situation in one theory that focuses on the meanings of each of these: meanings of the self (identities), meanings of the objects of action (attitudes), meanings of behavior, and meanings of the situation. Additionally, this extension of the concept of attitude may strengthen the relationship between attitudes and behavior.

I do not think that evaluation, potency, and activity are the only possible dimensions for attitudes. As studies of identities (self-attitudes) have shown, the dimensions of meaning are often contextual. Studies of specific behaviors may require specific semantic dimensions. Studies of general behaviors or multiple behaviors may be handled by semantic dimensions that are very general, like EPA.

Adding situations

We need to incorporate the situation more explicitly into our research. Whereas symbolic interactionists have long held that the self is situated, very little work has been done to incorporate the situation into theoretical models. My work with Franzoi (1988) shows that the meanings of identities do change with the situations in which people find themselves.

A particular identity does not have just one particular meaning, but apparently has a range of potential meanings; within that range, the manifest meaning seems to depend upon the situation.

Affect control theory has begun to take the situation or setting into account by showing how impressions are modified by settings. Additionally, and more importantly, Smith-Lovin (1988, this volume) has suggested that meanings of settings themselves are involved in a control system and are homeostatically maintained by individuals selecting behaviors that return transient deviations of situation meaning back toward the fundamental meanings. Most likely, the meanings of the situation, like the meanings of behavior, sustain and reinforce self-meanings (identities), and to the extent that self-meanings are not being sustained by the setting, behavior is selected to change the meaning of the situation. Thus the homeostatic process of which Smith-Lovin speaks assumes that the "fundamental" meaning of the setting is already congruent with the self-meanings. To the extent that this is not the case, then meanings of the situation may change in their fundamentals, as when we decorate our office or our home to be "us," or when we alter lighting and music to reflect our current mood or identity.

Again, it should be recognized that in some cases it may be the meaning of the identity that is changed and not the meaning of the situation. For this to happen, from the point of view of the model employed here, higher order identity processes must come into play. If we are in a situation whose meaning cannot be changed or cannot be changed easily, the outputs of higher-order identity processes (which are lower-order identities) may be changed to maintain congruency at both levels. Such might happen in a forced compliance situation where one's identity may change to agree with the meaning of the forced behavior.

Putting the dimensions together – self, attitude, situation, behavior

We need a principle of semantic congruency that incorporates the four components of identity, attitude, behavior, and situation. For example, much of my work deals with people choosing behaviors, the meanings of which are semantically congruent with their identities. If that behavior is directed toward an attitude object, then the meaning of that object becomes important. Assuming that meanings have direction, then we can think of good, strong, and active, for example, as positive and bad, weak, and passive as negative. Behaviors toward attitude objects thus may be chosen so that the product of the signs of the meanings for self, attitude, and behavior are positive on each dimension. Thus a good identity chooses a good behavior toward a good object, and a weak identity chooses a weak behavior toward a strong object.

When the meaning of the situation is taken into account, additional rules may be needed. My work with Franzoi (1988) has shown that people choose situations and identities such that the meanings of each tend to be similar. This is not to say that the meanings of identities and situations become fully congruent, only that people tend, for example, to view themselves more actively in active situations, more positively in positively evaluated situations, and so on. Whether this is the result of people selecting situations to "fit" their identities, or changing their identities to fit the situation, or, more likely, some combination of both, is not clear.

In any case, behavior choices may vary somewhat from the "three-product positive" rule discussed, depending upon the meaning of the situation. The meaning of the situation may augment or diminish the meaning of the behavior chosen along congruent dimensions. For example, a good person in a good situation acting toward a bad object may act less good than he or she would toward the same object in a bad situation.

Lessons from cognitive approaches to attitude research

Nonself

Cognitive approaches to attitudes that have focused on the retrieval of established attitudes have pointed out the need to be sure that measured attitudes are, in fact, established. We need to address the problem of identity/nonidentity in much the same way that the problem of attitude/nonattitude has been addressed (cf. Fazio et al., 1986). Thus far, the Burke–Tully (1977) procedure for measuring attitudes has proven quite successful. Yet, there has always been the question of the degree to which people "make up" responses to the adjectives provided and the degree to which they, in fact, already have established responses. Nonidentities, of course, do not guide the selection of behavior. Without some indication that we are indeed measuring identities when we say we are, we are unlikely to find many effects of measured identities on behaviors. It is only to the extent that people have identities that they can choose behaviors that are congruent with those identities.

The Burke and Tully (1977) procedure for measuring identities selects items that are relevant in discriminating one identity from another. This procedure is helpful in removing irrelevant items so that the shared established meanings of the identities can come through. The measurement of identity salience is another helpful tool in this quest. Identities that are high in the salience hierarchy are more likely to be identities as opposed to nonidentities. However, position in the hierarchy is not the same as existence, a more fundamental issue. It is possible (though perhaps unlikely) to have a salient identity but not to have established meanings. For example, one's ethnicity may be salient, but what it means to be black or Irish or Jewish is not necessarily clear.

The notion of an established response as an indication of the presence of an identity might be assessed by measuring the latency of a response to particular self-descriptors. The degree to which there is an established response would thus be indicated by the shortness of the latency, with more established responses yielding shorter latencies. This method has worked well to separate nonattitudes from attitudes (Fazio et al., 1986) and self-schemas from the absence of a schema (Markus, 1977).

Activation of identities

We need to address the issue of the activation of identities. It is clear that people's identities are not all active at the same time, but that they take on different identities in different situations or in different roles. This has been referred to as a *working copy of the self* (Burke, 1980) or as a *working self-concept* (Markus & Kunda, 1986; Nurius, this volume). We need to identify what cues (perceptions) activate given identities or deactivate those identities. To what extent are the cues characteristics of the setting? To what extent are the cues characteristics of the other people in the setting (classified by their identities)? To what extent do the cues reside in the meanings of other's behavior in the settings? What other possibilities are there? Are there master identities, as suggested by control theory, that serve to regulate, change, activate, and deactivate other identities that are lower in the control hierarchy? How can such be discovered and identified?

Conclusion

This chapter has reviewed two independent traditions for understanding and predicting behavioral choices: the study of identities and the study of attitudes. Because identities have been referred to in past literature as self-attitudes, I have suggested that bringing together these two traditions would be helpful to each. Identity theory can benefit from the cognitive, mediational approach of attitude theory to help understand how identities are formed in experience and activated in situations. Theories of attitudes can benefit from the inclusion of dimensions other than evaluation to predict behavior. Together, the two approaches will need to develop a principle of congruency that takes into account identity, attitude, situation, and behavior to understand the dynamic mixing and balancing of meaning among all these components along relevant dimensions of meaning. In this way behavioral selection can be better understood to be a complex result of identity, attitudes, and situation.

Notes

1 In some cases the counteridentity is not clear and may simply be persons who are *not* in a particular social position (group, role). Persons who have a given identity have certain characteristics in common *that set them apart from others*. It is this setting apart that is important for the development of an identity.
2 That is to say, we must understand the methods by which people develop, use, and change their identities in social situations.

References

Ajzen, Icek, & Martin Fishbein. 1977. Attitude–behavior relations: A theoretical analysis and review of empirical research. *Psychological Bulletin* 84: 888–918.

Bagozzi, Richard P. 1981. Attitudes, intentions, and behavior: A test of some key hypotheses. *Journal of Personality and Social Psychology* 41: 602–627.

Bem, Daryl J. 1967. Self-perception: An alternative interpretation of cognitive dissonance phenomena. *Psychological Review* 74: 183–200.

Bem, Daryl J. 1972. Self-perception theory. *Advances in Experimental Social Psychology* 6: 1–62.

Brown, Roger. 1965. *Social psychology*. New York: Basic Books.

Burke, Peter J. 1980. The self: Measurement implications from a symbolic interactionist perspective. *Social Psychology Quarterly* 43: 18–29.

Burke, Peter J. 1989. Gender identity, sex and school performance. *Social Psychology Quarterly* 52: 159–169.

Burke, Peter J., & Stephen L. Franzoi. 1988. Studying situations and identities using experiential sampling methodology. *American Sociological Review* 53: 559–568.

Burke, Peter J., & Donald C. Reitzes. 1981. The link between identity and role performance. *Social Psychology Quarterly* 44: 83–92.

Burke, Peter J., & Judy Tully. 1977. The measurement of role/identity. *Social Forces* 55: 880–897.

Campbell, Donald T. 1950. The indirect assessment of social attitudes. *Psychological Bulletin* 47: 15–38.

Cooper, Joel, & Robert T. Croyle. 1984. Attitudes and attitude change. *Annual Review of Psychology* 35: 395–426.

DeFleur, Melvin L., & Frank A. Westie. 1963. Attitude as a scientific concept. *Social Forces* 42: 17–31.

Fazio, Russell H. 1986. How do attitudes guide behavior? In R. M. Sorrentino & E. T. Higgins (Eds.), *The handbook of motivation and cognition: Foundations of social behavior* (pp. 204–243). New York: Guilford Press.

Fazio, Russell H., J. Chen, E. C. McDonal, & S. J. Sherman. 1982. Attitude accessibility, attitude–behavior consistency, and the strength of the object-evaluation association. *Journal of Experimental Social Psychology* 18: 339–357.

Fazio, Russell H., Martha C. Powell, & P. M. Herr. 1983. Toward a process model of the attitude–behavior relation: Accessing one's attitude upon mere observation of the attitude object. *Journal of Personality and Social Psychology* 44: 724–735.

Fazio, Russell H., David M. Sanbonmatsu, Martha C. Powell, & Frank R. Kardes. 1986. On the automatic activation of attitudes. *Journal of Personality and Social Psychology* 50: 229–238.

Fazio, Russell H., & Mark P. Zanna. 1978a. Attitudinal qualities relating to the strength of the attitude–behavior relationship. *Journal of Experimental Social Psychology* 14: 398–408.

Fazio, Russell H., & Mark P. Zanna. 1978b. On the predictive validity of attitudes: The roles of direct experience and confidence. *Journal of Personality* 46: 228–243.

Festinger, Leon. 1957. *A theory of cognitive dissonance*. Stanford: Stanford University Press.

Fishbein, Martin, & Icek Ajzen. 1975. *Belief, attitude, intention and behavior: An introduction to theory and research*. Reading, MA: Addison-Wesley.

Fuson, W. M. 1942. Attitudes: A note on the concept and its research context. *American Sociological Review* 7: 856–857.

Heider, Fritz. 1946. Attitudes and cognitive organization. *Journal of Psychology* 21: 107–112.

Heise, David R. 1977. Social action as the control of affect. *Behavioral Science* 22: 163–177.

Heise, David R. 1979. *Understanding events: Affect and the construction of social action*. Cambridge, UK: Cambridge University Press.

Krech, D., & Crutchfield, R. S. 1948. *Theory and problems of social psychology*. New York: McGraw Hill.

Lindesmith, Alfred R., & Anselm L. Strauss. 1956. *Social psychology*. New York: Holt, Rinehart and Winston.

Markus, Hazel. 1977. Self-schemata and processing of information about the self. *Journal of Personality and Social Psychology* 35: 63–78.

Markus, Hazel, & Z. Kunda. 1986. Stability and malleability of the self-concept. *Journal of Personality and Social Psychology* 51: 858–866.

McCall, George J., & J. L. Simmons. 1978. *Identities and interactions* (rev. ed.). New York: Free Press.

Mead, George Herbert. 1934. *Mind, self, and society*. Chicago: University of Chicago Press.

Osgood, Charles E., William H. May, & M. S. Miron. 1975. *Cross-cultural universals of affective meaning*. Urbana: University of Illinois Press.

Osgood, Charles E., George J. Succi, & Percy H. Tannenbaum. 1957. *The measurement of meaning*. Urbana: University of Illinois Press.

Powers, William T. 1975. *Behavior: The control of perception*. Chicago: Aldine.

Reitzes, Donald C., & Peter J. Burke. 1980. College student identity: Measurement and implications. *Pacific Sociological Review* 23: 46–66.

Rose, Arnold M. 1962. A systematic summary of symbolic interaction theory. In Arnold M. Rose (Ed.), *Human behavior and social processes* (pp. 3–19). Boston: Houghton Mifflin.

Rosenberg, Morris. 1979. *Conceiving the self*. New York: Basic Books.

Schulman, Gary I., & Charles R. Tittle. 1968. Assimilation-contrast effects and items selection in Thurstone scaling. *Social Forces* 46: 484–491.

Sherman, Steven J., C. C. Presson, L. Chassin, M. Bensenberg, E. Corty, & W. R. Olshavsky. 1982. Smoking intentions in adolescents: Direct experience and predictability. *Personality and Social Psychology Bulletin* 8: 376–383.

Smith-Lovin, Lynn. 1988. The affective control of events within settings. In Lynn Smith-Lovin & David R. Heise (Eds.), *Analyzing social interaction: Advances in affect control theory*. New York: Gordon and Breach Science Publishers.

Smith-Lovin, Lynn, & David R. Heise. 1988. *Analyzing social interaction: Advances in affect control theory*. New York: Gordon and Breach Science Publishers.

Snyder, Mark L., & D. Kendzierski. 1982. Acting on one's attitudes: Procedures for linking attitude and behavior. *Journal of Experimental Social Psychology* 18: 165–183.

Stone, Gregory P. 1962. Appearance and the self. In Arnold Rose (Ed.), *Human behavior and social processes* (pp. 86–118). Boston: Houghton Mifflin.

Stryker, Sheldon. 1980. *Symbolic interactionism: A social structural version*. Menlo Park, CA: Benjamin-Cummings.

Tittle, Charles R., & Richard J. Hill. 1967. Attitude measurement and prediction of behavior: An evaluation of conditions and measurement techniques. *Sociometry* 30: 199–213.

Zanna, Mark, & Joel Cooper. 1976. Dissonance and the attribution process. In J. H. Harvey, W. J. Ickes, & R. F. Kidd (Eds.), *New directions in attribution research* (pp. 199–217). Hillsdale, NJ: Erlbaum.

10   From changing selves toward changing society

Judith A. Howard

Virtually all discussions of the relationship between self and society contain some acknowledgment of, and often apology for, the fact that social psychologists have more often considered the impact of social systems on individuals than the impact of individuals on social systems. Integration of knowledge of macrosocial structures and processes, microsocial interaction, and individual psychology is necessary to understand this relationship (House, 1981). In this chapter I sketch the outline of one of the many possible such integrations.

Although in exceptional circumstances, one particular individual can affect social systems, more often than not people affect social systems through their individual decisions to engage collectively in social actions. Hence I focus on an account of individuals' decisions to participate in actions such as social movements. I argue that phenomena such as social movements can be understood fully only by directing explicit attention to the experienced selves of individual actors. Shott (1979), among others, maintains that self-control is an essential component of social control; consistent with her reasoning, I suggest that self-change is an essential component of sustained social change. As Turner (1983) states, "Movements seldom achieve substantial and lasting successes without strong components of personal transformation." Thus I attempt to identify those forces that impel the self to the redefinitions required to overcome the tendency toward self-definitional and hence social stability. I begin by reviewing sociological social psychological theories of the self and the relationship between self and society, emphasizing how these theories account (or fail to account) for changing selves. I then draw more briefly from the literature on social movements, referring primarily to models that incorporate individual agency. I conclude by proposing a model of the relationship between self-change and social change.

Sociological theories of self, identity, and self-change

Definitions

Sociological theories of the self derive almost entirely from a symbolic interactionist orientation (Gecas, 1989).[1] From this perspective, the self is defined primarily by the capacity for reflexive activity, that is, the human ability to make oneself the object of one's own consciousness. Self refers to both the process of reflexive activity and the specific products of this experience. Symbolic interactionism generally has emphasized the immediate situations and encounters in which social interaction occurs. Structural symbolic interaction incorporates the broader structural conditions that shape immediate contexts. At least three distinct symbolic interactionist versions of self reflect this structuralism by conceiving of self as defined by the relationship between person and social roles.[2]

McCall (McCall & Simmons, 1978) and Stryker (1980) both emphasize the importance of internal hierarchical organization of the self. McCall conceives of the elements of this organization as role-identities, the characters that an individual constructs for him or herself as an occupant of particular social positions. Role-identities are organized according to their relative prominence for the self. This prominence hierarchy of role-identities in turn merges with immediate contextual circumstances to create a relatively flexible situational self. The components of Stryker's identity theory (1980 and see chapter 1, this volume) are very similar. Stryker (1981) reasons that if self and society are reciprocal and society is highly differentiated, so too must be the self. Identities, internalized positional designations, thus reflect social differentiation; identities are the consequence of being placed as a social object and appropriating the terms of placement for oneself. Identities are organized into a hierarchy of salience, a hierarchy defined as the probability of various identities being invoked in a given situation. This salience hierarchy is the product of prior interactions in structured role relationships, and in turn affects future role performance. Identity theory goes further in proposing a useful account of the social construction of the salience hierarchy. Commitment, the degree to which important social relationships are premised on particular identities, determines in part the location of those identities within the salience hierarchy. Identity theory also suggests that the salience hierarchy of identities shapes the probabilities of particular behavioral choices (Stryker & Serpe, 1982; Callero, 1985). It is in this way that social structures, reflected in relationships, shape the probabilities of behavior.

Turner (1987) raises some fundamental challenges to these relatively

traditional conceptions of the self. He suggests that people do not necessarily have well-formulated and communicable self-conceptions. What is
important is that we appear to orient ourselves as if we had discoverable
and characterizable selves. Furthermore, Turner suggests that there may
be substantial variation in the affective valence of particular identities,
proposing that identities may be much more neutral than they have been
conceived to date, indicating simply potential milieus for action. Whereas
some identities will be more valued and thus some milieus ones in which we
will try to claim or assert a valued identity, others are neutral or, at best,
simply comfortable and accepted.

Turner adopts a self-discovery perspective that presumes that we hold
diverse and conflicting conceptions of self, and that these conceptions can
shape behavior without our conscious awareness. Turner and Gordon
(1981) suggest that we have both articulated and unarticulated identities,
contradicting assumptions prevalent in common measures of identity such
as the Twenty Statements Test. Unarticulated selves can be a vital part of
the customary self, and thus influential to behavior, without being salient.
This is not an incidental observation. If important self-conceptions can
be unarticulated, measures of the hierarchy of salience or prominence of
identities are necessarily limited in the degree to which they explain how
identity affects behavior. In response to this barrier to identity measurement, Turner suggests that we turn to behavioral indicators, considering
the carryover of behavior from one role to another. He adopts his own
suggestion in pointing to measures of self and role. Turner (1978) conceptualizes the relationship between self and role in terms of the degree to
which person and role are merged. According to Turner, all people play
many roles, but not with equal involvement. Role-person merger exists
when attitudes and behaviors associated with one role are brought into
other situations. Recognizing that the relationship between self and role
may not be articulated, he suggests that one indicator of role-person
merger is that the person continues to play a role in situations in which the
role does not apply.

These theorists use the term *identity* to refer to a cognitive representation of location in the social world. *Self* is a somewhat more troublesome
term. Symbolic interactionists view self as constituting reflexive activity
and the products of this activity, which are identities. What is missing is the
phenomenal, experienced sense of self. I use the term *self* to refer to an
underlying sense of the continuity and essence of one's own person, and
identity to refer to the cognitive awareness of specific, situated social
locations. Hewitt (1988: 113) expresses well my conception of the relationship between self and identity (although he uses the term *personal*

identity rather than self): "[Self] is a sense of self built up over time as the person participates in social life. . . . [It] underlies and makes possible the variety of situated identities the person assumes. . ., permits the person to become temporarily absorbed in a situated identity."

Stability and change in self and identity

The conceptual distinction between self and identity rests in part on the degree of stability or instability attributed to these concepts.[3] The relative stability of the self has been debated vigorously. Recent theorists (Zurcher, 1977; Tedeschi & Lindskold, 1976) have challenged a long-standing belief that self-conception is stable and enduring (Block, 1971; Costa & McCrae, 1980). Swann (1983) suggests that this debate is misguided, arguing that change-oriented research demonstrates transitory changes in self-image, akin to Burke's (1980) notion of self-images as working copies of identity, as opposed to changes in generalized self-conceptions. Rosenberg (1981) makes a similar assertion, contrasting Stryker's view of the self as a stable set of meanings attached to self as object with the situated self-concept, a view in which the self is a shifting adjustive process of self-presentation (Blumer, 1969).

These distinctions do not address two broader questions: (1) Does a generalized self-conception even exist? (2) Does change occur in generalized self-conceptions? Poststructuralist theorists argue forcefully that the very notion of a general sense of self is culturally and historically specific (Smith, 1977). For my purposes, it does not matter whether these theorists are correct in asserting that self is a delusion. Whether or not a self exists, individuals' beliefs in and about themselves affect their social behavior. As Turner (1987) asserts, what is important is that we act as if we have a sense of self.

I turn then to the former question, To what extent do these general conceptions of self change? Although no theorist would argue that self-conceptions are entirely fixed and immutable, answers to this question range from the widely accepted view of self as relatively durable to recent positions that the self is defined by change. Sampson (1985), for example, argues for a decentralized view of personhood as "continuous becoming." In perhaps the fullest elaboration of a similar idea, Zurcher (1977) proposes the mutable self, characterized by flexibility and diversity (a conception that does not receive strong empirical support in Wood & Zurcher, 1988). The answer to this question is critical for the larger question motivating this chapter, that is, under what circumstances self and identity motivate social action. The nature of those changes that occur in self or identities is highly likely to be associated with the type of social action in which an individual may become involved; sustained social action is more likely to follow from significant, enduring change in one's sense of self, whereas short-term, less committed action may result from the variability associated with situated identities.

Social mechanisms of self-change. To identify adequately the degree of potential change in a generalized sense of self, it is necessary to specify mechanisms that motivate or inhibit change. Evidence of psychological forces that enhance the stability of and inhibit change in the self is overwhelming. Swann (1983, 1987), for example, has demonstrated the ubiquity of the motivation for self-verification, the desire to verify pre-existing self-conceptions (and see Hoelter, 1985). Individuals create self-confirmatory opportunity structures through selective interaction and selective comparison processes (Tesser & Campbell, 1983), selecting self-confirmatory feedback (Swann, 1983), and selective interpretation. These processes work in tandem with a positivity bias (Greenwald, 1980; Baumeister, 1982); most people have positive self-conceptions and wish to verify these self-conceptions. (When these two motivations conflict, the desire for self-verification is apparently likely to prevail.) Della Fave's (1986a) account for the persistence of social inequities ultimately rests on this same motivation. Della Fave maintains that disadvantaged individuals develop an "investment in subordination" because their self-esteem rests on their ability to perform subordinate roles well. That is, they develop a commitment to role-identities located in subordinate positions in social systems. Despite these forces, individuals' selves and identities do change. From the perspective of these theories of self-stability, change is usually viewed as a failure of maintenance. Hormuth (1984) asserts that self-change should not be viewed simply as the reversal of maintenance processes; instead, it is important to explain self-initiated self-change. Extant theories of self and identity do provide explanations of this process.

From the perspective of identity theory, changes in the structure of the self are assumed to be related directly to the person's movements within the social structure, movements due either to choice or to circumstances. The degree of choice available among behavioral alternatives reflects the constraints that operate on any given set of identities. The more open the social structure, the greater the range of behavioral choices, and the greater the opportunity for role making (Turner, 1962), and hence shifts in identities. In an empirical analysis of change in identity across five be-havioral domains, Serpe (1987) reports that the influence of commitment on identity salience varies substantially according to the degree of choice associated with role performance in these areas. Serpe concludes that social structural constraints affect the processes by which identity is built, through defining the amount of choice associated with role performance. Although this study demonstrates the importance of social structure in constraining change in the self, it does not indicate the mechanisms through which the self changes, that is, why individuals initiate change, given that the opportunity to do so is available. Moreover, Serpe focuses on just one of several possible types of change.

Callero (1986) identifies four different types of change relevant to identity theory: ipsative, level, structural, and normative change. Ipsative change, the topic of Serpe's study, focuses on the intraindividual ranking of a number of role-identities; level change focuses on the magnitude of role-identity salience over time. Structural change refers to the stability of the dimensional structure of identity salience. Normative change refers to the interindividual ordering of actors in a particular group with respect to the salience of a particular role-identity. Each of these types of change is potentially relevant to the initiation of social action. Furthermore, a particular sequence of change seems likely. Ipsative change is likely to be the first indicator of change, and over time this is probably associated with level change as well. With sustained long-term role performance in accord with these changes, structural change may also occur, but structural change may depend also on the implications of ipsative and level change for other role-identities of the individual.

Callero draws on developmental analyses by Mortimer, Finch, and Kumka (1982), who consider whether there are systematic differences between those whose self-concepts remain stable and those whose self-concepts change over time. They observe that stability of personality is a function of constancy of environmental circumstances surrounding the individual. Some attitudes and values become more stable with age, they assert, because the social environment tends to become more stable after early adulthood. Nonnormative events lead to a redirection of the course of self-concept development. Echoing Serpe, they are careful to note that people are not passive in the face of change, selecting and molding situations where they have the choice to do so.

Mortimer's analysis parallels closely Wells and Stryker's (1988) recent exploration of stability and change in self over the life span. The life course involves movements in and out of social roles; these in turn lead to changes in the networks of social relationships and interactions, and hence commitments to particular identities. Those identities associated with statuses that cut across varied situations remain relatively stable, but they will change when these statuses shift in the context of the life course. Marital partner, for example, is a role that is vulnerable to change as individuals approach old age and potential widowhood. There may also be historical changes in the relative stability of these statuses. The marital partner role appears to be increasingly more vulnerable to change in the middle years of adulthood through divorce. Viewing self in terms of the life course foregrounds the dynamic character of self and identity without reducing this dynamism to momentary transient shifts. This perspective extends the model of self as an active constructive process by recognizing that self is time bound.

Identity theory locates the sources of self- and identity change primarily in social structural constraints that affect the process by which identity is built. Other sociological approaches to self-change draw more explicitly on the influence of social and historical conditions. Both Zurcher (1977; Wood & Zurcher, 1988) and Turner (1976) maintain that contemporary structural instability has produced societywide changes in the content of selves and identities. Zurcher (Wood & Zurcher, 1988) suggests that instability in the self is due to various forms of societal change, including: (1) the successful rationalization and secularization of industrial society, (2) the decline of the sense of historical continuity associated with secularization and modernization, (3) the overripe development of rationalistic Western culture, (4) accelerated social change, (5) the increasing importance of consumption as opposed to production values and orientations, (6) symbolic overload due to a rapid increase of cultural imagery. Zurcher (1977) traces the impact of these changes in his theory of the mutable self. He observes that students of the 1970s tended to favor "C" mode statements on the Twenty Statements Test (TST), statements describing personal traits and qualities or modes of expression and feeling, as opposed to the "B" mode responses favored by students of the 1950s, responses identifying self specifically with institutionalized statuses or roles. Zurcher argues that a self dependent on identification with social structures is not functional or adaptive when a society's institutional scaffolding is unstable or lacks legitimacy. A self that is less dependent upon identification with social structure is functional when that structure is undergoing rapid change.[4] According to Zurcher, if a given individual has experienced the four components of self identified in responses to the TST (physical, social, reflective, and oceanic) and conditions of social instability persist, a self-concept fully consistent with change will emerge. This mutable or postmodern self is able to move among these four components with ease. The sense of self thus is characterized by flexibility, tolerance, openness, and diversity. Although these characteristics may be functionally desirable for individuals, they may inhibit the expression of social action. The postmodern self is flexible, but also uncommitted; tolerant, but also individualistic. In a sense, the achievement of a self capable of coping with social upheaval comes at the possible societal expense of selves committed to changing and presumably improving social conditions.

Like Zurcher, Turner (1976) also attributes societal shifts in the definition of self to recent social change. He proposes that rapid social change has lead to a societal shift from a sense of real self located in institution to a sense of real self located in impulse. Repudiation of institutional identities is the product of a growing sense of unreality that derives from the institutional person's effort to be all her or his roles, an impossibility in times of substantial social upheaval. Given that social roles are an essential component of an institutional orientation, a shift toward a self rooted in impulse implies that identities based on institutional roles will move to lower positions on the hierarchy of identity salience. To the extent that institutional roles remain influential, their influence may be negative, directing role-distancing behavior.

Turner does not provide an explicit account of the microlevel processes through which change in self occurs, but it is possible to trace such an account through his conception of identity. Given that some identities are not articulated, then part of what we experience as change may be the process of articulating particular identities. The motor of this process of articulation may be rooted in the sentiment of authenticity or inauthenticity of the self. Turner suggests that we ask not only Who am I, but also Who am I not? The experience of (in)authenticity differs for individuals rooted in institutions and those rooted in impulse. His empirical work with Gordon (1981) reveals that the sense of an authentic and true self derives from the luxury of disregarding or transcending the institutional order (suggesting a self rooted in impulse), whereas a sense of inauthenticity or a "not me" derives from failures of integration, disruptions of the underlying order (suggesting a self rooted in institutions). Inauthenticity involves discord between the customary self and the social environment, whereas experiences of a true self are likely to occur in unusual, noncustomary circumstances. Unlike authenticity, then, the experience of inauthenticity generally is located in everyday interaction with the prevailing social structure.

The experience of inauthenticity may lead to identity change. In experiencing inauthenticity, individuals may come to recognize, to articulate, aspects of themselves of which they were not fully aware. Thus the experience of inauthenticity eventually may lead to incorporation of new (or rejection of old) elements in one's customary self. This suggests in turn that sustained social activism may derive from the persistent experience of inauthenticity, rather than from a drive to experience the true self, a factor often offered as a motivator of participation in the social movements of the late sixties and early seventies. Sustained activism, or for that matter, any form of sustained behavior, must eventually require support from individuals' customary selves. Moreover, in seeking to eradicate the experience of inauthenticity, an individual must achieve a new reconciliation or adjustment between self and social structure. Self-change and social change that require this kind of accommodation with social structure, changes that follow from the experience of inauthenticity, are more likely to persist than self- and social change located in attempts to separate oneself from the social environment, changes that accompany the experience of authenticity.

All of these approaches either explicitly or implicitly suggest that social conditions are responsible for change in self and identity. The identity theory perspective on change conceives of social conditions in a more limited, situation-specific sense, whereas Turner and Zurcher's analyses refer to the pervasive structural and historical shifts that extend throughout a given society or culture. None of these explanations refer to the intra-individual factors that might also motivate self-change. A comprehensive account of self-change must incorporate both social and individual factors.

Intraindividual mechanisms of self-change. Following Foote's (1951) notion that all motivation is a consequence of an individual's set of identities, most intraindividual accounts of self- and identity change rely on some form of motivation or affective stimulation. Gecas (see chapter 8 of this volume) maintains that the self-concept is associated with at least three significant motives: self-esteem, self-efficacy, and authenticity. The motive for authenticity, the striving for meaning, coherence, and understanding, presumably underlies the very development of identities and of self. Consistent with Turner, the experience of inauthenticity may motivate change in unsatisfying identity structures, although Gecas does not detail the processes whereby this might occur.

The notion of possible selves proposed by Markus and Nurius (1986, and see chapter 11 of this volume) holds particular promise in understanding the motivational merchanisms of self-change. Possible selves are the representations of how we think about our potential – the cognitive manifestation of enduring goals, aspirations, motives, and fears. Markus and Nurius derive this construct from symbolic interaction theory, citing Mead's notion that having a self implies the ability to rehearse possible courses of action. Through engaging in such rehearsals, we construct possible selves. This conception is analogous to Burke's notion of temporary self-images constructed from stable identity, but the concept of possible selves is broader, incorporating not only active selves, but also positive and negative inactive and only imagined selves.

Possible selves give specific cognitive form to various end states and thus provide a direct link between cognition and motivation. Markus and Nurius assert that possible selves both function as incentives for the future and provide an evaluative or interpretive context for the current view of self. The dynamics of change in possible selves have not yet been addressed by Markus and Nurius: How do we acquire new possible selves, or cast away old possible selves? Other treatments of the self suggest that one stimulus for such changes is environmental or social change. In the presence of situational or environmental changes, it may be the construction of possible selves that motivates the kinds of change Turner and Zurcher have identified. This construct thus may represent a critical mechanism of both self- and social change.

According to Markus and Nurius, identities are associated with particular emotions that are activated when the self is activated. The motivational quality of possible selves may lie in this affective or emotional association. A number of scholars have recently turned attention to the ways in which emotion is bound up with the self. The most historically prominent of these approaches is the study of self-esteem, a sentiment about the self that has affective correlates such as feelings of pride or shame and pervasive motivational effects. Rosenberg (1979) has identified both interpersonal and intraindividual processes that shape the formation of self-esteem, emphasizing the importance of understanding the immediate context in which phenomena such as social comparison and reflected appraisals occur. Gecas (chapter 8 of this volume) stresses the motivational effects of self-esteem; he maintains that the need for self-esteem motivates action designed to protect or increase favorable evaluations of oneself. The general motivational thrust is toward increasing self-esteem; clearly this may involve altering one's sense of self through adding or deleting particular identities, or altering the salience hierarchy of identities.

Della Fave's (1980, 1986a, 1986b) self-evaluation theory directly connects this motivation to enhance and protect self-esteem with the legitimation of societal institutions. He argues that those in disadvantaged social positions usually create positive self-esteem through focusing on those areas of life in which they are successful and avoiding attention to the social arenas in which they are disadvantaged, leading to an investment in subordination. He also articulates how identity may underly the delegitimation of such institutions through the development of counternorms, particularly norms of equality. Della Fave maintains that the source of the influence of norms is identity. The more significant an institution is for people's identities, the more influence it will have on the norms associated with that institution. For example, in certain historical times religious institutions can sow the seeds of political dissension through the dual importance of religion for individuals' identities and the emphasis of religion on equality. Della Fave's model is an exemplar of a multilevel analysis that links identity to social change through a mediating variable such as norms. The key motor of this model is the motivational power of self-evaluation.

Other theories focus specifically on the link between identity and emotion. Affect control theory posits that affective meanings of social identities and behaviors control interpersonal perception and social action (Heise, 1987; Smith-Lovin & Heise, 1988, and see chapter 7 in this volume). Definitions of situations are the framework for social interaction, but the social dynamics are governed by an affective system of motives and emotion. Classifications of places and the people in them are associated with a domain of feelings. Events generate new feelings about people; typically these will not be the same as the fundamental sentiments associated with those individuals' identities. Therefore we use emotion attributions to deflect these transient impressions away from the fundamental sentiments. The theory thus focuses on how individuals use emotions to maintain generally stable fundamental sentiments about others. If affect control enters the process of self-change, two additional questions must be addressed. Does the process obtain when we are dealing with emotions about ourselves and our own stable identities? Reversing Heise's emphasis, under what circumstances might these transient impressions fail to be deflected away from fundamental sentiments, and therefore prompt change, either in sentiments or the identities of others or ourselves?

Although identity theory has not explicitly incorporated emotion, the distinction between interactional and affective commitment facilitates such an incorporation (Stryker, 1987a, 1987b). Affective commitment refers to the emotional costs incurred by potential departure from a given role; these costs reflect the subjective importance of others with whom one interacts in this role. Following the logic of identity theory, the greater these emotional costs, the more salient the particular identity, and the greater the influence of this identity on role performance. Affect also enters identity theory by altering the probabilities of networks or role relationships forming and being maintained. Stryker draws on affect control theory in suggesting that emotion may enter the meaning of social objects, including self and others. Disparities in the affective values attached to self, other, and behavior may motivate and direct role performance.

Stryker observes that most sociologists who have dealt with affective aspects of relationships have focused on sentiments, defined as enduring affect, to the neglect of short-term affective outbursts, or emotions. From this more traditional perspective, sentiments, but not emotions, are viewed as socially organized. Contradicting this view, Stryker (1987b) suggests that emotion is critical to the interplay and negotiation of identity claims. He argues that emotional outbursts, momentary displays of emotion, occur when role partners behave in ways that contradict identity claims, whether affirming an identity one is trying to deny or denying an identity one is trying to affirm. Thus emotion is closely linked with interpersonal identity claim negotiation.

This approach also helps to elaborate the notion of emotion as a signal to the self (Hochschild, 1983). The more intense the emotional response, the more validity is attributed to this signal, and presumably the stronger one perceives his or her commitment to the identity to be. Heise's affect control theory suggests that minor emotional experiences or shocks are likely to generate actions to restore a customary preexisting affective balance. However, more substantial outbursts might alter the preexisting affective balance. This reasoning also illuminates, and is consistent with, Turner's exploration of the interplay between customary and (in)authentic selves. The notion of fundamental sentiments about identities suggests that sentiments are part of the customary self. Emotions are analogous to situated sentiments; an intense emotional experience may jolt an individual into more articulated consciousness of sentiments about the self, in addition to consciousness of cognitions. Furthermore, in an era of increasingly impulse-based selves, in which emotions are experienced as immediate, unmediated, spontaneous, and outside conscious control, it may be primarily through the experience of emotions that we draw inferences about who we really are. (Ironically, these same characteristics have lead some social scientists to presume that emotions are beyond the realm of theory.) Even in less impulse-oriented times, these several theories would argue that some portion of self-knowledge is triggered and validated by emotion, as well as by cognition.

Emotions may serve as a crucial link in explaining how identity motivates behavior. The approaches outlined here refer generally to the significance of emotion for everyday social interaction. How emotions may underly long-term change has yet to be explored. Issues of measurement also have barely begun to be addressed. Not only do we lack reasonable measures of emotion (as opposed to sentiment), but the ideas explored in the preceding discussion also have troublesome implications for measurement. For example, consider Stryker's observation that all social objects have an affective value of some sort. Presumably this affect is relatively routinized. Routinized affect, like the customary self, may have a pervasive influence on social interaction. If affect is routinized, however, it is unlikely to be salient, and hence may not be identified by individuals on measures that require conscious awareness. Creating inventive ways to assess the traces of emotion, or for that matter, of customary selves, is thus an important challenge.[5]

Behavioral mechanisms of self-change. There is one other approach to identity change that derives from a different strand of symbolic interactionism. Behavior itself may produce identity change. As Blumstein discusses in chapter 14 of this volume, Goffman's view of identity emphasizes impression management and the conscious construction of identities in situated interaction. Blumstein maintains that situated identity work may in fact create the self, a process fully compatible with Bem's (1972) theory of self-perception. Through the enactment of particular behaviors in identity work. Gecas's (see chapter 8 in this volume) emphasis on self- may change any time we enter roles or situations that require a new form of identity work. Gecas's see chapter 8 in this volume) emphasis on self-efficacy extends Blumstein's analysis to suggest other ways in which we might enter new arenas of identity work. Self-efficacy, the motivation to perceive oneself as a causal agent in the environment, clearly may instigate new forms of behavior that may in turn shape the sense of self. Gecas suggests that self-efficacy is especially relevant to the social structural domain and thus is particularly likely to inspire social action.

Summary. The circumstances for self- and identity change are located, in part, in the role-taking and role-making processes. When nonnormative events occur, individuals are thrown out of kilter in their role relationships. When others cease to confirm what we intend to convey as our identities, we have both affective reactions and behavioral responses. When these others are people with whom we share either or both high interactional and affective commitment, we are likely to respond with intensity. In the event that we cannot successfully alter the responses of others, and the new information is confirmed through responses of a variety of others, there is at least the potential for significant and enduring individual change.

This microlevel change occurs primarily through interaction. Instigators of this process of identity disconfirmation may lie either in personal or in social conditions. Disruptions in particular social networks, for example, may occur simply through changes in friendships and the vagaries of individual relationships. Another possibility is that individual change is impelled by boredom, by a reaction against habit and routine (see chapters 2 and 12 by Callero and Piliavin, respectively, in this volume). Significant societal shifts such as the several processes outlined by Wood and Zurcher (1988) also may impel the microlevel experience of identity disconfirmation. When large-scale environmental shifts are mediated through relationship interaction, they may lead to changes in self and identity.

One individual's self- and identity change, in turn, may prompt parallel (or reactive) changes in others with whom the individual is connected. When the instigators of identity change lie mainly in the specific conditions of the lives of particular individuals, that identity change is unlikely to have effects that extend beyond the immediate social networks of the individual. Even when the instigators of change lie in social conditions, social effects may not necessarily follow. Thus in the contemporary era in which, according to Turner and Zurcher, selves are rooted in impulse and spontaneity, change may be an expected, acceptable, and even normative component of the self. In this cultural environment, the experience of changing selves may occur in the absence of structural societal changes. Precisely because change is normative, identity change is unlikely to have enduring societal effects. For example, many U.S. citizens have come to rely on individual therapy as one positive route to change. This is a strategy that has visible interpersonal effects: Witness the social circles in which it is the odd member who has not gone through therapy and, indeed, has not shared the same therapist with his friends. A population of clients, however, is unlikely to initiate social action.

When the stimuli for change lie in social conditions, however, and more institutional conceptions of the self are prevalent, individual identity change may have social effects. To take just one example, it is widely believed that the feminist movement was moribund during the decades of the 1930s through the mid-1960s. This does not mean that individuals did not experience feminist awareness based on the individual circumstances of their lives, but the social environment did not facilitate the translation of individual identity shifts into a social movement. With the massive structural changes evidenced in patterns of labor force participation, changes in personal awareness became unified and solidified into the women's movement. Sociological theories of the self have not addressed how and when identity change may motivate social action. The literature on social movements provides some understanding of the process through which individual change evolves into social change.

Social movements

Elements of identity in social movements

Not all forms of social change are likely to involve enduring self- and identity change. Social movements, defined by Turner and Killian (1972) as a collectivity acting with some continuity to promote a change or resist a change in society, are perhaps the most relevant category of social change. Turner and Killian distinguish social movements from collective action in their considerable degree of organization, emergence of rules and tradition, and stability and continuity in time. Resource mobilization theory, the most prominent contemporary perspective on social movements, similarly views social movements as extensions of institutionalized rational actions oriented toward clearly defined goals, characterized by centralized organizational control over resources (Jenkins, 1983). Turner and Killian identify three general types of social movements, expressing respectively an orientation to values, power, or participation. Identity change conceivably could be implicated in each of these types of movements, but is most relevant for value-oriented movements.

Within this literature, the topic of recruitment of participants to a social movement most directly implicates identity and identity change. Zurcher and Snow (1981) suggest that the major mechanisms of recruitment are some degree of linkage among problematic structural conditions, social psychological attributes of potential and actual participants, and the goals and ideology of movements. Some of the specific motivators they cite directly implicate identity; the pursuit of meaning, the search for identity, social isolation, and the quest for community echo Turner's notion of a search for authenticity and Gecas's emphasis on the motivational drive of authenticity. Smelser and Smelser (1981) note that there have been intractable problems in addressing the issue of recruitment, including vagueness in definition of both micro- and macrolevels of analysis, difficulties in formulating the mechanisms linking the two levels, and failure to develop feedback models of psychosocial processes. Similarly, Jenkins (1983) identifies development of a more sophisticated social psychology of collective action as a necessary refinement of the basic resource mobilization model of social movements.

Identity theories may be helpful in formulating social psychological feedback models. One missing link in predicting which individuals are likely to join a movement and to remain involved, may be the degree to which cognitive and affective stimuli in the environment become linked to the self. Hundreds of thousands of young adults were supportive of anti-Vietnam activism during the late 1960s and early 1970s; but the number who participated actively in such movements is smaller, and the number who have remained dedicated activists in the years since is decidedly smaller. In a longitudinal study of the adult political behavior of those who were college students in the early 1960s, Fendrich and Lovoy (1988) report that those who were radical civil rights activists are more politically active as adults on each of a variety of dimensions of political behavior than those who were institutional activists or uninvolved undergraduates. Although Fendrich and Lovoy do not speculate about the mechanisms underlying these differences, I suggest that for the radical activists, the movement ideology may have become a part of their identity, or to use the terms of identity theory, they may have developed a role-identity as an activist.

A merger of identity theories and resource mobilization theory might provide substantial insight into the process whereby identity change leads to social change. Resource mobilization theorists have been plagued by the free-rider problem; presumably rational self-interested individuals will not contribute to movements if they can incur the benefits of those movements without contributing (Olson, 1968). Movements that have overcome this problem offer collective incentives of group solidarity and moral commitment (Gamson & Fireman, 1979; Jenkins, 1982). Moral commitment could not operate as an incentive if individual values, emotions, and identities were not a crucial aspect of individual decisions to join movements. Indeed, Tilly (1978) asserts that groups with strong and distinctive identities, as well as tight interpersonal networks exclusive to group members, are the most highly organized and the most readily mobilized into movements. Groups with weak identities, few networks, and strong ties to outsiders are much less likely to mobilize.

Identity theories account for the microlevel processes whereby the strong identities of some groups exert their effects on social behavior. What resource mobilization theories lend is the notion that identities are a form of resources available to individuals and groups alike. Identity theory tends to view identities as always constructed by the individual, rather than as cultural resources. A more sociological perspective might ask what identities exist as resources for action in particular cultures, which actors are likely to adopt these identities, and how particular identities are used in social action.[6] Thus according to an identity mobilization model of social movements: (1) a variety of latent identities is available in a given culture; (2) the particular circumstances of a social movement make more likely the activation of some of these identities, and work against the activation of other identities, in combination with the prior histories of individuals; (3) these identities have varying relevance for social movements – some identities will predict short-term participation, others will predict sustained long-term participation.[7] (The quasi-behaviorist model of identity suggests that the initial involvement in a social movement may be part of what creates the long-term identity.) Identity mobilization works in combination with other factors influential to social movements. Thus, for example, effective leaders may influence what identities become salient so as to create a movement of dedicated long-term participants.

Models of individual and group contributions to social movements

Several models of the process by which both individual and group interests create social movements have been proposed. Barry Adam's (1978) *The Survival of Domination*, a comparative study of several inferiorized groups, suggests the mechanisms of this process. The existence of a group of individuals who share a common (socially constructed) status preconditions the possibility of recognition of commonality among members of this group. Consciousness is the process through which commonality is translated into a community, a consciously recognized group. Adam, like Snow, emphasizes the critical role of communication in this process. Communicability, the sustained contact of similarly situated people over time, is necessary for the formation of a community. This analysis is compatible with a widespread emphasis on social networks, which by all accounts are critical to effective social movements. Participation in movements is unlikely without prior contact with a recruitment agent; individuals have to be informed about and introduced into a movement, and social networks are the most effective mechanisms for meeting these requirements.

Adam identifies three factors necessary for class consciousness to become mobilized toward action: (1) recognition of identity between self and similarly situated others; (2) recognition of the divergence of ingroup and outgroup interests, that is, recognition of the political basis of intergroup relations; (3) an ideology about the sources of intergroup differences and possible social alternatives. A universe of discourse must link prospective participants with the goals of the movement. Social networks also facilitate dissemination of ideology and channel the diffusion of these ideas. In this analysis, Adam (1978: 55) explicitly cites the importance of identity and identity change, and acknowledges the significance of self–other relationships in creating identity: "The development of self is thereby inhibited by (non)accessibility of acknowledging others, and all but precluded by a cultural milieu which refuses to recognize its existence." Placing power in the center of this process, Adam argues that only the acknowledgment of self reflected by those others who are able to influence or control one's life or survival necessarily organizes the self's priorities and orientations. Indeed, in this way the active experience of discrimination, which implies a reflected negative self-image, may be crucial to the development of new identities and of consciousness of those identities; in order to combat the negative identity, it is necessary to articulate or strengthen an alternative identity.

Importantly, Adam also proposes a number of situational and structural factors that enhance moving through these stages in the development of consciousness: (1) the existence of large numbers of individuals in the same status; (2) geographical concentration; (3) identifiable targets; (4) sudden events or rapid changes in social position; (5) intellectual leaders with readily understood goals, and (6) the perception of alternatives to the current system. These factors are by no means inconsistent with those identified by Turner and Zurcher as instigators of change in the nature of self, but these factors are more likely to instigate voluntary participation in movements of change.

In summary then, a social movement requires (1) a group of similarly situated individuals who have been defined as different through a social and ideological process of definition; (2) social networks that promote communication among such individuals; (3) objective details such as geographic concentration and identifiable targets; (4) and mechanisms that promote the perception of action as effective, for example, the presence of specific leaders with understandable goals, and the presence of viable alternatives to the present system.

Identity change and social movements. Although Adam incorporates the concept of identity into his model of social movements, the specific nature of these identity shifts is not fully articulated. In an early discussion of the subjective aspects of stratification, Morris and Murphy (1966) hypothesize a temporal sequence through which the perception of differences in status may lead to class action. The first step is awareness of the range of statuses and the ability to place oneself on that range. The next step is awareness of discrete categories of statuses, or strata. From this perception, one may move to stratum affiliation, and membership behavior that reflects a feeling of belonging to this stratum. It is at this stage that the creation or adoption of an identity on the basis of the stratum enters the model. From this position one may then move to stratum consciousness, which requires a commitment to stratum interests and ideology. Finally, this commitment may translate into stratum action, behavior intended to further the interests and ideology of the stratum.

In one of the few empirical studies of identity-related transitions relevant to social movements, Gurin, Miller, and Gurin (1980) explore class, race, sex, and age consciousness within a single survey study. They distinguish between identification and consciousness, defining identification as a cognition about a relation to others within a social stratum, analogous to Morris and Murphy's stratum affiliation, and consciousness as a cognition about a stratum's position within society. Political consciousness is defined empirically as a combination of power discontent and rejection of the legitimacy of the status quo. Lacking a measure of political action, the authors assess the presence of an action orientation, the view that collective action is the best means to realize the stratum's interests.

Gurin et al. suggest that deprivation of valued resources and conflict over prevailing structural conditions are primary determinants of both identification and consciousness. (Either of these variables could exist in the absence of the other; the apparently less likely presence of consciousness without identification could occur in times during which consciousness of inequality is salient in the society as a whole.) The development of consciousness is hypothesized also to depend on aspects of social networks: The authors hypothesize that when contact within a stratum is maximal, and contact with other strata minimal, consciousness is more likely to occur (a hypothesis consistent with Tilly's discussion of group mobilization). The factors that Gurin et al. identify as important determinants of individual identification and consciousness, structural subordination, the amount and quality of contact within and between strata, and the existence of an ideology, echo factors suggested by other scholars as important determinants of social movements. The authors predict that *both* identification and consciousness are necessary for the development of a collective orientation, a prediction that is borne out empirically. This finding supports the distinctive importance of identity, although the measure of identification is not equivalent to identity in the sense used here.

It is critical to recognize the importance of structural factors in promoting or inhibiting the development of a collective orientation. The importance of structural constraints is developed in a creative discussion by Tajfel (1976), drawing on the ideas of Hirschman. Tajfel discusses two forms of intergroup relations, social mobility and social change. Social mobility derives from the perception that improvement in one's position in a social system can be achieved as an individual; this perception assumes a flexible and permeable social system. This type of mobility is labeled "exit," meaning that one moves from one's position in a class through exiting the class as an individual. Social change, in contrast, derives from the belief that an individual cannot move out of a group as an individual; the only way to change conditions is together with other group members, an option labeled "voice."[8] Although identification may be implicated in both types of change, consciousness is implicated only in social change. Thus identity change alone is not sufficient to motivate social movements. Indeed, Serpe (1987) implies that identity change itself is blocked under structural conditions that admit of little behavioral choice.

A conceptual model of the cognitive underpinnings of collective action

This discussion is summarized by a two-part model that incorporates self- and identity change and how these changes lead individuals to participate in social movements.

Changing selves. The model begins with the assumption that individuals form a sense of self that includes not only social role identities, the primary emphasis of identity theory, but also personal characteristics (a component recently acknowledged more explicitly by Stryker, 1987a), affect, and physical qualities. Predictors of identity include variables such as structural characteristics and social networks (represented by the variable of commitment in identity theory). Social structures constrain the development of social relationships, and thus social networks, and, ultimately, identity. Stryker and Serpe (1982), for example, include age and income in an analysis of religious role performance, hypothesizing that age- and class-related roles are inversely associated with the salience of religious identities.

The few direct conceptualizations of identity change locate the source of change in shifting environmental conditions, whether these be societal shifts or the changes that occur in more immediate social circles. Implicit in a number of theoretical approaches is the influence of social networks on changing selves. Change in the members of particular networks may well motivate self- and identity change in other members of those networks. Structural changes may also effect self- and identity change indirectly through their influence on social networks.

One problematic aspect of this model is the very definition of identity change. Does identity change involve acquisition of a new identity, a new awareness of an old identity, changes in identity salience, or perhaps even deletion of an old identity, which then makes possible a shift in the salience of other identities? It is also important to specify how different elements of identity may contribute to the process of change and how changes in one aspect of the salience hierarchy of identities may promote other changes. Another weak link is the paucity of mechanisms that explain how selves and identity change. Recent work points to the significance of emotional experiences and their effect on motivation.

Changing society. In moving to social action, the range of identities narrows to those associated with membership in particular social groups. This section of the model is akin to a Guttman scale, in that each step toward social action is likely to be increasingly more costly, and thus to be taken by increasingly fewer individuals. The steps move from consciousness, awareness of the relevant group's position in society, to a collective action orientation, a narrower realm yet, and, finally, to collective action, that is, the translation of an orientation into action, a step fraught with the familiar problems of the relationship between attitudes and behavior. Moving from each step to the next is a costly action, and the model will need to specify both costs and benefits.

One critical mechanism in the interconnections between these models is social networks and the communication they make possible. Interpersonal contacts are important at varying stages both in changing selves and in changing society. Moreover, the nature of those interpersonal contacts may vary depending on the stage of change. In the shift from identity to consciousness, interpersonal contact with individual significant others might be more important, whereas in the shift from consciousness to collective orientation and from collective orientation to collective action, contact with social groups may be more important than contact with specific individuals. Emotional experiences are also an important mechanism for social change. Kanter's (1968) analysis of mechanisms of solidarity in utopian communities points to the importance of factors such as group cohesiveness, engendered through renunciation and communication, and work on collective action (although less so, social movements) emphasizes the emotional intensity of group action. Mechanisms such as social networks, communication, and emotional experience are important both for changing selves and changing society and thus, in a sense, may overdetermine the eventual outcomes.

Although the discussion has implied a unidirectional process, for at least some steps there must be some degree of feedback. In coming to consciousness about the social position of a group, for example, we may strengthen our identification with that group, and hence the identity salience of that identity. The steps to collective action are the most difficult; therefore, if action is not successful, there may well be negative feedback to a collective orientation, and perhaps even to identity (but probably not to consciousness, since this failure underscores recognition of the position of the group).

Footnote: A research agenda and example

At least three prongs of research are desirable: (1) a prospective study of individuals as they move through these stages; (2) a retrospective study in which a sample of those who are at the last stage, that is, social activists, is isolated and examined (e.g., Fendrich & Lovoy, 1988); (3) separate studies of samples of individuals at each transition point. Although no research of which I am aware has examined all of the steps in this model, I will conclude the chapter with a brief empirical tangent that is at least suggestive of the validity of some parts of the model, using data from a comprehensive survey of intimate relationships of both homosexual and heterosexual couples (Blumstein & Schwartz, 1983).

The interview schedule included questions about respondents' involvement in feminism and gay activism, two social movements prominent in the past two decades. The responses of lesbians are particularly relevant – in coming to recognize and act on their sexual orientation, the lesbians may have had the opportunity to question two dominant institutions in our society, heterosexuality and patriarchy. However, not all lesbians are feminists, and not all lesbians are gay activists. As a very preliminary exploration of whether the model presented here might hold water, then, I examined the associations between activism and a set of possible correlates, selected on the basis of the previous discussion.

Sexual identity. Issues of identity have been explored with much intensity and thoroughness in the domain of human sexuality. Jeffrey Weeks (1987) suggests that sexual identity is a fundamental concept, offering personal unity, social location, and, for some, a political commitment. The work of Foucault (1979), in particular, has had fundamental impact in a variety of both social sciences and humanities. Foucault argues that sexuality is fundamentally social and structured by power relations; sexuality is at once the essence of identity and the essence of power.

Plummer (1975) outlines four stages in the development of a homosexual identity that strongly echo the models of Adams, Morris and Murphy, and Gurin. In sensitization, the individual becomes aware of the possibility of being different; in signification, the individual begins to attribute a particular meaning to these differences; in subculturization, the individual begins to recognize herself or himself through involvement with others; and in stabilization, the individual comes to full acceptance of her or his feelings and way of life. Plummer, echoing the emphases of recent social psychologists, argues for an alternative to an individualist identity paradigm, describing what he calls a relationship paradigm. He expresses the need to examine the complicated net of relationships through which sexuality is always expressed and changes over time. Identity is always relational, in that identities exist in relation to other potential identities, and are always about relationships. A sense of identity is critical for establishment of relationships, and thus is critical for social movements.

Lesbian activism. There is one measure of involvement in gay activism: Respondents were asked to indicate their degree of involvement in the gay rights movement (1 = extremely active; 9 = not at all active). In addition, respondents were asked to indicate how involved they are in organized gay activities, lesbian activities, and feminist activities (1 = extremely involved; 9 = not at all involved). Responses to this question could include both political and social activities. There is no direct measure of sexual preference identity. The closest indicator is the respondents' degree of agreement with the statement, "I would not give up my homosexuality even if I could." I use this question as a proxy for sexual preference identity. I examined the correlations between a set of possible correlates of activism, selected on the basis of the prior discussion. Then I divided the sample on the basis of sexual preference identity, into those who responded with a 1 (65% of the sample) and those who responded 5 to 9 on this item (34% of the sample) and examined the same set of correlations separately within each subsample.

The correlates of activism fall into six sets: (1) a set of demographic variables; (2) a set of self-perceived personality descriptors; (3) a set of ideological variables pertaining to attitudes about being gay, feminism, and general political outlook; (4) a set of variables pertaining to the geographical closeness of family members, and attitudes about obligations of adult children to their parents; (5) a set pertaining to the degree of social immersion in a homosexual environment; and (6) a set pertaining to the relationship statuses of one's friends, both homosexual and heterosexual. I will report the correlations for the gay activism items first, then turn to those for lesbian activism and for feminist activism.[9]

Starting with the correlations for involvement in the gay rights movement and in gay activities more generally (the association between these variables is $r = .622$), greater involvement is associated with (1) more education and lower income; (2) being more outgoing, more aggressive, and more forceful (gay rights movement only); (3) being more feminist and more politically liberal, believing that one would not give up being homosexual if one could, disagreeing with the belief that life would be easier as a heterosexual, and with the belief that being gay is a conscious choice; (4) lack of agreement with the principle that one should visit one's partner's relatives (both items), and less frequent self-initiated contact with one's partner's parents, lack of agreement with the idea that adult children are obliged to keep in touch with their parents, should be with their parents in times of a serious illness, should pay their parents' medical bills, and should keep in touch with one's partner's parents (for all the preceding items, gay rights movement only); (5) more frequent attendance at gay bars and at other gay public places, greater number of gays living in one's immediate area, and higher proportion of gays in one's workplace; (6) higher numbers of lesbian friends, and, interestingly, the proportion of one's gay, lesbian, and heterosexual female friends who are currently living with a partner or married.

Turning to the correlations for involvement in lesbian and feminist activities, greater involvement is associated with (1) more education and lower income; (2) being more muscular, and (for feminists only) more outgoing, more competitive with one's partner, and more self-sufficient; (3) being more feminist and more politically liberal, less likely to believe that being gay is beyond one's control (feminist only), more likely to believe that one would not give up being homosexual if one could (lesbian only); (4) greater geographical distance from one's mother (feminist only), less frequent self-initiated contact with one's partner's parents (feminist only), less agreement with the idea that adult children are obliged to keep in touch with their parents (lesbian only), should keep in touch with one's partner's parents, and should be expected to visit one's partner's parents; (5) more frequent attendance at gay bars (lesbian only) and at other gay public places, greater number of gays living in one's immediate area, and higher proportion of gays in one's workplace; (6) higher numbers of gay male friends (lesbian only), and the proportion of one's gay, lesbian, and heterosexual female friends who are currently living with a partner or married.

The demographic variables, education and income, allow tests of structural influences on social activism, and the personality descriptors allow tests of the influence of individual traits. Ideology has been identified as an important predictor of social activism; this concept is examined by the third set of variables. Virtually all theorists of social movements also have identified social networks as influential; this notion is examined with the three remaining sets of variables. One set addresses whether one's family networks are influential; a second set considers the influence of network involvement with other people who are gay, and the extent to which this permeates the important arenas of one's life, residence, job, and social life; and the last set evaluates a different aspect of social networks, whether having single or coupled friends influences the degree of activism.

These associations indicate strong support for the association between ideology and social activism and between social networks and social activism. The variations in these associations suggests that the influence of networks is quite specific. It is involvement in gay networks and pervasiveness of these networks across significant life domains that predicts gay activism, and, interestingly, feminist activism as well, among these lesbians. Furthermore, these correlations point to the significance of particular structural variables and of some personality traits.

To examine whether sexual identity mediates these relationships, I recomputed these correlations within two groups, the 992 lesbians who responded with a 1, indicating strong agreement with the statement that they would not give up being homosexual if they could, and the 247 lesbians whose responses ranged from 5 to 9 on this item, indicating neutral to strong disagreement with this statement.[10] In general, the patterns of correlations are very similar, and most of the correlations are replicated. Of the full set of 95 significant correlations, 37 of the correlations are replicated within the sample who indicate a strong homosexual identity that are not replicated within the sample who indicate a weak homosexual identity. Although this is a highly questionable approach to assessing the role of identity in social movements, these results at least point to the mediating role of sexual identity in participation in gay rights activities. Taken together, these correlations indicate the complex web within which social movements originate, a web that weaves together structural and individual level variables and, importantly, social networks that connect the social and the individual.

Notes

1 Although beyond the scope of the present discussion, why other theories do not conceive explicitly of a self is an intriguing question. Exchange theorists, e.g., Emerson (1981), cast the actor as a neutral, self-interested, but undifferentiated entity. Identification of particular characteristics of individual actors is not required in this model, in which all actors are assumed to share a common motivation.

2 These conceptions of the relationship between person and society are structural in their emphasis on social roles, but they reflect the traditional symbolic interactionist inattention to social institutions. Any effects of social institutions are thought to be carried through the network of social roles in which individuals are embedded: "social structures affect individuals by conditioning the kinds of interactions and relationships within which individuals exist as social actors (Stryker, 1980: 203)

3 A related issue is whether a stable generalized self is unitary or multiple, and to what extent self-deception underlies a sense of a unitary self (see Elster, 1986).
4 This analysis relies on the debatable assumption that personal characteristics cannot be independent of social structures.
5 Research on self-schemas may provide promising measurement and conceptual leads (Markus, 1977). For example, findings that novel experiences and negative or unexpected occurrences prompt effortful, unscripted action, may point to ways in which unarticulated selves become articulated.
6 I am indebted to Peter Callero for discussion of this view of identities.
7 The characteristics of a social movement, which I do not have the space to discuss in this chapter, also change over time. Movements tend to evolve through a series of stages, and various identities may be more or less relevant to these stages.
8 Tajfel links the practice of social psychology to the relative emphasis on these two options. Most contemporary social psychology has been produced in the United States; social mobility assumptions are consistent with the American political system. Hence most explanations of intergroup behavior stress social mobility and the exit option. There has been little attention to social change, the voice form of intergroup relations. Tajfel suggests that the objective absence of access to exit (or the belief that access does not exist) may lead to voice forms of political action. Thus to understand social movement, Tajfel argues, we must use the social change structure of beliefs as the theoretical framework.
9 Due to the large sample size, I use a $p < .001$ level of significance.
10 I use a $p < .001$ level of significance for the analyses in the strong identity group, and a $p < .05$ level of significance for the weak identity group. Although different significance levels are generally not advisable, the strong identity group is four times larger than the weak group, and these probability levels work against the hypothesis.

References

Adam, Barry D. 1978. *The survival of domination: Inferiorization and everyday life*. New York: Elsevier North-Holland.

Baumeister, Roy. 1982. A self-presentational view of social phenomena. *Psychological Bulletin* 91: 3–26.

Bem, Daryl. 1972. Self-perception theory. In Leonard Berkowitz (Ed.), *Advances in experimental social psychology* (pp. 1–62). New York: Academic Press.

Block, J. 1971. *Lives through time*. Berkeley, CA: Bancroft.

Blumer, Herbert. 1969. *Symbolic interactionism: Perspective and method*. Englewood Cliffs, NJ: Prentice-Hall.

Blumstein, Philip, & Pepper Schwartz. 1983. *American couples: Money, work and sex*. New York: William Morrow.

Burke, Peter J. 1980. The self: Measurement requirements from an interactionist perspective. *Social Psychology Quarterly* 43: 18–29.

Callero, P. L. 1985. Role-identity salience. *Social Psychology Quarterly* 48: 203–214.

Callero, P. L. 1986. *The sociological self: A longitudinal analysis*. Unpublished grant proposal. ADAMHA.

Costa, P., & McCrae, R. 1980. Still stable after all these years: Personality as a key to some issues in adulthood and old age. In Paul B. Baltes & Orville G. Brim, Jr. (Eds.), *Life-span development and behavior* (Vol. 3, pp. 65–102). New York: Academic Press.

Della Fave, L. Richard. 1980. The meek shall not inherit the earth. *American Sociological Review* 45: 955–971.

Della Fave, L. Richard. 1986a. The dialectics of legitimation and counternorms. *Sociological Perspectives* 29: 435–460.

Della Fave, L. Richard. 1986b. Toward an explication of the legitimation process. *Social Forces* 65: 476–500.

Elster, Jon (Ed.) 1986. *The multiple self.* Cambridge, UK: Cambridge University Press.

Emerson, Richard M. 1981. Social exchange theory. In Morris Rosenberg & Ralph Turner (Eds.), *Social psychology: Sociological perspectives* (pp. 30–65). New York: Basic Books.

Fendrich, James Max, & Kenneth L. Lovoy. 1988. Back to the future: Adult political behavior of former student activists. *American Sociological Review* 53: 780–784.

Foote, Nelson N. 1951. Identification as the basis for a theory of motivation. *American Sociological Review* 16: 14–21.

Foucault, Michel. 1979. *The history of sexuality* (Vol. 1). London: Penguin Press.

Gamson, William, & B. Fireman. 1979. Utilitarian logic in the resource mobilization perspective. In Mayer N. Zald & John H. McCarthy (Eds.). *The dynamics of social movements* (pp. 8–45). Cambridge, MA: Winthrop.

Gecas, Viktor. 1989. The social psychology of self-efficacy. *Annual Review of Sociology* 15: 291–316.

Greenwald, Anthony G. 1980. The totalitarian ego: Fabrication and revision of personal history. *American Psychologist* 35: 603–618.

Gurin, Patricia, Arthur H. Miller, & Gerald Gurin. 1980 Stratum identification and consciousness. *Social Psychology Quarterly* 43: 30–47.

Heise, David R. 1987. Affect control theory: Concepts and model. *Journal of Mathematical Sociology* 13: 1–33.

Hewitt, John P. 1988. *Self and society: A symbolic interactionist social psychology.* Boston: Allyn and Bacon.

Hochschild, Arlie Russell. 1983. *The managed heart: Commercialization of human feeling.* Berkeley: University of California Press.

Hoelter, Jon W. 1985. A structural theory of personal consistency. *Social Psychology Quarterly* 48: 118–129.

Hormuth, Stefan E. 1984. Transitions in commitments to roles and self-concept change: Relocation as a paradigm. In Vernon L. Allen & Evert van de Vliert (Eds.), *Role transitions: Explorations and explanations* (pp. 109–124). New York: Plenum Press.

House, James S. 1981. Social structure and personality. In Morris Rosenberg & Ralph H. Turner (Eds.), *Social psychology: Sociological perspectives* (pp. 525–561). New York: Basic Books.

Jenkins, J. Craig. 1982. The transformation of a constituency into a movement. In J. Freeman (Ed.), *The social movements of the 1960s and 1970s* (pp. 52–70). New York: Longman.

Jenkins, J. Craig. 1983. Resource mobilization theory and the study of social movements. *Annual Review of Sociology* 9: 527–553.

Kanter, Rosabeth Moss. 1968. Commitment and social organization: A study of commitment mechanisms in utopian communities. *American Sociological Review* 33: 499–517.

Markus, Hazel. 1977. Self-schemas and processing information about the self. *Journal of Personality and Social Psychology* 35: 63–78.

Markus, Hazel, & Paula Nurius. 1986. Possible selves. *American Psychologist* 41: 954–969.

McCall, George J., & T. T. Simmons. 1978. *Identities and interaction.* New York: Free Press.

Morris, Richard T., & Raymond J. Murphy. 1966. A paradigm for the study of class consciousness. *Sociology and Social Research* 50: 297–313.

Mortimer, Jeylan T., Michael D. Finch, & Donald Kumka. 1982. Persistence and change in development: The multidimensional self-concept. In Paul B. Baltes and Orville G. Brim,

Jr. (Eds.), *Life-span development and behavior* (Vol. 4, pp. 263–312). New York: Academic Press.

Olson, Mancur. 1968. *The logic of collective action.* New York: Schocken.

Plummer, Kenneth. 1975. *Sexual stigma.* London: Routledge and Kegan Paul.

Rosenberg, Morris. 1979. *Conceiving the self.* Malabar, FL: Krieger.

Rosenberg, Morris. 1981. The self-concept: Social product and social force. In Morris Rosenberg & Ralph H. Turner (Eds.), *Social psychology: Sociological perspectives* (pp. 593–624). New York: Basic Books.

Sampson, Edward E. 1985. The decentralization of identity: Toward a revised concept of personal and social order. *American Psychologist* 40: 1,203–1,211.

Serpe, Richard T. 1987. Stability and change in self: A structural symbolic interactionist explanation. *Social Psychology Quarterly* 50: 44–55.

Shott, Susan. 1979. Emotion and social life: A symbolic interactionist analysis. *American Journal of Sociology* 84: 1,317–1,334.

Smelser, William T., & Neil J. Smelser. 1981. Group movements, sociocultural change, and personality. In Morris Rosenberg & Ralph H. Turner (Eds.), *Social psychology: Sociological perspectives* (pp. 625–652). New York: Basic Books.

Smith, Paul. 1977. *Discerning the subject.* Minneapolis: University of Minnesota Press.

Smith-Lovin, Lynn, & David R. Heise. 1988. *Affect control theory: Research advances.* New York: Gordon and Breach.

Stryker, Sheldon. 1980. *Symbolic interactionism, a social structural version.* Menlo Park, CA: Benjamin-Cummings.

Stryker, Sheldon. 1981. Symbolic interactionism: Themes and variations. In Morris Rosenberg & Ralph H. Turner (Eds.), *Social psychology: Sociological perspectives* (pp. 3–29). New York: Basic Books.

Stryker, Sheldon. 1987a. Identity theory: Developments and extensions. In Krysia Yardley & Terry Honess (Eds.), *Self and identity: Psychosocial perspectives* (pp. 89–103). New York: Wiley.

Stryker, Sheldon. 1987b. *The interplay of affect and identity: Exploring the relationships of social structure, social interaction, self and emotion.* Paper presented at the meeting of the American Sociological Association, Chicago.

Stryker, Sheldon, & Richard T. Serpe. 1982. Commitment, identity salience and role behavior: Theory and research example. In William Ickes & Eric Knowles (Eds.), *Personality, roles, and social behavior* (pp. 199–218). New York: Springer-Verlag.

Swann, William B., Jr. 1983. Self verification: Bringing social reality into harmony with the self. In Jerry Suls & Anthony G. Greenwald (Eds.), *Psychological perspectives on the self* (Vol. 2, pp. 33–66). Hillsdale, NJ: Erlbaum.

Swann, William B., Jr. 1987. Identity negotiation: Where two roads meet. *Journal of Personality and Social Psychology* 53: 1,038–1,051.

Tajfel, Henri. 1976. Exit, voice and intergroup relations. In Lloyd H. Strickland, Frances E. Aboud, & Kenneth J. Gergen (Eds.), *Social psychology in transition* (pp. 281–304). New York: Plenum Press.

Tedeschi, James T., & Sven Lindskold. 1976. *Social psychology: Interdependence, interaction and influence.* New York: Wiley.

Tesser, Abraham, & Jennifer Campbell. 1983. Self-definition and self-evaluation maintenance. In Jerry Suls & Anthony G. Greenwald (Eds.), *Psychological perspectives on the self* (Vol. 2, pp. 1–31). Hillsdale, NJ: Erlbaum.

Tilly, Charles. 1978. *From mobilization to revolution.* Reading, MA: Addison-Wesley.

Turner, Ralph H. 1962. Role taking: Process versus conformity. In A. Rose (Ed.), *Human behavior and social processes* (pp. 20–40). Boston: Houghton-Miffin.

Turner, Ralph H. 1976. The real self: From institution to impulse. *American Journal of Sociology* 81: 989–1,016.

Turner, Ralph H. 1978. The role and the person. *American Journal of Sociology* 84: 1–23.

Turner, Ralph H. 1983. Figure and ground in the analysis of social movements. *Symbolic Interaction* 6: 175–181.

Turner, Ralph H. 1987. Articulating self and social structure. In Krysia Yardley & Terry Honess (Eds.), *Self and identity: Psychosocial perspectives* (pp. 119–132). New York: Wiley.

Turner, Ralph H., & Steven Gordon. 1981. The boundaries of the self: The relationship of authenticity in the self-conception. In Mervin D. Lynch, Ardyth A. Norem-Hebeisen & Kenneth J. Gergen (Eds.), *Self concept: Advances in theory and research* (pp. 39–57). Cambridge: Ballinger.

Turner, Ralph H., & Lewis M. Killian. 1972. *Collective behavior.* Englewood Cliffs, NJ: Prentice-Hall.

Weeks, Jeffrey. 1987. Questions of identity. In Pat Kaplan (Ed.), *The cultural construction of sexuality* (pp. 31–51). New York: Tavistock.

Wells, L. Edward, & Sheldon Stryker. 1988. Stability and change in self over the life course. In Paul B. Baltes, David L. Featherman, & Richard M. Lerner (Eds.), *Life-span development and behavior* (pp. 191–229). Hillsdale, NJ: Erlbaum.

Wood, Michael R., & Louis A. Zurcher, Jr. 1988. *The development of a postmodern self. A computer-assisted comparative analysis of personal documents.* New York: Greenwood Press.

Zurcher, Louis A., Jr., 1977. *The mutable self.* Beverly Hills, CA: Sage.

Zurcher, Louis A., & David A. Snow. 1981. Collective behavior: Social movements. In Morris Rosenberg & Ralph H. Turner (Eds.), *Social psychology: Sociological perspectives* (pp. 447–482). New York: Basic Books.

11 Possible selves and social support: Social cognitive resources for coping and striving

Paula Nurius

The general goal of this chapter is to pursue a synthesis of the information-processing properties of the self-concept with prevailing models of social support processes and to explore their combined consequences for health outcomes. Although increasingly indicated in the cast of well-being and health outcome predictors, the roles of social support and the self-concept have been pursued relatively independent of one another. The objective here is to explore mechanisms that serve a social cognitive basis for "transactions" (cf. Lazarus & Folkman, 1984) between the two as well as the relevance of these transactional dynamics for coping and striving efforts and for personal health outcomes. An underlying premise is that the prevailing emphasis on cognitive features of the self-concept predisposes preventive and remedial interventions toward intrapsychic solutions, and that a better understanding of the social interface may argue for a more contextual approach.

Specifically, I will focus on elements within the self-concept and social support systems that bear significantly upon motivation and subsequent motivated or goal-directed activity. In particular, I will emphasize cognitive representations of possible selves, social support appraisals, and their interrelatedness. First, a formulation of the self-concept as both a social product and a social force will be described in terms of the working self-concept and possible selves. The relation of social support processes, particularly support appraisals, to coping processes and to health (including mental health) outcomes will then be sketched. This will be followed by a social cognitive analysis of linkages between support appraisals and possible selves and their implications for goal-directed activity. The chapter will conclude with implications for the changing self, and for primary prevention and treatment efforts.

The self-concept and social environment in transaction

Within both sociological and psychological approaches, two some-what paradoxical characterizations of the self-concept have been evident. One casts the self-concept in terms of its stable, tenacious, unifying features – the biographical and the schema-based self-concept (Block, 1981; Shrauger & Schoeneman, 1979). The other focuses on the "situated," responsive, and mutable features of the self-concept (Alexander & Wiley, 1980; McGuire & McGuire, 1981; see also Gecas, 1982; Greenwald & Pratkanis, 1984; and Zurcher, 1977).

One approach to resolving this tension between the stability and malleability of the self has pointed to the limits of working memory and awareness and to the differential accessibility of self-conceptions across circumstances (e.g., Higgins, King, & Mavin, 1982). In prior work, my colleagues and I have differentiated the very malleable *working self-concept* from the more enduring and monolithic repository of self-conceptions amassed over a lifetime (Markus & Kunda, 1986; Nurius, 1986; Nurius & Markus, 1990).

This working self-concept is the functionally relevant self-concept in the moment. It is a constantly shifting configuration of self-conceptions that wax and wane in salience according to the priming effects of currently relevant cues and events. By and large, these priming effects occur in a highly patterned and automatic or "mindless" fashion. Thus, in routine circumstances, this priming or activation is a highly efficient process with little need of conscious effort or awareness on the part of the individual. In other situations, perhaps under novel circumstances or those requiring focused attention or deliberate efforts to override a competing set of selves, the individual will be quite self-aware and willfully invoke certain subsets of self-conceptions.

As presented in Figure 1, some self-conceptions may form the core of the individual's sense of identity and be so continuously drawn upon that they become transsituationally salient. The majority, however, are likely to be primed, and thus brought into active service, on a much less frequent and more contingent basis. That is, differing sets of self-conceptions are likely to be primed in response to differing situations (e.g., following embarrassments or accomplishments), domains (e.g., athletics, romance), or tasks (e.g., delivering an important speech, negotiating an argument among one's family members), and thereby be salient and "working" for the individual on a more periodical basis.

Self-conceptions will vary in their importance to the individual, in their degree of cognitive elaboration and differentiation, and their likelihood of

SELF-CONCEPT

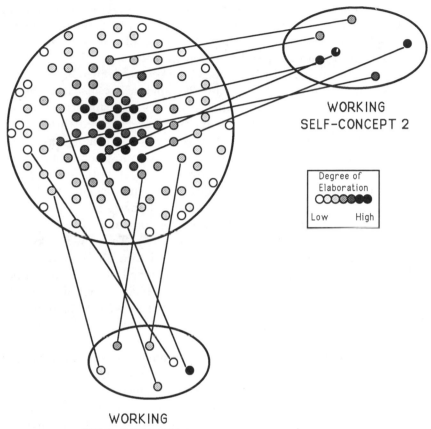

WORKING
SELF-CONCEPT 2

WORKING
SELF-CONCEPT 1

Figure 1. From "The self-concept: A social–cognitive update" by P. S. Nurius, 1988, *Social Casework*, 70, pp. 285–294. Copyright by Family Service America. Reprinted by permission.

being activated. For purposes of illustration, these are suggested through the varying sizes of the structures in Figure 1, the degree to which they are filled out, and their greater density and ordering in the central region. Self-conceptions vary across additional dimensions as well – valence is perhaps the most frequently noted – detailed discussion of which is beyond the scope of this chapter.

These subsets of primed self-conceptions serve as the basis for subsequent attributions and evaluations (by oneself and others in the immediate social environment) as well as for action alternatives. They thereby provide one concrete reflection of the Meadian interactionism that conceives of stimuli becoming objects only as they take on personal meaning and of objects as situationally constituted from the perspective of the participants in the ongoing activity. The working self-concept thus can be seen as one specific manifestation of the self-situation transaction.

Although how these "self-conceptions" can best be defined has not been fully resolved, multifaceted schema-based approaches are now widely embraced. Self-schemata are cognitive structures consisting of organized elements of information about the self that have evolved through experience and reflected appraisals – that is, views and evaluations of the self by others as perceived by the individual. As both generalizations and hypotheses about the self, self-schemata function as both plans *of* and *for* action (Alba & Hasher, 1983; Hastie, 1981). And, once formed, these structures are believed to operate in virtually all phases of the processing of self-relevant information, including perceptions and expectations of others (e.g., Markus, Smith, & Moreland, 1985). Thus, in speaking of self-conceptions, a cognitive structural view of the self consistent with schematic processing and schema theory is assumed. Within this framework, self-conceptions can vary considerably in their degree of specificity and elaboration (both ideational and affective) as well as their degree of rationality, veridicality, and personal importance, points that will be further explored later.

With respect to content, self-conceptions are not just repositories of the past and catalogues of the present, however active the role of self in constructing and maintaining these representations. Self-conceptions also carry both positive and negative beliefs about what could come to pass in the future and about what is possible. These *possible selves* are thus the future-oriented components of the self-concept; they personalize and give enduring cognitive form to one's goals, motives, and hopes and fears for the future.

More specifically, possible selves are representations (visual, semantic, symbolic, kinesthetic) of oneself in future states and circumstances; and as such would be expected to operate according to the same schematic processes that other self-representations follow. In this way possible selves give specific self-referent form to the selves individuals would like to become or are afraid of becoming (Markus & Nurius, 1986), including selves of one's past that are not presently true yet constitute personally salient future possibilities (e.g., the lonely "fat kid" of one's youth, the carefree world traveler of one's young adulthood). Possible selves provide structural content and form to what Mead (1934) described as one's anticipated future and to the "I want" dimension of self-reflection generally neglected by symbolic interactionists (Serpe, chapter 3 in this volume). Thus, possible selves are important links of the self-concept to motivation and to goal-directed action.

Although not always acknowledged, there are sources of data and verification regarding who one *is* – current and past roles, specific accomplishments, habitual and observable actions, and mood states. With respect to who one *could* be or become, self-symbolizing of hopes and fears renders a far broader and less data-based net of possibilities. More than conceptions of self in the present, possible selves are free from restraints of veridicality and apparent rationality. And their emotional weight can far exceed their likelihood of being realized. For example, the actual likelihood of being abandoned or publicly ridiculed or rejected is often far less than the emotional experience of risk or vulnerability, fueling a considerable amount of energy designed to avoid negative evaluation by others. Conversely, consider the inordinate distress we would feel if forced to acknowledge flatly the great improbability of some privately cherished dream.

In addition, the ability to construct, invoke, and sustain possible selves may be one critical determinant of actual goal achievement. This includes goals to strive toward, such as obtaining the necessary training to land a desired job or saving toward a prized acquisition, as well as goals depicting outcomes to avoid, such as losing one's job, developing a health problem, or becoming a victim of assault or abuse. Possible selves decrease the perceptual distance between one's current state and a possible future state (whether desirable or undesirable) and thus contribute toward galvanizing and organizing behavior relative to that goal. And, like schemata of past and present selves, possible selves carry affective valence and evaluations of their goodness or badness that become salient upon activation. They will vary in degree of specificity as a function of elaboration, of accessibility as a function of frequency of use, and of importance as a function of personal values and intensity of commitment to the future state by the individual (cf. Stryker's identity salience, 1980, chapter 1 of this volume; and Rosenberg's psychological centrality, 1979, chapter 6 of this volume).

When individuals strive to realize a desired future or to avoid or resist an undesired future, it is likely they have acquired or fashioned a vision of the new or changed self. Yet general goals often do not indicate specific actions or pathways toward achieving these end states. Nor do they sufficiently convey differences in the emotional weight or symbolic value of these end states across individuals. It is through exposure to and experience with others that these means–ends connections and valuations become elaborated and that more fully developed conceptions, or possible selves, evolve. And it is often through these social conduits that possible selves are reinforced when threatened and are energized toward shaping self-presentation, situation evaluation, and, ultimately, action.

Clearly, the self-concept is both a social force and social product. The self-concept is an active and central cognitive structure, and yet is continuously embedded within and in commerce with an equally active social environment. Social evaluation (from significant as well as generalized others such as the media) influences self-evaluation, and one's prevailing view of self – both present and future – colors and directs subsequent transactions and social functioning. One component of social evaluation that bears particularly upon the self-concept is that of the reflected or perceived self – how an individual *believes* others see her or him (Rosenberg, 1981), and to this I will turn next. The following section describes the relation of social support to coping, striving, and health outcomes. I will stress the role of social evaluation in the form of reflected support appraisals, especially esteem-enhancing appraisals, in mediating the influence of support on coping and striving.

Social support, coping, and health outcomes

There is general agreement that social ties are important factors associated with a broad spectrum of well-being and quality-of-life indicators (Broadhead et al., 1983; Cohen & Syme, 1985; Kessler, Price, & Wortman, 1985). But despite evidence that social support buffers and minimizes adverse effects of stress and strain (Cohen & Wills, 1985; Kessler & McLeod, 1985; Turner, 1983), we do not fully understand how social support works or the double edge of social supports as sources of burden or stress (Fischer & Phillips, 1982). What specific factors embedded within the often vaguely defined social support are responsible for observed health-protective effects? Research has focused on stress-related interpersonal aids such as emotional support, cognitive restructuring, and instrumental aid. Of growing interest also is the individual's subjective experience or perception of social support.

It is not yet clear what constitutes the primary component of perceived support. One view is that esteem-enhancing appraisals stemming from one's appraisal of others' views of self form this primary component (Heller, Swindle, & Dusenbury, 1986; Thoits, 1985). This, of course, speaks to symbolic interactionists' emphasis on reflected appraisals (Mead, 1934; Rosenberg, 1981; Stryker, 1980; several contributors to this book). Yet it also acknowledges an active role on the part of the individual in

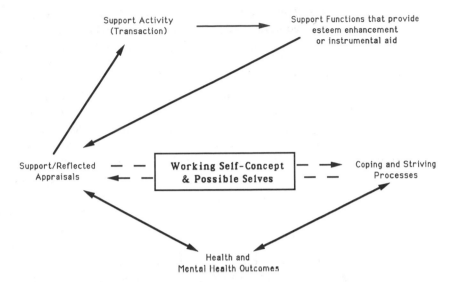

Figure 2. From "Component social support processes: Comments and integration" by Heller, Swindle, & Dusenbury (1986), *Journal of Consulting and Clinical Psychology* 54:466–470. Copyright 1986 by the American Psychological Association. Adapted by permission.

mediating these appraisals from others, both in seeking out and shaping these appraisals and assigning meaning and value to them.

As presented in Figure 2, social activity and support functions deriving from them influence *support appraisals*, which in turn shape the nature of future social interactions as well as support functions sought and experienced by the individual. Support appraisals also influence and are influenced by coping efforts, and both can independently influence health outcomes. Therefore, social support is seen here as influencing health outcomes *through* appraisal processes; through the individuals' cognitive-emotional filter that assigns value and meaning to others' actions, to one's self (past, current, and future), and to coping efforts.

Clearly, rather than being a passive recipient of "social support," the individual plays an active role in shaping networks, eliciting input from others, and then interpreting the meaning and value of these. Yet it is not clear what internal resources or cognitive tools the individual brings to bear in this appraisal and translation process. For example, if bolstered self-esteem, morale, and sense of well-being can significantly influence health independent of coping efforts, how does this occur? What are the cognitive underpinnings? What differentiates those for whom this effect is greater than others? And what are the mechanisms through which interactions with others have enduring and cumulative effects on self-esteem, motivation, and problem management (i.e., coping, striving, resisting)?

An information-processing analysis of the working self-concept and possible selves addresses these questions by specifically linking social ties, individual mediation, and coping and striving behaviors. The following sections will explore the roles of possible selves and the working self-concept in social support appraisal processes and the influence of social ties in developing and engaging the self-system. Specifically, these interrelationships will be considered in terms of (1) the personalization of motivation through the development of possible selves, (2) the elicitation and validation of biased sets of self-conceptions, including possible selves, and (3) the consequences for striving and coping.

Development of possible selves

The developing child receives a plethora of messages about who she is and isn't and the relative "goodness" or "badness" of these attributes, roles, skills, and talents. Although more subtle, the child is also inundated with messages about what she can and can't become, what would be wonderful and terrible to become, and what she "ought," like it or not, to develop into (cf. Higgins, Strauman, & Klein, 1985), and these social communiques continue throughout life. Who and what constitutes the most powerful set of social influencers changes over the life course. Nonetheless, in the same fashion that "who we are" is contingent upon our roles, relationships, and the reflected appraisals of credible and valued others, so too are our conceptions of our possible selves – both positive and negative.

An individual, theoretically, is free to create any variety of possible selves. Yet, as with other aspects of our socially constructed realities, our pool of possible selves derives mainly from the categories and domains made salient by our particular sociocultural and historical context and from the models, images, and symbols provided by the media and by our social experiences. Possible selves have the potential to reveal the inventive and constructive nature of the self, but they also reflect ways in which the self is socially determined and constrained. Although individuals can, and do, contemplate a wide band of future scenarios and ways of being, possible selves are not likely to become elaborated and thereby either motivationally or behaviorally effective unless valuing them and believing in them are supported or encouraged by significant others. Thus the parameters for the possible selves one will contemplate, develop, and maintain depends greatly on the nature of one's social environment. This would include cultural and social identity variables as well as social structural constraints and opportunities (e.g., the constraints of poverty, racism, sexism, ageism, and homophobia).

The individuals in one's social environment, for example, provide information on what attributes, talents, roles, and abilities are valued, and set evaluation standards regarding the extent to which the individual possesses (or could possess) any given attribute. The more consistent and the longer the duration of such social evaluations, the more likely the individual is to adopt others' perspective on the self – both present and possible self – and to incorporate this conception into his or her decision-making, coping, and striving behaviors. This is readily apparent, for example, in the effects of sex-role socialization in stipulating qualitatively different self-conceptions and possibilities as appropriate for males and females, and a narrower scope of alternatives for females (Russo, 1985; Weinraub & Brown, 1983). And although analysis of self-concept development and change has been biased toward youth, effects of the social environment on the self-concept and of the self-concept on health and well-being are evident across the life span (McCrae & Costa, 1988; Guidano, 1987: chapter 11; Leahy, 1985).

Taking the role of the other with respect to one's own self-definition has long been pursued in terms of social identities, particularly as defined and enacted through role relationships. One's set of identities give meaning and guidance to behavior. Whereas the risk of role conflict and strain do exist, theorists have also argued that multiple role involvements offer important benefits. The greater the number of identities held, the stronger one's sense of meaningful, guided existence and thus of psychological health and security (cf. Marks, 1977; Sieber, 1974). Verbrugge (1983) and Thoits (1983) recently found support for this identity accumulation hypothesis. Thoits (1986) and Potts (1987) replicated this finding, yet also found that in addition to the *number* of identities, the *types* of identities (how personally meaningful, how socially valued) and the structural factors associated with them (e.g., access to and support for role opportunities such as employment) differed significantly by gender and confounded the identities-health relationship. The notion of possible selves as *potential* social and role identities provides an additional dimension to study of multiple identities and of identity accumulation, and to specification of links among social referents, self-identity, and goal-directed activity.

The presence of well-specified, achievable, self-referent goals has consistently been found critical for effective performance, particularly when external cues are lacking or ambiguous. Positive possible selves carry both means–end information about who to be like (what social identity to emulate) and what to do (how to go about manifesting or enacting that identity), as well as positive mood associated with the anticipated goal and regard of others.

In contrast, negative possible selves are more likely to reflect what *not* to become, who not to be like, and, in some cases, what not to do. Models of negative possible selves (e.g., of embitterment and loneliness in old age) may suggest alternatives (e.g., of a positive outlook and lots of friends), yet often do not carry means–ends information about *how* to avoid one and realize the other. By themselves, therefore, negative possible selves are less likely to be effective in directing one's actions about what *to do*. Similarly, a *lack* of positive possible selves (e.g., among the seriously depressed) renders individuals less able to self-regulate their bahavior effectively in new, constructive directions, and thus less able to garner positive mood and social rewards associated with effective coping and striving.

Elicitation and validation of possible selves

The subset of self-schemata that constitute the working self-concept at any given point are those either invoked by the individual or elicited through some association (e.g., a sensory experience, emotion, or social cue). And, whether consciously or not, individuals learn to use these cueing functions strategically to establish (or maintain) a desired state within the self-system. For example, many of us respond to bruising work experiences by calling a friend or relative for an "ego boost." In the process of this interaction, attention will likely be directed back in time (e.g., to prior evidence of competence) and forward in time (e.g., to the longer-term goals and the rewards to come), or perhaps to other domains (e.g., affirming one's value as a good friend). In other words, social support is functioning as coping assistance (cf. Thoits, 1986). The social activity is facilitating a reconfiguration of the prevailing working self-concept through priming of biased sets of self-conceptions (elicitation) and through mood and belief altering esteem-enhancing appraisals (validation).

The strategic element is in initiating and manipulating these contacts, using social ties to reconfigure prevailing conceptions of current and future self as one means of coping. Other activities could produce similar effects, for example, leafing through prior work or evaluations extolling one's expertise, or turning to other activities with a high likelihood of success or affirmation. One might also be strategic in *avoiding* individuals or events likely to activate negative conceptions of self (e.g., a rival sibling or elitist coworker). Or, as in relapse prevention, one might fortify oneself for a challenging experience by invoking a particular working self-concept biased toward a sense of self-efficacy and self-worth (Nurius, Lovell, & Edgar, 1988).

The resultant working self-concept is likely to be configured largely by positive possibility – including former selves one can again become (e.g., I've had great speaking experiences before) as well as future selves one is striving toward (e.g., images of oneself as a confident and impressive orator, sought after, admired, and a model for others). This effect is implicitly assumed by clinical self-management interventions, wherein the individual is taught to stop himself or herself under certain circumstances and deliberately to invoke a more functional set of memories, self-statements, or goals. Yet the clinical literature is also replete with evidence that skill building and informational interventions are often insufficient to effect enduring change in individuals' behavior and responses.

One missing link involves integrating general information into the self-system, of formulating and elaborating representations of *oneself* as being or behaving in the desired fashion (Guidano & Liotti, 1983). Information that has not been categorized and assimilated as self-defining – either potentially or "actually" – is unlikely to be as influential in self-regulation efforts as information that has been organized within the associated network of self-knowledge or current concerns (cf. Carver & Scheier, 1982; Klinger, 1975). And one central means of validating new self-conceptions or self-hypotheses is through interpersonal confirmation. It is seldom sufficient to introduce an alternative self-conception. Others (specific or generalized) must legitimate and validate this self-conception as real or possible for it to become a stable component of the self-system (Rosenberg, 1981).

The most direct way to validate possible selves is by taking direct action to manifest or achieve them, or their antithesis in the case of undesired selves. How one goes about this is determined by the plans and strategies activated or constructed (Cantor & Kihlstrom, 1987; Pervin, 1982), by self-efficacy expectations for achieving particular goals (Bandura, 1986), and by the person's ability to control action with respect to situational opportunities and constraints (Heckhausen & Kuhl, 1985; Kuhl, 1985). Yet direct action is not always possible. Alternatively, one may attempt to symbolize the possible self, to convey to oneself and others that he or she does possess or could achieve the desired self, or not possess the undesired possible self.

Research by Steele (1988) and Wicklund and Gollwitzer (1982), for example, indicates that use of symbols (e.g., wearing crucifixes for a religious self-definition, wearing lab coats by science-oriented students) enables subjects to resolve dissonance and to maintain their self-attitudes and goal-directed motivation in the face of challenge. A more maladaptive example involves evidence that adolescent girls tend to initiate and move to habitual smoking for self-definitional reasons; out of a desire to symbolize a desired possible self derived from a social image – of the independent, glamorous, successful woman of today – or to reduce the possibility of a negative social image – being fat, undesired, and unsuccessful (Gilchrist, Schinke, & Nurius, 1989; Jacobson, 1982).

In summary, self-conceptions of past, present, and possible self constitute latent or potential *resources* for coping and striving. To become an active part of coping or striving *activity*, they must be mobilized. They are pressed into service through elicitation and fortified in their believability or viability through validation. And this mobilization is a social phenomenon – either explicitly through social interactions and reflected appraisals or implicitly through the socially impregnated "dialogues" we entertain in our own minds. (For a more fully developed discussion of latent and active components see Gore, 1985.)

Striving and coping consequences

A sense of competence and related motivational constructs like perceived self-efficacy, personal control, positive expectancies, ego strength, hardiness, and willpower have all been shown to have a positive impact on performance, coping, and well-being, and even on physical health (Lazarus & Folkman, 1984; Marlatt & Gordon, 1985; Salovey & Rodin, 1985; Taylor & Brown, 1988). The underlying premise of this chapter is that their common effect derives from one important element. They all involve the ability to create a bridge of self-representations between one's current self and one's desired or hoped-for self as well as one's feared selves. This is consistent with research that emotional support from others appears to exercise its remediating influence (e.g., mitigating depression) indirectly through promoting self-esteem and a sense of mastery (Pearlin, Lieberman, Menaghan, & Mullan, 1981). And the ability to imagine oneself in the end state facilitates construction of the self at subgoals and substages, thus promoting agentic and effective instrumental behavior. In this way, possible selves function as the proximate mediators of long-term motivation, as well as of ongoing coping and striving processes.

The question of realism, of the importance of actual probability of possible selves, has not yet been adequately addressed. The clinical literature emphasizes the importance of the ability to *generate* alternatives (e.g., Meichenbaum, 1977; Spivack, Platt, & Shure, 1976) and to weigh their relative utility for a particular goal or situation. Also evident have been the constraining effects of social and cultural forces in producing premature closure of potential role identities and pursuits. For example, females tend to have fewer and more tentative possible self-conceptions, a tendency that becomes increasingly marked as the world of work and childbearing enter adolescents' lives (e.g., Rosenberg, 1985; Thoits, 1986). At latter phases of life, options for and conceived by elders become increasingly more narrow and less positive (Rodin & Langer, 1980). And, of course, the influence of ethnicity, race, and culture are often enormous and all too often overlooked (cf. McGuire & McGuire, 1988).

It may be that possible selves serve a variety of functions. In some cases they are the embryonic forms of what will develop into well-elaborated self-schemata (e.g., Chris Evert's childhood images of becoming a great tennis player). In other cases they may serve as personally important symbols of possibility and sources of motivation, even if judged as unrealistic or inappropriate by the outside world (e.g., the vision of becoming a physician by the youth who is a third-generation welfare recipient). In some cases they may serve balancing functions between positive and negative possibility (e.g., the battered wife having conceptions of self as becoming more physically and psychologically injured *and* as becoming economically independent and free of her abusive relationship); the two sets combine the emotional motivation to change and the means–ends guides for how to accomplish the change. Finally, the development of possible selves constitutes an important training ground of sorts – for exercising one's creative capacity to see and generate possibility, for "trying on" various roles and attributes and testing the social waters for reaction. The ability to conceive alternatives and to flexibly adapt are hallmark contributors to health and well-being, and possible selves can be seen as a critical resource in these efforts.

In summary, the social support model in Figure 2 suggests that it is not social ties or activity per se that are health protective, but how these are perceived and interpreted. What I have suggested here is that general social support models, even those attentive to the importance of support appraisals, typically do not go far enough toward specifying components of the self-system that are brought into play in these appraisal and subsequent coping and striving processes.

Discussion

This exploration of possible selves and social support appraisals demonstrates their potential for reducing psychological and health vulnerability as well as for enhancing social functioning and well-being. As cognitive appraisals of self are increasingly implicated as a key mediating factor in the coping process, so are they increasingly recognized as important for prevention and relapse prevention (Heller & Swindle, 1983). It is becoming evident that approaches involving skills training and social support interventions that fail to attend to commensurate change in underlying belief systems about oneself and one's future often are not sufficient to sustain enduring change (Glass & Arnkoff, 1982; Schwartz & Gottman, 1976).

To prevent outcomes such as dropping out of high school, it is generally agreed that a high-risk student must both value this end state and believe she or he is capable of attaining it. In addition, there is some evidence that the presence of negative possible selves to avoid (e.g., being trapped in dead-end jobs due to dropping out) can provide additional motivational force *if* they are paired or balanced with positive possible selves in the same domain (Oyserman & Markus, 1988). In addition, the ability to *generate* new possible selves and relationships with family members, teachers, or friends who might help to elicit, validate, and strengthen more adaptive alternatives also appears to be a differentiating factor with respect to coping and striving (Markus, Cross, & Wurf, 1990; Nurius & Dunn, 1988).

Thus, within interventions designed to promote coping, striving, and prevention, the role of possible selves – their creation, elaboration, balance, and reinforcement – holds promise. To be functionally relevant, however, these possible selves must be recruited into the working self-concept that is salient within the relevant social circumstances. Thus, as part of a broader self-management plan, for example, individuals would be aided best by learning to use social exposure and experiences strategically to (1) develop new self-schemata, (2) activate or explicitly make salient these developing conceptions of possibility, both hoped for and feared, and (3) seek validation and reinforcing input from their social environment. (For a more detailed discussion of schema-based self-concept change, see Winfrey & Goldfried, 1986.)

To be sure, a great many features of the very complex affect-cognition-behavior environment interplay have not been addressed in detail here. One example of particular relevance to this volume is the multiplicity of identities – present and potential – and its relation to well-being. As a reflection of social ties and opportunities that the individual has had, does have, or is expected to possess in the future, multiplicity is generally regarded as a positive indicator. Linville (1987), for example, has suggested that the more complex (defined in terms of independence of self-representations) one's system of "self-aspects," the less extreme are his or her swings in affect and self-appraisal, the less deflatable is one's self-esteem, and the less vulnerable one is to the myopia, uncertainty, and spillover (from one self-domain to another) effects of negative input or emotion.

Thoits (1983, 1986) pursued the question of multiplicity with greater emphasis on the social etiology and overlap of one's self-conceptions (Stryker & Serpe, 1982). She found that effects of identity gain or loss are conditional upon one's relative degree of social isolation or integration and upon the degree of overlap of one's social relationships and their resultant role identities. The more socially integrated individual benefited more from identity gain and suffered more from identity loss. Not surprisingly, degree of investment in (commitment to) the identities was positively associated with degree of impact, both the cost of loss and the enhancement of gain.

In addition to the number of distinct self-conceptions and the degree of overlap or multiplexity across social roles and ties, several have argued for the importance of a time dimension in considering the issue of multiplicity of identities (Lens, 1987; Nuttin, 1984; Stryker, chapter 1 in this volume). As the cognitive representations of and scaffolds for a different or changing self, possible selves offer a structural link among the reciprocal influences of social structure, the self-concept, and motivated strategies. That is, as do current social and role identities, identities reflecting conceptions of self in the future would be expected to motivate interactional performance whose function it is to reaffirm through interaction that one is – or in the case of aversive possibility, is not – the kind of person defined by the identities (Stryker, 1987).

The preponderance of attention to future identities has emphasized positive or appropriate goals such as ideal or ought selves. Although consistent with fundamental motives for self-enhancement, this emphasis may also reflect the achievement, goal-striving orientation of mainstream thought. It may well be that one is not likely to project a future self in negative terms, except in the sense of anticipating what one does not wish to become. Yet in many cases, dreaded or undesirable possible selves are not only expected but also highly likely possible selves (e.g., the anticipated effects of aging, illness, deprivation, or isolation).

More specifically, the potentially powerful influence of negative conceptions and expectations for one's future self has been well documented in the form of depression, learned helplessness, self-handicapping, withdrawal, alcohol or drug misuse, and related maladaptive responses. We do indeed project negative possibilities for the self, and we spend a considerable amount of time contemplating these possibilities – worrying about them, defending against them, and planning and rehearsing strategies (cf. Serpe, chapter 3 in this volume). And, given that our social environment often does not offer balanced models (e.g., neglected or abused children rarely have good parenting models available in their immediate social networks), there is no reason to assume possible selves would necessarily be bipolar in nature.

In some instances, we are suddenly thrust into new identities for which we have little or no prior self-conceptualization, such as identities of spinal cord injury, infertility, or young widowhood. In contrast, the vast majority of our identities evolve more incrementally through our social relationships and experiences, and through our own cognitive differentiation. Identities, particularly those of greatest personal relevance, are not easily "lost" or "gained." Possible selves expand our time perspective of identities and of the evolving, differentiating nature of the self-concept over time. Within a social information-processing context, possible selves provide one mechanism through which embryonic representations of possibility – both dreaded and desired – make contact with the social world of the present and either languish or thrive. And, like other structures that constitute our "assumptive world," possible selves both exert and reflect social influence.

In closing, it is important to remember the sometimes harsh and disabling effects of the social world, the constraining and disheartening effects of poverty, prejudice, ignorance, and abuse on actual opportunities and on what is perhaps one of the most elemental aspects of the self – that of imagining. To a large extent, the social environment determines the opportunity and support structure for individual adaptation and change, and provides the models, images, and symbols for framing these end states and efforts.

The self-system shapes and personalizes motivation. Yet the social and cultural environment shapes the self, including what conceptions of possibility the person will likely embrace or construct as well as how these conceptions are made salient, affirmed, and elaborated in the context of social transactions. The future challenge is to specify further both the unique and the interactive self and societal factors, as well as the means to marshal these better toward health-protective and health-promotive ends.

References

Alba, J. W., & L. Hasher. 1983. Is memory schematic? *Psychological Bulletin* 93: 207–231.
Alexander, C. N., Jr., & M. G. Wiley. 1980. Situated activity and identity formation. In M. Rosenberg & R. H. Turner (Eds.), *Social psychology: Sociological perspectives* (pp. 269–289). New York: Basic Books.

Bandura, A. 1986. *Social foundations of thought and action: A social cognitive theory.* Englewood Cliffs, NJ: Prentice-Hall.

Block, J. 1981. Some enduring and consequential structures of personality. In A. I. Rubin et al., (Eds.), *Further explorations in personality.* New York: Wiley.

Broadhead, W. E., B. H. Kaplan, S. A. James, E. H. Wagner, V. J. Schoenbach, R. Grimson, S. Heyden, G. Tibblin, & S. H. Gehlbach. 1983. The epidemiologic evidence for a relationship between social support and health. *American Journal of Epidemiology* 117: 521–537.

Cantor, N., & J. Kihlstrom. 1987. *Personality and social intelligence.* Englewood Cliffs, NJ: Prentice-Hall.

Carver, C. S., & M. F. Scheier. 1982. Control theory: A useful conceptual framework for personality, social, clinical, and health psychology. *Psychological Bulletin* 92: 111–135.

Cohen, S., S. L. Syme (Eds.). 1985. *Social support and health.* New York: Academic Press.

Cohen, S., & T. A. Wills. 1985. Stress, social support, and the buffering hypothesis. *Psychological Bulletin* 98: 310–357.

Fischer, C. S., & S. L. Phillips. 1982. Who is alone? Social characteristics of people. In L. A. Peplau & D. Perlman (Eds.), *Loneliness* (pp. 21–40). New York: Wiley.

Gecas, V. 1982. The self-concept. *Annual Review of Sociology* 8: 1–33.

Gilchrist, L. D., S. P. Schinke, & P. S. Nurius. 1989. Reducing onset of habitual smoking among women. *Preventive Medicine* 18: 235–248.

Glass, C. R., & D. B. Arnkoff. 1982. Thinking cognitively: Selected issues in cognitive assessment and therapy. In P. C. Kendall (Ed.), *Advances in cognitive-behavioral research and therapy* (Vol. 1, pp. 35–71). New York: Academic Press.

Gore, S. 1985. Social support and styles of coping with stress. In S. Cohen & S. C. Syme (Eds.), *Social support and health* (pp. 263–278). New York: Academic Press.

Greenwald, A. G., & A. R. Pratkanis. 1984. The self. In R. S. Wyer & T. K. Srull (Eds.), *Handbook of social cognition* (pp. 129–178). Hillsdale, NJ: Erlbaum.

Guidano, V. F. 1987. Principles of lifespan developmental psychopathology. *Complexity of the self* (chapter 11). New York: Guilford Press.

Guidano, V. F., & Liotti, G. 1983. *Cognitive processes and emotional disorders: A structural approach to psychotherapy.* New York: Guilford Press.

Hastie, R. 1981. Schematic principles in human memory. In E. T. Higgins, P. Herman, & M. P. Zanna (Eds.), *Social cognition: The Ontario symposium* (pp. 39–88). Hillsdale, NJ: Erlbaum.

Heckhausen, H., & J. Kuhl. 1985. From wishes to action: The dead ends and short cuts on the long way to action. In M. Frese & J. Sabini (Eds.), *Goal-directed behavior: Psychological theory and research on action* (pp. 133–159). Hillsdale, NJ: Erlbaum.

Heller, K., & R. W. Swindle. 1983. Social networks, perceived social support, and coping with stress. In R. D. Fulner, L. A. Jason, J. N. Moritsugu, & S. S. Farber (Eds.), *Prevention psychology: Theory, research, and practice* (pp. 87–103). New York: Pergamon Press.

Heller, K., R. W. Swindle, & L. Dusenbury. 1986. Component social support processes: Comments and integration. *Journal of Consulting and Clinical Psychology* 54: 466–470.

Higgins, E. T., G. A. King, & G. H. Mavin. 1982. Individual construct accessibility and subjective impressions and recall. *Journal of Personality and Social Psychology* 43: 35–47.

Higgins, E. T., T. Strauman, & R. Klein. 1985. Standards and the process of self-evaluation: Multiple effects from multiple stages. In R. M. Sorrentino & E. T. Higgins (Eds.), *Handbook of motivation and cognition: Foundations of social behavior* (pp. 23–63). New York: Guilford Press.

Jacobson, B. 1982. *The ladykillers: Why smoking is a feminist issue.* New York: Continuum.

Kessler, R. C., & J. D. McLeod. 1985. Social support and mental health in community samples. In S. Cohen & S. L. Syme (Eds.), *Social support and health* (pp. 219–240). New York: Academic Press.

Kessler, R. C., R. H. Price, & C. B. Wortman. 1985. Social factors in psychopathology: Stress, social support, and coping processes. *Annual Review of Psychology* 36: 531–572.

Klinger, E. 1975. Consequences of commitment to and disengagement from incentives. *Psychological Review* 82: 1–25.

Kuhl, J. 1985. Volitional mediators of cognition-behavior consistency: Self-regulatory processes and action versus state orientation. In J. Kuhl & J. Beckmann (Eds.), *Action control: From cognition to behavior* (pp. 101–128). New York: Springer-Verlag.

Lazarus, R. S., & S. Folkman. 1984. Coping and adaptation. In W. D. Gentry (Ed.), *The handbook of behavioral medicine*. New York: Guilford.

Leahy, R. L. (Ed.). 1985. *The development of the self*. New York: Academic Press.

Lens, W. 1987. Future time perspective, motivation, and school performance. In E. DeCorte, J. Lodewijks, R. Parmentier, & P. Span (Eds.), *Learning and instruction: European research in an international context* (Vol. 1, pp. 181–189). Oxford; UK: Pergamon Press.

Linville, P. W. 1987. Self-complexity as a cognitive buffer against stress-related illness and depression. *Journal of Personality and Social Psychology* 52: 663–676.

Marks, S. 1977. Multiple roles and role strain: Some notes on human energy, time, and commitment. *American Sociological Review* 42: 921–936.

Markus, H., S. Cross, & E. Wurf. 1990. *The role of the self-system in competence*. In R. J. Sternberg & J. Kolligian (Ed.), *Competence considered* (pp. 205–225). New Haven, CT: Yale University Press.

Markus, H., & Kunda, Z. 1986. Stability and malleability of the self-concept. *Journal of Personality and Social Psychology* 51: 858–866.

Markus, H., & P. S. Nurius. 1986. Possible selves. *American Psychologist* 41: 954–969.

Markus, H., J. Smith, & R. L. Moreland. 1985. Role of the self-concept in the perception of others. *Journal of Personality and Social Psychology* 49: 1,494–1,512.

Marlatt, G. A., & J. R. Gordon. 1985. *Relapse prevention*. New York: Guilford Press.

McCrae, R. R., & P. T. Costa. 1988. Age, personality, and the self-concept. *Journal of Gerontology* 43: S177–185.

McGuire, W. J., & C. V. McGuire. 1981. The spontaneous self-concept as affected by personal distinctiveness. In M. D. Lynch, A. Norem-Hebeisen, & K. Gergen (Eds.), *Self-concept: Advances in theory and research* (pp. 147–171). Cambridge, MA: Ballinger.

McGuire, W. J., & C. V. McGuire. 1988. Content and process in the experience of self. *Advances in Experimental Social Psychology* 21: 97–144.

Mead, G. H. 1934. *Mind, self, and society*. Chicago: University of Chicago Press.

Meichenbaum, D. 1977. *Cognitive behavior modification: An integrated approach*. New York: Plenum.

Nurius, P. S. 1986. A reappraisal of the self-concept and implications for counseling. *Journal of Counseling Psychology* 33: 429–438.

Nurius, P. S., & B. Dunn. 1988. *Possible selves, coping, and adaptation among street youth*. Unpublished manuscript, University of Washington, Seattle.

Nurius, P. S., M. Lovell, & M. Edgar. 1988. Self-appraisals of abusive parents: A contextual approach to study and treatment. *Journal of Interpersonal Violence* 3: 458–470.

Nurius, P. S., & H. Markus. 1990. Situational variability in the self-concept: Appraisals, expectancies, and asymmetries. *Journal of Social and Clinical Psychology* 7: 316–333.

Nuttin, J. 1984. *Motivation, planning, and action*. Hillsdale, NJ: Erlbaum.

Oyserman, D., & H. Markus. 1988. *Possible selves and delinquency*. Unpublished manuscript, University of Michigan, Ann Arbor.

Pearlin, L. I., M. A. Lieberman, E. G. Menaghan, & J. T. Mullan. 1981. The stress process. *Journal of Health and Social Behavior* 22: 337–356.

Pervin, L. A. 1982. The stasis and flow of behavior: Toward a theory of goals. *Nebraska Symposium on Motivation* (pp. 1–53). Lincoln: University of Nebraska Press.

Potts, M. K. 1987. *The effects of role multiplicity on health status, illness rates, and illness behavior in men and women: A test of the scarcity and expansion hypothesis.* Unpublished doctoral dissertation, Purdue University, West Lafayette, IN.

Rodin, J., & E. Langer. 1980. Aging labels: The decline of control and the fall of self-esteem. *Journal of Social Issues* 36(2): 12–29.

Rosenberg, M. 1979. *Conceiving the self.* New York: Basic Books.

Rosenberg, M. 1981. The self-concept: Social product and social force. In M. Rosenberg & R. H. Turner (Eds.), *Social psychology: Sociological perspectives* (pp. 593–624). New York: Basic Books.

Rosenberg, M. 1985. Self-concept and psychological well-being in adolescence. In R. L. Leahy (Ed.), *The development of the self* (pp. 205–246). New York: Academic Press.

Russo, N. 1985. Sex-role stereotyping, socialization, and sexism. In A. Sargent (Ed.), *Beyond sex roles*. St. Paul: West Publishing.

Salovey, P., & J. Rodin, 1985. Cognitions about the self: Connecting feeling states and social behavior. In P. Shaver (Ed.), *Self, situation and social behavior: Vol. 6. Review of personality and social psychology* (pp. 143–166). Beverly Hills, CA: Sage.

Schwartz, R. M., & J. M. Gottman. 1976. Toward a task analysis of assertive behavior. *Journal of Consulting and Clinical Psychology* 44: 910–920.

Shrauger, J. S., & T. J. Schoeneman. 1979. Symbolic interactionist view of self-concept: Through the looking glass darkly. *Psychological Bulletin* 86: 549–573.

Sieber, S. D. 1974. Toward a theory of role accumulation. *American Sociological Review* 39: 567–578.

Spivack, G., J. J. Platt, & M. B. Shure. 1976. *The problem-solving approach to adjustment.* San Francisco: Jossey-Bass

Steele, C. M. 1988. The psychology of self-affirmation: Sustaining the integrity of the self. In L. Berkowitz (Ed.), *Advances in experimental social psychology* (Vol. 20, pp. 261–302). New York: Academic Press.

Stryker, S. 1980. *Symbolic interactionism: A social structural version.* Palo Alto, CA: Benjamin-Cummings.

Stryker, S. 1987. Identity theory: Developments and extensions. In K. Yardley & J. Honess (Eds.), *Self and identity: Psychosocial perspectives* (pp. 89–104). Chichester, UK: Wiley.

Stryker, S., & R. T. Serpe. 1982. Commitment, identity salience, and role behavior. In W. Ickes & E. S. Knowles (Eds.), *Personality, roles, and social behavior* (pp. 199–218). New York: Springer-Verlag.

Taylor, S. E., & J. D. Brown. 1988. Illusion and well-being: A social psychological perspective on mental health. *Psychological Bulletin* 103: 193–210.

Thoits, P. A. 1983. Multiple identities and psychological well-being: A reformulation and test of the social isolation hypothesis. *American Sociological Review* 48: 174–187.

Thoits, P. A. 1985. Social support and psychological well-being: Theoretical possibilities. In I. G. Sarason & B. R. Sarason (Eds.), *Social support: Theory, research, and applications* (pp. 51–72). The Hague, The Netherlands: Martinus Nijhoff.

Thoits, P. A. 1986. Social support as coping assistance. *Journal of Consulting and Clinical Psychology* 54: 416–423.

Turner, R. J. 1983. Direct, indirect, and moderating effects of social support on psychological distress and associated conditions. In H. B. Kaplan (Ed.), *Psychological stress: Trends in theory and research*. New York: Academic Press.

Verbrugge, L. 1983. Multiple roles and physical health of women and men. *Journal of Health and Social Behavior* 24: 16–30.

Weinraub, M., & L. Brown, 1983. The development of sex-role stereotypes in children: The crushing realities. In V. Franks & E. Rothblum (Eds.), *The stereotyping of women: Its effects on mental health* (Vol. 5, pp. 30–58). New York: Springer-Verlag.

Wicklund, R. A., & P. M. Gollwitzer. 1982. *Symbolic self completion*. Hillsdale, NJ: Erlbaum.

Winfrey, L. P. L., & M. R. Goldfried. 1986. Information processing and the human change process. In R. E. Ingram (Ed.), *Information processing approaches to clinical psychology* (pp. 241–258). New York: Academic Press.

Zurcher, L. A. 1977. *The mutable self: A self-concept for social change*. Beverly Hills, CA: Sage.

12 Is the road to helping paved with good intentions? Or inertia?

Jane Allyn Piliavin

With the current emphasis within psychological social psychology on cognitive processes, and within sociological social psychology on the self, social psychology has largely ignored the concept of habit. Identity theorists (Burke, this volume; Burke & Tully, 1981; McCall & Simmons, 1978; Stryker, 1980, this volume; Turner, 1978; Turner & Billings, this volume) have used only the concepts of role-identity salience, role-person merger, and the like, which suggest conscious thought in relationship to action. The popular psychological theory of reasoned action (Fishbein & Ajzen, 1975; Ajzen & Fishbein, 1980) includes only attitudes, subjective norms, and intentions as predictors of behavior. Attribution theory (Kelley, 1967; Jones and Davis, 1965; Weiner, Russell, & Lerman, 1978) until very recently has assumed a very active, analytic "lay scientist" model of social information processing and action.

Habit as a concept was popular among the early theorists in sociology but fell out of favor with the rise of Watsonian behaviorism in psychology (Camic, 1986). I will use habit here to mean actions that "are relatively unmotivated" (Giddens, 1979: 218), actions in which "means-ends relations...are [from the actor's standpoint] not subject to argument" (Hartmann, 1939: 91). Following Camic (1986: 1,044) "the term 'habit' generally denominates a more-or-less self-actuating disposition or tendency to engage in a previously adopted or acquired form of action." I am not suggesting that such behavior is mechanical or lacking in meaning, in the sense used by symbolic interactionists. Rather, Camic (1986: 1,047) points out that "habitual action does exhibit a 'meaningful character' – a meaningful character either taken for granted by the actor or lodged in the unconscious."

All habits initially begin when an actor consciously chooses to engage in the behavior, carefully weighing its costs and benefits. Once established, however, the only "decision" in which the actor is involved has to do with the timing of the action. And that timing is often also programmed in some

259

way. If it is Sunday morning, my husband plays tennis; if it is Friday night, he plays poker. He no longer has to decide whether or not he wants to engage in these activities; he long ago performed those mental calculations and decided that the benefits outweigh the costs. The timing, too, is now rather automated. This is not meant to suggest that habits, once established, can never be changed. It is probably the case that the potential for change exists when the actor is forced into a new cost-reward calculation, such as is occasioned for smokers every time there is a new report from the surgeon general.

Probably the best known sociological theorist who dealt with habit extensively was Emile Durkheim (1905–1906: 152), who wrote, "it is not enough to direct our attention to the superficial portion of our consciousness, for the sentiments, the ideas which come to the surface are not, by far, those which have the most influence on our conduct. What must be reached are the habits...these are the real forces which govern us." Max Weber also discussed habit, going beyond Durkheim to suggest that "customs are frequently transferred into binding norms....The mere fact of the regular recurrence of certain events somehow confers on them the dignity of oughtness....What were originally plain habits of conduct owing to psychological disposition, come later to be experienced as binding" (as quoted in Camic, 1986: 1,059). Although he was discussing an institutional concept of habit, Weber also referred to "the inertia of the habitual," suggesting that to continue along as one has always done was a strong force against cultural innovations.

But if habits are meaningful and can come to be experienced as binding, how are they related to identities, which can be described in similar terms? We might consider them as akin to the "scripted behavior" discussed by Abelson (1976) or to "mindlessness" as explored by Langer (1978). As such, habits can be very closely related to identities or completely divorced from them. Abelson's favorite example of a "script" is the "restaurant script." He claims that most adults have a well-developed set of verbal and behavioral responses that they carry out sequentially when going to a restaurant. I doubt very much, however, that many people attach an "identity" to their restaurant-going activities. On the other hand, parents frequently engage in bedtime rituals with their children that are very "scripted." I suspect that these habitual behaviors are very closely tied to parental identities. For any given habit, then, I am suggesting that the ties to the actor's identities are not knowable a priori.

Two recent analyses by Charng, Piliavin, and Callero (1988) and Piliavin and Callero (1991) have demonstrated that a measure of the strength of the blood donation habit predicts future donation history over and above the effects of intentions or role-identities. Other recent research (Bagozzi, 1981; Bentler & Speckart, 1979, 1981; Fredricks & Dossett, 1983; Godin, Valois, Shephard, & Desharnais, 1987; Manstead, Proffitt, & Smart, 1983; Mittall, 1988) has also demonstrated the importance of habit for the prediction of continuation in a variety of activities.

In an attempt to revitalize habit as a theoretically important determinant of behavior, I here introduce the concept of *inertia*. I see inertia as the *force* in the phrase "force of habit." I suggest that in the absence of other contradictory motivations, or even sometimes in opposition to them, we have a strong tendency just to keep doing what we have been doing. I am, then, using the concept of inertia in a manner analogous to the original physics definition, "that property of matter by which it retains its state of rest or of uniform rectilinear motion so long as it is not acted upon by an external force" (*American College Dictionary*, 1952). Some might suggest that this concept applies to physical but not to mental energy. For heuristic purposes, I would prefer not to reintroduce the mind–body dichotomy. I will use the concept of inertia to represent the energy that inheres in habit. To those who doubt the inherent force in habit, I propose that you think of the last time you intended to do an errand on the way home that would take you out of your normal route, but then just stopped thinking about it for a moment.

The concept of inertia has not been used much in the social science literature. Hannan and Freeman (1984), in an influential paper, discussed structural inertia and organizational change. They suggest that structural characteristics such as age, size, and complexity of an organization as well as features of its environment are the forces leading to slowness to change. This macrolevel use of the term has also been employed in the area of the sociology of development and in political sociology (see, e.g., DeJong & VanDonge, 1983; Franklin & Mackie, 1983). A popular model of migration employs the concept of cumulative inertia (Huff & Clark, 1978; Myers, McGinnis, & Masnick, 1967), which means that the longer one has lived in a place the less likely one is to move, excluding all other relevant variables.

"Brand choice inertia" has been used as an explanation for longer than expected runs of buying one of a set of relatively interchangeable brands in a competitive market (Jeuland, 1979). Pitz (1969; Geller & Pitz, 1968) reports an "inertia effect" involving resistance to changing one's estimates of the likelihood of a particular event. These researchers find that there is more inertia following the occurrence of *predicted* events than unpredicted events. That is, information consistent with a hypothesis to which one has committed oneself carries more weight than does inconsistent information.

Havassy and Tschann (1983) used the term *inertia* to reflect the continuation of past behavior into a situation with potential for change. In an experimental study of a methadone treatment program, they found that baseline illicit opiate use and level of methadone dose at entry remained the strongest predictors of illicit use during the experiment.

The immediate impetus to the present chapter, however, came from a paper on fertility. In this study, two conditions – one of "rest" and one of "motion" – were compared, a strategy that has not been used explicitly in any other research. In two separate studies, Davidson and Beach (1981) found that among married couples, prediction of deviations from the status quo resulted in a higher proportion of prediction errors than prediction of nondeviation. That is, the accuracy of predictions that couples would decide to *become* pregnant was lower than the accuracy of predictions that couples would decide not to become pregnant. The authors suggest that a stronger motivational force is required to compel a person to elect a change from the status quo than is required to *maintain* the status quo. They (1981: 485) suggest that "it would be of value to extend the examination of the hypothesis using...other content areas."

Study one

All of my tests of the concept of habit-based inertia use data on blood donation. In the first study, I examine its impact on the relationship between stated intentions and actual donation behavior in two samples of blood donors: an American sample and a Polish sample. These samples were obtained in quite different ways, although both are quite representative of their respective populations. The American donors represent a stratified random sample of donors taken from the records of three blood donation centers in the state of Wisconsin and one in Iowa. The sample was stratified by number of prior donations. The selected donors were sent a questionnaire in the mail, and their donation records were followed for 6 months. The return rate was 80%. All donors can be viewed as altruistic, since they receive no compensation for their donations.

The Polish donors were obtained at the time of a donation at the central blood collection facility in Warsaw, Poland. They were interviewed face-to-face, usually immediately after donation, and usually in the donation center. The interview schedule was a translation of the questionnaire used in the first study. The Polish donors can also be viewed as altruistic, since they did not receive money for their donation.[1]

In both samples there is a very strong relationship between stated intentions and actual donation. Using a measure of the probability of giving blood within the next 6 months (on a scale from 1, very likely, to 7, very unlikely), 67.5% of U.S. donors saying "very likely" ($N = 538$) gave in that time period, whereas among those giving any other answer ($N = 110$), only 45.5% gave. The chi-square for this relationship is 19.15 ($p < .001$), and only 34.5% of donors are misclassified by using dichotomized intention to predict behavior. In the Polish sample, the relationship is even stronger: 70.7% of those saying "very likely" ($N = 181$) actually gave, whereas only 19.8% of those checking any other response ($N = 48$) did so. (Chi-square $= 42.63$; $p < .001$; only 27% of donors are misclassified.)

In the U.S. sample, a smaller proportion of those who said it was "very likely" that they would give failed to give, and a higher proportion of those who were less certain actually gave than one would expect by chance (chi-square $= 4.50$, $p < .05$). In Poland, this pattern is reversed. Only 14.5% of the errors consist of "not certains" who give, although they make up 21% of the sample of donors. This difference is not significant.

The inertia hypothesis asserts that the more habitual a particular course of action has become, the less conscious motivation it will require to engage in that action. By analogy to physical energy, we can compare habit to the speed at which a vehicle is rolling and compare intention to the strength of a push that is given to it. Just as a smaller push is required to move something a certain distance if it is already rolling than if you have to get it started, we propose that a less strong intention is needed to lead to continued donation among habitual donors than among "rookies."

For donors of all levels of experience, we expect intentions to predict behavior. However, for those who say it is "very likely" that they will give, we would expect more failures to follow the intention among those for whom the actions are not yet habitual. Similarly, among those donors who do *not* say that it is "very likely" that they will give again, repeat donors should be more likely to give than should first-time or early-career donors, because to give is, for them, to just keep doing what they are doing. There is thus a clear prediction regarding the relative number of errors of "commission" and of "omission" to be expected as one moves from the status of a "rookie" donor to that of an "old hand". Relatively more of the errors should be of omission – not giving when predicted to do so – among rookies, and relatively more should be of commission – giving when predicted not to – among long-term donors.

Table 1 gives the number and percentage of donors of various categories of past donation history who gave within a specified time period in the U.S. and Polish samples. For both U.S. and Polish donors, data are presented showing behavior for a 6-month period, and behavior over a year is presented for the Polish donors. It is clear that performing the act of

Table 1. *Number and percentage of donors giving within a specified time period, among groups defined by past donation history*

Donors	U.S., 6 months		Poland, 6 months		Poland, 1 year	
	Gave	Didn't give	Gave	Didn't give	Gave	Didn't give
Rookies	15 (43%)	20 (57%)				
2-timers[a]	46 (57%)	35 (43%)	16 (31%)	36 (69%)	19 (37%)	32 (63%)
3–4-timers	63 (58%)	45 (42%)				
5–8-timers	79 (58%)	57 (42%)	17 (52%)	16 (48%)	20 (61%)	13 (39%)
9–16-timers	69 (61%)	45 (39%)	37 (67%)	18 (33%)	41 (74%)	14 (26%)
17+-timers	122 (81%)	28 (19%)	67 (76%)	21 (24%)	72 (82%)	16 (18%)

[a] Because of small sample size, one- through four-time donors in Poland are combined.

donation becomes more likely the more times one has done so in the past. And once a person has given blood at least five times in either the U.S. or the Polish system, it is more likely than not that the donor will give again within 6 months.

There is an interesting difference between the countries in the speed with which a donor becomes behaviorally committed, as suggested by these data.[3] Two- to four-time donors in the U.S. system already resemble those in the 5–8-time category – 57% to 58% in all three groups returned within 6 months. In the Polish sample it appears that it may take more donations to lead to commitment; of the entire group of rookies to 4-time donors, only 31% return within 6 months. Once the 5–8 donations point has been reached, however, donors in the two countries do not differ in their likelihood of return.

Inertia in relationship to intentions

These results suggest that with an increasing number of prior donations, something is changing with regard to the continued likelihood of giving again. Some form of inertia *not* to give is being overcome, and a habit of giving is being established. According to my hypothesis, the relationship between intention and donation should take a somewhat different shape as we move from the uncommitted donors (rookies in the U.S., 1–4-timers in Poland) to the committed donors (five or more donations in both countries, possibly 2–4-timers in the U.S.). Whereas prediction of donation from intention should be strong within all categories of donors, the distribution of errors of prediction should be different for the committed as compared to the uncommitted donors. Among early career, uncommitted donors there should be more errors of *omission*, and among late-career, committed donors there should be more errors of *commission*.

The simplest test of this prediction is to examine the difference in the percentage of errors between those predicted to give and those predicted not to give at each level of donation experience. That is, I will divide the donors by level of past experience (our measure of habit) and compare the proportion who gave after expressing a weak intention (errors of commission) with the proportion who did not give after expressing a strong intention (errors of omission). The inertia hypothesis suggests that the first proportion should be greater than the second among committed donors, and the reverse among early career donors.

In Table 2 I present the number and percentage of donors giving again, categorized by their number of past donations and their expressed intention to give again. In the United States the followup period was 6 months; in Poland we have used two lengths of followup, 6 months and 1 year.[2] Note that in all of the groups, with the single exception of those in the United States with 3–4 prior donations, intentions significantly predict donation. This is indicated in the table in the row titled "Chi-square (overall)." The table also presents results for the test just discussed – a critical ratio for the difference between the proportions of errors of omission and errors of commission.

Although not all of these tests show significant differences, all of the differences are in the direction predicted by the inertia hypothesis. That is, among the uncommitted donors, those at the top of the table, there are more errors of omission than of commission. The least committed donors, the 1–4 donation Poles, show the largest differences, as we might expect. Among the more committed, the 3–4 donation Americans and all of the 5+ donation groups, there are consistently more errors of commission than of omission. In three of the seven outcomes, the differences are significant, and in one, the difference reaches the .10 level (all tests are one-tailed).

Clearly the results just presented could also be described as reflecting the operation of a second variable in a multiple regression, once the first is controlled. When such a regression is run, habit as indexed by past donations makes a significant additional contribution to the prediction of return donation in both countries. This fact does not speak to the mechanism by which it occurs. For such an explanation, I refer you to a comparison of the 6-month and 1-year data in the Polish sample, which represent the same individuals over time. Note that there is essentially no difference between the 6-month and 1-year data among the rookie–4 donation group

Table 2. *Predicting future donations based on expressed intentions: U.S. data and Polish sample for specified time period (predictor is estimated likelihood of donation)*

Donors and predictor	U.S., 6 months		Poland, 6 months		Poland, 1 year	
	Didn't give	Gave	Didn't give	Gave	Didn't give	Gave
1–2 priors[a]						
Giving less than very likely	24	13	23	3	20	4
	(64.9)	(35.1)	(88.5)	(11.5)	(83.3)	(16.7)
Giving very likely	31	48	13	13	13	15
	(39.2)	(60.8)	(50.0)	(50.0)	(46.4)	(53.6)
Chi-square (overall), *p*	5.65 < .05		7.31 < .01		6.08 < .05	
CR[b], diff. in prop., *p*	<1, n.s.[c]		2.25 < .01		1.54 < .10	
3–4 priors						
Giving less than very likely	11	13				
	(45.8)	(54.2)				
Giving very likely	34	50				
	(40.5)	(59.5)				
Chi-square (overall), *p*	<1, n.s.					
CR, diff. in prop., *p*	<1, n.s.					
5+ priors						
Giving less than very likely	24	24	16	6	14	16
	(50.0)	(50.0)	(72.7)	(27.3)	(46.7)	(53.3)
Giving very likely	106	246	39	115	29	117
	(30.1)	(69.9)	(25.3)	(74.7)	(19.9)	(80.1)
Chi-square (overall), *p*	6.74 < .01		17.98 < .001		8.29 < .01	
CR, diff in prop., *p*	2.27 < .05		<1, n.s.		3.31 < .01	

[a] One- through four-time donors among the Polish sample.
[b] CR = critical ratio
[c] n.s. = not significant

of donors. Nineteen percent of the errors of prediction among these donors are errors of commission over the 6-month period; this increases only to 24% over 1 year. This is a 20% increase. However, among "committed" donors, the proportion more than doubles, from .125 to .35. These are essentially the same donors over time. What this appears to reflect is the continued operation of an inertial force; the longer the time period, the more likely it is that the old habit will assert itself, over and above the less than total expressed intention to give.

It is possible that stronger recruitment attempts may have been applied during the interim period to the more experienced as compared to the less experienced donors. It is also possible that the *intention* may have changed in the interim period – toward non-donation for rookies and toward donation for the more experienced donors. The obtained results would then simply reflect those changed intentions, not inertia based on habit. There is no way to check either of these possibilities. The potential utility of the concept of inertia for the understanding of behavior that deviates from stated intentions is, however, at least suggested by this analysis.

Inertia in relationship to role-identity

Charng, Piliavin, and Callero (1988) have recently suggested that quite stable intentions can be based on developed role-identities. Less change in role-identities than in intentions would be expected over a 6-month or 1-year period, since role-identities are locked into an entire self-structure and set of social relationships. And we certainly expect blood donation behavior to follow from a developed role-identity, just as we do from an expressed intention. This has been demonstrated by Callero (1985) and by Piliavin and Callero (1991).

The inertia hypothesis would also suggest that as the donor moves from an initial donation through a donation "career" – as habit begins to develop – errors in predicting blood donation from expressed role-identities will follow a similar pattern. That is, among early-career donors, I would expect the ratio of errors of commission to errors of omission to be less than among late-career donors. In this case, an error of commission consists of an individual with a low score on a measure of role-person merger[4] making a donation, whereas an error of omission is the failure of a donor with a high score to make a donation. For the purpose of this analysis, we have used donors in the upper and lower thirds of the distribution on this measure in each of the two countries.

There is, overall, a highly significant relationship between scores on the role-person merger measure and donation. Among American donors in the lower third of the sample on this scale, 54.6% gave blood within the next 6 months, whereas 68.9% of donors in the upper third of the distribution did so. This difference yields a chi-square of 8.81, significant at $p < .01$. Among Polish donors, 37.3% of those in the lower third of the distribution gave blood within the next 6 months, whereas 77.2% of those in the upper third did so. This yields a chi-square of 22.46, significant at $p < .001$.

Results relevant to the prediction derived from the inertia hypothesis are shown in Table 3. First note that in all but the U.S. 3–4 donations group, role-person merger does indeed tend to predict continued donation, at $p = .10$ or better. Prediction is confirmed more strongly in the Polish data set

Table 3. *Predicting future donations based on role-person merger: U.S. and Polish samples for specified time period*

Donors and predictor	U.S., 6 months		Poland, 6 months		Poland, 1 year	
	Didn't give	Gave	Didn't give	Gave	Didn't give	Gave
1–2 priors[a]						
Merger, lowest third	27	17	20	6	19	7
	(61.4)	(38.6)	(76.9)	(23.1)	(73.1)	(26.9)
Merger, highest third	10	17	2	6	1	7
	(37.0)	(63.0)	(25.0)	(75.0)	(12.5)	(87.5)
Chi-square, p	5.33 < .10		8.69 < .05		10.59 < .01	
CR, diff. in prop., p	<1, n.s.		<1, n.s.		<1, n.s.	
3–4 priors						
Merger, lowest third	16	23				
	(41.0)	(59.0)				
Merger, highest third	15	23				
	(39.5)	(60.5)				
Chi-square, p	<1, n.s.					
CR, diff. in prop., p	1.22, n.s.					
5+ priors						
Merger, lowest third	46	67	17	16	15	18
	(40.7)	(59.3)	(51.5)	(48.5)	(45.5)	(54.5)
Merger, highest third	43	106	16	55	14	57
	(27.9)	(72.1)	(22.5)	(77.5)	(19.7)	(80.3)
Chi-square, p	5.23 < .10		8.96 < .05		10.30 < .01	
CR, diff. in prop., p	3.92 < .001		2.22 < .01		2.97 < .001	

[a] One- through four-time donors among the Polish sample.

(always at .05 or higher), and the significance level of the relationship increases as the length of time increases. Table 3 also indicates that there are no significant differences in the proportion of errors of omission and of commission among the early-career donors. That is, using role-person merger as the basis for prediction, we find no evidence for the operation of "resting" inertia here. The proportions giving when predicted not to give are very similar to the proportions not giving when they were predicted to give.

There is some evidence for "moving" inertia among the 3–4 donation donors in the U.S. sample; 59% of those predicted *not* to give – those who are low on role-person merger – gave, whereas only 39.5% of those predicted to give failed to do so. This difference is not significant. How-ever, among all groups of 5+ donation donors, U.S. and Polish, we find a significantly higher proportion of errors of commission as compared to errors of omission. Among the Polish donors tracked for a year, the difference is very large: 54.5% vs. 19.7%.

Study two

In the spring of 1984, roughly 1,800 donors giving in one of six American Red Cross regions in the South and Midwest of the United States were asked to fill out before-and-after donation questionnaires. The questionnaires included measures of the intention to continue donating, and the donors' records were followed for the next 6 months. Somewhat over half of these donors were giving at mobile collection sites, and the other half were giving at walk-in centers like those at which the donors in the research just discussed gave.

The distinction between these settings is that a walk-in center provides constant access; a motivated (or habit-driven) donor is able to act on his or her inclinations to give at almost any time except Sundays and holidays. Mobile collections, on the other hand, are set up in small towns, at work places, or at schools on an intermittent schedule. The most common interval is every 3 to 4 months. All of the mobile collection donors in our sample would have had at least one more opportunity to donate in the next 6 months. Another difference between the two settings is that recruitment efforts before mobile drives are frequently intense. Because the occasion for donation is only periodic, those charged with recruitment make a concerted effort to involve all potential donors at that occasion. If that occasion is missed, however, the donor is free of pressure for the next interval before the bloodmobile returns.

What would the inertia hypothesis suggest about the differences we might expect in this situation? First, it is clearly easier to act on an intention at a walk-in center, but it is also easier to get "roped in" to going if one doesn't really want to. With mobile collections, it is easier to *avoid* donation, by coming up with one excuse for one day. Thus it should be harder to act *positively* on an intention, but also easier *not* to act when one has no intention. Thus one clear prediction would be for relatively fewer errors of commission among early-career donors at mobile sites than at fixed centers.

With regard to late-career donors, the expectation is, I think, different. A well-developed habit can be attuned to periodicities. The donor who gives at a center cannot give more often than every 8 weeks. Yet that regularity of donation is maintained, often by writing the date of eligibility on a calendar. An habitual donor who must give at mobile sites is very

Table 4. *Predicting donation on the basis of expressed likelihood of return, 1984 U.S. sample for a six-month time period*

Donors and predictor	Fixed sites		Mobile sites	
	Didn't give	Gave	Didn't give	Gave
0–1 priors				
Return less than very likely	13	7	45	23
	(65.0)	(35.0)	(66.2)	(33.8)
Return very likely	28	26	73	39
	(51.9)	(48.1)	(65.2)	(34.8)
Chi-square, *p*	<1, n.s.		<1, n.s.	
CR, diff. in prop., *p*	<1, n.s.		2.80 < .01	
2–8 priors				
Return less than very likely	9	6	25	12
	(60.0)	(40.0)	(67.6)	(32.4)
Return very likely	56	84	91	86
	(40.0)	(60.0)	(51.4)	(48.6)
Chi-square, *p*	1.48, n.s.		2.60, n.s.	
CR, diff. in prop., *p*	<1, n.s.		1.52 < .10	
9+ priors				
Return less than very likely	6	10	11	15
	(37.5)	(62.5)	(42.5)	(57.7)
Return very likely	95	196	99	187
	(32.6)	(67.4)	(34.6)	(65.4)
Chi-square, *p*	3.98 < .05		3.54 < .07	
CR, diff. in prop., *p*	1.77 < .05		1.69 < .07	

likely to be attuned in a similar way to the cues that the drive is coming. I would therefore expect to find no difference between regular donors and fixed-site donors. Both should show the pattern of more errors of commission than of omission.

Inertia in relationship to intentions

As in the other samples, intentions are very significantly related to donation. Among donors saying it was very likely that they would give in the next 6 months, 55.9% did so, and only 37.5% who were less than certain actually gave during that time. The percentages were different at bloodmobiles and at centers. Of the 706 mobile-site donors, 54% gave; 63% of center donors did so. This is a highly significant difference (chi-square = 12.78, $p < .001$).

Table 4 presents the relationship between intentions to donate and donation within the following 6 months for donors broken down two ways: by site of donation (mobile vs. center) and by experience (0–1 prior donation, 2–8, and 9 or more). First note that intentions do not predict donation very strongly in this data set, once we have controlled for the level of donor experience. At both centers and mobile sites, it is only among the quite experienced donors (9 or more donations) that intentions predict donation, and the relationship is not at all strong. There is no good explanation for why there should be such a difference between this data set and study one.

Expectations based on the inertia hypothesis are for the most part confirmed by these data. For early-career donors at both mobile and fixed sites, there are more errors of omission (not giving when the donor said it was "very likely") than of commission (giving when the donor said it was "less than very likely"), but the difference is significant only among mobile-site donors. In the middle range of experience there is no tendency toward either errors of omission or errors of commission among fixed-site donors. The mobile-site donors make somewhat fewer errors of commission than of omission, but the difference only approaches significance at the .10 level. It is also interesting that at both of these levels of experience, there is more *defection* from a strongly expressed intention among mobile-site donors than among fixed site donors (CR's = 1.64, p = .08 and 2.02, p < .05 for 0–1 and 2–8 donation groups, respectively). This is quite consistent with our expectation that it is harder to act positively on an intention – and therefore easier to follow the path of one's resting inertia – under mobile-site than under fixed-site conditions.

Among the experienced (9 or more donations) donors, the mobile-center distinction is unimportant. Both groups make more than the expected number of errors of commission. The critical ratios in both cases suggest a significant difference (p-levels of .05 and .07, respectively). Among these most experienced donors, there is no evidence of greater defection from a strongly expressed intention among mobile-site donors.

Inertia in relationship to identity

We do not have a measure of role-person merger in this data set. We do have a single-item measure of self-definition, however, which was worded as follows: "Would you say that you are: a first-time donor, an occasional donor, or a regular donor?" The first answer can, of course, only be given by rookies, and a person with one prior donation who defines himself or herself as a regular donor has no basis for that statement. Thus we have restricted this analysis to donors with two or more prior donations.

Table 5. *Predicting return based on self-definition as a regular donor, 1984 sample (donors separated by number of past donations and site)*

Donors and predictor	Fixed sites		Mobile sites	
	Didn't return	Returned	Didn't return	Returned
2–8 priors				
Occasional donor	35	32	77	30
	(52.2)	(47.8)	(72.0)	(28.0)
Regular donor	42	66	64	77
	(38.9)	(61.1)	(45.4)	(54.6)
Chi-square, p	2.47, n.s.		16.44, < .001	
CR, diff. in prop., p	<1, n.s.		2.20, < .05	
9+ priors				
Occasional donor	19	26	28	25
	(42.2)	(57.8)	(52.8)	(47.2)
Regular donor	104	203	116	202
	(33.9)	(66.1)	(36.5)	(63.5)
Chi-square, p	<1, n.s.		4.45, <.05	
Chi-square, p	2.46, <.01		<1, n.s.	

This measure could be criticized as not reflecting a role-identity, but rather as simply reflecting the individual's past donation behavior. In other words, it could be suggested that all the donors will be telling us in response to this question is how habitual a donor they are. However, although donors are more and more likely to call themselves regulars as they move through their careers, there are at every level of experience donors who say "occasional" and donors who say "regular" in response to that question. Thus it would seem to carry some psychological meaning over and above a simple report about their past donation behavior. Table 5 presents the relationship between this self-definition and having donated in the next 6 months, separately among mobile- and center-site donors at two levels of prior experience. Self-definition predicts donation significantly only among mobile-site donors, a finding that is not readily explainable. However, the pattern of results predicted by the inertia hypothesis reappears. There are significantly more errors of omission than of commission among relatively early-career mobile-site donors, and the opposite pattern is found among late-career fixed-site donors. In the other two categories of the table, there are no significant differences between the two kinds of errors. The lowest percentage of errors of commission (28%) and the highest percentage of errors of omission (45.4%) is found among 2–8 donation mobile-site donors, and the highest percentage of errors of commission (57.8%) and the lowest percentage of errors of omission (33.9%) is found among the 9+ fixed-site donors.

It is possible that what donors who call themselves "occasional" may be telling us is that they do not give as many times *per year* as do those who call themselves "regulars." That is, they may take longer to return than do regulars, even though they have made as many total donations in the past. Since our followup period was only 6 months, this could be the reason why more regulars than occasionals have given in that period. It also might explain why the difference is greater at mobile sites, where waiting to give means missing the opportunity.

Study three

Another way of looking at the concept of inertia might involve not only the frequency of past behavior, but also its recency. People who have done something more recently should – other things being equal – be more likely to do it again than should those who have done it longer ago, if what we are dealing with is some kind of "habit strength" that decays over time. The early learning theorists who dealt with habit used to say that habits were strengthened by use and weakened by disuse. People who have given blood only once should, of course, still be less likely to do it again than those who have donated more often, holding recency constant. Another structural aspect of the situation must also be considered, as in the preceding analysis of fixed and mobile sites. This is the ease with which the act can be performed. An opportunity that comes to you – as does a mobile drive – other things being equal, should be taken advantage of more than one that you have to seek out.

I have a fourth sample of blood donors obtained in the fall and spring of the 1978–1979 academic year in four high schools in Madison, Wisconsin. Some had given blood only at the fall drives, some only at the spring drives, and some at both. Of those giving only in the spring, I have selected out for special attention a group who were 17 years old, assuming that these were mainly juniors who would have a greater opportunity to give after school let out than would seniors. More seniors go away for the summer and/or the following fall for work or college. Thus we expected that "inertia" would work in the direction of increasing donation among these spring-only juniors. On the other hand, we have assumed that fall-only donors have decided *not* to give. They had an easy opportunity in the spring drives and avoided it. Thus we feel that inertia for them means not continuing – remaining at rest. Although inertia for two-time donors and for the spring-only seniors means continuation – remaining in motion –

Table 6. *Relationship between prior record and donation in response to a summer appeal (horizontal percentages are given in parentheses)*

Prior donations	Didn't give in summer	Gave in summer	Total
One time, fall	91 (75.8)	29 (24.2)	120
One time, spring, seniors	49 (81.7)	11 (18.3)	60
Two times	69 (71.1)	28 (28.9)	97
One time, spring, juniors	40 (58.8)	28 (41.2)	68
Total	249	96	345

Chi-square = 9.04, $p < .03$

structural considerations (and unreliability of measurement because of them) may preclude finding any strong effects for them.

During the summer, as many of these donors as could be reached were called and asked in a personal appeal to go to the central donation site and give because of summer shortages. In January, all of the donors were called on the phone and asked about donations during the fall semester. The local Red Cross records of all donors were then followed for about 2 years. In Table 6, we present the percentages of donors who gave in the summer for each of the four categories. As the table shows, record prior to the summer predicts giving in response to the appeal in the summer, with those who gave only in the fall and spring-only seniors being underrepresented and spring-only juniors being overrepresented. The relationship is significant at $p < .03$ (chi-square = 9.04, $df = 3$).

We do not have a measure of intention to continue donating for these donors at the time at which they were asked for a summer donation. Thus we will use whether or not they actually gave in response to that request as a proxy for intentions to continue. (Since intentions are often used as a proxy for behavior, there is precedent for this.) Clearly this is not ideal, but it is the best available substitute. Thus our inertia analyses will be based on the relationship between giving in the summer and giving after the summer. Our predictions are that those who previously had given only in the fall will show higher than expected errors of omission, and spring-only juniors will show higher than expected errors of commission.

In Table 7, we present the relationship between giving in the summer and reporting that one has given in the period immediately after the summer (for donors who could be reached the following January) as well as the relationship between giving in the summer and our two-year institutional measure of continued donation, for the total sample and our three subgroups. These two measures are both imperfect, in different ways.

Table 7. *Relationship between summer and later donation for a high school sample (horizontal percentages are in parentheses)*

Gave in summer?	Self-report: January		Two-year record	
	Didn't give after summer	Gave after summer	Didn't give after summer	Gave after summer
Total sample				
No	141 (69.8)	61 (30.2)	168 (67.5)	81 (32.5)
Yes	38 (49.4)	39 (50.6)	42 (43.7)	54 (56.3)
Chi-square, *p*	10.14, <.01		16.37, <.001	
CR, diff. in prop., *p*	2.40, <.01		1.56, <.10	
One time, fall				
No	65 (84.4)	12 (15.6)	73 (80.2)	18 (19.8)
Yes	13 (52.0)	12 (48.0)	16 (55.2)	13 (44.8)
Chi-square, *p*	19.29, <.001		5.95, <.02	
CR, diff. in prop., *p*	2.96, <.01		2.93, <.01	
Two time + one time, spring, sr.				
No	57 (60.0)	38 (40.0)	77 (65.0)	41 (35.0)
Yes	16 (52.0)	15 (48.0)	18 (46.0)	21 (54.0)
Chi-square, *p*	<1.00, n.s.		4.48, <.05	
CR, diff. in prop., *p*	<1, n.s.		<1, n.s.	
One time, spring, jr.				
No	19 (63.3)	11 (36.7)	18 (45.0)	22 (55.0)
Yes	9 (42.9)	12 (57.1)	8 (28.6)	20 (71.4)
Chi-square, *p*	1.35, n.s.		6.05, <.02	
CR, diff. in prop., *p*	<1, n.s.		2.05, <.05	

The self-report could be distorted in the socially desirable direction, and the sample size is reduced, because we were unable to reach some of the donors. The measure taken from Red Cross records will underestimate the donations of anyone who moved out of the Badger Region.

Summer and later donations are consistently significantly related for all three subgroups, if we look at the longer time period provided by the institutional record. They are significantly related only among the fall-only donors in the short term. However, the relationship is in the same direction for all groups.

As in previous similar tables, we are looking at errors of commission (giving when not predicted to) and errors of omission (not giving when predicted to). In this case, however, the prediction is based on the summer behavior as a proxy for intention or self-definition. We are saying that, other things equal, we would expect summer donation to predict later donation, as it does. But we expect more errors of commission among those with moving inertia – the spring one-time juniors (based on the recency of their prior donation, and a likely opportunity) – and more errors of omission among those with resting inertia – the fall one-time donors (based on their having chosen not to give at an intervening opportunity in the spring, and therefore a possible self-definition as a nondonor).

The table bears out the latter prediction quite strongly. Using either measure of continuation, self-report or institutional records, the fall one-time donors make far more errors of omission than of commission – two-and-one-half to three times the percentage. One-time spring junior donors show no significant effect on the short-term measure of continuation but do on the longer-term measure, having nearly twice the percentage of errors of commission than of omission. The other two groups show no effects on either measure, showing slightly more defections than errors of commission. Recall, however, that the long-term records for these donors will be inadequate at capturing any of their donations made out of state. Thus we cannot really conclude too much about them, except to note that the "resting inertia" effect found among the fall-only donors – for whom the same methodological and structural problems apply – does *not* appear.

It is also interesting to note that as we move from the one-time fall donors to the one-time spring juniors, the percentage of errors of commission on the 2-year record rises from 19.8 to 35 to 55%, whereas the percentage of errors of omission decreases from 55.2 to 46 to 28.6%. Using the self-report measure, the only real difference appears to be between the one-time fall donors and the rest, on errors of commission. About 40% of donors in the other three groups who did *not* give in the summer gave during the fall, indicating some degree of moving inertia. Only the fall-only donors who did not give in the summer, who should therefore have a lot of resting inertia, show a low level of continuation – only 15.6%.

The contribution of this analysis to our understanding of the workings of inertia is, first, to rule out some simple explanation of our previous analyses based on the regression of the number of future donations on the number of past donations. Similarly, we can rule out differential recruitment in explaining the differences between the fall and spring seniors in their patterns of donation beyond the summer. The increase in errors of commission between the January measure of return and the longer record among one-time spring juniors – if it is a real effect – also is hard to explain on the basis of differential recruitment. The fall drive in their high schools would have been their first exposure to more recruitment in the fall. But this is not where the effect shows up. Rather, it is in the longer record. This again suggests more the operation of an inertial force in response to a positively structured environment.

Conclusions

In this chapter I have attempted to show how the concept of inertia, or "force of habit," can help us understand the deviations we find when attempting to predict behavior from measured identities or intentions. I have attempted to lay out some implications of considering inertia based on habit as a possible counterweight to the heavy emphasis on cognitive processing and the influence of self-structures in social psychology today. In the course of this first investigation I have suggested that there are at least two aspects to past behavior that contribute to the force of habit: the number of past experiences with the behavior and the recency of the last experience. I have also alluded to the possible relevance of the spacing of experiences; perhaps more closely spaced experiences lead to greater "moving inertia." I have suggested that an intervening occasion not taken advantage of can decrease "moving" inertia and contribute to the reinstatement of "resting" inertia. Throughout this chapter I have ignored the possible cognitive correlates of this inertial force. That is, I have not dealt with the possibility that all of the effects operate by means of the impact of the timing, spacing, and repetition of past behavior on the self-image. If one were to take such a view, one would be claiming that habit is just another aspect of identity. The fact that measures of habit predict behavior over and above measures of identity, intention, and so on would then be attributed solely to faulty measurement of these cognitive variables. As I noted in the introduction, it is possible to take this position; however, I find it hard to defend in relationship to some habitual behavior. Furthermore, it seems unnecessary baggage to bring along on this particular trip, the goal of which is to see how far a much simpler conceptualization can take us. Freud once said, "Sometimes a cigar is just a cigar." Maybe, sometimes a habit is just a habit, and we don't need to invoke cognition in order to understand it.

Notes

1 In Poland, altruistic donors receive a meal, a day off work with pay, and some small gifts in exchange for their donation; however, they do not perceive these amenities as payment.
2 Following the suggestions of Ajzen and Fishbein (1977), the measures of intention match the behaviors. For the analysis of the 1-year measure among Polish donors, we used a question asking about likelihood of giving again within the year.
3 I am using the term *commitment* here to indicate that the behavior pattern has become a meaningful aspect of the self. It may be that this is the necessary step that must be taken before the inertial force to continue donation in the absence of conscious intentions develops.

4 This measure, developed by Callero (1985), consists of the sum of responses on an agree–disagree scale, to the following five statements: (1) Blood donation is something I rarely even think about (reversed). (2) I would feel a loss if I were forced to give up donating blood. (3) I really do not have any clear feelings about blood donation (reversed). (4) For me, being a blood donor means more than just donating blood. (5) Blood donation is an important part of who I am.

References

Abelson, R. P. 1976. Script processing in attitude formation and decision-making. In J. S. Carroll & J. W. Payne (Eds.), *Cognition and social behavior* (pp. 33–47). Hillsdale, NJ: Erlbaum.

Ajzen, I., & M. Fishbein. 1977. Attitude-behavior relations: A theoretical analysis and review of empirical research. *Psychological Bulletin* 84: 888–915.

Ajzen, I., & M. Fishbein. 1980. *Understanding attitude and predicting social behavior.* Englewood Cliffs, NJ: Prentice-Hall.

American College Dictionary. 1952. New York: Random House.

Bagozzi, R. P. 1981. Attitudes, intentions, and behavior: A test of some key hypotheses. *Journal of Personality and Social Psychology* 41: 607–627.

Bentler, P. M., & G. Speckart. 1979. Models of attitude-behavior relations. *Psychological Review* 86: 452–464.

Bentler, P. M., & G. Speckart. 1981. Attitudes "cause" behaviors: A structural equation analysis. *Journal of Personality and Social Psychology* 40: 226–238.

Burke, P. J., & J. Tully. 1981. The measurement of role/identity. *Social Forces* 2: 83–92.

Callero, P. C. 1985. Role-identity salience. *Social Psychology Quarterly* 85: 203–215.

Camic, C. 1986. The matter of habit. *American Journal of Sociology* 91: 1,039–1,087.

Charng, H., J. A. Piliavin, & P. C. Callero. 1988. Role-identity and reasoned action in the prediction of repeated behaviors. *Social Psychology Quarterly* 51: 303–317.

Davidson, A. R., & L. R. Beach. 1981. Error patterns in the prediction of fertility behavior. *Journal of Applied Social Psychology* 11: 475–488.

DeJong, L., & J. VanDonge. 1983. Communication and ward development committees in Chipata: A Zambian case-study of administrative inertia. *The Journal of Modern African Studies* 21: 141–150.

Durkheim, E. 1905–1906. The evolution and the role of secondary education in France. In *Education and sociology* (pp. 135–153). (Sherwood D. Fox, Trans.). Glencoe: Free Press.

Fishbein, M., & Ajzen, I. 1975. *Belief, attitude, intention, and behavior: An introduction to theory and research.* Reading, MA: Addison-Wesley.

Franklin, M. N., & T. T. Mackie. 1983. Familiarity and inertia in the formation of governing coalitions in parliamentary democracies. *British Journal of Political Science* 13: 275–298.

Fredricks, A. J., & D. L. Dossett. 1983. Attitude-behavior relations: A comparison of the Fishbein-Ajzen and the Bentler-Speckart models. *Journal of Personality and Social Psychology* 45: 501–512.

Geller, E. S., & G. F. Pitz. 1968. Confidence and decision speed in the revision of opinion. *Organizational Behavior and Human Performance* 3: 190–201.

Giddens, A. 1979. *Central problems in social theory.* Berkeley: University of California Press.

Godin, G., P. Valois, R. J. Shephard, & R. Desharnais. 1987. Prediction of leisure-time exercise behavior: A path analysis (LISREL V) model. *Journal of Behavioral Medicine* 10: 145–158.

Hannan, M. T., & J. Freeman. 1984. Structural inertia and organizational change. *American Sociological Review* 49: 149–164.

Hartmann, H. 1939. *Ego psychology and the problem of adaptation* (David Rapaport, Trans.). New York: International University Press.

Havassy, B. E., & J. M. Tschann. 1983. Client initiative, inertia, and demographics: More powerful than treatment interventions in methadone maintenance? *The International Journal of the Addictions* 18: 617–631.

Huff, J., & W. A. V. Clark. 1978. Cumulative stress and cumulative inertia: A behavioral model of the decision to move. *Environment and Planning – A* 10: 1,101–1,119.

Jeuland, A. P. 1979. Brand choice inertia as one aspect of the notion of brand loyalty. *Management Science* 25: 671–682.

Jones, E. E., & K. E. Davis. 1965. From acts to dispositions: The attribution process in person perception. In L. Berkowitz (Ed.), *Advances in experimental social psychology* (Vol. 2, pp. 220–266). New York: Academic Press.

Kelley, H. H. 1967. Attribution theory in social psychology. In D. Levine (Ed.), *Nebraska symposium on motivation* (Vol. 14, pp. 192–241). Lincoln: University of Nebraska Press.

Langer, E. 1978. Rethinking the role of thought in social interaction. In J. Harvey, W. Ickes, & R. Kidd (Eds.), *New directions in attribution research* (Vol. 2, pp. 36–58). Hillsdale, NJ: Erlbaum.

Manstead, A. S. R., C. Proffitt, & J. L. Smart. 1983. Predicting and understanding mother's infant-feeding intentions and behavior: Testing the theory of reasoned action. *Journal of Personality and Social Psychology* 44: 657–671.

McCall, G. J., & J. L. Simmons. 1978. *Identities and interactions* (rev. ed.). New York: The Free Press.

Mittal, B. 1988. Achieving higher seat belt usage: The role of habit in bridging the attitude-behavior gap. *Journal of Applied Social Psychology* 18: 993–1,016.

Myers, G. C., R. McGinnis, & G. Masnick. 1967. The duration of residence approach to a dynamic stochastic model of internal migration: A test of the axiom of cumulative inertia. *Social Biology* 14: 121–126.

Piliavin, J. A., & P. C. Callero. 1991. *Giving blood: The development of an altruistic identity.* Baltimore: The Johns Hopkins University Press.

Pitz, G. F. 1969. An inertia effect (resistance to change) in the revision of opinion. *Canadian Journal of Psychology* 23: 24–33.

Stryker, S. 1980. *Symbolic interactionism: A social structural version.* Menlo Park, CA: Benjamin-Cummings.

Turner, R. 1978. The role and the person. *American Journal of Sociology* 84: 1–23.

Weiner, B., D. Russell, & D. Lerman. 1978. Affective consequences of causal ascriptions. In J. H. Harvey, W. Ickes, & R. F. Kidd (Eds.), *New directions in Attribution Research* (Vol. 2, pp. 59–90). Hillsdale, NJ: Erlbaum.

13   Social structure and the moral self

Michael L. Schwalbe

For cognitive developmentalists working in the tradition of Piaget and Kohlberg, morality is largely a matter of abstract reasoning about problems of justice and equity (see Rest, 1986, for a review). The most capable moral problem solvers in this view are those who can transcend the particulars of situations and formulate principled solutions to whatever justice and equity problems they pose. Because role taking is held to be an important part of the social cognition underlying this kind of moral problem solving, and because of his association with the concept, G. H. Mead has often been cited as providing theoretical grounding for this approach. But in fact his views are almost diametrically opposed.

Mead rejected the idea that intelligent moral action is equivalent to facility with formulas or abstract principles (see Mead, 1934: 379–389; 1908/1964; 1924–1925/1964; 1929/1964; 1930/1964). For Mead, moral action is practical problem solving – a matter of trying to reconcile within concrete situations the impulses that simultaneously impel action in different directions. He argued that although thought is necessary to generate hypotheses about how conflicting impulses might be reconciled, solving a moral problem requires linking thought to overt action. He conceived of moral development in terms of "enlarging the self" by learning how others perceive, interpret, and respond to the world – in other words, by improving role-taking abilities.

Mead's social psychology and ethical theory can be used to develop a more sociological approach to moral action – one that recognizes how social structures shape both the competence and performance of individuals as moral problem solvers in concrete situations. Because of its centrality to Mead's thought, the self is necessarily central to this approach. One purpose of this chapter is thus to show how a Meadian view of moral action, with the self as its focal point, can help us see better the social embeddedness of individuals as moral actors. A larger purpose of this is to recover moral action as a subject for sociological analysis and to

281

show its relevance for what are usually considered more macrosociological issues, such as the reproduction of social structure.

Moral problem solving and the moral self

To understand Mead's ethical theory it is necessary to understand the social psychology on which it is premised. This section will thus begin with a brief review of Mead's conception of the self. It will proceed then to offer a Meadian view of moral action and of how it depends upon the moral self.

Mead's conception of the self

In Mead's view (1934: 144–200), selves emerge as individuals develop the ability to call forth in imagination the responses that their overt acts would evoke in others. The development of a fully social self rests on the ability to use symbols or imagery to call forth in precise fashion the complex responses of diverse others to our overt acts. In this sense, the Meadian self can be described as an internalization of the social process. The self can also be described in terms of the impulses it comprises. Mead associated one set of impulses with the "I," which consists of one's own biologically rooted tendencies to act; the other set he called the "Me," which consists of others' cognitively appropriated tendencies to act.[1] The former might be thought of as primary impulses – they are prepotent or "ready to fire," so to speak, when objects in the environment trigger their release; these impel habitual and other forms of nonreflective behavior. The latter might be thought of as secondary impulses, which may arise in response to an ambiguous object or in response to the imagined consequences of an intended act. When this occurs, behavior becomes reflective; the self comes fully into play.

Mead saw these internalized impulses of others not simply as constituents of an undifferentiated "Me," but as organized into perspectives that correspond to the specific persons, groups, and larger communities with which the individual is familiar. This organization of mind – which corresponds to the organization of society as the individual experiences it – enables the individual to adopt the perspectives of specific others, as well as the synthetic perspectives of groups and communities. By alternately adopting these perspectives in thought, individuals can discover how they overlap and diverge and how they might be further synthesized into more inclusive perspectives. This is a large part of what constitutes social cognition in Mead's view (see Callero, this volume).

In Mead's view, the thinking individual is thus thoroughly social; in fact, there could be no individual thought at all if not for the existence of communal life based on the creation and use of symbols. Moreover, the very forms that thought can take are constrained by the symbols in use in a community, the rules that govern their manipulation, and the ways they are used to organize perspectives. There is of course always the possibility for the creative use of symbols and the reorganization of perspectives, but individuals must begin thinking with the symbolic equipment provided by the community. As such, it is impossible to adequately understand individual cognition by abstracting it from the context of communal life (Morgan & Schwalbe, 1990).

Levels of conduct and phases of action

Two distinctions may be helpful to better grasp the Meadian analysis of moral action that follows. The first is among three levels of conduct.[2] As already implied, a preliminary distinction can be made between habitual and reflective conduct. Although the former may involve some low level of routine self-awareness, only the latter, which involves role taking in imagination, brings the self fully into play. Further useful distinctions in levels of conduct can be made by considering more precisely the kinds of role taking involved.

The first level of conduct involves no role taking. It is directed toward immediate satisfaction of impulses, with no regard for how the consequences of this conduct will affect others. Much habitual conduct may be of this egocentric type. Conduct moves to the second level only when there is some awareness of conflicting impulses to act. This conflict occurs and inhibits conduct because the individual does not know which rule to follow. Role taking occurs here, but it is of a simple kind: The individual takes only the perspective of the group to try to determine which specific behavior will be approved or disapproved. Once this is determined, action resumes. Although such rule-following behavior is often described as implicating morality, it is largely a matter of ritual conformity entailing no complex moral cognition.

It is at the third level of conduct that moral cognition becomes more complex and interesting. At this level, the inhibiting conflict involves at least three perspectives: those of the community members whose values and interests conflict, and that of the community as a whole (i.e., the generalized other). Now it is no longer possible simply to choose which rule to follow; multiple interests and values – embodied in divergent perspectives – must be reconciled. The role taking involved is correspondingly more complex. Individuals do not just take the perspective of the group over against themselves, but take the perspectives of all those persons or groups whose interests and values are at stake in the situation. It is at this level of conduct that true moral dilemmas arise. The moral problem solving that is of foremost interest from a Meadian perspective is of this polycentric type.

The second distinction that may be helpful is between two phases of action: covert and overt. In Mead's view, thinking and behavior are simply parts of a process of adaptive action. Behavior driven by impulses gives rise both to satisfaction of impulses and, because inhibiting problems often arise, to thinking. Thinking in turn guides attempts to overcome problems; it thus serves behavior and the need to satisfy impulses. New behaviors may then lead to new problems demanding new thinking, and so on. Action in the world is thus a continuous process that alternates between the overt phase of behavior and the covert phase of thought.

Moral problem solving occurs at the third level of conduct and of course involves these two phases of action. There is the covert phase that constitutes moral cognition, which involves, principally, the role taking through which the individual seeks to reconcile conflicting values and interests and find a way for action to proceed; and there is the overt phase of observable behavior, through which attempts are made to put tentative solutions into practice. To solve moral problems in the real world requires both phases of action. What I am calling moral action should thus be understood as comprising both moral cognition and the behavior it guides.

Moral problems and moral problem solving

In Mead's view there is no sharp break between social and moral problems. Problems of any kind arise in social life when habits alone are inadequate guides to action. Habits are recognized as inadequate when an actor is confronted by a novel situation that calls forth conflicting impulses to act. Under such circumstances, action is impeded until conflicting impulses can be reconciled and some way to proceed determined. Such reconciliation might be achieved by repressing some impulses and carrying through others, by identifying other, more readily attainable objects that will satisfy impulses originally directed toward incompatible objects, or by giving new meaning to objects such that the logical incompatibility of the values attached to them is eliminated. Solving a problem is thus a matter of finding a way to keep action moving toward its goal.

The problem-solving demands of social life will vary depending on its complexity. More problems will arise, for example, in a community where elaborate projects, such as building roads or governments, are undertaken by individuals with divergent perspectives than in a community of homogeneous individuals whose only collective activities are governed by ritual. Of course, some kinds of problems will arise in even the simplest, most homogeneous communities. Problems of *interpretation* – that is, of correctly inferring intention and of anticipating the response tendencies of others – arise in all human communities. Human fallibility and creativity ensure it.

Moral problems can be distinguished from simple interpretive ones, in the Meadian view, with respect to the degree of consensus prevailing regarding the ends or "objects" of action. When there is agreement about the objects of action but action is impeded by imperfect communication, the problem is interpretive rather than moral. Action thus impeded can continue when understanding is reestablished. But action can also be impeded because it is pulled in conflicting directions by values attached to objects whose attainability appears mutually exclusive. Such a situation can also be described in terms of conflict over ends, conflict over the values that identify some ends as more important than others, or conflict over the interests that various ends would serve. However described, such a situation presents a moral problem (Mead, 1908/1964; see also Broyer, 1973).

In the Meadian view these are not problems of individual conscience, although conscience, in the form of the generalized other, is implicated in their recognition and solution. Moral problems are always social problems in the sense of entailing conflicts between interests and values arising in a community – even if the locus of the immediate conflict is an individual. Attempts by individuals to reason about and solve moral problems are thus inherently social; there is always interaction between a self and internalized others.

One implication of the previously presented view of levels of conduct should be made explicit: Any behavior has the potential to become morally problematic. This is so because it is always possible for impulsive or habitual behaviors to entail consequences that, under certain circumstances, will conflict with the previously unconsidered values and interests of others. Dewey used the example of acting on an impulse to open a window in an uncomfortably warm room. Doing so would not seem to entail any great moral dilemma. But in the presence of someone who feels cold, the act can take on moral significance, for now another perspective must be taken into account and a potential conflict dealt with.

Smoking in public is another example. This same behavior can occur at any level of conduct, depending on the values and interests perceived to be at stake when it occurs. For the habitual smoker oblivious to the interests of others, it may represent no moral problem; under other circumstances the problem may be the simple one of which rule to follow; under still other circumstances the problem may become the complex one of reconciling conflicting interests in personal freedom, pleasure, and health. The point is that the moral significance of any behavior is determined by the situation and the relationships it creates between the values and interests present within it. No behavior is inherently morally problematic, though any behavior might become so.

The importance of role taking

For Mead the most important thing that occurs in thinking about moral problems is role taking. It is by adopting alternative perspectives in something of a round-robin fashion that one sees where both conflicts and common values lie.[3] What the moral problem solver must do, in other words, is successively adopt all the perspectives that are represented in the problematic situation and attempt to discern precisely how they conflict and how they converge (cf. Kohlberg, 1973). The preferred solution to a moral problem is one that best respects all the values and interests relevant to the problem, provided they are compatible with furthering the social process.

The idea of furthering the social process as the goal of moral action warrants some explanation. In Mead's view this means several things (see Mead, 1908/1964; 1934: 379–389). First, it means preserving community and the cooperation upon which it depends; second, it means extending and refining the shared perspective, or generalized other, that links members of a community; third, it means enhancing individual role-taking abilities; and fourth, it means continuing to transform the physical and social worlds to satisfy impulses more readily. The best solutions to moral problems are those that, all relevant and reasonably foreseeable consequences considered, will do the most to improve individual and communal life in these ways. Role taking is how the covert phase of moral action proceeds toward these goals.

The cognitivist perspective also acknowledges the importance of role taking (see Selman, 1971; Kohlberg, 1973; Rest, 1986). But it holds that moral reasoning involves other basic perceptual and cognitive abilities (Weinreich-Haste, 1983; Hoffman, 1984). This is undeniable. To solve moral problems people must be able, among other things, to understand types of situations and types of social actors, to understand types of social relationships, to appreciate the value of feelings, and to make logical inferences about persons, situations, and the consequences of various lines of action for people's feelings and for the creation of new situations.

Moral thinking can be some of the most demanding and complex that humans must do; and indeed it involves more than role taking. But the importance of role taking depends in large part on how moral problems are defined. If they are defined in terms of dilemmas arising from competing justice and equity claims, then formal operational thought (in Piaget's sense) becomes more important than role taking. In this view moral problems are essentially logical puzzles to which formal rules can be applied to arrive at correct, or at least the "most principled," solutions (cf. Harding, 1985). As noted earlier, this is the conception of moral problems that is generally embraced by cognitivists such as Kohlberg (1969, 1984) and those who have adopted his approach (see Rest, 1986, for a review).

If moral problems are defined, however, in terms of conflicting values and interests embodied in partially overlapping perspectives, then role taking assumes preeminent importance. This view of moral problems does not ignore matters of justice and equity, but sees them as "potential considerations" in particular cases. It also rejects the notion that moral problems are primarily logical puzzles solvable by use of universal principles. If they are puzzles of any kind, they are communicative ones whose solutions arise out of negotiating new meanings and social relationships, not out of decontextualized philosophizing. If general ethical principles prove useful in this process, that is fine. But their use cannot substitute for the hard task, as Mead put it (1929/1964: 365), of trying to realize the common value in the experience of conflicting groups and individuals in concrete situations.

Some readers might recognize the parallels here to Habermas's (1984, 1985) communicative ethics. Like Mead, Habermas is concerned with the postconventional (i.e., beyond Mead's second level of conduct) reasoning required to solve complex moral problems. He is also concerned, like Mead, with how this reasoning is shaped by social relations. Moreover, what Habermas discusses as communicative action seems to be the sort of action Mead expects individuals to undertake when facing moral problems at the third level of conduct. For the individual the goal is to develop the ability to adopt a perspective from which he or she can reflect on the very process by which values and principles for realizing them are created. The communal goal, for both Mead and Habermas, is to achieve the highest possible degree of mutual understanding through a process of universal role taking. It seems also that the implied teleology of Mead's ethical theory is Habermas's ideal speech community.

Whereas Habermas gives more attention to social structural constraints on moral action, the advantage of Mead's perspective derives from the more elaborate social psychology of the self on which it is premised. This makes it possible to see more clearly just how an individual's competence and performance as a moral actor are shaped both by large-scale social structures and by features of situations. In turn this allows, as I will try to show, a more complete view of the reciprocity between moral action and social structure.

The moral self

My conception of the moral self builds on the interpretation of Mead presented, draws also on the work of John Dewey, and incorporates several ideas from more recent theories of the self. I use the term *moral self* not to suggest the existence of some entity distinct from the social self in general, but to refer to a set of self-related cognitive elements that underlie moral action. These include (1) impulses to role-take that are rooted in the "I," (2) the expansiveness of the generalized other or what I will call *role-taking range*, (3) conceptions of the self as an object possessing moral characteristics, and (4) a sense of self-efficacy that motivates action in the face of moral problems. The first two elements concern the self as it functions in shaping the perception and processing of social information. The latter two concern the self as an object about which information is possessed and processed.

If the recognition and solution of moral problems depends on role taking, then the moral actor must possess impulses to role-take. There must be, in other words, a propensity to consider one's acts and their consequences from the perspectives of others. This is not synonymous with the *ability* to role-take, as abilities may be possessed without the inclination to use them (cf. Stotland, 1969; Keller, 1976; Staub, 1979: 69–86). I am proposing that we think of role-taking propensity as that element of the self that inclines individuals to apply whatever role-taking abilities they possess. I see this propensity as both subject to contextual influences and as a disposition that exhibits a baseline stability across situations. As a disposition, it is that part of the self that might be described as the will to moral responsibility.

This view reflects Dewey's (1908/1960) notion of the moral self as one that "strenuously pursues virtue." To do so, according to Dewey, is to strive to reinforce impulses to pursue objects that are judged good in "calm moments of reflection," to be sympathetic, to reflect on the consequences of acts, to increase knowledge of self and others, to discover new values and to revise old ones. The *will* to cultivate the moral self was for Dewey (1908/1960: 168) the cornerstone of moral character:

The very problem of morals is to form an original body of impulsive tendencies into a voluntary self in which desires and affections center in the values which are common; in which interest focusses in objects that contribute to the enrichment of the lives of all.

Mead would agree that this is indeed the key problem of individual morality.[4] He described this in terms of striving to enlarge the self.

Motivation to take alternative perspectives on a problematic situation is thus one key element of the moral self. The ability to do this, widely and flexibly, depends on role-taking *range*, which refers to the diversity of perspectives represented in an individual's consciousness. Here I am thus referring to a developed quality of mind that facilitates discovery of solutions to moral problems (for further discussion of role-taking propensity and range, see Schwalbe, 1988b). In the terms of contemporary social cognition, this is analogous to the ability to apply diverse schemas to interpreting the information that is present in a moral problem-solving situation (cf. Weinreich-Haste, 1983). The more such schemas an individual can employ, the more likely is the discovery of a solution that best serves all the interests and values at stake.

Information about the self as an object is organized into self-conceptions, which can also affect moral action (cf. Wegner, 1980; Blasi, 1984; Damon, 1984; Hogan & Busch, 1984). For example, an individual might think of himself or herself as honest, tolerant, caring, fairminded, compassionate, and so on. These are conceptions of the self as virtuous. Assuming a powerful self-esteem motive that can be satisfied, in part, through action consistent with positive self-conceptions (see Gecas, this volume), the likelihood of morally responsible behavior will be increased to the extent that the self is defined in virtuous terms (cf. Cheek & Hogan, 1983; Backman, 1985). The more central these definitions of the self as virtuous are to an individual's overall conception of self, the greater will be their motivating force.

Carol Gilligan (1982, 1987) has offered a somewhat different analysis of how morality is linked to what might be called existential self-affirmation. She has argued that men and women, although both capable of approaching moral problems from either a justice or a care orientation, tend to choose one or the other. This choice, which determines how moral problems are perceived and how attempts are made to solve them, is said to derive from the fundamentally different ways that men and women affirm their existence as persons: men through autonomous action and women through relationships with others. Gilligan's argument, in brief, is that men tend to embrace justice ethics that prescribe inviolable boundaries between self and others, thus protecting the autonomy of the self. Women, on the other hand, tend to embrace an ethic of care because care preserves connections between self and others, thus protecting a self premised on those connections.

Gilligan's argument is sometimes taken to mean that men and women are creatures with distinct kinds of moral selves. It is perhaps more accurate, however, to say that *gendered selves* are affirmed by different kinds of experiences, and that the different values thus attached to these experiences affect judgments about what are acceptable solutions to moral problems. Values and interests that are seen as important from one gendered perspective may not be seen as important, or seen at all, from the other. From a Meadian perspective, we might say that gender socialization inhibits role-taking propensity and range, such that men and women characteristically have trouble dealing with different aspects of moral problems. Drawing on both Mead and Gilligan, we might say that learning to perceive and appreciate all the justice and care issues that complex moral problems typically entail helps enlarge the moral selves that are narrowed in the process of creating gendered beings.

The three elements of the moral self already described are primarily implicated in the covert phase of moral action; they shape the perception and processing of information about the problem. But the moral self also includes an element that motivates attempts to put hypothesized solutions to moral problems into practice. This element is a sense of efficacy. The competent moral problem solver, in other words, must be motivated not only to think about moral problems and possible solutions, but willing to test those solutions in action.[5] Self-efficacy underlies this willingness. What is involved is a belief that one possesses the abilities to do whatever is necessary to put a proposed solution into practice. Without this sense of efficacy, moral action never gets beyond the covert phase; it remains the moral cognition that cognitive developmentalists have mistaken for morality in toto (cf. Bandura, 1986: 488–498).

These elements of the moral self undergird effective moral action. They also vary in degrees of development. By implication, an individual's capabilities as a moral problem solver are limited by the development of these elements of the self. Obviously, however, moral action is never solely a function of abilities or dispositions. It is a function of how the features of a concrete situation stand over against the abilities and dispositions of an individual at a given point in time. Under minimally demanding circumstances even a poorly developed moral self might be an adequate basis for effective moral action; under extremely demanding circumstances even a highly developed moral self might be overwhelmed (cf. Haan, Aerts, & Cooper, 1985).

Social structure and the moral self

Development

Social structure can be linked to the moral self as a force shaping its development. It is misleading, however, to reify "social structure" and speak of it as an agent in itself. I see it rather as a matter of persisting patterns of action and interaction involving large numbers of people. These are patterns that people are born into and drawn into for various reasons over the course of their lives. What shapes individual development are the experiences provided by or precluded by particular locations in the pattern. Of interest here are the experiences that affect development of each element of the moral self.

The moral self was said to comprise a propensity to role-take, role-taking range, self-conceptions of virtuous character, and self-efficacy. A full discussion of the structurally engendered experiences that might affect each of these elements is beyond the scope of this chapter.[6] My treatment of these matters will thus be only suggestive. The point I hope to establish nonetheless is that the development of capacities for moral action must be seen as a part of the larger process whereby social structure shapes development of the social self.

First, then, what social-structure related experiences might affect the development of role-taking propensity? What sort of experiences, in other words, might foster a disposition to take the perspectives of others? We can look first to how such a disposition might be instilled as a matter of moral socialization. It seems that this is what parents who use "person-oriented appeals" or "inductive social control" to discipline their children are doing, that is, attempting to teach self-control by explaining how improper behavior will harm others (Schantz, 1975). These strategies seek, in effect, to instill role-taking propensity, to make the taking into account of others' perspectives a habit of mind. These are socialization strategies empirically associated with the middle- and upper-middle classes; working- and lower-class parents tend to use strategies emphasizing strict rule following or punishment and reward (Bernstein, 1973; Cook-Gumperz, 1973). These socialization strategies in turn reflect parents' adaptations to their own positions in the larger political economy (Kohn, 1969; Gecas, 1979). Hence arises one link to the class structure of society.

Among adults, the impulse to role-take might be reinforced by demands for role taking and by observing that it leads to desired results. The workplace is one arena in which such role-taking experiences commonly arise. In the workplace, both the demands and consequences of role taking can vary by social structural location (e.g., occupation, class position, organizational role). Depending on the nature of one's work, role-taking demands may be great and the consequences of role taking significant and adaptive. Engineers and managers, for example, are faced with continual demands to take alternative perspectives (within the universe of the capitalist workplace), the effectiveness of their work resting on their abilities to do so successfully. Production-line workers, on the other hand, are faced with relatively few such demands in the course of their work. Impulses to role-take may thus tend to be reinforced among managers and engineers, and diminished, in relative terms, among production workers (see Schwalbe, 1986: 92–98, 130–135). This is another way in which role-taking propensity can be linked to social structure.

I am referring here to role-taking propensity as a characteristic disposition to take others' perspectives into account when contemplating some course of action that might affect others' well-being. The preceding points are thus intended to suggest how this characteristic disposition, as an element of the moral self, is associated with certain experiences in the family and the workplace. Experiences in other institutional realms – education, religion, sports, art, politics, and so on – are also potentially consequential. The point is that social structural location will shape an individual's opportunities to have the sort of experiences (in any of these realms) that will either foster or inhibit development of role-taking propensity (cf. Staub, 1979). This foundational element of the moral self is thus inextricably linked to the patterns of social life that initially shape the child and continue to influence adult character.

The development of role-taking range will also depend on opportunities for specific kinds of interaction and problem-solving experiences. Individuals must have opportunities to encounter others with dissimilar perspectives under circumstances that demand role taking. Circumstances that require cooperation to achieve jointly sought goals should be most conducive to development of role-taking range. By the same token, the segregation of racial, ethnic, sexual, or other subcultural groups will tend to inhibit development of role-taking range. Lack of opportunities to confront alternative perspectives through literature, film, and other forms of art will have similar limiting effects. This element of the moral self is thus also a systematic product of social experience, in that it can develop only out of circumstances that demand serious consideration of others' perspectives. The enlargement of the self in this way reflects the complexity of social life that structure forces upon individuals and the complexity they are able to find when seeking it for self-stimulation (cf. Coser, 1975).

With respect to role-taking propensity and range, I have discussed in very general terms the importance of development-enhancing and development-inhibiting experiences. I have said little about the specific content of these experiences, because the developmental effect of interest would seem to derive more from the form than the content of experience. The same point applies less to self-conceptions of virtue, since these are specific beliefs about the self. Some examples used earlier were tolerance, caring, and honesty – though the list could be extended almost indefinitely. The developmental issue in this case is how individuals come to apply these particular meanings to themselves. This would seem to depend directly on the content of experience.

If we think of these self-conceptions as deriving from reflected appraisals, social comparisons, and self-perceptions, we can say that individuals must have opportunities to derive from a least one of these sources information affirming their virtue. Lacking opportunities to receive positive reflected appraisals, to make favorable social comparisons, and to perform virtuous actions, it would seem difficult to develop self-conceptions of virtue. But still the reference to opportunities-in-the-abstract does not explain how an individual might come to think of himself or herself as honest, caring, tolerant, and so on. What this suggests is that development of certain elements of the moral self may be more subject to the idiosyncrasies of biography than others. The moral self as it is constituted by self-conceptions of virtue may be the best example. It may take only one memorable experience to establish or destroy such self-conceptions.

The real issue for moral action remains, however, how a particular self-conception is interpreted (e.g., what it means to be caring or tolerant). This implies a link between the moral self and moral culture as providing the symbolic resources drawn upon to construct self-conceptions of virtue. The meaning of "honest" as a possible self-conception depends on what it means in the culture or subculture from which it is drawn. It seems likely, for example, that this self-label will mean different things to bank tellers, politicians, priests, and drug dealers. Understanding how specific self-conceptions of virtue will affect moral action thus requires looking beyond specific selves to the cultural contexts in which self-labels acquire their meanings.

Conceptions of the self as efficacious may likewise depend upon cultural standards, but they can also be linked to general features of social organization, such as the distributions of power and wealth. Developing a sense of self-efficacy requires, in general, that individuals have opportuni-ties to feel responsible for producing some set of intended, positively valued effects on the world (see Gecas & Schwalbe, 1983, for an elaboration). An imbalance in the distribution of resources needed to produce effects on the world is likely to produce an imbalance in the distribution of self-efficacy (cf. Della Fave, 1980). Individuals in relatively poor and powerless groups may, in other words, be systematically dis-advantaged when it comes to developing a sense of efficacy. A potential result would be inhibited development of one element of the moral self.[7]

In treating self-efficacy as an element of the moral self we get away from a conception of morality or moral character that is strictly a matter of reasoning ability. Considering self-efficacy takes us into the realm of action where, in the pragmatist view, morality ultimately lies. On the individual level it is thus necessary to consider the development of the will to act. If this will to act can be described in terms of self-efficacy – a belief that one is capable of acting on the results of moral cognition – then social structure can again be tied to moral action via effects on the development of self-efficacy.

Situated action

In the preceding section I have tried to suggest how patterns of social life can affect development of the moral self. But the elements of the moral self that develop out of social life are only foundations for moral action; they enable and constrain morally responsible action but do not determine it. To understand what individuals do or fail to do as moral actors in any given case it is necessary also to take circumstances into account. Moral action is always situated action.

If there is any single aspect of social structure or pattern to social life that seems to have preeminent consequences for the moral self, it is inequality. Under some circumstances, any dimension of material or symbolic in-equality might be relevant. But for the present discussion I shall limit my consideration to inequality in the distribution of power (defined as the ability to access and mobilize whatever material or symbolic resources as are necessary to create intended effects, on people or objects, in a given situation). To say that power is inequitably distributed in situations is to say that some individuals will sometimes be able to make others think, feel, and act in ways that override the best interests of those whose thoughts, feelings, and actions are so manipulated. This is also to describe a form of life where it is possible to use human beings as means to ends.

Situations characterized by such power imbalances can affect moral action via effects on various elements of the moral self. For example, it seems that power imbalances can undermine role-taking propensity (Maccoby, 1959; Thomas, Franks, & Calonico, 1972; Schwalbe, 1986; Morgan & Spanish, 1987). This is so because the psychic and material interests of the powerful do not require for their satisfaction serious consideration of the perspectives of the powerless. *This is not to say that the powerful do not role-take*; they must of course do so to the extent necessary to maintain communication and ideological control. In relative terms, however, when the powerful and powerless interact it is the powerless who must do the greater share of role taking, because satisfaction of their psychic and material interests is more dependent on doing so. Being able to discern what the boss is thinking is often necessary to preserve both employment and dignity.

In any given situation where such power imbalances obtain, the powerful will have little material or psychic incentive to do the demanding work of discerning the perspectives of the powerless. In consequence, should overt conflicts arise, the powerful cannot act in fully deliberative, morally responsible ways, since their propensity to take all relevant values and interests into account has been undermined by their own power; in fact, they are unlikely even to perceive the moral problems inherent in wielding their power (cf. Sorokin & Lunden, 1959). In further consequence of a lack of role taking, the powerful will likely claim that challenges to their power are unreasonable or even nonsensical, and hence cannot be responded to rationally. The immorality of power, it might thus be said, tends to be self-perpetuating in part because of its distorting effects on the moral selves of the powerful.

Power imbalances might in this way have far-reaching effects on the development of moral selves, as I will consider again in the next section. My intent here is simply to show how the moral self mediates the effects of circumstances on moral action. Another way inequality affects moral action, via the moral self, is by undermining self-efficacy.

As an element of the moral self, a sense of efficacy was said to be essential to motivating action based on the results of moral cognition. It is, in other words, what gives the individual the confidence to risk putting thought into action; short of this, morality remains a safe philosophical exercise. If efficacy depends on power, then a relative lack of it in a situation where values and interests are in conflict is likely to undermine an individual's sense of being able to put the results of any moral thought into action. This might tend to undermine commitment to pursuing moral thought or problem-solving dialogue in the first place. What is the point, one might think, if there is no hope of being taken seriously or of taking effective action? In some situations, then, power imbalances will undermine commitment to intelligent, good faith participation in moral problem solving by undermining the sense of efficacy necessary to sustain this commitment. The moral self can thus be disempowered along with the individual as a whole.

The argument that self-conceptions of virtue ought to foster moral action presumes underlying self-esteem and self-consistency motives: Persons possessing self-conceptions of virtue should tend to behave in morally responsible ways because doing so reaffirms their valued self-conceptions and enhances self-esteem (see Gecas, this volume). One problem, however, is that power imbalances might negate the positive effects of particular self-conceptions of virtue. The immediate reflected appraisals of powerful audiences might overwhelm the effects of self-conceptions of virtue, as when, for example, adolescents who otherwise might think of themselves as kind and respectful behave quite the opposite within a delinquent group (cf. Wells, 1978; Kaplan, 1980). If some audiences stake their approval on actions that are not consistent with self-conceptions of virtue – and if such approval is subjectively deemed more important for self-esteem in a given situation – then moral action may be subverted.

The linear form of my discussion might seem to imply that each element of the moral self operates independently in a moral problem-solving situation. This is not really so. Whereas it is likely that different elements may be more or less important depending on the nature of the situation and the power imbalances obtaining within it, the moral self always operates as a whole. Role-taking propensity, role-taking range, self-conceptions of virtue, and self-efficacy are all to a degree implicated in each attempt to solve a moral problem. From a cognitivist perspective concerned principally with logical reasoning by autonomous individuals, this might seem like crowding too much into the analytic frame. But in the Meadian view it can be no other way, since moral problem solving is a form of social action that requires participants with fully social selves.

Reproduction of social structure

The self mediates the process of reproducing social structure. When individuals act in ways that are consistent with the self-conceptions that have been instilled in them, they reproduce the patterns of social life. The same occurs when they act to maintain or enhance self-esteem by conforming to the perceived expectations of others or by otherwise striving for competence in socially approved ways. But these are not the only ways the self functions in reproducing social structure. It is possible to more fully illuminate the structure-reproducing effects of the self in general by considering the moral self in particular.

First, the moral self can come into play in exactly the ways suggested: by motivating behavior that is consistent with instilled conceptions of virtue, thus reproducing moral culture; and by motivating esteem-seeking behavior that conforms to the perceived expectations of others or to rules for demonstrating competence in approved ways, thus also reproducing culture and traditional patterns of behavior. The moral self thus plays a mediating role in the reproduction of moral culture, that is, in reproducing a body of shared beliefs about the objects and forms of conduct that are good, and of patterns of behavior based on those beliefs.

Of course, reproduction per se does not depend on highly developed moral selves. Consider that role-taking propensity and range might remain so poorly developed among some individuals that they never recognize the moral significance of their actions. For such people, the level of conduct where complex moral problems arise may never be reached. Beyond demanding knowledge of appropriate rules of conduct, life is perceived as presenting no moral challenges. The habitual, amoral behavior of such individuals nonetheless contributes to the reproduction of social structure. But there is no contribution through moral problem solving to the reorganization of perspectives that underlies the evolution of social structures and moral culture.

Self-efficacy is implicated in the reproduction of social structure in much the same way. But here it is a *weak* sense of efficacy that may promote untroubled reproduction, in that a weak sense of efficacy may tend to inhibit struggles to change existing social arrangements. In turn this would tend to undermine the moral self as a force for social change. Even if other elements of the moral self are active and spark interest in change, or if the solution to a moral problem demands it, without a sense of efficacy to undergird action, social structures may not be seriously challenged. The reproduction effect in this case is not limited, however, to overt behaviors. When action is inhibited because of a lack of efficacy, the moral self as a whole is weakened, or is at least "unreinforced." The long-term effect may be a solidification of destructive social structures that disempowered moral selves are unable to change.

The reproduction of social structure can also be affected by role-taking propensity and role-taking range, both tending to accelerate change. A propensity to take the perspectives of others is, as described earlier, essential to perceiving conflicts between values and interests and, by implication, also to appreciating the need to reconcile these conflicts. This is another way of describing awareness of the need for change. Role-taking range is a developed quality of mind, a sort of intellectual flexibility, that also facilitates reconciliation. This is another way of describing a cognitive ability conducive to making change happen. The moral self in which these elements are highly developed is thus both predisposed and more able to find ways of forging new perspectives and more adaptive social relations.

As can a weak sense of efficacy, diminished role-taking propensity and limited role-taking range can inhibit the operation of the moral self as a force for change. Lack of a disposition to take others' perspectives inhibits perception of the need for change. Lack of the ability to take alternative perspectives or, more simply, to grasp how others perceive and respond to the world, precludes creative thought and serious consideration of possible avenues for pursuing change. The narrowed moral self, or the moral self that harbors no impulse to enlarge itself, will have the sort of conservative reproduction effect described, as it poses little threat to the existing social arrangements that give rise to moral problems.

It should be clear that my conception of the highly developed moral self is as a potentially powerful force for change. The propensity to role-take, the ability to take diverse perspectives, possession of self-conceptions of virtue, and a strong sense of efficacy are elements not just of a moral self but of a dynamic self. This is a self that is able to perceive needs for change arising out of moral problems, is able to intelligently and objectively reflect on possible changes, and is motivated to try to make change happen. The moral self in the ideal is, following Dewey and Mead, what might be called a pragmatic, progressive self.

I have explored the function of the moral self in moral action because it is through moral action that social structures are both modified and preserved. This focus has also served to show the social construction and embeddedness of the individual as a moral actor, and how the self can operate to uncritically reproduce or to challenge and modify existing social structures. In this view, moral action as it is driven by the moral self is thus much more than a matter of clever thinking about moral dilemmas. It is a matter of thinking and acting in ways that lead either to furthering the social process or to its decay and possible termination.

Possible directions for research

It might seem that psychologists and educators have cornered the market, so to speak, on research concerning moral development and moral judgment. What can sociologists-come-lately hope to contribute? A great deal, I think, provided we frame our questions about moral action in sociological terms and do not limit ourselves to cognitivist conceptions of morality as logical reasoning about justice and equity dilemmas. Using Mead's social psychology and ethical theory to put moral action back into social context suggests both new questions and new avenues for research.

One set of questions suggests an avenue for research that runs parallel to that most often taken by cognitivists: How does the moral self develop? What are the key experiences that shape it? How do individual differences come about? The answers to these questions are important, but for sociologists they should not be ends in themselves. The point of studying development and identifying differences between individuals is to make it possible to link these differences to differences in social experience. The sociological end, in other words, should be to discover how moral problem-solving competence develops out of social experience and is thus a consequence of particular social structures. How, for example, do the experiences associated with social class position affect the development of moral selves? How do sex and race come into play in sexist and racist societies?

Since social structure is not something that only children and adolescents confront, research on the development of the moral self must look at adults as well. The cognitivist view, based on Piagetian notions of stages of development in reasoning ability, holds that by late adolescence one's highest level of cognitive and moral development is more or less fixed. This leaves little room for exploring variability in the moral problem-solving competence of adults. In contrast, the Meadian view considers development of the moral self as a process that can continue throughout the life span. A new line of research into individual development might thus focus on how the moral selves of adults are shaped by the problem-solving demands particular environments force upon them, and by the problems adults seek out for themselves.

Sociologists ought also to study the function of the moral self in the face of moral problems that arise in natural settings. Despite hundreds of studies of moral reasoning, knowledge of what people do when they confront real moral problems in everyday life is quite limited (cf. Sabini & Silver, 1982; Haan et al., 1985; Jackall, 1988). Laboratory and survey studies create the impression that solutions to moral problems are arrived at through thought experiments or are predetermined as a function of "moral attitudes." This impression is thoroughly misleading, as it is based on an image of the individual as a moral problem solver in vacuo. A sociological view must emphasize features of the situation as determinants of moral action in the real world. This view suggests that research should be directed to understanding just how elements of the moral self come into play both in thought *and in interaction*, as individuals try to resolve moral problems in concrete situations. Getting at these processes will require more field studies of moral problem solving in everyday life.

Finally, there is the matter of the reproduction of social structure through moral problem solving. Perhaps this is better described as the study of how social structure and culture are preserved and modified through moral action. Here there is much to learn about moral action and the social construction of reality. The sociological emphasis ought to be on this process as it evolves interactively and as it is shaped by power imbalances and other forms of inequality.[8] Of particular value would be more studies of how strong moral selves, as might be found in political and organizational dissidents, lead to troublemaking and to political and organizational change. The issue might also be turned around and the question asked, How does the mass weakening of moral selves function to perpetuate destructive forms of social organization? How does this occur through elite use of ideology and repressive institutions?

The concept of the moral self is one theoretical tool that may be helpful for answering these questions. It can be used to better understand how the covert and overt phases of moral action arise out of and function to reproduce social life. Herein lies its value for sociological analysis. The concept can also be used to better understand how social structures might be changed to foster rather than undermine moral action. Herein lies its value for furthering the social process.

Notes

1 The Meadian terminology seems to imply that some impulses are more "fully owned" than others. This is not really the case. All the impulses that the self comprises, whether described as belonging to the "I" or the "Me," belong to the individual. To say that the "Me" phase of the self is made up of the internalized impulses of others is only to say that these particular impulses can be identified with others. They are for this no less part of the individual who has internalized them.

2 In discussing levels of conduct my usage departs somewhat from Mead's. In his 1927 Introductory Ethics course Mead distinguished three levels of moral conduct: personal, socially determined, and rational (see Broyer, 1973: 185; Mead, n.d.). The personal level involves taking the perspective of a specific other; the socially determined level involves taking the perspective of a group; and the third level involves taking an abstract, universal perspective. At the third level, the individual reflects on the social process itself and attempts to discover new values. This is where what others would call "post-conventional moral reasoning" occurs. My discussion of levels of conduct is intended simply to introduce the idea that it is important to understand social behavior in terms of the degree and scope of reflexiveness it entails.

3 Role taking in round-robin fashion is what Kohlberg (1973) calls ideal role taking or playing "moral musical chairs." This sort of cognition is necessary to achieve fair solutions to moral problems, according to Kohlberg. Fair solutions are those that exhibit a reversibility of moral judgments among all the stakeholders in the problem. Achieving reversibility calls

for moral actors to first imagine themselves in each person's position in the situation and to consider all the claims that could be made from each position, including their own; then they must imagine that they do not know who they are in the situation and to ask whether they would still uphold all claims considered; and finally, to act in accordance with only those claims that are reversible in the situation. In this process the moral actor must be able to take the perspectives of all parties to the situation, but not just reciprocally. The actor must also be able to take other perspectives *from other perspectives*, that is, to imagine how all parties to a problematic situation would respond if they were each to look at the situation from every other perspective. What Kohlberg seems to have in mind is Mead's notion of the social process operating at a very high level.

4 In his course on ethics, Mead used the Dewey and Tufts text *Ethics*, from which the quoted Dewey passage originally derives.

5 Working from what she calls an "interactionalist" perspective on morality, Norma Haan and her colleagues (Haan, Aerts, & Cooper, 1985) have shown that sophistication in justice reasoning may actually inhibit effective moral problem solving in concrete situations. This is because sophisticated reasoning in the abstract is often used in a self-defensive way to avoid confronting the real points of conflict. The best moral problem solvers, she found, were those who were willing to endure the emotional stress of coping straightforwardly with moral conflicts (cf. Dewey 1908/1960: 128–129).

6 I have attempted to address these matters more fully in other papers. See Schwalbe (1988a, 1988b).

7 Some readers may be uncomfortable with the implication that the powerless and oppressed might have weaker moral selves, on the average, than those in more privileged groups. If so, I would like to point out three things. First, this reaction has no bearing on the validity of the argument, which stands or falls on other grounds. Second, the argument carries no implication that members of powerless and oppressed groups are, on the average, any less honest, caring, or concerned for justice than anyone else. And third, I suggest that whatever uneasiness the implication of unequal development of moral selves evokes be redirected toward the far more vast inequalities in material well-being that make full self-development an impossibility for those who must struggle merely to survive.

8 If problems of public policy formation can be thought of as attempts to solve moral problems, then some forms of policy analysis might be described as doing essentially this. There nonetheless remains a need for social psychological analyses that take the moral self explicitly into account. The public policy arena might be an especially good one in which to study the overwhelming of the moral self.

References

Backman, C. 1985. Identity, self presentation, and the resolution of moral dilemmas: Towards a social psychological theory of moral behavior. In B. Schlenker (Ed.), *The self and social life* (pp. 261–289). New York: McGraw-Hill.

Bandura, A. 1986. *Social foundations of thought and action*. Englewood Cliffs, NJ: Prentice-Hall.

Bernstein, B. 1973. *Class, codes, and control, II: Applied studies toward a sociology of language*. London: Routledge and Kegan Paul.

Blasi, A. 1984. Moral identity: Its role in moral functioning. In W. M. Kurtines & J. L. Gewirtz (Eds.), *Morality, moral behavior, and moral development* (pp. 128–139). New York: Wiley.

Broyer, J. A. 1973. Mead's ethical theory. In W. R. Corti (Ed.), *The philosophy of G. H. Mead* (pp. 171–192). Winterthur, Switzerland: Archiv fur genetische Philosophie.

Cheek, J. M., & R. Hogan. 1983. Self-concepts, self-presentations, and moral judgments. In J. Suls & A. Greenwald (Eds.), *Psychological perspectives on the self* (Vol. 2, pp. 249–273). Hillsdale, NJ: Erlbaum.

Cook-Gumperz, J. 1973. *Social control and socialization: A study of differences in the language of maternal control*. London: Routledge and Kegan Paul.

Coser, R. L. 1975. The complexity of roles as the seedbed of individual autonomy. In L. A. Coser (Ed.), *The idea of social structure: Papers in honor of Robert K. Merton* (pp. 237–263). New York: Harcourt Brace Jovanovich.

Damon, W. 1984. Self-understanding and moral development from childhood to adolescence. In W. M. Kurtines & J. L. Gewirtz (Eds.), *Morality, moral behavior, and moral development* (pp. 109–127). New York: Wiley.

Della Fave, L. Richard. 1980. The meek shall not inherit the earth: Self-evaluation and the legitimacy of stratification. *American Sociological Review* 45: 955–971.

Dewey, J. 1960. *Theory of the moral life*. New York: Holt, Rinehart and Winston. (Original work published 1908)

Gecas, V. 1979. The influence of social class on socialization. In W. R. Burr, R. Hill, F. I. Nye, & I. L. Reiss (Eds.), *Contemporary theories about the family* (Vol. 1, pp. 365–404). New York: Free Press.

Gecas, V., & M. L. Schwalbe. 1983. Beyond the looking-glass self: Social structure and efficacy-based self-esteem. *Social Psychology Quarterly* 46: 77–88.

Gilligan, C. 1982. *In a different voice*. Cambridge: Harvard University Press.

Gilligan, C. 1987. Moral orientation and moral development. In E. F. Kittay & D. T. Meyers (Eds.), *Women and moral theory* (pp. 19–33). Totowa, NJ: Rowman and Littlefield.

Haan, N., E. Aerts, & B. A. B. Cooper. 1985. *On moral grounds: The search for practical morality*. New York: New York University Press.

Habermas, J. 1984. *The theory of communicative action*. Boston: Beacon Press.

Habermas, J. 1985. Philosophical notes on moral judgment theory. In G. Lind, H. Hartmann, & R. Wakenhut (Eds.), *Moral development and the social environment* (pp. 3–20). Chicago: Precedent.

Harding, C. G. 1985. Intention, contradiction, and the recognition of dilemmas. In C. G. Harding (Ed.), *Moral dilemmas: Philosophical and psychological issues in the development of moral reasoning* (pp. 43–55). Chicago: Precedent.

Hoffman, M. L. 1984. Empathy, its limitations, and its role in a comprehensive moral theory. In W. M. Kurtines & J. L. Gewirtz (Eds.), *Morality, moral behavior, and moral development* (pp. 283–302). New York: Wiley.

Hogan, R., & C. Busch. 1984. Moral action as autointerpretation. In W. M. Kurtines & J. L. Gewirtz (Eds.), *Morality, moral behavior, and moral development* (pp. 227–240). New York: Wiley.

Jackall, R. 1988. *Moral mazes: The world of corporate managers*. New York: Oxford University Press.

Kaplan, H. B. 1980. *Deviant behavior in defense of self*. New York: Academic Press.

Keller, M. 1976. Development of role-taking ability. *Human Development* 19: 120–132.

Kohlberg, L. 1969. Stage and sequence: The cognitive-developmental approach to socialization. In D. Goslin (Ed.), *Handbook of socialization theory and research* (pp. 347–480). Chicago: Rand McNally.

Kohlberg, L. 1973. The claim to adequacy of a highest stage of moral judgment. *Journal of Philosophy* 70: 630–646.

Kohlberg, L. 1984. *Essays on moral development: Vol. II. The psychology of moral development*. New York: Harper and Row.

Kohn, M. L. 1969. *Class and conformity: A study in values*. Homewood, IL: Dorsey.

Maccoby, E. 1959. Role-taking in childhood and its consequences for social learning. *Child Development* 30: 239–252.

Mead, G. H. 1934. *Mind, self and society* (C. W. Morris, Ed.). Chicago: University of Chicago Press.

Mead, G. H. 1964. The genesis of the self and social control. In A. J. Reck (Ed.), *Selected writings: George Herbert Mead* (pp. 267–293). New York: Bobbs-Merrill. (Original work published 1924–1925)

Mead, G. H. 1964. National-mindedness and international-mindedness. In A. J. Reck (Ed.), *Selected writings: George Herbert Mead* (pp. 355–370). New York: Bobbs-Merrill. (Original work published 1929)

Mead, G. H. 1964. Philanthropy from the point of view of ethics. In A. J. Reck (Ed.), *Selected writings: George Herbert Mead* (pp. 392–407). New York: Bobbs-Merrill. (Original work published 1930)

Mead, G. H. 1964. The philosophical basis of ethics. In A. J. Reck (Ed.), *Selected writings: George Herbert Mead* (pp. 82–93). New York: Bobbs-Merrill. (Original work published 1908)

Mead, G. H. n.d. *Mead collection*. Unpublished notes, Box VI, "Ethics" envelope, University of Chicago.

Morgan, D., & M. L. Schwalbe. 1990. Mind and self in society: Linking social structure and social cognition. *Social Psychology Quarterly* 53: 148–164.

Morgan, D., & M. Spanish. 1987. *Post-crisis social psychology: An integration of role-theory and social cognition*. Paper presented at annual meetings of Pacific Sociological Association, Eugene, Oregon.

Rest, J. R. 1986. *Moral development: Advances in theory and research*. New York: Praeger.

Sabini, J., & M. Silver. 1982. *Moralities of everyday life*. New York: Oxford University Press.

Schantz, C. 1975. The development of social cognition. In E. M. Hetherington (Ed.), *Review of child development theory and research* (Vol. 5, pp. 257–323). Chicago: University of Chicago Press.

Schwalbe, M. L. 1986. *The psychosocial consequences of natural and alienated labor*. Albany: State University of New York Press.

Schwalbe, M. L. 1988a. Meadian ethical theory and the moral contradictions of capitalism. *Philosophy and Social Criticism* 14: 26–51.

Schwalbe, M. L. 1988b. Role taking reconsidered: Linking competence and performance to social structure. *Journal for the Theory of Social Behavior* 18: 411–436.

Selman, R. 1971. The relation of role-taking to the development of moral judgment in children. *Child Development* 42: 79–91.

Sorokin, P. A., & W. A. Lunden. 1959. *Power and morality*. Boston: Porter Sargent.

Staub, E. 1979. *Positive social behavior and morality: Vol. 2. Socialization and development*. New York: Academic Press.

Stotland, E. 1969. Exploratory studies of empathy. In L. Berkowitz (Ed.), *Advances in experimental social psychology* (Vol. 4, pp. 271–314). New York: Academic Press.

Thomas, D., D. Franks, & J. Calonico. 1972. Role-taking and power in social psychology. *American Sociological Review* 37: 605–614.

Wegner, D. M. 1980. The self in prosocial action. In D. M. Wegner & R. R. Vallacher (Eds.), *The self in social psychology* (pp. 131–157). New York: Oxford.

Weinreich-Haste, H. 1983. Social and moral cognition. In H. Weinreich-Haste & D. Locke (Eds.), *Morality in the making: Thought, action, and the social context* (pp. 87–108). New York: Wiley.

Wells, L. E. 1978. Theories of deviance and the self-concept. *Social Psychology Quarterly* 41: 189–204.

14   The production of selves in personal relationships

Philip Blumstein

Introduction

Innumerable words have been written and uttered on the fundamental relationship between the person and society, many of them inspiring discussion of the *social* nature of the self. As Rosenberg (1981: 593) summarizes,

social factors play a major role in...formation [of the self]....[It] arises out of social experience and interaction; it both incorporates and is influenced by the individual's location in the social structure; it is formed within institutional systems ...; it is constructed from the materials of the culture; and it is affected by immediate social and environmental contexts.

The significance of this simple point cannot be overstated: It has been one of sociology's guiding principles for many years, it has been offered as an epiphany to generations of undergraduates, and it has inspired countless research studies. Nevertheless, the concrete social processes captured in the simple but elegant notion of the social creation of the self remain, after all these years, only vaguely understood. The picture is incomplete. Surely social interaction generates selves, but the question that continues to deserve our attention is *how*.

From the early work of Cooley (1902), it has been a commonplace to locate much of the development of self in *primary groups*, by which is generally meant families and similar intimate relationships. This classical theme is the point of departure for this chapter, in which I address the question of how selves are created, maintained, and changed by virtue of the structure of intimate relationships and the nature of interaction that occurs in them.

Self and identity

The terms *self* and *identity* have been used in a dizzying diversity of ways, and no definitional synthesis will be attempted here. My approach

305

here is largely dramaturgical, relying on the numerous discussions of self and identity that followed the 1959 publication of Goffman's *Presentation of Self in Everyday Life* (e.g., Messinger, Sampson, & Towne, 1962; Weinstein & Deutschberger, 1963; McCall & Simmons, 1966; Gergen, 1968; Blumstein, 1975). In my usage, *self* is a personal intrapsychic structure and is only knowable by the person to whom it belongs. In this view the self can be part of the mechanics that motivate the actor's behavior (McCall & Simmons, 1966; Blumstein, 1975; Rosenberg, 1981; Swann, 1987). In contrast, I will use the term *identity* as a shorthand for *situational* or *situated identity* (Weinstein & Deutschberger, 1963; Alexander & Wiley, 1981), referring to the *face* that is publicly displayed, perhaps quite fleeting, in interaction. In this usage, identity is Goffman's *presented self* and, as such, it requires no private commitment on the part of actor or audience to its being a valid reflection of the "true" self.

Numerous attempts have been made to characterize the relationship between identity and self (McCall & Simmons, 1966; Gergen, 1968; Blumstein, 1975; Swann & Read, 1981; Wiley & Alexander, 1987). First, it is necessary to consider the relationship between self and behavior. Although the various approaches to this question differ in detail, a common theme can be identified: The self finds expression in behavior, even if that expression may be mediated in complex ways. The actor's behavior, according to the most general model, invokes a response in alter. Out of that response ego receives information with implications for his or her self, information that ultimately may modify that self. The self, it is posited, has enormous motivation consequences for interactive behavior, and all interactive behavior, it is further posited, can be analyzed in terms of the situated identities being presented. Perhaps the best articulated version of the view that self produces identity is found in McCall and Simmons's (1966: 73) discussion of individuals' ubiquitous motive to seek *role-support*, which they define as "a set of reactions and performances by others the expressive implications of which tend to confirm one's detailed and imaginative view of himself. . . . Role-support is centrally the implied confirmation of the specific *content* of one's idealized and idiosyncratic imaginations of self." Since people are universally motivated to seek role-support for cherished aspects of the self, they tend to present (enact) identities consistent with that self in order to maximize the likelihood of receiving that role-support.

I have no quarrel with this view of the relationship between self and identity. However, in this chapter I wish to explore a different causal ordering, one less commonly considered, that is, that identity affects self. Going back to the work of Bem (1972), numerous social psychologists have argued that actors perceive their own behavior (whatever its sources), and in the process they make attributions to the self. If one translates this into a dramaturgical framework, instead of *behavior,* one may speak of the *identities* people project. Individuals observe the identities they project, and in some circumstances they may attribute this enactment to a true expression of the self. In spite of any constraints the self may place on the identities presented (Blumstein, 1975), these enacted behaviors may frequently have nothing to do with any sincere underlying dimensions of self.

A central assertion of this chapter is that if identities are projected frequently enough, they eventually produce modifications in the self. In searching for a term to capture this process whereby repeated enactment of identities produce selves, I have chosen the concept of *ossification.* Whereas the work of people on self-attribution has dealt with the intrapsychic process whereby one's own behavior is observed and inferences are made about it, I focus more on the interpersonal aspects of how and why identities ossify into selves.

The process of ossification is very slow and gradual, and consequently is not easy to study with our conventional research methods. It is the process that we infer has occurred when we awaken one morning to discover we are not the same person we were twenty years earlier. Or more commonly when we encounter a person from our past and are reminded by the interaction of how much our self has drifted over the years. Surely the meanderings of our social environment are responsible for the drift, but I would argue that it is particularly in our intimate relationships that the ossification process takes place. To say that the self is subject to drift does not contradict the idea of ossification. Indeed the two concepts may be seen as constituting two ends of a continuum. Drift occurs as a function of changes in the individual's interpersonal environment. Ossification has as a necessary condition continuity in the interpersonal environment, and accelerates during those periods of continuity. Ossification means that we enact identities with great frequency and we *become* the person whom we have enacted.

Why, in so much writing about the self has the idea of ossification (or some equivalent) not been prominent? The answer lies in a shortcoming of dramaturgical analysis, that is, its inattention to the development of durable social structures. Microsociology seems recently to have undergone a shift away from an exclusive focus on interaction to a greater recognition of ongoing relationships. When the model, especially in Goffman's work, was built on unanchored, situationally bounded, evanescent exchanges between near strangers, the implications for self of the identity presented seemed trivial. But so much of social life occurs in relationships that, even if not always intense, have histories and futures, and for that reason the identities that are enacted in intimate relationships should have important implications for the self.

Couple identity work

There is a form of seemingly insignificant talk heard frequently from husbands, wives, and from partners in other kinds of intimate marriagelike relationships. Possibly it is occasionally heard in the speech of close friends. Here are three simulated examples:

My husband can't be allowed into the kitchen. He wouldn't know how to boil water. He would ruin it and make a mess in the process.

We are different about dirt. I hate it and clean it up the minute it appears. She waits until it begins to accumulate and then goes after it with a vengeance. We are both very clean, just different about it.

We are not like other couples. They are all interested in showing what they earn and what they can buy, but we prefer to content ourselves with a more spiritual approach to life.

This form of verbal behavior, *couple identity work*, is often heard when one interviews couples, as well as in the spontaneous speech of ordinary people. It is frequently directed to persons outside the relationship, but I believe it also arises when intimates are alone talking together about themselves and about their relationship. As is clear from the examples, these are not ponderous discussions of "the relationship," but instead rather mundane characterizations of who the two partners are, frequently with a tone of who they are vis-à-vis one another.

I have called this process couple *identity* work; what does it have to do with the *self*? Although there is certainly identity work going on in the examples, it has already been acknowledged that situated identities and selves are not the same. However, one of the important ways in which personal relationships differ from simple Goffmanesque interaction is that in the former situated identities are potentially much more apt to have long-lasting implications for the self. Again, this is the process I have called ossification.

One might argue that these couples are only announcing the truth about themselves and their partners. Indeed this is a compelling observation because who will be more keenly aware of the dispositions of another than his or her spouse or partner? The very nature of intimacy implies that two people have developed a profound awareness of who the other is. It is, however, the publicness of the display, the apparent felt necessity of locating oneself, one's partner, and the relatedness of the two in some kind of conceptual space that suggests that the relationship engenders or demands reality creation work that is separate and apart from the simple reporting on a preexisting reality (cf. Goffman, 1971, on tie-signs). In these interactions couples are displaying a reality they have created, while at the same time they are allowing us to witness a sample of the processes through which this reality was created over the months and years.

Motivation

A husband may learn for the first time that he cannot cook as his wife describes his culinary failures to a group of assembled friends. If he hears such commentary with sufficient frequency, both in front of guests and in solitary conversation with his wife, one may expect that he will come to incorporate culinary incompetence into his self. Moreover, if no circumstances arise to propel him into the kitchen, he will have no opportunity to challenge that aspect of self. This example is particularly useful because it leads to speculations about motivation: What goals or purposes would a wife be likely to achieve by fostering the reality that her husband is incompetent in the kitchen? What goals or purposes does a husband achieve in passively acceding to that definition of the situation? One can ask a further set of questions, more on the level of social structure, such as, What is it about the institution of marriage that led to this bit of reality creation in which, ultimately, both spouses have colluded? Moreover, in what ways did this minute exercise in reality creation contribute to the reproduction of the marital institution?

A fundamental concept in dramaturgical analysis is *interpersonal control* (Weinstein, 1969). It links the motivational states of purposive actors to the self-presentational strategies they employ. It draws attention to the connection between hedonistic actors and processes of reality presentation and reality negotiation. A focus on interpersonal control lends motivational enrichment to the dramaturgical model, with the simple principle that actors' purposes (desires, goals) can best be served by the identities they choose to enact and the identities into which they are able to cast their interaction partner(s) (Weinstein & Deutschberger, 1963, 1964; Weinstein, 1969). If one accepts that frequently enacted identities eventually may ossify into selves, then the implication of interpersonal control as a motivational concept is that selves grow out of motivational states (both ego's and alter's – the opposite of the usual position on causality).

In close relationships, just as in Goffman's disconnected focused gatherings, it must be acknowledged that ego takes active, though perhaps not conscious, involvement in shaping alter's identity, and his or her motivation may frequently be purely selfish. Ego may best pursue his or her desired outcomes in interaction and/or relationship by shaping the distribution of identities (both ego's and alter's) that are incorporated into the working consensus. But intimate relationships are significantly different from the interactions that Goffman analyzed. Among intimates, who have durable relationships with anticipatable futures, it is generally much more efficient to shape the underlying self of alter, such that by simply *being* that self, alter will assume a situated identity congruent with ego's goals. The less efficient alternative would be for ego to try to manipulate alter's situational identity afresh in each encounter. For example, once a husband has incorporated as a part of his self a sense of ineptitude in the kitchen, then his wife need never again altercast him in that light because his sense of self keeps him from entering her mysterious domain.

So far, little has been said about the content of actors' motivational systems. Aside from the everyday motivations – scratch my neck, take the children off my hands, do not drink too much in front of my parents – I would posit one central motivation in close relationships: the desire to keep alter committed to the relationship, and equally or more committed than oneself. The first part of this motivation involves the creation of solidarity through interdependence; the second involves the potential creation of hierarchy, that is, a partner who is either equal or inferior in terms of power and status. Both can be achieved if one finds ways to encourage alter's dependency (Emerson, 1962). But alter's dependency is encouraged at the same time that he or she is encouraged to perform services that increase his or her worth and consequently ego's own dependency (Emerson, 1972).

Definitions of reality

The process of identity negotiations should be viewed as ubiquitous because there are identity implications (hence potential self-implications) in even the most insignificant nuances of communication. For example, in a study of the division of labor in conversation, Kollock, Blumstein, and Schwartz (1985), showed that interruptions (violations of turn-taking norms) appear to be the right of the powerful. It is reasonable to argue a related phenomenon, that is, that actors infer from how much they successfully achieve interruption, or how often they are successfully interrupted, what their power or status is in an encounter. Some evidence indirectly supports this assertion: In an experimental study Robinson and Reis (1988) found that people who interrupt are more likely than those who do not to be perceived as more masculine and less feminine. Based on the research of Kollock et al. (1985), it could be argued that the dimensions being measured by Robinson and Reis as perceived masculinity and perceived femininity are really perceived hierarchy in the relationship between the speakers. If research subjects make such judgments about third parties who interrupt, it seems very reasonable that ordinary people make similar judgments about the interruptions that occur in their own on-going relationships. To be interrupted at alter's will is to learn the worth of one's contribution, and if this pattern is experienced repeatedly, it should affect the self in significant ways, even if alter is not intentionally trying to altercast ego into a subordinate position by his or her interruptions.

Another example of this logic comes from a study of influence tactics used by couples (Howard, Blumstein, & Schwartz, 1986) that found the weaker partner tends to use indirection to get his or her way. By extension, one might expect that by using indirection, one *becomes* a certain kind of person in the shared definition of reality, and that eventually this is incorporated into the self. Additionally, Goody (1978) has argued very convincingly that the simple act of asking a question is, for the lowly, one of the few legitimate avenues for inducing a high-status other into conversation. How one is required to enter a conversation, with head raised or bowed, sets a situational identity, and if this scenario occurs repeatedly, it eventually shapes the self.

Situations of open conflict have particular capacity for creating realities that may force modifications in the self. Frequently in the opening rounds of conflict in intimate relationships one partner offers a definition of the situation, usually a narrative containing complaints easily translatable into assertions about both situational identities and about dispositions, that is, selves, of the actors (see Turner, 1970, for an analysis of conflict between intimates). Information expressed in conflict situations has the patina of deep veracity because the extreme emotions are believed to undermine the expressive control necessary for strategic interaction. The other partner may find the asserted characterizations of self that emerge during intense conflict enormously discontinuous with respect to the self held dear, and must come to grips with what may be a persuasive but unsettling definition offered by a person who has been granted unparalleled permission to define situations. Alter may also have a counterdefinition to offer, one that may neutralize the self-implications of ego's statements. Nevertheless, alter has learned a possibly new way of framing the self, and even if ego recants his or her asserted truth, that truth, once uttered, continues to exist as a potential resource in the production of self for alter.

An intimate dyad has two fundamental properties when it comes to defining reality: (1) By being intimate, each partner grants the other enormous authority to shape the collective reality of the pair, and (2) by being a dyad, there may often be little in the way of third-party adjudication as to whose definition of reality – definition of selves – bears resemblance to some reality above or beyond the couple (a reality that actors take to be objective). This is why members of couples in conflict feel a need to discuss their problems with third parties, in order to bring the weight of validation to bear on one or the other of the potentially competing realities. And, of course, central to the realities being crafted are the selves of both parties.

This brings us back to dependency. Even in a structure as simple as a dyad, the process of reality construction can be very complex. Two of the many factors that enter into the process are *power* and *competence*. For the relationship to be close, both partners are highly dependent on one another and therefore both are very powerful. Nevertheless, in most cases one is likely to be even more powerful than the other, reflecting differences in resources and alternatives (Emerson, 1962). The generally more powerful partner, one might expect, will not only have greater capacity to get his or her way, but also in more subtle ways to control the definition of the situation, and by extension, the selves expressed within that definition (Scheff, 1968).

Not all forms of power are the same, and indeed one should expect that power that reflects one partner's particular expertise will be especially useful in defining relevant realities. For example, modern women have been granted the right of expertise over the subject of love (Cancian, 1985), and as a consequence, one would expect women in heterosexual relationships to have legitimacy in defining their partner's competence at such qualities as expressiveness, tenderness, and the like. This does not mean that these women are either generally more powerful or generally more capable of shaping the collective definition of the situation.

Interpersonal competence is an aggregation of skills that allow one actor to prevail over another in defining the situation, that is, in assuring that the working consensus captures a reality that supports his or her goals and desires. It includes such qualities as role-taking ability and the possession of a large and unfettered repertoire of lines of actions (Weinstein, 1969). Competent actors will generally be more successful at shaping their partner's identity *and* their partner's self, even without being relatively more powerful. Indeed the less powerful partner is more likely to resort to interpersonal tactics of indirection (Howard et al., 1986), and one form of indirection may be the subtle yet constant efforts to change alter's self so that he or she will behave more cooperatively. Following this line of argument, one encounters an interesting paradox: The more powerful partner is in a better position to change alter's definition of himself or herself, yet the less powerful partner has a greater desire to change alter's self because he or she does not have as many alternative means to change alter's behavior.

Another aspect of reality work in relationships is worth noting: In the everyday negotiation of reality, there is a norm of passive acceptance such that if the costs are small to endorsing alter's definition of the situation, then people will permit that definition to prevail. Given this premise, dramaturgically astute actors can gradually create a definition of the relationship and the selves of its members that will take enormous effort, and possibly engender hostility and conflict, if alter wishes to amend it. Collective meanings may accrue that one partner feels unable to modify, even though he or she neither believes in them nor feels strategically safe by accepting their implications. This is why such culturally significant relationships as marriage have developed rich elaboration around defining the relationship in an inescapable way. For example, ego's proposal of marriage is a last chance, however fraught with risk of momentary unpleasantness and discomfort, for alter to say that the inadvertent accretion of meaning that may have occurred cannot be sustained.

Roles and relationships

The motivational states of the actors are not the only place to look for sources of the reality-creating processes in intimate relationships whereby selves are likely to be produced. Other places include the social structure and the structure of intimacy.

There is evidence in the work of social psychologists that roles shape selves (e.g., Huntington, 1957; Kadushin, 1969; Turner, 1978). The role structure of heterosexual marriage, in particular, has clear self-producing properties. Marital roles set important markers that are widely used to define traits or dispositions of role incumbents. The *provider* role, the *homemaker* roles, the *parent* role, the *lover* role, and so on, all have highly elaborated cultural standards that can be used to measure one's own and one's partner's adequacy as a person, as a man, as a woman, and so on. I will not attempt it here, but I think it would be a fruitful enterprise to analyze some of the subtleties in the content of marital roles with respect to the potential for self-implications. For example, what are the implications for the self to live under the conception that one's house can never be too clean, that one can never earn too much money, or that the delinquency of one's children reflects upon the quality of their home life?

Intimate relationships are at the same time *role relationships* and *personal relationships* (Blumstein & Kollock, 1988). As role relationships they provide common cultural scripts for their enactment, and these scripts, I have argued, shape selves. As personal relationships they have a set of internal processes, growing from the structure of intimacy, that also shape selves. Unlike roles, which are scripted particularly for each type of relationships, these internal processes have more to do with the structure of intimacy per se.

I would posit two dynamics in intimate relationships, particularly those that involve the complex coordination problems of living together – the *centripetal* and *centrifugal*. They are akin to the dual and contradictory needs for security/inclusion and autonomy/freedom. The former leads to projections of similarity or sameness; the latter to projections of difference or uniqueness (Maslach, 1974; Snyder & Fromkin, 1980). Projections of difference are very risky because they easily and inadvertently (perhaps inevitably) shade off into hierarchy.

In order to predict when these two dynamics will occur, one must consider both the motivational states of the actors and the constraints of social structure. What can ego accomplish by being similar to or the same as his or her partner? What can ego accomplish by being different? better? How does the relationship function when there is a shared reality of sameness? if there is a shared reality of difference?

Differentiation

Differentiation is one of the internal processes inherent to close relationships. Some differentiation comes with the role structure, as in the case of traditional heterosexual marriage, although the institution of marriage seems to be losing some of its role rigidity. However, this does not mean that as the cultural and structural sources of difference wither, spouses will not create differences, perhaps smaller, more subtle, more idiosyncratic, and personally less repugnant, but differences nevertheless.

There are several connections between forces of differentiation and self-production processes – the contrast effect, the division of labor, and the avoidance of competition. The first, and most evident is the *contrast effect*. Inevitably, as two people become intimately acquainted with one another, they simply will note that they react differently to a situation. The question is how such a simple set of personal observations may enter the interpersonal realm, and from there be elaborated upon to the point where they have potency in the production of selves.

The situation occurs frequently when there are serious potential coordination problems that are being exacerbated by the perceived difference.

A good example is in the realm of sexuality, where small differences in sexual appetite or preferred sexual scripts can become highly elaborated under some circumstances. The coordination problems help to heighten each partner's awareness of his or her own dispositions, and this awareness in itself can transform a disposition into a feature of self. But at another level, the couple may need to achieve a shared conceptualization to account for enduring imperfection or compromises in their solutions to the problems of sexual coordination. The consequence is that the dispositional differences are magnified, abstracted, reified, and typified. Through this process, the small differences become a more real feature of the individuals' selves.

Much of our thinking about intimacy derives from a heterosexual marital or dating context. Here a wealth of cultural resources is available for the creation of differences, and it is interesting to wonder whether this availability increases or decreases the potential impact on selves. Returning to the example of sexual coordination, one might wonder what occurs when a wife has a ready cultural basis for understanding the difference between her sexual appetite and that of her husband (i.e., Men are more sexual than women). What are the consequences for her self? In structuring an answer to this question, it might prove fruitful to contrast the wife's situation to that of a partner in a lesbian couple where a similar asymmetry of initiating and declining sex is present. In this case, it is much more difficult to find relevant cultural materials for contextualizing the observed differences between the two partners. Without an obvious categorical basis of observed differences, then any differences are likely to be treated as idiosyncratic (cf. Jones, Davis, & Gergen, 1961). The questions, then, become: In which kind of couple – two sexes or one – are the problematics of sexual coordination more likely to become part of the shared consciousness and rhetoric? In which kind of couple is that shared definition going to lead to a creation of a reality of dispositional difference? In which kind of couple will the creation of a reality of difference become ossified in the selves of the actors? Given the cultural belief that women have less sexual appetite than men, it would seem that the wife in our example would have as a central feature of her self her female sex, but that the *typical* aspects associated with her sex would in general not feature centrally in her self. The lesbian in our example does not have any category membership to account for her comparatively low sexual appetite and so her uniqueness (relative to her partner) would make sexual appetite a more salient dimension of self-organization. Indeed she may carry her typification of self as a person low in sexual appetite into a subsequent relationship where the facts might cast her self-perception in doubt.

The second force of differentiation is the tendency for all forms of social organization to create a *division of labor* even when there is none pre-assigned. In my research I have observed that struggle as some couples might to avoid differentiation in household tasks and other instrumental activities, they face a monumental uphill battle. The antagonism to a division of labor seems to have two sources: (1) a fear that it will resemble the traditional patriarchal divisions of heterosexual marriage with their attendant inequality, and (2) a desire to perform tasks together in order to maximize the amount of shared couple time. Couples report, however, that the pressures of efficiency, differences in aptitude, and different tastes all conspire to push them into a division of labor even when they fervently wish to avoid one.

The third process has some parallels to the creation of a division of labor. It involves the *avoidance of competition.* Inspiration for focusing the discussion of competition avoidance comes from the work on self-evaluation maintenance processes described by Tesser (1988). Couples face the problem of competitiveness whenever their selves are constructed such that the realms in which competence is salient are the same for both of them. This means that rather than identifying with the other's success, each may feel diminished by it. The powerful bonds of identification (Turner, 1970) are inhibited by the evils of social comparison processes (Festinger, 1954; Suls & Miller, 1977). According to Tesser's model, there are two dynamic processes: *reflection processes,* which involve what has been called identification by others, such that the successful performance of a person with whom we are close reflects favorably on us (see Cialdini & Richardson 1980), and *comparison processes*, which involve the sense of diminished worth of our own performance in comparison to the superior performance of the other. Turner (1970) has argued persuasively that bonds based on identification are salutary for intimate relationships, and by implication, the competitiveness that can grow out of comparison processes is detrimental.

The traditional differentiation of gender and its institutionalization in marital roles provided a significant buffer against competitiveness between spouses. However, as these institutions have changed, as men's and women's lives have become more similar and the distinction between their realms (private versus public) has withered, couples have clearly developed an increased potential for competition. Although many couples are probably crippled or brought to dissolution by that competition, I believe I have observed among couples I have interviewed that many others find ways of moving away from the conditions that lead to competitiveness.

Based on my impressionistic observation, I would suggest that couples whose similarity in skills, talents, and performances makes them vulnerable to competition rather than identification work collectively to create rich elaborations on tiny differences. Initially this is an act of reality construction, and eventually an act of self-production. By focusing and elaborating on small and apparent differences, they eventually *become* different. The couple who early in their relationship develop a shared hobby of cooking discovers that one is slightly better at desserts and the other slightly better at salads. Years later they may be discovered to have one salad-maker and one pastry chef, with each taking pride in the other's "unique" talent. Of course, the system is self-perpetuating, that is, the more each partner comes to define herself or himself as different from the other, the more that partner will come to behave differently and thereby be validated in the reflection from others in that self-definition. There is not a lot of strong evidence on the consequences of such differentiation for couples, but one study suggests that when couples can agree on which partner has greater knowledge in various domains, they also express greater satisfaction with their relationship (Wegner, 1986).

Sameness

The creation of differentness, both symbolic and real, must have limits in order for close relationships to survive. Indeed, it might be hypothesized that relationships can only create differentness to the extent that their solidarity or bondedness (Turner, 1970) is secure. Indeed, similarity abounds. Homogamy among married couples is one of the most durable empirical facts in the social sciences (Buss, 1984, 1985; Buss & Barnes, 1986), and there is also recent evidence for homogamy in same-sex couples (Kurdek & Schmitt, 1987; Howard, Blumstein, & Schwartz, 1989) as well as in friendship choice (Verbrugge, 1977; Duck & Craig, 1978; Kandel, 1978; Feld, 1982). The usual discussion of homogamy is based on assumptions of similarity of stable values, opinions, social statuses, and personality traits, all qualities the partners bring to the relationship. Without denying the validity of the literature on homogamy, I would suggest that homogamy in the "softer" areas, that is, values, opinions, *perceived* dispositions, may be something that couples *achieve* together once in the relationship. They accomplish the achievement through interpersonal processes of reality construction layered with supporting self-modifications.

Some examples of the social construction of sameness come from my study in collaboration with Pepper Schwartz on four types of couples:

married couples, heterosexual cohabitors, lesbian couples, and gay male couples (Blumstein & Schwartz, 1983). One of the lesbian couples was striking in this regard. When they arrived for their interview they wore the same hairstyle and virtually identical clothes. During the interview one partner exemplified couple identity work directed at sameness (Blumstein & Schwartz, 1983: 454):

I could honestly believe in reincarnation. We think so much alike and we have so much in common and we do these dumb things like get the same clothes on. We buy the same things. We bought each other the same valentine at different stores at different times. . . . We go out and buy the same groceries, not having discussed what we wanted ahead of time. . . . We'll shop at the same place and drift into each other. We drive up nose to nose in the same parking lots at the same moments.

There is little to be gained in treating these coincidences as either valid facts or as hallucinations. Rather one can look at these *stories* (which in the interview did not seem to be told for the first time), and the narrative they formed. One can understand how this narrative allows the couple to key into deep cultural themes of *love as merger*, and thereby multiply the symbolic solidarity and perfect taken-for-grantedness of the *happily ever after scenario* for their relationship. One can also understand how by the telling of these stories by both women (or when one woman tells them in the other's presence and the latter does not balk or object), each is saying something, either actively or passively, about her self and about the self of her partner. And if one is cynical about it, one can imagine each woman awaking in the morning and subconsciously choosing what clothing to wear in order to enhance the likelihood of confirming that they have "dis-covered" the uniquely perfect match in partners. I would suggest that she would choose that dress, not because she is consciously taking the role of her partner, but rather because she has come to see herself as "the kind of person who looks good in and likes wearing pastel colors." The motive is to construct togetherness through coincidence; the product is a pair of selves that will allow that motive to succeed.

Another example (Blumstein & Schwartz, 1983) comes from a partner in a gay male relationship, who said:

We go to the opera and I know that at the first intermission he will have a strong opinion one way or the other. Sometimes I have a gut level reaction to the opera, but generally I fall somewhere in the middle. The opera is somewhere between pretty good and quite bad, and I'm really not sure how I feel. But I do know that I feel a need to have an opinion to express at the intermission. And I realized the other night as I sit there, I'm getting anxious about what my opinion will be. So I asked myself why I was anxious about having an opinion, and I realized that when we both spontaneously love something, or we both spontaneously hate something, I feel this great, euphoric sense of rapport, of we-ness, that we are well matched and are therefore a "natural," "meant-to-be" couple. And when we disagree, or see the same thing very differently, I feel distant and alienated from him. It's like the spell has been broken. So as I sit in the opera wondering what my opinion is, I am really hoping that I will wind up with the opinion that will allow us to blend into one sweep of unanimity and be overwhelmed with that warm glow of coupleness.

This couple may not be typical; many couples feel free to disagree over heartfelt issues without any constraint to create a mystical couple reality, and do not experience their relationship as diminished by the agreement to disagree. They have learned that they agree on enough basic matters that a few displays of uniqueness is not distressing. Indeed such displays may be salutary in precisely the ways described in our discussion of differentiation processes. Examples such as this are probably most common in the early phases of relationships, where the participants may be eager to give assistance to whatever emerging similarities they may be discovering in one another. They feel genuine in the exaggerated sameness they project, but as I have argued, the projection of a self has the grave potential for the becoming of a self.

Anchors against drift

A fundamental fact about close relationships is that their attractiveness emerges from their predictability (Kelly, 1955; Bateson 1972; Kelley & Thibaut, 1978). Costs associated with learning new scripts with each new person one meets are reduced, role taking is simplified, coordination problems are minimized. How do couples accomplish this predictability? It is more than simply learning the other; rather it is by imposing a set of constraints on selves such that partners actually *become* more predictable. I would posit a fundamental overarching obligation in close relationships: to live up to the dispositional qualities that have become part of the working consensus (Athay & Darley, 1981; Swann, 1984). That is why personal relationships are inherently conservative, because an actor is constrained today to be the same person he or she was yesterday. Because of the constraints on actors to exhibit stable dispositional traits, close relationships can depart rather markedly from cultural scripts as the two participants create and maintain their own private culture.

Many people might object to this view of the conservative effects of intimate relationships. They would see close relationships as vehicles of personal growth and change (Cancian, 1987; Aron & Aron, 1989). They would argue that the extreme interdependence found in close relationships would provide a safe haven for the partners to explore alternative definitions of self. Although this logic is very persuasive, it ignores the fact that the selves of the partners are finely interwoven. One partner cannot express a self if there is no complementary self with which to resonate. One cannot enact incompetent dependency unless one's partner plays effective authority. To the extent that each partner has cathected the elements of his or her self, then that person is deeply invested in the complementary aspects of the self of the other. Certainly relationships can sometimes survive significant and abrupt changes in one of the selves. But it is indeed a matter of survival, because newly adopted selves create new demands on the other to give role-support, demands that cannot always be met, even with the best of intentions.

References

Alexander, C. Norman, Jr., & Mary Wiley. 1981. Situated activity and identity formation. In M. Rosenberg & R. H. Turner (Eds.), *Social psychology: Sociological perspectives* (pp. 269–289). New York: Basic Books.

Aron, Arthur, & Elaine Aron. 1989. *New research on the self-expansion model.* Paper presented at the Nags Head Conference on Interaction Process and Analysis, Nags Head, NC.

Athay, M., & John M. Darley. 1981. Toward an interaction centered theory of personality. In N. Cantor & J. F. Kihlstrom (Eds.), *Personality, cognition, and social interaction* (pp. 281–308). Hillsdale, NJ: Erlbaum.

Bateson, Gregory. 1972. *Steps to an ecology of mind.* New York: Ballantine.

Bem, Daryl J. 1972. Self-perception theory. In Leonard Berkowitz (Ed.), *Advances in experimental social psychology* (Vol. 6, pp. 1–62). New York: Academic Press.

Blumstein, Philip W. 1975. Identity bargaining and self-conception. *Social Forces* 53: 476–485.

Blumstein, Philip, & Peter Kollock. 1988. Personal relationships. *Annual Review of Sociology* 14: 467–490.

Blumstein, Philip, & Pepper Schwartz. 1983. *American couples: Money, work, and sex.* New York: Morrow.

Buss, David M. 1984. Toward a psychology of person-environment (PE) correlations: The role of spouse selection. *Journal of Personality and Social Psychology* 47: 361–377.

Buss, David M. 1985. Human mate selection. *American Scientist* 73: 47–51.

Buss, David M., & Michael Barnes. 1986. Preferences in human mate selection. *Journal of Personality and Social Psychology* 50: 559–570.

Cancian, Francesca. 1985. Gender politics: Love and power in the private and public spheres. In Alice S. Rossi (Ed.), *Gender and the life course* (pp. 253–264). New York: Aldine.

Cancian, Francesca. 1987. *Love in America: Gender and self-development.* New York: Cambridge University Press.

Cialdini, Robert B., & K. D. Richardson. 1980. Two indirect tactics of image management: Basking and blasting. *Journal of Personality and Social Psychology* 39: 406–415.

Cooley, Charles Horton. 1902. *Human nature and the social order.* New York: Scribner's.

Duck, Steve W., & R. G. Craig. 1978. Personality similarity and the development of friendship. *British Journal of Social and Clinical Psychology* 17: 237–242.

Emerson, Richard M. 1962. Power-dependence relations. *American Sociological Review* 27: 31–41.

Emerson, Richard M. 1972. Exchange theory, part II: Exchange relations and networks. In J.

Berger, M. Zelditch, & B. Anderson (Eds.), *Sociological theories in progress* (Vol. 2, pp. 58–87). Boston: Houghton Mifflin.

Feld, Scott L. 1982. Social structural determinants of similarity among associates. *American Sociological Review* 47: 797–801.

Festinger, Leon. 1954. A theory of social comparison processes. *Human Relations* 7: 117–140.

Gergen, Kenneth J. 1968. Personal consistency and the presentation of self. In C. Gordon & K. J. Gergen (Eds.), *The self in social interaction* (pp. 299–308). New York: Wiley.

Goffman, Erving. 1959. *The presentation of self in everyday life.* New York: Doubleday.

Goffman, Erving. 1971. *Relations in public: Microstudies of the public order.* New York: Basic Books.

Goody, Esther N. 1978. Toward a theory of questions. In E. N. Goody (Ed.), *Questions and politeness: Strategies in social interaction* (pp. 17–43). London: Cambridge University Press.

Howard, Judith A., Philip Blumstein, & Pepper Schwartz. 1986. Sex, power, and influence tactics in intimate relationships. *Journal of Personality and Social Psychology* 51: 102–109.

Howard, Judith A., Philip Blumstein, & Pepper Schwartz. 1989. *Homogamy in intimate relationships: Why birds of a feather flock together.* Paper presented at the annual meeting of the American Sociological Association, San Francisco.

Huntington, Mary Jean. 1957. The development of a professional self image. In R. K. Merton, G. G. Reeder, & P. Kendall (Eds.), *The student physician* (pp. 179–187). Cambridge: Harvard University Press.

Jones, Edward E., Keith E. Davis, & Kenneth J. Gergen. 1961. Role playing variations and their informational value for person perception. *Journal of Abnormal and Social Psychology* 63: 302–310.

Kadushin, Charles. 1969. The professional self-concept of music students. *American Journal of Sociology* 75: 389–404.

Kandel, Denise B. 1978. Homophily, selection and socialization in adolescent friendships. *American Journal of Sociology* 84: 427–436.

Kelley, Harold H., & John W. Thibaut. 1978. *Interpersonal relations: A theory of interdependence.* New York: Wiley.

Kelly, George A. 1955. *The psychology of personal constructs.* New York: Norton.

Kollock, Peter, Philip Blumstein, & Pepper Schwartz. 1985. Sex and power in interaction: Conversational privileges and duties. *American Sociological Review* 50: 34–46.

Kurdek, Lawrence, & J. Patrick Schmitt. 1987. Partner homogamy in married, heterosexual cohabiting, gay, and lesbian couples. *Journal of Sex Research* 23: 212–232.

Maslach, Christina. 1974. Social and personal bases of individuation. *Journal of Personality and Social Psychology* 29: 411–425.

McCall, George J., & J. L. Simmons. 1966. *Identities and interactions.* New York: Free Press.

Messinger, Sheldon L., with Harold Sampson & Robert D. Towne. 1962. Life as theatre: Some notes on the dramaturgical approach to social reality. *Sociometry* 25: 98–110.

Robinson, Laura F., & Harry T. Reis. 1988. *The effects of interruption, gender, and leadership position on interpersonal perceptions.* Paper presented at the International Conference on Personal Relationships, Vancouver, Canada.

Rosenberg, Morris. 1981. The self-concept: Social product and social force. In M. Rosenberg & R. H. Turner (Eds.), *Social psychology: Sociological perspectives* (pp. 593–624). New York: Basic Books.

Scheff, Thomas J. 1968. Negotiating reality: Notes on power in the assessment of responsibility. *Social Problems* 16: 3–17.

Snyder, C. R., & Howard L. Fromkin. 1980. *Uniqueness: The human pursuit of difference.* New York: Plenum Press.

Suls, Jerry M., & Richard L. Miller (Eds.). 1977. *Social comparison processes: Theoretical and empirical perspectives.* Washington, DC: Hemisphere.

Swann, William B., Jr. 1984. Quest for accuracy in person perception: A matter of pragmatics. *Psychological Review* 91: 457–477.

Swann, William B., Jr. 1987. Identity negotiation: Where two roads meet. *Journal of Personality and Social Psychology* 53: 1,038–1,051.

Swann, William B., Jr., & S. J. Read. 1981. Self-verification processes: How we sustain our self-conceptions. *Journal of Experimental Social Psychology* 17: 351–372.

Tesser, Abraham. 1988. Toward a self-evaluation maintenance model of social behavior. In Leonard Berkowitz (Ed.), *Advances in experimental social psychology* (Vol. 21, pp. 181–227). San Diego: Academic Press.

Turner, Ralph. 1970. *Family interaction.* New York: Wiley.

Turner, Ralph. 1978. The role and the person. *American Journal of Sociology* 84: 1–23.

Verbrugge, Lois M. 1977. The structure of adult friendship choices. *Social Forces* 56: 576–597.

Wegner, Daniel M. 1986. Transactive memory: A contemporary analysis of the group mind. In B. Mullen & G. R. Goethals (Eds.), *Theories of group behavior* (pp. 185–208). New York: Springer-Verlag.

Weinstein, Eugene A. 1969. The development of interpersonal competence. In D. A. Goslin (Ed.), *Handbook of socialization theory and research* (pp. 753–775). Chicago: Rand McNally.

Weinstein, Eugene A., & Paul Deutschberger. 1963. Some dimensions of altercasting. *Sociometry* 26: 454–466.

Weinstein, Eugene A., & Paul Deutschberger. 1964. Tasks, bargains, and identities in social interaction. *Social Forces* 42: 451–456.

Wiley, Mary Glenn, & C. Norman Alexander. 1987. From situated activity to self-attribution: The impact of social structural schemata. In K. Yardley & T. Honess (Eds.), *Self and identity: Psychosocial perspectives* (pp. 105–117). Chichester, UK: Wiley.

15   Conclusion

Peter L. Callero

In this final chapter we will undertake an analysis of some general theoretical issues that are largely implicit in the preceding chapters. In particular, we would like to focus on the common sociological frame of reference of this volume. In our introductory chapter we highlighted the importance of cognition, emotion, and action in our understanding of the self–society link. Here we will take a more macro approach and turn to the common themes reflected in the various conceptualizations of society.

For the most part, the contributors to this volume are representative of a body of American social psychologists whose theoretical roots can be traced to the early American pragmatists. Indeed, the influence of James, Peirce, Cooley, and especially Mead is evident in many of the preceding chapters. This early pragmatic tradition can be said to have been the source of a number of distinct theoretical perspectives in both psychology and sociology, with psychology drawing more heavily from James, and sociology from Mead (cf. Lewis & Smith, 1980). Although there is no doubt a gulf between the psychological and sociological traditions on a number of theoretical issues, the self has served over the years as a conceptual bridge linking the two social psychologies. A particularly good example of this common conceptual focus can be found in the chapters by Stryker (chapter 1), Gecas (chapter 8), and Rosenberg (chapter 6) where the traditional psychological concerns of cognition, motivation, and emotion are explicitly developed from a sociological perspective. In all three chapters, the self is used as the key conceptual mechanism for linking the psychological and sociological traditions. Moreover, each author is very clearly eclectic in his use of theory and research on the self, drawing freely from relevant work in both psychology and sociology. Thus, as we noted in the introduction, amid diversity in conceptions of the self there exists a common ground that often brings the two social psychologies together.

This is not to say that there are no differences between psychologists and sociologists in the definition and use of the self-concept. There are clear theoretical lines that mark the boundary between the two disciplines. The work in the sociological tradition, for example, is framed by an interest in understanding how the concept of self is relevant to the concept of society. In fact, it would be fair to argue that for sociologists, the self is relevant *because* it aids in the understanding and articulation of social structure. In the psychological tradition, on the other hand, the self finds its greatest conceptual utility as a variable in the explanation of individual action; little, if any, attention is given to social structure, institutions, or other large-scale patterns of interaction.

Whereas this volume at one level seeks to transcend the barriers separating the two social psychologies, it is unapologetically sociological in its frame of reference. What emerges is a distinctly sociological perspective on matters that have traditionally been the province of psychology. Thus, even though the contributors to this volume have not made the problem of society an explicit analytical concern, it is evident that understanding the society side of the self–society relationship is central in a larger theoretical sense. In this final chapter we will draw out the sociological side and examine the implicit conceptions of society evident in the individual chapter contributions. We will also take a brief look at the implications some of the analyses have for understanding the issue of social change.

Conceptions of society in theories of self and social cognition

As noted, a general observation that can be made about the chapters in this volume is that even though the focus is on seemingly individualistic concerns of cognition, emotion, and action, the theoretical orientation has not been an individualistic one. On the contrary, what leaps out is a pervasive sociological approach to problems that are traditionally framed from a more psychological perspective.

Most of the contributors have been clearly influenced by the work of Mead, and a number explicitly work from a symbolic interactionist tradition. Consequently, there are some basic theoretical assumptions that are at least implicitly held by most of the authors. Three are particularly noteworthy:

1. The individual and society are not separate. They are mutually supportive and dependent.
2. Action, emotion, and cognition are limited, changed, and sometimes determined by forces greater than the individual.
3. Society is sustained in the dynamic processes of interaction.

Thus, at this very general level we can see that there is a common concern for the dynamic relationship between self and society. Yet, as we would expect, there are also key differences in the explicit articulation of the social process. In sifting through the individual chapter contributions we have identified four characteristic ways of conceptualizing society. Although these conceptualizations are not in opposition (most authors draw on more than one), they do have subtle consequences for explaining the self–society relationship. In fact, we will argue that each conceptual approach can be viewed as possessing a particular theoretical utility.

Society as patterns of interaction

A common emphasis in a number of chapters is that society is sustained in reoccurring patterns of interaction. This conceptualization is most explicit in the contributions of Callero (chapter 2), Carley (chapter 4), and Schwalbe (chapter 13), but it is also a conceptualization consistent with identity theory, and is thus more or less advocated in the contributions by Stryker (chapter 1), Serpe (chapter 3), Smith-Lovin (chapter 7), and Burke (chapter 9).

Schwalbe notes that a particular advantage of this view of society is that it protects us from the problem of reification and the tendency to speak of social structure as an agent in itself. To be sure, society is still seen as a powerful force, but it is a force that is experienced as a participant in the stream of interaction where interpersonal power plays a significant role.

Callero also affirms the idea that society is "carried in reproduced practices and relationships," but he directs our attention to the question of how such patterns emerge. In other words, how can we explain the tendency and stability of certain patterns? He argues for the differentiation among types of interaction patterns and emphasizes that it is important to recognize the role played by cognition in the process.

Carley also sees society as expressed in opportunities of interaction and as dependent upon cognition. In a dynamic model of knowledge acquisition and exchange, she illustrates a promising technique for representing the relationship between microlevel interaction and the more macrolevel social structures. Carley's contribution is in fact a good example of an analysis that makes use of two different conceptualizations of society. On the one hand she views society as a system of interaction and as the product of cognitive processes. On the other hand, however, there is also an emphasis on the distribution of discrete items of knowledge, and the suggestion that society is at least partially a system of beliefs and norms – a point of view that is also represented in the work of a number of other contributors to this volume.

Society as a system of beliefs and norms

Accepting the dual premises that society is organized and patterned and that social structure to a degree determines action, leads inevitably to the question of how the force of society influences the actor. One quite traditional conceptual approach has been to emphasize the idea that society is a system of beliefs and norms. Through various processes of socialization the individual is said to internalize general cultural standards. Thus, social control is achieved through adherence to a normative system. It is clear that none of the contributors to this volume advocates this position uncritically, yet the utility of this particular conceptualization is evident in a number of chapters. Rosenberg (chapter 6) makes the most extensive use of this approach in his elaboration of emotional self-objectification. He describes, for example, the importance of "emotional norms...anchored in social roles" and notes that depending upon our position in society we are subject to various rules regarding appropriate feelings and the expression of affect. Moreover, Rosenberg suggests that these norms function to serve basic societal needs of control and integration. Yet, this is only a small part of a far-reaching eclectic analysis. Rosenberg is quick to point out that this is not all of the self–society relationship. Indeed, the central focus of the Rosenberg chapter is the self-regulation of emotional experiences that are seen as "spontaneous and involuntary responses to unplanned events." It is quite possible, therefore, to integrate elements of a normative conceptualization of society into a broader, more dynamic understanding of the self–society relationship.

In a similar way Gecas (chapter 8) also uses a conceptualization of society that is defined in part by a "system of meaning, values, and beliefs," what he refers to as the "cultural domain." Yet, Gecas is explicit in his acknowledgment that the cultural domain is only one level of a multilayered social system that is also defined by face-to-face interaction and hierarchies of power and status. The real value of Gecas's analysis in this respect, however, is his suggestion that particular self-motives are associated with each of the domains, thus articulating the importance of self.

Normally, conceptualizing society as a system of beliefs and norms is limited by a failure to appreciate the dynamic and creative side of action. Individual actors are typically seen as internalizing societal standards in a highly deterministic, one-directional process. However, by making the self an explicit component, Carley, Gecas, and Rosenberg have shown that a conceptualization of society in terms of shared knowledge is not necessarily inconsistent with the more dynamic aspects of the self. Moreover, the clear advantage of this particular conceptualization of society is that it takes into account the constraints and limits that exist as a consequence of our dependence upon a shared knowledge base. Clearly, as actors we are not free to construct *any* pattern of interaction. In fact, we are very much restricted by the resources provided by our culture – our shared language, knowledge, rules, and values.

In addition to a system of values, beliefs, and norms, there is also a relatively organized system of social positions and identities. These particular societal resources structure interaction and define both the self and the social structure. The emphasis on this aspect of society is also a dominant theme in a number of chapters.

Society as a system of positions and identities

Perhaps the most pervasive general conceptualization of society in this volume is that of a social structure defined by a system of positions and identities. This view is rooted in the work of Park, Kuhn, and Mead and is in line with the traditional symbolic interactionist dictum that self and society are only two sides of the same coin. In other words, self-structure mirrors social structure.

Society as a system of positions and identities is represented very clearly in Stryker's identity theory, which is the background for not only his chapter, but is also very clearly the frame of reference for the contributions by Serpe (chapter 3), Burke (chapter 9), and to some extent Smith-Lovin (chapter 7), Callero (chapter 2), and Howard (chapter 10).

The clear attraction of this conceptualization of society is that it unambiguously allows for the influence of social structure on the self in a way that avoids the problems of a strict determinism. Thus, although Stryker acknowledges that "it is social structures – including systems of positions and related roles as well as larger principles (e.g., age, sex, race, class) around which societies are organized – that shape interaction," the influence of society is one that goes through the self, thus leaving open the possibility for novel behavior and social change. Consequently, Stryker and Serpe are both able to develop models of a highly self-conscious and cognitive actor within the framework of identity theory.

The precise manner in which society and self link up under this conceptualization varies. Serpe uses one's self-structure of identities as a starting point. Social structural constraints are reflected in the availability of certain identities. Choice, however, enters in the commitment to available identities, a commitment that Serpe shows is determined by cognitive activity as well as structural factors. Stryker, on the other hand, focuses on the social structural constraints in the self–society relationship, asserting that cognitions are not random. What we think is also the product of socially structured interaction and experience.

Burke and Smith-Lovin emphasize another aspect of the self–society link within an identity framework. Drawing in part from the work of Heise (1979), both authors note that identity processes can be viewed as a control system that seeks to balance the semantic meaning or affective response generated by others, the situation, and the self. In addition, in both contributions traditional psychological constructs are addressed from a sociological perspective. Smith-Lovin uses the identity-based affect control model to explain the processes of cognition and emotion, and Burke uses a similar control systems approach to put a uniquely sociological twist on the classic social psychological problem of attitude-behavior consistency.

What makes the analyses by Burke and Smith-Lovin distinct is the guiding assumption that an overarching conceptualization of society is required for a complete explanation of their subject matter. Their general perspective clearly supports the view of society as a system of positions and identities, but they also rely heavily on the notion that society is defined by our shared cultural resources. What is emphasized, however, is not shared values, norms, and rules in the traditional sense already outlined, but rather shared sentiments and meanings. Their conceptual approach to society is valuable in that it illustrates the subtle processes of societal constraint at work in the situation. Society is a system of identities, it is shared sentiments, but it is also a predictable pattern of interaction that emerges at the level of the situation.

Society as situated

Whereas most of the contributors to this volume have identified the social in large macrosystems of norms, identities, and interaction patterns, at least two authors remind us that society is also experienced at the level of the situation – in interaction itself. First, Turner and Billings (chapter 5) argue that the social context, or self-in-situation, is experienced at both an objective (i.e., shared agreement on the facts) and a subjective level (similar to W. I. Thomas's definition of the situation), and that self-experience depends upon these situational experiences. In an empirical coding of student responses to open-ended questions, Turner and Billings identify a number of key elements of situations. In the process they demonstrate the microcomplexity of social structure. Thus, we see the importance of the physical properties of the setting, the cast of characters, and whether others in the setting are close friends or formal relations. We are also reminded that the occasion may be more or less casual, routine, even ceremonial, and at times the situation may be unique or novel. The nature of the activity is also relevant. Is it one involving contemplation, conversation, or recreation? The important point is that the self is experienced differently depending upon the social context. In other words, society affects the self in the complexities of subjective and objective situations.

Blumstein (chapter 14) is the other contributor to rely on a conceptualization of society as situated. Using the intimate personal relationship as a substantive case, he convincingly argues that the self as a somewhat enduring, personal characteristic is a product of the more public and fleeting features of situated identities. His focus actually turns upside down the more common emphasis on the stable self as a source of situated identities. In other words, instead of focusing on the manner in which a general and enduring self guides action in particular and novel settings, Blumstein reverses the causal order and examines how situation-specific identities affect the development of a more general cross-situational self. The value of this analysis is that it allows us to see more clearly the processes that lead to the emergence of society as we experience it.

Self, society, and social change

It is clear that all of the contributors to this volume accept the idea that society undergoes periods of both relative change and stability. At the same time, however, there are differences in whether emphasis is placed on the dynamic or static dimension. In chapter 12, Piliavin presents a unique analysis that explicitly addresses the issue of stability. Drawing from both the psychological and sociological literature, she shows how the concepts of habit and inertia can be used to explain the social psychology of repeated behavior. Moreover, her analysis raises some challenging questions concerning the methods and concepts we use to explain change and stability. For example, how central is the self in the production of repeated behavior? Piliavin reminds us that the self has its limits and that change is not ubiquitous.

But what about those historical periods when major structural change does occur? In what way does the self enter as an important explanatory concept? Traditionally, the self has not played a central role in analyses of social change. In fact, when the self is implicated, it is viewed almost exclusively as a product of changes in social structure. It is quite rare to find analyses that center on the self as a source of social change. Although it is undoubtedly the case that social structural change is never solely the consequence of changing selves, it is equally true that changes in self have at least the potential to impact social structure.

One consequence of the uniquely sociological social psychology of this book is that many of the chapters offer some intriguing, although sometimes subtle, proposals for the explanation of self-based social change. Explicating these proposals should help not only in our understanding of the self–society relationship, but should also provide fertile theoretical ground for the further development of our understanding of social change.

How then are changes in the macrosystems of society initiated at the microlevel? Most of the contributors suggest that the process is a gradual, accumulative one. This is the argument implicit in the chapters written from the perspective of identity theory, which sees large social structures built upon the small social structures of interaction. Stryker, for example, uses self-complexity theory to argue that a potential source of social change can be found in modifications of the cognitive structure linking claimed identities. Such a change in cognitive structure will necessarily alter the behavioral choices of the actor, and could lead to actions that ultimately stabilize in the form of institutionalized behavior.

Social change emerging from the cognitive structures tied to roles or identities is also suggested in the chapters by Callero, Serpe, Smith-Lovin, and to some extent Carley. It is in the contributions of the latter two authors that we can get a sense of the promise computer simulations hold for our understanding of the microbasis of social change. If in fact social change initiated at the microlevel is accumulative and gradual, the process will prove to be very difficult to examine empirically. Yet, by modeling microinteraction with a simulated model we get an intriguing look at how cognitive, affective, and interaction processes work to change our social structural parameters as part of a dynamic system.

The chapters by Gecas (chapter 8) and Nurius (chapter 11) also suggest some novel conceptual tools for examining social change from the bottom up. Gecas, in his call for a renewed focus on self-based motivation, discusses how motives associated with self-esteem, self-efficacy, and authenticity may have consequences for changing society. The value of this proposal is twofold. First, by linking change to self-based motivation we are reminded that one source of energy for propelling change is the individual. Whereas the explicit motivation to change society is by no means inherent, the potential for change is always with us. Second, Gecas's differentiation among three self-motives emphasizes that change, although often emanating from the self, does not necessarily emerge from a singular source. There are in fact a diverse set of self-based processes that operate to initiate social structural changes.

One increasingly influential concept that may prove to play a critical role in discussions of self-based changes in social structure is the concept of *possible selves* (Markus & Nurius, 1986). Although Nurius's contribution does not directly focus on this concept as a source of major social change, she clearly recognizes its potential in this regard. By directing our attention to the dynamic "working self-concept," Nurius, like Gecas, shows that the dynamics of social change are a defining component of the fully developed self.

As noted, the discussions of social change in most of the chapters assumes a gradual, accumulative process. However, in the only chapter that is explicitly concerned with the problem of social change, Howard (chapter 10) develops a persuasive conceptual model that suggests that in addition to gradual change, the self can also be instrumental in the initiation of changes in social structure that are more revolutionary and abrupt. For Howard, self-change initiates the process of collective action by producing the necessary social consciousness and identities that support participation in change-oriented social movements. It is then collective action that leads to changes in society. One particularly valuable feature of Howard's model is that it draws from the extant theory and research on the self and social cognition and shows how our understanding of the self is directly relevant to the explanation of societal change.

Conclusion

The cognitive revolution in psychology has been criticized by social psychologists for its failure to account for the sociological features of thought. In a similar manner, symbolic interactionists have traditionally been reprimanded for their emphasis on the self to the neglect of social structure. This collection of work indicates, however, that the social is currently alive and well on both fronts. Moreover, by exploring the importance of cognition, emotion, and action in the self–society relationship, we are approaching a more complete understanding of human social behavior.

References

Heise, D. R. 1979. *Understanding events: Affect and the construction of social action.* Cambridge, UK: Cambridge University Press.

Lewis, J. D., & R. L. Smith. 1980. *American sociology and pragmatism: Mead, Chicago sociology, and symbolic interaction.* Chicago: University of Chicago Press.

Markus, H., & P. Nurius. 1986. Possible selves. *American Psychologist* 41: 954–969.

Author Index

Subject Index